Beckett's afterlives

Manchester University Press

Beckett's afterlives

Adaptation, remediation, appropriation

Edited by Jonathan Bignell, Anna McMullan
and Pim Verhulst

MANCHESTER UNIVERSITY PRESS

Copyright © Manchester University Press 2023

While copyright in the volume as a whole is vested in Manchester University Press, copyright in individual chapters belongs to their respective authors, and no chapter may be reproduced wholly or in part without the express permission in writing of both author and publisher.

Published by Manchester University Press
Oxford Road, Manchester M13 9PL
www.manchesteruniversitypress.co.uk

British Library Cataloguing-in-Publication Data
A catalogue record for this book is available from the British Library

ISBN 978 1 5261 5379 1 hardback
ISBN 978 1 5261 7896 1 paperback

First published 2023

The publisher has no responsibility for the persistence or accuracy of URLs for any external or third-party internet websites referred to in this book, and does not guarantee that any content on such websites is, or will remain, accurate or appropriate.

Typeset
by New Best-set Typesetters Ltd

Contents

List of figures — page vii
Notes on contributors — viii

Introduction — 1
Pim Verhulst, Anna McMullan and Jonathan Bignell

1 Beckett's 'adaphatroce' revisited: towards a poetics of adaptation — 19
Pim Verhulst

2 Adaptation and convergence: *Beckett on Film* — 34
Jonathan Bignell

3 'Imprecations from the Brighton Road to Foxrock Station': the effect of place on Mouth on Fire's stagings of *All That Fall* — 50
Feargal Whelan

4 Engines of reverence? Beckett, festivals and adaptation — 66
Trish McTighe and Kurt Taroff

5 Passing by, gazing upon: gendered agency in adaptations of *Come and Go* and *Happy Days* — 81
Katherine Weiss

6 'last state last version': adaptation and performance in Gare St Lazare Ireland's *How It Is* — 96
Dúnlaith Bird

7 Intermedial embodiments: Company SJ's staging of Beckett's *Company* — 111
Anna McMullan

8 Beckett, neurodiversity and the prosthetic: the posthuman turn in contemporary art — 126
Derval Tubridy

9 Beckett and new media adaptation: from the literary corpus to the transmedia archive — 140
David Houston Jones

10 Opera as adaptation: György Kurtág's *Samuel Beckett: Fin de partie, scènes et monologues* 155
Olga Beloborodova

11 Questioning norms in three Beckettian choreographic projections: Maguy Marin, Dominique Dupuy, Joanna Czajkowska 171
Evelyne Clavier

12 'I'll give you just enough to keep you from dying': power dynamics disclosed in Tania Bruguera's *Endgame* 186
Luz María Sánchez Cardona

13 *Godot* noir: Beckett in black and whiteface 202
S. E. Gontarski

14 Deferred dreams: waiting for freedom and equality in Nwandu and Beckett 218
Graley Herren

15 'How can you photograph words?': expanding the *Godot* universe from adaptation to transmedia storytelling 233
Luciana Tamas and Eckart Voigts

16 The figure of Beckett in four contemporary novels 249
Paul Stewart

Index 263

List of figures

2.1 Michael Gambon at the launch of *Beckett on Film*, RTÉ news. — *page* 40

3.1 Audience at Tullow Church for *All That Fall*, 23 March 2019. (Photo Melissa Nolan.) — 57

7.1 Raymond Keane in Company SJ's *Company*. Sculptural figure by Roman Paska. (Photo Futoshi Sakauchi.) — 118

12.1 *Endgame*. A production by BoCA Biennial (Lisbon). Courtesy of Estudio Bruguera. (Photo Ricardo Castelo.) — 192

13.1 Flyer for *Purlie Victorious*, *Waiting for Godot* and *The South Shall Rise Again*. (Free Southern Theater records, Amistad Research Center, New Orleans.) — 210

14.1 Jon Michael Hill (left) as Moses and Julian Parker (right) as Kitch in Antoinette Nwandu's *Pass Over* (Steppenwolf Theatre, Chicago). Directed for stage by Danya Taymor (2017). Directed for film by Spike Lee (40 Acres & A Mule Filmworks/Amazon Studios, 2018). — 221

15.1 Close-up of a text message Godot sends to Vladimir and Estragon. Screenshot from *While Waiting for Godot* (director Rudi Azank, 2013), https://vimeo.com/252586094. — 245

Notes on contributors

Olga Beloborodova is a postdoctoral researcher at the University of Antwerp's Centre for Manuscript Genetics. She has published articles and book chapters on Samuel Beckett, cognition and genetic criticism. Together with Dirk Van Hulle and Pim Verhulst she co-edited *Beckett and Modernism* (Palgrave Macmillan, 2018) and she is a member of the Editorial Board of the Beckett Digital Manuscript Project (www.beckettarchive.org). Her first monograph, *The Making of Samuel Beckett's 'Play' / 'Comédie' and 'Film'*, was published with UPA/Bloomsbury in 2019. Her second monograph, *Postcognitivist Beckett*, came out in 2020 as part of the new *Elements in Beckett Studies* series (Cambridge University Press).

Jonathan Bignell is Professor of Television and Film at the University of Reading. He works primarily on television drama and the methodologies of television and film analysis. His work on Beckett includes a monograph, *Beckett on Screen: The Television Plays* (Manchester University Press, 2009), and several articles in *Samuel Beckett Today / Aujourd'hui* and the *Journal of Beckett Studies*. He has published chapters on Beckett's screen drama in *Writing and Cinema* (Routledge, 1999), which he also edited, *Drawing on Beckett* (Assaph, 2003), *Beckett and Nothing* (Manchester University Press, 2010) and *Pop Beckett* (Ibidem, 2019). He is a Trustee of the Beckett International Foundation and member of the Samuel Beckett Research Centre. He has led teams of researchers on several major collaborative externally funded research projects focusing on TV drama of the past in the UK and US, most recently the screen work of Harold Pinter.

Dúnlaith Bird is Senior Lecturer in English at the Université Paris 13 and co-editor of *Études anglaises*. Her current research explores the role of electricity in the work of Samuel Beckett and she has most recently presented at conferences in Paris, Brussels and Prague. In 2010 she organised the 'Beckett Between' conference at the École Normale Supérieure in Paris and co-edited the collection *Beckett Between / Beckett entre deux*, with Sjef Houppermans for *Samuel Beckett Today / Aujourd'hui* (2013). She is also the founder of the Beckett Brunch, the third iteration of which, 'Beckett Beyond', took place in March 2019 at the Centre Culturel Irlandais, Paris.

Evelyne Clavier is the author of a PhD on 'Dancing with Samuel Beckett', defended at the Université Bordeaux Montaigne. She has conducted various dance experiments based on Beckett's works and their choreographic projections, including one with disabled students. She has contributed a chapter on modern dance to *Beckett and Modernism* (Palgrave Macmillan, 2018) and she has written several articles and book chapters in French: 'Samuel Beckett et l'humour comme fissure dans la catastrophe théâtrale' (Faculté des Lettres et des Sciences Humaines Ben M'Sik Casablanca, 2016), 'Portrait de Václav Havel dans *Catastrophe* de Samuel Beckett (1982)' (Éditions Universitaires de Dijon, 2017) and 'Le retour du pire dans *mirlitonnades* (1976–1978) de Samuel Beckett' (*Cahier Erta: Autour du retour*, Best, 2019).

S. E. Gontarski is Robert O. Lawton Distinguished Professor of English at Florida State University. He has edited *The Beckett Critical Reader: Archives, Theories, and Translations* (2012) and *The Edinburgh Companion to Samuel Beckett and the Arts* (2014), and his monographs, *Creative Involution: Bergson Beckett, Deleuze* (2015) and *Beckett Matters: Essays on Beckett's Late Modernism* (2016), have all appeared from Edinburgh University Press. His *Revisioning Beckett: Samuel Beckett's Decadent Turn* appeared with Bloomsbury in 2018 and was followed by *Burroughs Unbound: William Burroughs and the Performance of Writing* in 2021.

Graley Herren is Professor of English at Xavier University in Cincinnati. He is the author of *Samuel Beckett's Plays on Film and Television* (Palgrave Macmillan, 2007), *The Self-Reflexive Art of Don DeLillo* (Bloomsbury, 2019) and *Dreams and Dialogues in Dylan's 'Time Out of Mind'* (Anthem Press, 2021). He is a former member of the executive board for the Samuel Beckett Society and former editor of the society's newsletter, *The Beckett Circle*.

David Houston Jones is Professor of French and Visual Culture at the University of Exeter. His books include *Installation Art and the Practices of Archivalism* (Routledge, 2016; paperback, 2018), *Samuel Beckett and Testimony* (Palgrave Macmillan, 2011) and (with Marjorie Gehrhardt) *Paddy Hartley: Of Faces and Facades* (Black Dog, 2015). He has co-edited a special issue of the *Journal of War and Culture Studies* (2017) entitled 'Assessing the Legacy of the *Gueules cassées*: From Surgery to Art'. His current work focuses on the intersection of intermediality, the archival and the forensic.

Anna McMullan is Professor Emerita in Theatre at the University of Reading. She is author of *Samuel Beckett's Intermedial Eco-Systems* (Cambridge University Press, 2021), *Performing Embodiment in Samuel Beckett's Drama* (Routledge, 2010) and *Theatre on Trial: The Later Drama of Samuel Beckett*

(Routledge, 1993), and co-editor of *Reflections on Beckett* (University of Michigan Press, 2009) with Steve Wilmer. She was Principal Investigator on the AHRC-funded Staging Beckett project (https://research.reading.ac.uk/staging-beckett/) and co-edited, with David Pattie, a special issue of *Samuel Beckett Today / Aujourd'hui* on 'Staging Beckett at the Margins' (29.2, 2017) and, with Graham Saunders, a special issue of *Contemporary Theatre Review* on 'Staging Beckett and Contemporary Theatre and Performance Cultures' (28.1, 2018).

Trish McTighe is Lecturer in Theatre at the University of Birmingham. Previously, she lectured at Queen's University, Belfast and was an AHRC postdoctoral researcher on the Staging Beckett project at the University of Reading (2012–15). Her book *The Haptic Aesthetic in Samuel Beckett's Drama* was published with Palgrave Macmillan in 2013, and she recently co-edited the two-volume *Staging Beckett in Ireland and Northern Ireland* and *Staging Beckett in Great Britain* (Bloomsbury/Methuen, 2016). She has published in the journals *Modern Drama*, *Samuel Beckett Today / Aujourd'hui*, and the *Irish University Review*. She is also the theatre reviews editor for the *Journal of Beckett Studies*.

Luz María Sánchez Cardona is a scholar-artist based at Universitat Oberta de Catalunya and the Kunstakademiet/The Art Academy KMD of Bergen University. She is an Artistic Member of the National System of Art Creators (SNCA) and of the National System of Researchers (SNI/CONACYT) in Mexico and convenes the arts, sciences, humanities and citizenship theme. Recent publications include her monographs *Sound · Beckett · Object* (UAM, 2022), *Electronic Samuel Beckett / Cochlear Samuel Beckett* (UAM, 2016) and *The Technological Epiphanies of Samuel Beckett: Machines of Inscription and Audiovisual Manipulation* (Fonca/National Trust of Culture and Arts, 2016). She is a member of the Executive Committee of the Samuel Beckett Society and the founder of the Beckett-Mexico initiative.

Paul Stewart is Professor of Literature at the University of Nicosia. He is the author of two monographs on Beckett – *Sex and Aesthetics in Samuel Beckett's Works* (Palgrave Macmillan, 2011) and *Zone of Evaporation: Samuel Beckett's Disjunctions* (Rodopi, 2006) – as well as the co-editor of *Pop Beckett: Intersections with Popular Culture* (Ibidem, 2019) with David Pattie. He has also produced two novels, *Now Then* (Armida, 2014) and *Of People and Things* (Armida, 2019).

Luciana Tamas is a visual artist, scholar, curator and translator. The first recipient of a full scholarship for Arts from the DAAD (2012–17), she is currently working as a lecturer and writing her PhD thesis at TU Braunschweig on 'Avant-Garde Rupture and the New Theatrical Vocabulary'. She has participated in and organised over 140 cultural events – solo and group exhibitions, artist talks and lectures – and has been granted several awards, most recently the DAAD Prize for Art History (2018).

Kurt Taroff's main area of interest is 'monodrama', plays which attempt to communicate the world as subjectively experienced by a protagonist with such intensity that the spectator feels as though they have merged with that protagonist. He is also engaged in a new project looking at non-profit theatres in New York's East Village area from 1990 to the present, examining how the rapid gentrification of the area and changes in audiences and public funding have affected the programming choices of these theatres. In connection with his work as a Co-Investigator on the AHRC-funded 'Living Legacies, 1914–18' project, he is exploring community engagement with the First World War through theatre and performance, as well as investigating uses of the war through public performance by the UVF commemoration parades of 2013–15. Further research interests include adaptation and translation in the theatre, American theatre, political theatre, theatre and cognition, and virtual reality theatre.

Derval Tubridy is Professor of Literature and Visual Culture at Goldsmiths, University of London. Author of *Samuel Beckett and the Language of Subjectivity* (Cambridge University Press, 2018), and *Thomas Kinsella: The Peppercanister Poems* (UCD Press, 2001), she has published widely on Modernism and Irish Studies with a focus on the visual arts, philosophy and performance. She is co-director of the London Beckett Seminar and Vice-Chair of the British Association of Irish Studies. Her research has been funded by the Fulbright Commission, the British Academy and the Arts and Humanities Research Council.

Pim Verhulst is a postdoctoral researcher at the University of Oxford and a teaching assistant at the University of Antwerp. His research on Beckett has appeared in *Variants*, *Samuel Beckett Today / Aujourd'hui*, *Genetic Joyce Studies* and the *Journal of Beckett Studies*, of which he was an assistant editor; he has contributed to edited volumes such as *Beckett and BBC Radio* (Palgrave Macmillan, 2017), *Beckett and Modernism* (Palgrave Macmillan, 2018; co-edited with Dirk Van Hulle and Olga Beloborodova), *Pop Beckett* (Ibidem, 2019), *Beckett and Technology* (Edinburgh University Press, 2021) and *Beckett and Media* (Manchester University Press, 2022). Pim is also an editorial board member of the Beckett Digital Manuscript Project (www.beckettarchive.org). He co-edited and co-authored the modules on *Molloy*, *Malone meurt / Malone Dies* and *En attendant Godot / Waiting for Godot*, which received an MLA Prize in 2018. His monograph *The Making of Samuel Beckett's Radio Plays* is forthcoming with Bloomsbury in 2023.

Eckart Voigts is Professor of English Literature at TU Braunschweig, Germany, and was President of the German Society for Theatre and Drama in English (2010–16). He co-edited (with Jeanette R. Malkin and Sarah Jane Ablett) the *Companion to British-Jewish Theatre since the 1950s* (Bloomsbury, 2021) and (with Katja Krebs and Dennis Cutchins) *The Routledge Companion to Adaptation* (2018). Further publications include *Adaptations – Performing Across Media and Genres* (WVT, 2009), *Reflecting on Darwin* (Ashgate, 2014), *Dystopia, Science Fiction, Post-Apocalypse* (WVT, 2015) and *Transforming Cities* (Winter, 2018).

Katherine Weiss is the Associate Dean of the College of Arts and Letters at California State University, Los Angeles. Her scholarly publications include *Samuel Beckett: History, Memory, Archive* (co-edited with Seán Kennedy; Palgrave Macmillan, 2009), *The Plays of Samuel Beckett* (Methuen/Bloomsbury, 2013), *A Student Handbook to the Plays of Tennessee Williams* (Bloomsbury, 2014), *Samuel Beckett and Contemporary Art* (co-edited with Robert Reginio and David Houston Jones; Ibidem, 2017) and *Simply Beckett* (Simply Charly Press, 2020). She has published articles in the *Journal of Beckett Studies* and *Samuel Beckett Today / Aujourd'hui*.

Feargal Whelan is Research Associate with the Centre for Beckett Studies at Trinity College Dublin and Co-director of the annual Samuel Beckett Summer School. He has presented and published widely on the works of Beckett and twentieth-century Irish writing and drama, contributing, among others, chapters to *Staging Beckett in Ireland and Northern Ireland* (Bloomsbury/Methuen, 2016), *Beckett and Modernism* (Palgrave Macmillan, 2018), *The Gate Theatre Dublin: Inspiration and Craft* (Peter Lang, 2018), *Beckett and Politics* (Bloomsbury, 2019) and various articles in journals, including a special issue of *Estudios Irlandeses* on 'Beckett and Biopolitics' (2019). In collaboration with Mouth on Fire Theatre company he has been involved since its inception with Beckett in Foxrock, the annual celebration of the author in his parish church, and he also edits *The Beckett Circle*. His monograph *Beckett and the Irish Protestant Imagination* was published by Ibidem in 2019.

Introduction

Pim Verhulst, Anna McMullan and Jonathan Bignell

Since Beckett's death in 1989 adaptations of his work have proliferated, from performances of the radio or prose texts to resited performances in non-traditional spaces, theatre plays transposed to the large or small screen, or traces of Beckett's work in fiction, artworks and digital media. Beckett's canonical status and ubiquity as a globally recognised cultural reference in the new millennium have no doubt animated these vibrant and diverse afterlives. This is the first collection of essays devoted specifically to Beckett and issues of adaptation, focusing on a range of case studies of (mainly) posthumous revisionings of his work in various genres and media. We have taken a broad approach to what counts as adaptation and both this introduction and the first chapter on Beckett's own adaptations of his work situate the collection historically and theoretically.

The transformed creative treatment of Beckett's work in the public sphere goes hand in hand with a step-change in the field of adaptation studies which has also expanded, reflecting critically on earlier debates and taking account of new media. Before we proceed to the case studies, therefore, this introduction briefly discusses some of those key developments in the field of adaptation studies, which we also see reflected in the more recent approaches to Beckett's work.

Adaptation, appropriation, remediation

Following on from Thomas Leitch's article 'Twelve fallacies in contemporary adaptation theory' (2003), which focused on the book-to-screen variety and was a first systematic attempt to address the frequently heard critique that the field of adaptation studies was heavily undertheorised, in 2006 Linda Hutcheon and Julie Sanders published the first editions of their *A Theory of Adaptation* and *Adaptation and Appropriation*. These were expanded with second editions in 2013 and 2016, incorporating a broader selection of genres and media ranging from film, prose and theatre to opera, musicals, comics and graphic novels, historical fiction, video games, the internet and various kinds of transmedially constructed storyworlds. Also, the first issues of *Adaptation* (Oxford University Press) and *The Journal of Adaptation in Film & Performance* (Intellect) appeared in 2008, providing scholarly forums to facilitate ongoing theoretical discussions. These pioneering endeavours have, in turn, occasioned dozens of monographs (Elliott, 2020), edited volumes (Bruhn et al., 2013) handbooks (Leitch, 2017), reference works (Cartmell and Whelehan, 2022) and book series (e.g. Palgrave Studies in Adaptation and Visual Culture) that further consolidated the field, from which Beckett studies could greatly benefit and on which the present collection builds.

As Hutcheon points out, in 2006 the so-called 'fidelity debates' were still going on and 'adaptations were being judged in terms of quality by how close or far they were from their "original" or "source" texts' (2013: xxvi). The further the distance, the more negative the assessment, which, as Hutcheon notes, is actually 'a late addition to Western culture's long and happy history of borrowing and stealing or, more accurately, sharing stories' (2013: 4), one that goes back to (neo)classicist principles of *imitatio* and *aemulatio* (2013: 20). Indeed, as Sanders concludes: 'Adaptation has, perhaps, suffered from an overemphasis in post-Romantic Western culture on a highly singular notion of creativity and genius but is finding new purchase in the era of global circulations and the digital age of reproduction and re-makings' (2016: 33). In recent years, owing to the cultural upsurge of postmodernism and notions central to it such as intertextuality, parody and pastiche, all enhanced by the internet, works of literature have come to be recognised as far less unique than we often like to think. Additionally, for Hutcheon – aligning herself with theorists such as Julia Kristeva or Roland Barthes – 'adaptations remind us there is no such thing as an autonomous text or an original genius that can transcend history, either public or private. They also affirm, however, that this fact is not to be lamented' (2013: 111). Every text, whether an adaptation or not, always creatively repurposes existing material in one way or another, which makes the dominant notions of 'originality' and 'fidelity' less desirable or even inadequate as tools for criticism.

Alternatively, for Rachel Carroll, every 'adaptation of a prior cultural text – no matter how "faithful" in intention or aesthetic – is inevitably an *interpretation* of that text: to this extent, every adaptation is an instance of textual *in*fidelity' (2009: 1). Sanders is slightly more nuanced when she states that 'the aim is in part to move us away immediately from any rigid concepts of fidelity or infidelity in the adaptive process and towards more malleable and productive concepts of creativity' (2016: 9). As a consequence, the normative assessment of whether an adaptation is 'good' or 'bad', and to what extent it is diminished by 'lack or loss' (2016: 17), are irrelevant because, as Hutcheon stresses, 'there will always be both gains and losses' (2013: 16). Concepts such as 'source text' or 'original' sustain a normative approach, and 'adapted text' does not immediately provide an elegant solution, so a change of mindset in addition to a terminological one is needed. Recognising that an 'adaptation is a derivation that is not derivative – a work that is second without being secondary' (2013: 9) signifies an important step forward, but again such language is hardly neutral. Hutcheon's recalibration of adaptation as the amalgamation of 'repetition with variation, … the comfort of ritual combined with the piquancy of surprise' (2013: 4) is a more positive and fruitful one, and so is Sanders' characterisation as 'the tension between the familiar and the new, and the recognition of both similarity and differences' (2016: 17). Only then can adaptation studies be 'understood as a field engaged with process, ideology and methodology, rather than encouraging polarized value judgments' (2016: 24). This leads to the conclusion that it inevitably involves change, which should be the object of our interpretation, not our (e)valuation. There is, however, a matter of degree.

In Hutcheon's opinion, while adaptation is 'always a double process of interpreting and then creating something', the result is either 'an act of appropriating or salvaging' (2013: 21). Sanders theorises this notion of appropriation in more depth as 'a revised point of view from the original, adding hypothetical motivation or voicing what the text silences or marginalizes' (2016: 23). In doing so, 'appropriation frequently effects a more decisive journey away from the informing text into a wholly new cultural product and domain' (2016: 35). Important to keep in mind as well is that 'a political or ethical commitment shapes the writer's, director's or performer's decision to reinterpret a source text' (2016: 3) so that it 'frequently adopts a posture of critique, overt commentary and even sometimes assault or attack' (2016: 6). This also affects how adaptations or appropriations self-identify. While the former quite 'openly declare themselves as an interpretation or re-reading of a canonical precursor', for the latter category that 'relationship may be less explicit or more embedded' (2016: 3). Still, Sanders assuages the dichotomy as well, for 'as the notion of hostile takeover present in an embedded sense at least in a term such as "appropriation" implies, adaptation can also be oppositional, even subversive. There are as many opportunities for divergence as adherence, for assault as well as homage' (2016: 12). To allow for more leeway, Yvonne Griggs (2016) has presented a different, three-tier model of 'classic treatment', 're-visioning' and 'radical rethink', which avoids the terms adaptation and appropriation altogether, but the categories are not mutually exclusive. In fact, they often co-exist in the same act of creative reworking, so a line cannot always be drawn.

While Sanders notes that appropriation often entails 'the movement from one genre to others', she also cautions that it 'may or may not involve a generic shift' (2016: 35). Quite contentious therefore, at least confusing, is her equation of 'adaptations' with 'mediations' and 'appropriations' with 'remediations' (2016: 3) – a term popularised by Jay David Bolter and Richard Grusin (2000) to indicate that 'new' media often just recycle existing modalities into different constellations or forms driven by technological advancement. For Hutcheon, in turn, when 'adaptations are to a different medium, they are re-mediations, that is, specifically translations in the form of intersemiotic transpositions from one sign system (for example, words) to another (for example, images)' or, alternatively, a 'transmutation or transcoding, that is, as necessarily a recording into a new set of conventions as well as signs' (2013: 16). Sanders characterises this transposition of expressive codes from one medium to another as 'movements of proximation or cross-generic interpretation' (2016: 37). Again, we see there are two creative forces in play here: the first attempting to establish correspondence, which may call for cuts and/or changes depending on the nature of the media involved; the second actively seeking to deviate, where alterations are not necessarily driven by matters of form. Sometimes the two go hand in hand, when the upgrade from a non-technological medium is accompanied by what Sanders calls 'updating' (2016: 23). Indeed, '[m]ost often adaptations are not backdated but rather updated', Hutcheon confirms, 'to shorten the gap between works created earlier and contemporary audiences' (2013: 146). This often entails revisions, some more radical than others, but these can also occur within the same medium or genre if the time span is long enough, so remediation actually straddles adaptation and appropriation, not fully coinciding with either one.

Remediations, in particular, have made it so that 'adaptations are often compared to translations', because '[j]ust as there is no such thing as a literal translation, there can be no literal adaptation' (Hutcheon, 2013: 16). As with adaptation, 'in most concepts of translation, the source text is granted an axiomatic primacy and authority, and the rhetoric of comparison has most often been that of faithfulness and equivalence' (2013: 16). Similarly, like adapters, translators have been rehabilitated from mere mouthpieces, working within the contours of a so-called 'original', to being recognised as inventive and creative agents in their own right, especially when authors are no longer around to 'authorise' the translations of their work. This is why adaptation and translation have recently been put in dialogue as acts of textual rewriting, following the 'cultural turn' in translation studies that urges scholars to consider adaptation as a form of intersemiotic translation (Raw, 2012). In addition to a transposition of language, and thus of medium or code, Sanders regards translation studies as 'an important cognate field to adaptation studies' in that 'all translation' is a form of 'cultural negotiation', not unlike adaptation, and since 'all adapters are translators' and 'all translators are creative writers', so are adapters (2016: 9). A term such as 'tradaptation', invented by Michel Garneau in the context of his Shakespeare translations from English into French (Hellot, 2009: 86), epitomises just how embedded adaptation is within the practice of translation, especially in the case of transcultural translation across historical periods. Thus, the freer a translation, the closer it converges on adaptation, yet the more liberal an adaptation – and thus the more independent it becomes as a work of art – the harder it is to delineate from yet another cognate field, namely that of intertextuality.

In Hutcheon's view, 'adaptation *as adaptation* is unavoidably a kind of intertextuality *if the receiver is acquainted with the adapted text*' (2013: 13; original emphasis). Yet she is also adamant that 'allusions to and brief echoes of other works would not qualify as extended engagements' (2013: 9). Sanders seems to agree when stating that 'citation is different again from adaptation, which constitutes a more sustained and deeper engagement … than the more glancing act of allusion or quotation, even citation allows'. But she does show more lenience by adding that the interaction is 'usually with a single text or source' (2016: 6). This is not always the case, as subspecies of adaptation like the 'mash-up', 'remix' or 'hack and sample' combine various existing texts into a new iteration, employing techniques such as 'montage' or 'collage' (2016: 5), often but not necessarily in a different medium. Here, each individual reference has the short duration of an intertextual allusion but the ensemble of invocations, taken as a whole, amounts to the more prolonged interaction that adaptation seems to require, so the two concepts partially overlap. Contemporary art and installation practices, which can also be highly allusive, present an even greater challenge to divisions hinging on the criterion of sustained or deeper engagement.

A similar case is the 'rewrite', which 'invariably transcends mere imitation, serving instead in the capacity of incremental literature' by 'adding, supplementing, improvising, innovating, amplifying'. 'The aim', Sanders concludes, 'is not replication as such, but rather complication, expansion rather than contraction' (2016: 15). A notorious example of this kind is Jean Rhys's *Wide Sargasso Sea*, which, being a prequel of sorts to Charlotte Brontë's *Jane Eyre*, rewrites that novel indirectly and thus qualifies as both adaptation and intertextuality. In Chapter 15 of this book, Luciana Tamas and Eckart Voigts analyse Matei Vișniec's theatrical appropriation, *Le dernier Godot* (1998), in which Beckett the author meets Godot, his creation. Hutcheon, by contrast, is notably stricter when stating that 'sequels and prequels are not really adaptations' (2013: 9). She regards them instead as 'spin-offs', positioned at the far end of the adaptation spectrum (2013: 171). This may appear strange, considering that Hutcheon and Sanders both embrace the literary genre of historical fiction, in other words 'the appropriation of historical "fact" and so-called real-life subjects' (Sanders, 2016: 16), wholesale as a form of adaptation without further ado. To motivate this decision, Sanders contends that '[t]he discipline of history is … in truth a history of textualities, of stories told by particular tellers according to particular ideologies and viewpoints' (2016: 189), which Hutcheon theorises more extensively in light of her work on postmodernism and the concept of 'historiographic metafiction' (1988). This notion will become particularly relevant for Chapter 16 in the collection, where Paul Stewart analyses four contemporary 'historical' novels that are based on Beckett's life.

Author, authority and authorisation

It thus seems safe to conclude that all adaptation is an (exaggerated) form of intertextuality, though not the other way around. Less straightforward, however, is to position adaptations in an 'intratextual' relationship with the precursors to which they owe their existence in the first place. For Sanders, one 'useful way of thinking about adaptation is as a form of collaborative writing across time and sometimes across culture or language' (2016: 60). But would this not make adapters co-authors and adaptations an integral part of the work, as some scholars have argued about third-party translators and translations, for example in the context of Joyce's multilingual *oeuvre* (see O'Neill, 2005)? It seems uncontroversial to include the author's own adaptations in the Beckett canon, as for example Ruby Cohn does with the German TV version (*Was Wo*) of the stage play *Quoi où* / *What Where* (2005: 377–8). But granting third-party adaptations, like the ones discussed in this book, the same status may for many seem a bridge too far. Furthermore, 'adaptations often adapt other adaptations' (Sanders, 2016: 16), which has by now led to a tradition of third-party engagement with Beckett that new creative reworkings can reflect on, assimilate or reject, to forge intertextual bonds with the adapted texts alongside intratextual ones with the foregoing adaptations or 'epitexts' – to bend Genette's term slightly for our purpose here. Yet, as we have seen before, the 'neatness of identification' that Beckett himself mistrusted (1984: 19) is once again subverted, for how within that tradition do third-party adaptations relate to the author's own: as intertextual, intratextual or both?

'For unknowing audiences, adaptations have a way of upending sacrosanct elements like priority and originality', Hutcheon remarks (2013: 122), but also intertextuality. For a 'knowing audience', adaptation instigates a conscious 'interpretive doubling, a conceptual flipping back and forth between the work we know and the work we are experiencing' (2013: 139). 'Would this experience be the same', she asks intriguingly, 'for the audience that knows the adapted text as it is for the one that does not', or would the latter 'simply experience the adaptation as we would any other work?' (2013: 120) Put differently, 'what if we never read the novels upon which they are based? Do the novels then effectively become the derivative and belated works, the ones we experience second and secondarily?' (2013: 122). This reality is what places the estate of Samuel Beckett in such a difficult position, charged as it is with looking after the author's legacy, preserving or conserving his work as much as allowing it to continue, at least in the short term, until copyright legally expires. Beckett's case is a typical example of Sanders' observation that '[m]odern legal notions of copyright have complicated the freedom with which writers seek to engage explicitly with the work of others' (2016: 46), so that adaptation, but even more so appropriation, can give rise to 'questions of intellectual property, proper acknowledgement and, at its worst, the charge of plagiarism' (2016: 43). For an '"out of copyright" author' such as Shakespeare, the work becomes 'a form of open access content available to the global community for glorious reinvention'. By contrast, '[w]here the work is "owned" by a living author or performer', or by an estate that intervenes on their behalf, 'the ramifications of reworkings are more complex' (2016: 195)

Apart from the copyright issue, another factor that renders Beckett's situation more complex than Shakespeare's – or any prewar author, for that matter – is the fact that he not only adapted his own work or consulted on it but did so across a wide range of genres and media. His estate therefore has to rule by following Beckett's poetics of adaptation, in so far as something of the kind can be reconstructed from his practice, which is not so very different from a court of law that passes a verdict on the basis of precedent or principle where there is no clearly stipulated rule. As this process is inevitably a matter of interpretation, the outcome is destined to be inconsistent – but so, too, was Beckett's own policy and his execution thereof. For example, while the estate appears to be more conservative when it comes to the ethnicity of actors portraying Beckett's characters, it has been loyal in enforcing the author's staunch refusal to let women star in *Godot* while being more permissive about gender for other plays. In some cases, this has resulted in a situation where an adaptation is officially denied, for the reason that it is too much of an appropriation, but then goes ahead regardless in the form of a 'parody', which invokes 'the right to comment critically on a prior work' and is much harder to police from a legal perspective (Hutcheon, 2013: 90). A recent example is the play *Godot Is a Woman* (2021) by clown theatre company Silent Faces (Wyver, 2020), in which a 'trio [of female and non-binary actors] are waiting for the Beckett estate to answer their call about performance rights for Godot' (Armitstead, 2021).

The more critical acclaim authors receive, the more institutionalised they become and the more they are perceived as the representatives of a cultural establishment. This can trigger two types of responses, as Sanders illustrates once more with the example of Shakespeare: 'Some authors are ... seeking to authenticate their own activities by attaching Shakespeare's name to their writing. In such cases an honorific approach is assumed. Others are seen to be less deferential, iconoclastic even, in their intent, rewriting and "talking back" to Shakespeare from an overtly political position' (2016: 59). A similar pattern emerges for Beckett, with the exception of course that his work is not a free-for-all and adaptations need to be authorised in advance, which indirectly invites deference and puts a curb on iconoclasm. As antithetical as these two treatments may seem at first sight, they both corroborate that '[a]daptation appears both to require and to perpetuate the existence of a canon, although it may in turn contribute to its ongoing reformulation and expansion' (2016: 11). Indeed, adaptation can also be a matter of 'investigating its edges and sometimes reviving and recuperating texts that may actually have fallen out of regular readership in the process' (2016: 124). The recent upsurge in adaptations of Beckett affirms the canonical status of his work, and that of particular texts in it, yet we also see that more peripheral titles are being rediscovered, as Trish McTighe and Kurt Taroff detail in Chapter 4 of this book. Adaptation can thus have a re-canonising effect in bringing renewed attention to 'minor' works – even if this is often because they are deemed less untouchable than the major ones, so there is still a double standard involved here, intensified by the estate's authority.

That same interplay of fidelity/reverence v. infidelity/irreverence is aptly reflected in a striking analogy that Hutcheon draws between adaptation and Darwin's theory of evolution: 'Natural selection is both conservative and dynamic; it involves both stabilizing and mutating' (2013: 167). Still, Hutcheon distinguishes 'biological evolution' from what she calls 'cultural evolution' – inspired by Richard Dawkins' concept of 'memes' derived from 'genes' – which also 'involves migration to favorable conditions', in that 'stories travel to different cultures and different media', yet with the crucial exception that they 'adapt just as they are adapted' (2013: 31). The term 'variation', which is central to Hutcheon's Darwinian take on adaptation, Sanders uses to argue that it is 'in musicology that some of the more enabling metaphors for the adaptation process might be located' (2016: 51). Similar to 'symphony and polyphony', it equips us with 'a more active vocabulary' that is 'derived from the performing arts', a more 'kinetic vocabulary' that is 'dynamic, enabling adaptation studies to constantly move forward as much as it is backward looking, and one that embraces ideas of composition and creativity' (2016: 50). True as this may be, it also flattens out the difference between types or degrees of adaptation. Then again, the analogy with evolution more readily implies a judgement of value and – especially in the more socially dubious (mis)interpretations of the concept – it contravenes the traditionally negative perception surrounding adaptation as a cultural phenomenon by valuing later mutations and variations, at least those that survive natural – here cultural – selection, as superior to the ancestors from which they derive, not as inferior. Beckett already anticipates this dilemma through his own fascination with Darwin (see Nixon and Van Hulle, 2013: 200–6), exploring alternatives like 'devolution' and 'dysteleology' in his writing; or, as he quipped in a letter to Nuala Costello of 27 February 1934, 'mere gress' (Beckett 2009: 186), annulling the traditional binary of 'progress' and 'regress'. In this sense, adaptation could be considered a continuation of that Beckettian 'gress', of going 'on', for better or for worse, but always changed and different.

The structure of the book

In another metaphorical comparison that still connects to the biological one but tinges it with a hint of the Gothic, Hutcheon states: 'An adaptation is not vampiric: it does not draw the life-blood from its source and leave it dying or dead, nor is it paler than the adapted work. It may, on the contrary, keep that prior work alive, giving it an afterlife it would never have had otherwise' (2013: 176). And, as Sanders does well to remind us, '"after" need not mean belated in a purely negative sense. Coming after can mean benefitting from accrued wisdom or experience; it can mean finding new angles and new points of entry into the supposedly familiar' (2016: 208). It is this spirit that the present collection of essays takes its title from. All of the chapters in *Beckett's Afterlives* come 'after' Beckett chronologically (also mostly after the 2006 centenary), in the sense that they examine posthumous reimaginings of his work. Even if some contributors refer to adaptations from Beckett's lifetime, this is usually for contrastive purposes. At the same time, they discuss productions that were made 'after' Beckett meaning 'in the style of' or 'imitating' the author – what in French would be called *d'après* or *à la façon de* Beckett – in that, like all adaptations, they rely on the complex, Derridean interplay of repetition and difference for their effect. The emphasis on the plural 'afterlives' is deliberate, for Beckett's work continues to live on in a variety of forms, genres and media, more diverse than the ones he took inspiration from, explored and incorporated into his own artistic practices, which already constitutes an impressive sweep.

In doing so, this volume offers the first systematic book-length study of Beckett and adaptation. Only *Waiting for Godot* has been the subject of a similar project before, by Lance Duerfahrd (2013), who was responsible for staging the play during the Occupy Wall Street protests at Zucotti Park in Lower Manhattan, New York, in 2011 (Duerfahrd, 2017). Similarly, the two edited volumes that emerged from the Staging Beckett project at the Universities of Reading and Chester minutely trace the performance histories of his plays in Great Britain and (Northern) Ireland, without an explicit focus on adaptation but touching on similar issues (McTighe and Tucker, 2016; Tucker and McTighe, 2016). Additionally, the chapters in this collection resonate with recent studies that have recontextualised Beckett's work from the perspectives of world literature (Chakraborty and Toribio Vazquez, 2020), global translation (Fernández and Sardin, 2021), contemporary art (Reginio et al., 2017), technology or media (Tajiri, 2007; Maude, 2009; Adar et al., 2021; Nixon et al. 2022) and popular culture (Murphy and Pawliuk, 2016; Pattie and Stewart, 2019). Finally, the *Journal of Beckett Studies* has long featured the 'Performance Reviews' section, where adaptations are often discussed yet rarely theorised, and the journal *Samuel Beckett Today / Aujourd'hui*, owing to its bilingual and international outlook, often features contributions on the subject. We have grouped individual case studies introduced below to create a series of dialogues between the works analysed and the different approaches to adaptation processes and media.

In the opening chapter, Pim Verhulst reassesses Beckett's peculiar neologism 'adaphatroce' in light of the author's selected correspondence as recently published. He attempts to reconstruct Beckett's poetics of adaptation and how his views on the matter changed over the decades, to nuance the cliché that he was simply 'against' it. This is contradicted not only by the dozens of adaptations Beckett himself was involved in or authorised – however reluctantly at times – as well as saw or read, but equally by some of the more inherent aspects of his work, such as, for example, inter- and transmediality, intertextuality, self-translation and self-directing. As a result, adaptation is revalued as something not alien or even dangerous to Beckett's work but in fact a natural or logical extension of his own experimental practices.

Jonathan Bignell's chapter on the *Beckett on Film* project (2000) relies on a similar premise and argues that its high-profile screen versions of Beckett's theatre plays together comprise a demonstration of the inherent adaptability of Beckett's work. While the idea of putting the plays on screen originally derived from a desire to preserve performances at The Gate Theatre Dublin's Beckett Festival of 1991, the project developed into an ambitious opportunity for diverse directors, actors and other creative personnel to interpret the dramas in a wide range of ways. The adaptations were shown at film festivals, broadcast on television, sold as a DVD box set and distributed via online video streaming. Bignell argues that *Beckett on Film* suited an emergent culture of media convergence around the end of the twentieth century, in which boundaries between media were being renegotiated. The chapter discusses the project's production, which drew together staff and facilities from theatre, cinema and television, and also the marketing of the adaptations towards specialist, general and educational audiences. Within the constraints imposed by Beckett's estate and the promotion of his authorship, the project had the capability to change and adapt, exemplifying the resilience of Beckett's work and its ability to survive in new circumstances.

One aspect of that resilience is how Beckett's work has been adapted to twenty-first-century contexts of theatre-making and event curation outside of traditional theatre buildings. The next two chapters discuss examples of how historical locations in Foxrock and Enniskillen linked to Beckett's biography have been adapted as sites for the performance, celebration and commemoration of his work. The reclaiming of Beckett as an Irish author, ongoing since the late 1980s, is acquiring new inflections. Feargal Whelan looks at two site-specific performances of *All That Fall* by Mouth on Fire, staged for blindfolded audiences at Tullow Church in Foxrock and Áras an Uachtaráin in Dublin, the official residence of Irish president Michael D. Higgins. In contrast to previous stagings by the Pike Theatre in Dublin, Out of Joint and Jermyn Street, Whelan argues that the Mouth on Fire versions were not so much explorations of Beckett's view that adaptations of his radio plays should be done as 'straight readings' or 'come out of the dark'. Instead, he analyses them as part of the commemorative Beckett in Foxrock and Culture Night events to assess the effect of space on the content of *All That Fall*, the problematic history of Beckett's work in Ireland and his ambiguous status as an Irish writer and citizen, while tallying what is gained rather than lost in transposition.

Following on from Whelan's analysis, Trish McTighe and Kurt Taroff reflect on the phenomenon of celebration more broadly and internationally through the cultural framework of festivalisation, in particular the 1991 Gate Theatre festival and the 2006 Centenary Festival, which both took place in the author's native Dublin, and the Happy Days Enniskillen Beckett Festival in Northern Ireland, where he went to school. Their chapter highlights the tension between reverence and preservation, on the one hand, and the need to breathe new life into Beckett's work, on the other, through a focus on matters such as canon formation, audience expectation, national identity and cultural capital, in addition to specific adaptation practices. In doing so, McTighe and Taroff attempt to explain how a further remove in time and space seems to allow more freedom in the adaptation process, as well as greater formal experimentation across the boundaries of genres and media formats.

Space is also central to Katherine Weiss's chapter, which combines four cases: Mabou Mines' production of *Come and Go*, first for the outdoor Brooklyn Bridge Festival in 1970 before moving to an indoor off-off-Broadway theatre venue four years later; Peter Brook and Marie-Hélène Estienne's 2015 staging of the same play; Canadian director Patricia Rozema's screen adaptation of *Happy Days* for the *Beckett on Film* project (2000); and Arlene Shechet's performance art piece *Passing By* (2018), set in New York's Madison Square Park and based on Theatre for a New Audience/Yale Repertory Theatre's production of *Happy Days* (2017). Weiss pays specific attention to the act of seeing and being seen. She explores the agency of women as well as the patriarchal and heteronormative gaze in Beckett's plays, arguing that adaptation invites spectators to question socially fabricated and gendered power structures through the use of location, props such as mirrors, casting choices and cross-dressing.

From site-specific productions we move into the realm of intermediality with Dúnlaith Bird's contribution on Gare St Lazare Ireland's stagings of *How It Is* (Part 1 and Part 2) at the Everyman Theatre in Cork (2018/2019). By observing that the prose text already questions notions such as source, origin and authority, with the narrator's speech being referred to as reported, recorded and repeated, or even just wrong, Bird argues that approaching adaptations of Beckett's work as secondary products that derive from a fully realised antecedent is not helpful. Instead, both could be more constructively understood in terms of a process rather than a product, investigating imperfection and incompleteness through different means, so that neither is the 'last state last version'. GSLI's renditions of *How It Is* self-reflexively occupy a position in-between theatre and prose, much like Beckett's own 'novel' is shaped by and alludes to other forms of media, contradicting his earlier comments against collaboration between the arts.

Anna McMullan investigates the problematic embodiment and spatial representation of prose texts in performance, touched upon by Bird, on the basis of Sarah Jane Scaife and Company SJ's adaptations of *Company* (1990/2018). Since no stage directions have to be negotiated with the estate of Samuel Beckett, theatre-makers have more creative freedom in the multisensory context of theatre. This allows for an intermedial dialogue between novel and performance, involving a projection of phrases from the text onto the back of the stage, as well as double embodiment (actor/sculpture) and recorded voice. The interplay of identities that *Company* depicts as a series of devisers devised is thus reimagined. Its ontological blurring and layering of creature/creator are achieved on stage through a digital scenography influenced by the audio-visual media or technologies that Beckett was familiar with and that the text draws on to convey the experience on the page, in addition to kinetic and choreographic elements. Informed by Beckett's own experiments with lighting and sound in his late theatre, Company SJ's production, like GSLI's *How It Is*, employs new digital technologies to undermine the apparent unity and ontological 'presence' of the body on stage.

The next group of chapters analyses the responses to Beckett's work by artists across different media. Derval Tubridy extends the discussion of intermedial adaptation to Rebecca Horn's art (1970s–2010s), in particular her recent engagement with Beckett's prose text *The Lost Ones* (2015), Anne Niemetz's and Andrew Pelling's sound work *Dark Side of the Cell* (2004) and Touretteshero's production of *Not I* with Jess Thom (2017), in turn related to a performance piece, *10 Minutes of Nothing* (2015), that she collaborated on with Matthew Pountney and artist Will Renel at the South London Gallery. In this chapter, embodiment, subjectivity and agency are investigated from the perspective of posthumanism, incorporating the machinic, the prosthetic and the neurodiverse. It illustrates how present-day art and performance, with their remediative and appropriative strategies, continue to be crucial experimental spaces for Beckett's work, forming the mode and material for new constructions and behaviours already present in his work, but expanded to highlight non-normative human agency and embodiment.

David Houston Jones continues this exploration of what he calls 'borderline' forms of adaptation into the realm of new media such as simulations and video games. Arguing that Linda Hutcheon's exclusion of 'brief echoes' of works from her theory of adaptation is no longer tenable for certain types of remediation, he also situates the problem in Beckett's own writing, where fragmentation is a structural principle and thematic concern, along with (un)ending, narratorial reflexivity and 'intra-intertextuality'. Houston Jones interprets John Gerrard's *Exercise (Djibouti)* (2012), *Exercise (Dunhuang)* (2014) and Simon Meek's *Beckett* (2018) as part of a 'heterocosm', a media ecology or transmedia archive, the implications of which for key notions like 'authorship' or 'media-specificity' are teased out in the chapter. It reconceives adaptations not as versions of a pre-existing essence but rather as instances in an iterative, diachronic elaboration of one or more works, which – although Beckettian – in turn clashes with adaptation's imperative to create 'repetition without replication'.

Olga Beloborodova focuses on György Kurtág's *Samuel Beckett: Fin de partie, scènes et monologues* (2018). Against the backdrop of the author's own views on music and opera, she examines the relationship between adaptation and its so-called 'original'. Unlike Houston Jones, Beloborodova takes issue with John Bryant's concept of the 'fluid text', which views all forms of revisioning (whether authorial or not) as part of the work's (epi) genesis, but she also approaches the matter through Linda Hutcheon's foregrounding of reception instead of production. As an example of 'cultural revision' or non-authorial adaptation, Kurtág's opera constitutes a fascinating test case that seeks to retain fidelity to the source material but at the same time has to deviate from it for the purpose of a transgeneric and transmedial adaptation. To make her point, Beloborodova discusses the libretto and scenography of Kurtág's opera, as these are elements that Beckett the playwright and director might have weighed in on himself.

From opera we proceed to dance. Evelyne Clavier discusses three choreographic productions based on Beckett's works: Maguy Marin's *May B* (1981), Dominique and Françoise Dupuy's *La petite dame* (2002) and Joanna Czajkowska's *All This This Here* (2015). She prefers the term 'projections' or 'filiations' over the more standard 'adaptation' or (intermedial) 'transposition', as they alter Beckett's texts beyond recognition and mix several together. However, because the interaction is quite sustained, this practice stretches the meaning and applicability of concepts such as 'intertextuality' and 'allusion'. Beckett's work urged Marin, the Dupuys and Czajkowska to question norms and adapt their aesthetics in relation to the body and psychological or realistic acting styles, creating new possibilities of gesturing for choreographers and dancers. Clavier's chapter thus illustrates how Beckett changed choreography and, in turn, the extent to which it has transformed our conception and reception of his work, in some cases re-psychologising and re-activating it, as with *Quad*.

A series of chapters on Beckett and the politics of adaptation is spearheaded by Luz María Sánchez Cardona, who situates Tania Bruguera's rendition of *Endgame* at the BoCA Biennial (2017) in the context of her work and life, in particular the Cuban government's crackdown on artists and activists. After a brief overview of Bruguera's social initiatives and art projects, including *10,148,451* (2018), as well as series such as *Tatlin's Whisper* (2008–9) and *Studies for Endgame* (2005–6), Sánchez Cardona illustrates how Bruguera's direction of Beckett's play at once taps into the historical circumstances of the 1930s–40s that shaped it, such as famine and oppression, while connecting them to more contemporary geopolitical conditions and the framework of Michel Foucault's 'Panopticon'. She thus 'reenacts' and 'appropriates' *Endgame* into her own practice, as a 'strategy' to position the work outside of the contemporary art landscape and move it into a transdisciplinary arena.

After Europe and Cuba, S. E. Gontarski sets the scene in the United States with his chapter on all-black performances of *Waiting for Godot*. Starting out with a more general consideration of how, in the realm of commercial theatre, 'all performance is adaptation' up to a point – a truth Beckett finally understood and accepted – Gontarski minutely reconstructs the history behind the first African American performance of the play, which previewed at Boston's Schubert Theatre before premiering at the Ethel Barrymore Theatre on Broadway in 1957, produced by Michael Myerberg and directed by Herbert Berghof. The chapter traces how this landmark production cut across American society, with its racial segregation and Jim Crow laws, while paving the way for the later production by the Free Southern Theater in the 1960s, in full swing of the Civil Rights movement, as well as Christopher McElroen and Chan Park's more recent staging of the play in post-Katrina New Orleans (2007).

Gontarski lays the foundation for Graley Herren's chapter on Antoinette Nwandu's play *Pass Over*, which premiered at Chicago's Steppenwolf Theatre in 2017 before it was staged at New York's Lincoln Center Theater in 2018, with changes, and filmed by Danya Taymor and Spike Lee. It is a modern-day reworking of *Waiting for Godot*, relocated to a street corner in urban America. 'Mashing up' Beckett's play with the Book of Exodus and plantation life, it triangulates adaptation and appropriation with intertextuality to reflect on freedom and slavery in their various guises, both historical and fictional. A pun on the Jewish Passover and being 'passed over' or ignored, among others, Nwandu's play melds the biblical undertones of *Godot*, her own Christian heritage and that of Martin Luther King Jr with the Black Lives Matter movement, creating a transformed sense of Beckettian absurdism and existential crisis. Following Nwandu's example, Herren makes a passionate plea for more inclusive approaches to adapting Beckett's work.

In a final chapter on *Godot*, Luciana Tamas and Eckart Voigts look at transmedial adaptations of the play that expand its fictional universe. After drawing our attention to the inherent multiplicity of Beckett's *Godot*s, they offer a selective overview of the play's many global 'tradaptations'. They zoom in on two productions to investigate power, be it political, cultural or authorial. Rudi Azank's *While Waiting for Godot* (2013) is also set in New York yet designed for a webseries format and the different screen sizes of social media. It blends a televisual and cinematic monochrome aesthetic with the sitcom genre, as Godot sends Didi and Gogo text messages on their stolen cell phones. In his theatrical appropriation *Le dernier Godot* (1987/1998), Matei Vișniec stages both Godot and the author behind the scenes, the character reproaching his maker for not giving him an entrance. Godot even starts to question his creator's existence, which renders Beckett as elusive as his iconic creation.

The author figure is also central to Paul Stewart's chapter, the last in the collection, which approaches adaptation from the angles of fictionality, historiography and biography. He singles out three recent novels inspired by Beckett's life: Jo Baker's *A Country Road, A Tree* (2016), Annabel Abbs's *The Joyce Girl* (2016), Alex Pheby's *Lucia* (2018) and Sam Thompson's

Jot (2018). The scarcity or, in some cases, total absence of archival information is a call for novelists to imaginatively fill in the narrative gaps, often by resorting, in different ways, to Beckett's own work as if it were a testimony of lived experience – not unlike his biographers. Stewart ponders the ethical as well as theoretical implications of Beckett's life being appropriated for the purposes of fiction, also in light of the author's own habit of sourcing biographical materials for works such as *Dream of Fair to Middling Women*, *More Pricks Than Kicks* and *Human Wishes*.

One of the major themes recurring throughout these chapters is that the adaptation process for contemporary artists, across the many genres and media discussed, acts as a catalyst for creativity, as indeed it did for Beckett. These posthumous reworkings have in turn engendered new responses and interpretations. As a canonical author whose work remains in copyright and is regularly invoked in celebrating national identity, especially in Ireland but also in France, such revisionings are necessarily engaged in interpretative, commemorative and evaluative frameworks. Informed by debates in adaptation studies, the essays in this volume suggest a range of critical approaches that do not simply compare the 'adaptation' with the 'original' in terms of fidelity but consider how the new work has creatively repurposed or responded to Beckett's own. The proliferation of versions of Beckett, of other Becketts and others' Becketts, across languages, cultures and media in the twenty-first century, is now an integral part of Beckett's afterlives, and of the ongoing vitality and relevance of his *oeuvre*.

References

Adar, E., G. Kiryushina and M. Nixon (eds) (2021). *Samuel Beckett and Technology*. Edinburgh: Edinburgh University Press.

Armitstead, C. (2021). '*Godot Is a Woman* review – cheeky, geeky take on Beckett's men-only rule', *Guardian*, 10 June, www.theguardian.com/stage/2021/jun/10/godot-is-a-woman-review-silent-faces-samuel-beckett (accessed 9 December 2021).

Beckett, S. (1984). *Disjecta: Miscellaneous Writings and a Dramatic Fragment*. Ed. R. Cohn. New York: Grove Press.

Beckett, S. (2009). *The Letters of Samuel Beckett, Volume I: 1929–1940*. Ed. M. Dow Fehsenfeld and L. More Overbeck. Cambridge: Cambridge University Press.

Bolter, J. D., and R. Grusin (2000 [1998]). *Remediation: Understanding New Media*. Cambridge, MA: MIT Press.

Bruhn, J., A. Gjelsvik and E. F. Hanssen (eds) (2013). *Adaptation Studies: New Challenges, New Directions*. London and New York: Bloomsbury.

Carroll, R. (2009). 'Introduction: textual infidelities', in R. Carroll (ed.), *Adaptation in Contemporary Culture: Textual Infidelities*. London and New York: Continuum, pp. 1–7.

Cartmell, D., and I. Whelehan (eds) (2022). *Adaptations: Critical and Primary Sources*. 3 vols. London: Bloomsbury.
Chakraborty, T., and J. L. Toribio Vazquez (eds) (2020). *Beckett as World Literature*. London: Bloomsbury.
Cohn, R. (2005 [2001]). *A Beckett Canon*. Ann Arbor: The University of Michigan Press.
Duerfahrd, L. (2013). *The Work of Poverty: Samuel Beckett's Vagabonds and the Theater of Crisis*. Columbus: Ohio State University Press.
Duerfahrd, L. (2017). 'Precarious theatre: staging *Waiting for Godot* at the Occupy Wall Street protest', *Samuel Beckett Today / Aujourd'hui*, 29.2, 350–60.
Elliott, K. (2020). *Theorizing Adaptation*. Oxford: Oxford University Press.
Fernández, J. F., and P. Sardin (eds) (2021). *Translating Samuel Beckett around the World*. New York and London: Palgrave Macmillan.
Griggs, Y. (2016). *The Bloomsbury Introduction to Adaptation Studies: Adapting the Canon in Film, TV, Novels and Popular Culture*. London and New York: Bloomsbury.
Hellot, M.-C. (2009). 'Le poète qui traduit: entretien avec Michel Garneau', *Jeu: Revue de théâtre*, 133.4, 83–8.
Hutcheon, L. (1988). *A Poetics of Postmodernism: History, Theory Fiction*. New York and London: Routledge.
Hutcheon, L., and S. O'Flynn (2013 [2006]). *A Theory of Adaptation*. London: Routledge.
Leitch, T. (2003). 'Twelve fallacies in contemporary adaptation theory', *Criticism*, 45.2, 149–71.
Leitch, T. (ed.) (2017). *The Oxford Handbook of Adaptation Studies*. Oxford: Oxford University Press.
Maude, U. (2009). *Beckett, Technology and the Body*. Cambridge: Cambridge University Press.
McTighe, T., and D. Tucker (eds) (2016). *Staging Beckett in Ireland and Northern Ireland*. London and New York: Bloomsbury/Methuen.
Murphy, P. J., and N. Pawliuk (eds) (2016). *Beckett in Popular Culture: Essays on a Postmodern Icon*. Jefferson, NC: McFarland.
Nixon, M., B. Rapcsak and P. Schweighauser (eds) (2022). *Beckett and Media*. Manchester: Manchester University Press.
Nixon, M., and D. Van Hulle (2013). *Samuel Beckett's Library*. Cambridge: Cambridge University Press.
O'Neill, J. (2005). *Polyglot Joyce: Fictions of Translation*. Toronto: University of Toronto Press.
Pattie, D., and P. Stewart (eds) (2019). *Pop Beckett: Intersections with Popular Culture*. Stuttgart: Ibidem.
Raw, L. (ed.) (2012). *Translation, Adaptation and Transformation*. London and New York: Bloomsbury.
Reginio, R., D. Houston Jones and K. Weiss (eds) (2017). *Samuel Beckett and Contemporary Art*. Stuttgart: Ibidem.
Sanders, J. (2016 [2006]). *Adaptation and Appropriation*. London and New York: Routledge.

Tajiri, Y. (2007). *Samuel Beckett and the Prosthetic Body: The Organs and Senses in Modernism*. Houndmills and New York: Palgrave Macmillan.

Tucker, D., and T. McTighe (eds) (2016). *Staging Beckett in Great Britain*. London and New York: Bloomsbury/Methuen.

Wyver, K. (2020), 'Not waiting for Godot: new show tackles Beckett's ban on women', *Guardian*, 18 October, www.theguardian.com/stage/2020/oct/18/not-waiting-for-godot-new-show-tackles-becketts-ban-on-women (accessed 9 December 2021).

1

Beckett's 'adaphatroce' revisited: towards a poetics of adaptation

Pim Verhulst

On 23 March 1975, Beckett wrote to American director Alan Schneider regarding a reprise of *Godot* he was overseeing at the Schiller Theater in Berlin, where ten years earlier the German premiere of the play had taken place under the direction of Deryk Mendel with the author's help. In that letter, Beckett stated: 'Berlin wasn't too bad in the end. We were nearly there. There will be a film of a performance, purely documentary, no *adaphatrôce* [sic]' (1999: 324). This portmanteau neologism – a compound of '*adaptation*' and '*atroce*', the spelling in the middle of the word hinting at '*aphteux*' ('ulcerous') – could be paraphrased as 'dreadful' or 'atrocious adaptation' (Bignell, 2009: 32; 2020: 100). It is certainly a 'pejorative pun', as Maurice Harmon, editing the Schneider correspondence, remarks in his annotations (Beckett, 1999: 324n2). Still, perhaps this is not quite the straightforward or wholesale rejection of adaptation it has often been taken to mean in the field of Beckett studies. What if it merely signals a difference between 'bad' and 'good' adaptations? But then how can we make that distinction between 'failure' or 'success' and – more relevant here – how did Beckett? In the words of Everett Frost and Anna McMullan: 'When does adaptation become *adaphatroce*?' (2003: 223).

In order to find an answer, it is imperative that we move beyond the 'old chestnuts' of the critical discourse surrounding Beckett's work, based on a small number of long-published letters that have come to dominate our view on his thinking about adaptation, which is mostly a negative or dismissive one. The specimen cited above is one example, but only to provide a starting point for the discussion. What this chapter sets out to do is offer a select overview of adaptations that Beckett was involved in directly or authorised during his career, in order to foreground some of the lesser-known comments he made about them and to reconstruct his poetics of adaptation. Thanks to the four-volume edition of his selected letters (2009–16), we are now better equipped to understand his stance on the matter, which turns out to be a less straightforward one, prone to evolution and – above all – contradiction. In their book on *Experimental Beckett*, Jonathan Heron and Nicholas Johnson point out: 'There is almost no prohibition that Beckett made in one case that was not transgressed in another. Partly on these grounds, we challenge the discourse that Samuel Beckett's drama is not already a terrain for experimental practice' (2020: 2). This claim could very well be generalised to his entire body of work so that the phenomenon of adaptation is not anathema to it, as often seems to be the perception, but actually constitutes its natural or logical extension.

Beckett and adaptation

It is, however, understandable that Beckett was wary of adaptation in the early stages of his career, especially when he took to theatre. As James Knowlson reminds us, '[r]equests started to flow into Lindon's office throughout 1953 for … permission to translate or "adapt" *Godot* into English' (1996: 398). As soon as the BBC got hold of a French copy, they deemed it necessary to have a 'free hand' at the translation, even rejecting Beckett's own (Tonning, 2017: 66–7). In Dublin, at the Pike Theatre, director Alan Simpson staged a heavily Irishised version that made small though considerable adjustments to the script – or 'improvements', as Beckett sarcastically called them (2011: 561) – and he was entirely shut out from talks about the London *Godot* production, directed by Peter Hall, which made him repudiate the stage design as looking like a Salvator Rosa painting (2011: 548) and which had severe consequences for the publication history of the play in the UK (Van Hulle and Verhulst, 2017a: 113–34). On the American front, too, Beckett found out that 'Clov carries skis at the end of *Endgame*' in Schneider's 1958 production of the play at the New York Cherry Lane Theatre (1999: 44), oversight being much easier to maintain in France, with his trusted friend and director Roger Blin. This made Beckett feel his work was being tampered with from all sides, so trying to maintain control, or at least being defensive and protective about it, was a natural response for him. Therefore, it is also necessary to keep this context in mind for a proper framing of his comments on adaptation from the 1950s. Nonetheless, in view of Beckett's misgivings, it is striking how many such projects he became entangled in, however marginally, or approved without involvement over the next three decades.

On 27 September 1957, he rejected a proposal by the French film and television producer François Beloux for a 'cinema adaptation' of *Molloy*, stating: 'I do not want films to be made of my writings and I shall always hold out against it' (2014: 66). Just a few months later, on 27 April 1958, Beckett reneged on his decision, reporting to Schneider: 'Talk also of a film

(Alain Resnais) of the French *All That Fall*. I have not yet given the green light for this, but so admire Resnais that I probably shall' (1999: 45). It would not be made until 1962, for French television (RTF) and by a different director (Michel Mitrani),[1] but this was the first in a series of adaptations across multiple genres and media, most of which have garnered some critical attention: *Molloy, From an Abandoned Work* (1957), *Malone Dies* (1958) and *The Unnamable* (1959) for radio (BBC Third Programme), read by Patrick Magee with music by John Beckett;[2] *Krapp's Last Tape* for chamber opera with the Romanian–French composer Marcel Mihalovici (1961);[3] *Play* for radio (1966), film (1966) and television (1976) with the Rothwell Group, the BBC and Marin Karmitz;[4] again *Krapp's Last Tape* for television with Schneider, but also WDR and the BBC, in the late 1960s and early 1970s;[5] *Lessness* for BBC Radio 3 (1971);[6] and *Not I* for a BBC2 ('Lively Arts') TV programme on Beckett entitled *Shades* (1977),[7] to name only the most prominent ones.

He also translated Robert Pinget's radio play *La Manivelle* – 'A bit too free and Irish', as he told Barbara Bray on 13 November 1959 (2014: 254) – by transposing it into Hiberno-English and relocating it from Paris to London as *The Old Tune* (Weller, 2015; Pilling, 2017). Although this would be the only explicit 'adaptation' he undertook in his lifetime, could not Beckett's reworkings of Nicolas Chamfort's maxims in the poem cycle *Long after Chamfort* be seen as such? And what about his role in the now lost play *Le Kid*, which was performed at Dublin's Peacock Theatre for Trinity College Dublin's Modern Language Society in 1931 and mingled Pierre Corneille's *Le Cid* with the Charlie Chaplin film *The Kid* and a pinch of Bergson (Knowlson, 1996: 122–6)? Or the aborted dramatic fragment *Mittelalterliches Dreieck*, for which Beckett drew on a scene from Ludovico Ariosto's *Orlando Furioso* (Van Hulle and Verhulst, 2017a: 29–34)? Additionally, while he condemned the New York staging of Dylan Thomas's radio play *Under Milk Wood* as a 'crime', despite the author's own involvement in the adaptation process (Cleverdon, 1969; Brinnin, 1989),[8] he lauded Mary Manning Howe's stage adaptation of *Finnegans Wake* (*The Voice of Shem*) as '[v]ery ingenious' (Beckett 2014: 179). And neither did he have a problem with encountering Marguerite Duras's novel *Le Square* (*The Square*) first on French radio (Beckett 2014: 10–11, 13, 15) before going to see it in the theatre (2014: 144–6), liking both very much and recommending them warmly to friends whenever he had an opportunity, even advising Barbara Bray on her translation and adaptation for the BBC Third Programme (2014: 79–80, 105). This reveals a somewhat inconsistent or double standard, as apparently the need to experience other authors' literary work in the original had become less pressing by the late 1950s and early 1960s.

Furthermore, Beckett's heavy reliance on intertextuality and his sustained practice of self-translation, which often took the form of rewriting and created a bilingual double *oeuvre* of false mirror images, are also forms of adaptation by proxy, not to mention the scores of theatre productions he was either consulted on or directed himself. As Julie Sanders notes, 'performance is in itself an inherently adaptive art; we might even argue that each individual performance is an adaptation' (2016: 60). Linda Hutcheon, too, states that 'live performance works are likewise fluid in that no two productions of one printed play text or musical score, or even two performances of the same production, will be alike' (2013: 170). Yet Beckett took the inherently mutable state of theatre to new extremes, changing some of his plays so radically in later productions that he was even accused by one critic of appropriating his own work. After seeing Beckett's 1984 San Quentin version of *Godot*, Colin Duckworth deplored what he considered as an act of 'textual vandalism, perpetrated on some of the most magical moments of the play' (1987: 190), which rendered it 'more portentous' and 'unfunny' (1987: 183), indicative of 'the vision Beckett now has of a greyer world, glimpsed through the filter of his own later work' (1987: 191). For the author, the experimental nature of his theatre was closely linked to performance as variation on a pre-existing text, even with 'performance as text' (Gontarski, 1998), which is not so very different from the rationale of adaptation.

Beckett's media awareness

Interestingly, we start to see a shift in Beckett's attitude about adaptation when he branches out from the traditional genres of poetry, prose and theatre into the technological realms of radio, television and film, a process that began in the mid-1950s and lasted until the close of his career in the late 1980s. Even if many of the productions touched upon below remained unrealised, they do shed light on Beckett's awareness of and sensitivity to central issues of adaptation. As his comment on the filmed theatrical production of *Godot* in Berlin shows, Beckett was well attuned to the distinction between a recording of a play as performed onstage and a genuine adaptation for the television medium, the latter requiring substantial re-(en)visioning. Capturing a dramatic performance from a fixed point of view, much like a spectator would perceive it in the audience, is not identical to watching it on the small TV screen. Not only would we lose the physical presence of the actor(s) but also the wide-open space of the theatre would be reduced. That this was an important element of the *Godot* experience is clear from Beckett's 1961 dismissal of television as 'a medium for fleas' (2014: 423).

To replicate a similar effect of vastness – one that would be easier to achieve on the big screen of cinema or later widescreen home television sets – actors would have to be the size of pin heads.

However, it seems that Beckett also came to appreciate TV as lending itself better to closeness or intimacy as well as confinement. This may have resonated with performances of *Godot* in prisons that started to take place in the late 1950s and early 1960s, for example at Lüttringhausen in Germany and San Quentin in the US by actors such as Karl-Franz Lembke and Rick Cluchey (Knowlson, 1996: 410, 611–14; Tophoven, 2015; Little, 2020). On 9 December 1961, Beckett told his Danish translator Christian Ludvigsen: 'I think the problem is how to give the space on the small screen. Roughly speaking I think the solution is in a counterpoint of long shots and close-ups' (2014: 448). This is not quite the aesthetic followed in the PBS version, directed by Alan Schneider, to which the comments here allude. Even though Beckett had given pointers by letter for this production and camera angles did alternate, the play was shot entirely in a cramped studio setting. 'Saw Godot on TV and that cured me – of my bright idea', he told Elliseva Sayers at the time (2014: 423). Still, when he learned about (unrealised) plans for a film version to be set on the west coast of Ireland, he again gave permission (2014: 498), perhaps because it would allow for greater distance and depth.

From his elaborate suggestions to Shivaun O'Casey on 13 January 1965, for a staged production of *From an Abandoned Work* that was to tour the US with Theatre Group 20 but never actually did, it also appears that Beckett had well-developed thoughts on the dramatic presentation of his prose texts (2014: 647). Similarly, when Joseph Chaikin asked permission to stage *How It Is* or *Texts for Nothing*, Beckett's reply shows that every production had to be judged on its own terms, writing on 26 April 1980: '*Texts for Nothing* perhaps. Seated. Head in hands. Nothing else. Face invisible. Dim spot. Speech hesitant. Mike for audibility' (2016: 526). Although not included in his published correspondence, Beckett sent Chaikin 'highly detailed suggestions for adapting' (2016: 532n1), but their exchange is equally insightful for the author's views about the difference between staging one text as opposed to more, even the entire series:

> The method I suggest is only valid for a single text. The idea was to caricature the labour of composition. The concentration is on one particular inanity to be accomplished before the next can be undertaken. If you prefer extracts from a number of texts you will need a different approach. (2016: 532)

Beckett went as far as to suggest a different title – 'Inania Verba (Virgil)', borrowed from the *Aeneid* – signalling an awareness that transposing *Texts for Nothing* from the page to the stage would result in a significantly different work. After giving Chaikin carte blanche on *Texts for Nothing*, Beckett could still not help but wonder 'How stage bodilessness? That groping <u>vox inanis</u>?' (2016: 546), which sees him reflecting on the problem of embodiment that any stage performance of a prose text inevitably raises.

Especially with people that he knew and trusted, Beckett allowed more freedom in the 1970s and 1980s. Although he occasionally still made suggestions by letter, he would often present them as provisional, and many of his responses contrast with the blatant refusals of the 1950s and 1960s. On 18 July 1979, he wrote to David Warrilow:

> I have confidence in your feeling for my work and shd. be happy for you to direct a TV <u>Lost Ones</u>. Also for you to direct & perform <u>Eh Joe</u> with Helen Bishop. There is no question of any special light on Joe in this TV play. In an eventual stage presentation, not to be encouraged, light might be used in an attempt to suggest progression towards final close-up, i.e. gradually brought up on the actor, finally on the face alone, while on all else correspondingly down. (2016: 508)

On 20 November 1969, he impressed on Jérôme Lindon, regarding a proposed cycle of his plays by the Compagnie Renaud-Barrault at the Théâtre Récamier: 'No question of *Dis Joe* in the theatre' (2016: 198). But his letter to Rick Cluchey of 25 December 1985 is more nuanced and tempered: '<u>Eh Joe</u> is not theatre. ... Together we might have talked it into some kind of stage shape. But on paper from afar, & in ignorance of your stage conditions, I don't know what help I can offer. These few thoughts <u>faute de mieux</u>' (2016: 665). Beckett then made some suggestions for the set, the lighting, Joe's body and voice, only granting Cluchey permission as compensation for a cancelled BBC TV remake that was to star him and Billie Whitelaw. All too often, these instances have been rationalised or explained away as Beckett doing a favour for a friend or an acquaintance. But the level of detail that qualifies these 'few thoughts' also betrays a genuine interest or intrigue, not just a feeling of protection.

To be sure, Beckett turned down more requests than he sanctioned, and the ones that he did see the outcome of were usually judged as failures rather than successes. But what does such a verdict mean for an author who came to measure the 'success' of his work in terms of 'failure', a continuous attempt to 'fail better' as *Worstward Ho* has it (Beckett 2009: 81, 82, 89), and who called *Film* an 'interesting failure', one that in the transmedial conversion from script to film – another type of adaptation, we might argue – 'acquired a dimension and a validity of its own that are worth far more than any merely efficient translation of intention' (Beckett 2014: 631)? Beckett was an author for whom the breakdown of one work often led to a breakthrough with another, whose writing process was 'ended' or 'stopped' rather than 'finished' or 'completed', and intersected with several other activities, a dynamic that Dirk Van Hulle (2021) has called 'creative concurrence' and which equally accommodates creative dead ends. In many ways, for Beckett, as for Stephen Dedalus in the 'Proteus' chapter of James Joyce's *Ulysses*, 'errors' – though not necessarily 'volitional' – were 'the portals of discovery' (1986: 156). Together with self-translation, which Beckett similarly decried as a 'losing battle' (Knowlson, 1996: 438), adaptation is perhaps not to be cast aside as disconnected from or tangential to, but rather as an integral part of his work, particularly during its later stages.

The first draft of *Words and Music* was begun the day after Beckett saw a run-through of Mihalovici's *Krapp* opera, concluding that the music had left his 'text rather obliterated' (2014: 399), which may have led to the more balanced treatment of the two components that we observe in the radio play (Verhulst, 2023). The French version of *All That Fall*, which he thought was done '[b]adly' (Beckett 1999: 135), left a mark on *Film* and *Eh Joe* (Kiryushina, 2021). And the failure to distinguish the six different voices in the *Lessness* adaptation for radio, just enough so they could still be perceived as emanating from the same consciousness, is closely connected to Beckett's exploration of the same idea in *That Time*, which uses prerecorded voices on stage (Stewart, 2017: 215). *Company* absorbs elements of theatre and audio-visual media (Flynn, 2016), even recycling a paragraph from *A Piece of Monologue* (Nugent-Folan, 2021: 330–2); *What Where* was soon transferred to television in German (Herren, 2007: 181–8); *Ohio Impromptu* looks like it could be one of Beckett's staged readings, amalgamating a multitude of genres (Dowd, 2006); and *Quad* is a hybrid crossover of drama and dance with television, extended off the cuff by means of a monochrome version during recording (*Quad II*), which could itself already be considered an instant adaptation (Wakeling, 2021: 34). As these examples suggest, increasingly in later decades, Beckett was interested not so much in keeping his genres apart as in what it is that keeps them apart, deepening his understanding of them, helping him explore and eventually transgress their boundaries. Adaptation was another important driving force of this process, alongside inter- and transmediality.[9]

Whose Beckett?

Closely bound up with the question of adaptation are notions such as author, authority and authorisation, even property. In this respect, too, we can discern an evolution in Beckett's relationship to his own texts from the 1960s onward. In his letter of 9 December 1961 to Judith Schmidt at Grove Press, he was still thinking about adaptation in terms of an outside influence tainting the purity of his work: 'You may authorize Canadian TV to do

Godot. It has been so battered by now that a little more or less can't make much difference. We'll just try and keep the others clean' (2014: 447). However, not everyone asked him for permission. On 17 September 1965, he complained to Patrick Magee about a film Paul Joyce had made of *Act Without Words II*: 'There are 2 mimes and I wonder which he has done. Foolish as you say without permission. Same things a few days ago with *Murphy* or similar. Film script by some woman out of the blue which no question of at any price' (2014: 674). The next time Beckett was in London, he saw Joyce's film and 'retroactively granted permission for *The Goad, adapted from Act Without Words, by Samuel Beckett*' (2014: 675n1). It is unknown what he thought of the result, but the fact that it was explicitly framed as an adaptation and given a different title may have been a mitigating factor.

It seems it also made a difference if Beckett was unfamiliar with the target medium. In a letter to Bray from early 1965, he states: 'Did work on *All That Fall*. Mrs R. presented by an animated line' (2014: 677). Or again to Bray on 19 January 1975: 'Tuesday appointment with one [i.e. German film director Ernst] Reinboth who has made some puppet film – if I understand right – of Le Dépeupleur (Der Verwaiser) with extracts spoken by [actor Ernst] Schroeder' (2016: 385). In fact, the 'puppet animation' was a mash-up featuring 'two other texts' of Beckett's, with music by György Ligeti and Michael Schwarz, retitled *Der Sucher (The Seeker)* (2016: 386n4). On 5 February, having seen the result, he wrote to his German publisher, Siegfried Unseld: 'The Reinboth film is not good, and has no connection with *Der Verwaiser*. But he's a young man and needs a helping hand. If when you've seen the film, or someone of your choice has seen it, you're not absolutely against, I won't mind' (2016: 390). Perhaps the possible connection with Heinrich von Kleist's essay 'On the marionette theatre' intrigued him (Knowlson, 1996: 584), but again it was more Reinboth's work than Beckett's, and again it carried a title clearly distinguishing it from *The Lost Ones*.

Even if reworkings kept their original labels, it gradually became easier for Beckett to take a distance from them. On 19 April 1970, he told Harold Pinter he was 'upset' by Roger Croucher putting on *Cascando* 'without permission' (2016: 229). It was 'played in total darkness', largely faithful to Beckett's well-known directives for dramatisations of his radiophonic work, so technically it was 'not a staged production' (2014: 229n2). It is easy to see how such clever sophistry could get on the author's nerves, and a younger version of himself might have taken action, but the incident did not prevent Beckett from eventually authorising the staging, this time for a double bill featuring a prose text as well. He wrote to Con Leventhal about it on 14 September 1976: 'N.Y. Mabou Mines doing their Lost Ones in the National Gallery opening yesterday & following up with a by all accounts regrettable Cascando' (2016: 435). The latter, directed by JoAnne Akalaitis, now had 'five actors seated at a table in the corner of a cluttered room' (2016: 435n5), so it deviated even further from Beckett's directives. Still, his referring to the production as 'theirs' is a sign of his growing awareness that it was not his work being performed but someone else's (re)interpretation of it.

As much as Beckett was advising trusted directors like Schneider about his plays to 'do them your own way' around this time (2016: 566), he slowly but surely ceded authority when it came to adaptations. His response of 26 April 1980 to a cassette tape recording of Chaikin's reading from *Texts for Nothing* and *How It Is* is telling in this regard: 'I listened to it with much interest. I thought the utterance too brisk & lively, especially end of How it is, for such consternation & extremity. But you know what authors are' (2016: 526). We can still detect a note of irony or sarcasm in Beckett's response, but he does acknowledge – however reluctantly – that his own artistic conception and his own definition of 'loss' need not be the guiding principles for adaptations across genres and media. That realisation was not restricted to friends or professionals Beckett admired but also included others, especially when they confronted him with accomplished facts. As he wrote to Bray on 1 October 1981: 'Letter from director Gérard Philippe [sic] pleading ignorance of fait accompli: stage adaptation instead of simple reading as authorized (Premier amour)' (2016: 559). This performance, 'set on the bridge of a boat' (2016: 559n2), shows that Beckett was starting to lose his grip on creative reworkings of his texts. By 1982, the tables seemed to have turned completely, others no longer encroaching on his work but the other way around. On 6 May of that year, he wrote to Alfred Behrens and Michael Kuball about their cinematic treatments of sections from *Murphy*: 'I have no suggestions. I don't want to intervene in any way' (2016: 581).

Especially with regard to Beckett's infamous veto on all-female productions of *Godot*, a Greek staging directed by Adonis Vouyoucas is fascinating: 'I remember writing to Beckett to ask if my wife could play Lucky, because I wanted his role to be genderless, with Lucky dressed in a white suit, wearing a smart tie, entirely white-faced, eyebrows very high, and with his famous wig. He gave me his permission because the idea appealed to him' (qtd in Beckett, 2016: 673). Although Beckett's note from April 1986 to Lindon about the matter does not convey much allure, it is revealing in its terseness: 'Permission granted and sod it' (2016: 673). In addition to it being a production outside of France, Germany, the UK or the US, which Beckett often judged less stringently, the sheer number of creative reworkings that crop up in his letters from the 1970s and 1980s – whether approved or not – must have made it clear to him that adaptation was fast becoming a cultural force to be reckoned with. In the late twentieth century, all the more so with the advent of 'new media' in the early twenty-first century, the literary work had become creative public property long before its copyright officially expired, a cultural trend difficult if not impossible to stop, let alone regulate or police.

Post-Beckett

In this regard, the period between Beckett's death in 1989 and the centenary of his birth in 2006 is a transitional phase. While the publication of the *Theatrical Notebooks* series (1992–99) unfixed the plays by including facsimiles and transcriptions that document the revisions Beckett made as a director of his own work, to a certain extent they also enshrined them by means of the 'revised texts' they contained. Together with Knowlson's critically acclaimed biography, *Damned to Fame* (1996), this surrounded the author and his work with an aura of adoration, eventually culminating in the *Beckett on Film* project (2001–2) and the centenary celebrations organised in Dublin in 2006. For Hutcheon, the *Beckett on Film* project was an example of 'reverential treatments':

> Sometimes homage is all that is possible – or allowed. In 2005, RTE, Channel 4, Tyrone Productions, and the Irish Film Board sponsored 19 short film adaptations of the work of Samuel Beckett by directors either experienced with or influenced by the playwright. But in the name of fidelity, the Beckett estate would allow no changes to the texts whatsoever. (2013: 93)

However, because these were transpositions of essentially theatrical works to film, with links to television, the ways in which the plays had been conceptualised for their original source medium had to be reconfigured. And even though the texts themselves did not undergo any major alterations, the stage directions were not adhered to stringently, which characterises the *Beckett on Film* project more accurately as a crucial watershed between fidelity and freedom, though still falling more on the side of the former than the latter.[10] Ironically, as a side effect of Beckett's 'authorised' versions having been recorded for posterity, literally through the DVD release of *Beckett on Film* but also with Faber's reissue of the *Theatrical Notebooks* in more accessible and cheaper paperback format (2019–21), the demand for 'unauthorised' versions only seems to have increased.

Recent years have brought instability as well, the *Letters of Samuel Beckett* showing sides of him that were hitherto unsuspected – as we have seen – but also the Beckett Digital Manuscript Project (2011–present).[11] Not only does the BDMP chart the inconsistencies of Beckett's published texts, it also highlights the sometimes radically different draft versions that preceded them and relates them to books in his personal library and notes, which often reveal surprising sources of interest. Particularly unhinging are unfinished and unpublished texts. 'Last Soliloquy', an abandoned dramatic dialogue originally situated in 1958 (Cohn, 2005: 241) but now redated to 1981 (Nixon, 2014: 298–9), is a pertinent illustration. What starts out in the spirit of fidelity soon takes the form of an iconoclastic adaptation. As two characters are rehearsing a classic suicide scene reminiscent of Shakespeare, P[rompter] says to A[ctor] 'You swoon too soon' after he gulps down a goblet and drops to his knees. When A asks P 'if I did? Who'd be ~~the wiser~~ know? [sic]' and the latter replies 'The author', he gets a cutting retort: 'Fuck the author. Fuck all authors' (qtd in Nixon, 2009: 26). Cohn and Nixon connect the fragment to *Catastrophe*, finished soon thereafter, but while that play stages an actor who rebels against a dictatorial director – an exaggerated self-representation of the late Beckett – the consequences of an author undermining his own authority over his own texts through his own work would have been far more incendiary and subversive. It is tempting to read this passage in light of 'intentionalism' and Roland Barthes' essay on 'The Death of the Author' – which he saw as a necessary price to pay for the 'birth of the reader' (Barthes, 1977: 148) – but it also has significance for the notion of adaptation.

Before the fragment breaks off, P asks A what at first sight appears to be a question but is in fact a statement, making it rhetorical or at least ambiguous: 'Are we sticking to the book or are we not' (qtd in Nixon, 2009: 26). The fact that Beckett abandoned yet preserved this fragment fits in with the ambivalence regarding authorship and creative reworkings of his texts that we see in letters from the 1970s and 1980s. With this gesture, he relegated 'Last Soliloquy' to the so-called 'grey canon' (Gontarski, 2006), perhaps because he realised that authors cannot proclaim themselves dead while still alive, not even through their fictional characters. Ever since the mid-1950s, Beckett had been very conscious of what he called his 'Posthumous Droppings' (2011: 446), and in the 1980s – across multiple genres – he was preoccupied with the question of what literary epitaph to end his career on. 'Last Soliloquy' is one of the discarded, but to this list we might well add 'Epilogue', an aborted piece of prose-theatre from 1981 (Nixon, 2014: 297), or 'Hörendspiel', an unpublished radio sketch from 1988 (Beckett, 2016: 704). 'Comment dire' / 'what is the word' was eventually the poem he decided to 'Keep!$^{\text{for end}}$', as the top of the manuscript reads (Van Hulle, 2011: 104), leaving the rest to wander as ghosts in his literary afterlife. From that posthumous place they keep revivifying the Beckett canon. This dichotomy between the official and the unofficial

Beckett, the on-the-record and the off-the-record author, is what posthumous adaptations of his work have to negotiate and come to terms with. Perhaps more so than Barthes' 'death', Beckett's 'fuck' is the perfect motto for this dynamic, as it captures the love-hate feeling that typifies all non-authorial adaptation.

Notes

1 See Zilliacus (1976: 181–2) and Kiryushina (2021).
2 See Feldman (2014), O'Reilly et al. (2017: 134–41), Van Hulle and Verhulst (2017b: 108–17).
3 See Knowlson (1996: 466–8) and Van Hulle (2015: 126–7).
4 See Zilliacus (1976: 151–2), Esslin (1980: 138–9), Bourgeois (2001), Herren (2007: 175–81) and Beloborodova (2019: 122–8).
5 See Zilliacus (1976: 203–8) and Van Hulle (2015: 108–15).
6 See Zilliacus (1976: 153), Esslin (1980: 140–1) and Stewart (2017).
7 See Esslin (1980: 152), Whitelaw (1996: 131–2), Knowlson (1996: 619–20), Bignell (2009: 147–8) and Little (2021: 107–9).
8 Beckett made this comment in an unpublished letter to Alan Simpson on 15 January 1958 (TCD 10731-56). It is quoted in full in Verhulst (2023; forthcoming).
9 Transmediality and intermediality are two phenomena that have been attracting increasing attention in recent years, taking as their scope either a specific work, a period or Beckett's career at large. See, for example, Engelberts (2001), McMullan (2010, 2021), Verhulst (2021, 2022), as well as the 'Beckett and Intermediality' special issue of *Samuel Beckett Today / Aujourd'hui*, guest-edited by Trish McTighe, Emilie Morin and Mark Nixon (32.1, 2021).
10 For a more thorough discussion of the creative double bind that marks *Beckett on Film*, see Frost and McMullan (2003).
11 See www.beckettarchive.org (accessed 23 December 2021).

References

Barthes, R. (1977). *Image-Music-Text : Selected Essays*. Trans. S. Heath. Glasgow: Collins.
Beckett, S. (1999 [1998]). *No Author Better Served: The Correspondence of Samuel Beckett & Alan Schneider*. Ed. M. Harmon. Cambridge, MA: Harvard University Press.
Beckett, S. (2009). *Company, Ill Seen Ill Said, Worstward Ho, Stirrings Still*. Ed. D. Van Hulle. London: Faber and Faber.
Beckett, S. (2011). *The Letters of Samuel Beckett, Volume II: 1941–1956*. Ed. G. Craig, M. Dow Fehsenfeld, D. Gunn and L. More Overbeck. Cambridge: Cambridge University Press.

Beckett, S. (2014). *The Letters of Samuel Beckett, Volume III: 1957–1965*. Ed. G. Craig, M. Dow Fehsenfeld, D. Gunn and L. More Overbeck. Cambridge: Cambridge University Press.

Beckett, S. (2016). *The Letters of Samuel Beckett, Volume IV: 1966–1989*. Ed. G. Craig, M. Dow Fehsenfeld, D. Gunn and L. More Overbeck. Cambridge: Cambridge University Press.

Beloborodova, O. (2019). *The Making of Samuel Beckett's 'Play / 'Comédie' and 'Film'*. Brussels and London: University Press Antwerp and Bloomsbury.

Bignell, J. (2009). *Beckett on Screen: The Television Plays*. Manchester: Manchester University Press.

Bignell, J. (2020). 'When *Beckett on Film* migrated to television', *Literary History*, 51.169, 97–108.

Bourgeois, C. (ed.) (2001). *'Comédie' / Marin Karmitz / Samuel Beckett*. Paris: Éditions du Regard.

Brinnin, J. M. (1989). *Dylan Thomas in America*. New York: Paragon House.

Cleverdon, D. (1969). *The Growth of 'Milk Wood'*. London: Dent.

Cohn, R. (2005 [2001]). *A Beckett Canon*. Ann Arbor: The University of Michigan Press.

Dowd, G. (2006). '*Ohio Impromptu*, genre and Beckett on Film', in G. Dowd, L. Stevenson and J. Strong (eds), *Genre Matters: Essays in Theory and Criticism*. Intellect: Bristol and Portland, pp. 69–83.

Duckworth, C. (1987). 'Beckett's new *Godot*', in J. Acheson (ed.), *Beckett's Later Fiction and Drama: Texts for Company*. Basingstoke: Palgrave Macmillan, pp. 175–92.

Engelberts, M. (2001). *Défis du récit scénique: formes et enjeux du mode narratif dans le théâtre de Beckett et Duras*. Geneva: Droz.

Esslin, M. (1980). *Mediations: Essays on Brecht, Beckett, and the Media*. London: Eyre Methuen.

Feldman, M. (2014). 'Beckett's trilogy on the Third Programme', *Samuel Beckett Today / Aujourd'hui*, 26, 41–62.

Flynn, D. (2016). 'The form and function of dialectical *cinécriture* in Beckett's *Company*', *Journal of Beckett Studies*, 25.2, 188–205.

Frost, E., and A. McMullan (2003). 'Questions of adaptation, aesthetics and audience in filming Beckett's theatrical canon', in L. Ben-Zvi (ed.), *Drawing on Beckett: Portraits, Performances and Cultural Contexts*. Tel Aviv: Assaph Books, pp. 215–38.

Gontarski, S. E. (1998). 'Revising himself: performance as text in Samuel Beckett's theatre', *Journal of Modern Literature*, 22.1, 131–45.

Gontarski, S. E. (2006). 'Greying the canon: Beckett in performance', in. S. E. Gontarski and A. Uhlmann (eds), *Beckett after Beckett*. Gainesville: University Press of Florida, pp. 141–57.

Herren, G. (2007). *Samuel Beckett's Plays on Film and Television*. New York: Palgrave Macmillan.

Hutcheon, L., and S. O'Flynn (2013 [2006]). *A Theory of Adaptation*. London: Routledge.

Johnson, N. E., and J. Heron (2020). *Experimental Beckett: Contemporary Performance Practices*. Cambridge. Cambridge University Press

Joyce, J. (1986). *Ulysses*. Ed. H. W. Gabler. New York: Vintage.

Kiryushina, G. (2021). '"A medium for fleas": Beckett, Mitrani and 1950s–1960s French television drama', in E. Adar, G. Kiryushina and M. Nixon (eds), *Beckett and Technology*. Edinburgh: Edinburgh University Press, pp. 125–41.

Knowlson, J. (1996). *Damned to Fame: The Life of Samuel Beckett*. London: Bloomsbury.

Little, J. (2020). *Samuel Beckett in Confinement: The Politics of Closed Space*. London: Bloomsbury.

Little, J. (2021). *The Making of Samuel Beckett's 'Not I' / 'Pas moi', 'That Time' / 'Cette fois' and 'Footfalls' / 'Pas'*. Brussels and London: University Press Antwerp and Bloomsbury.

McMullan, A. (2010). *Performing Embodiment in Samuel Beckett's Drama*. London: Routledge.

McMullan, A. (2021). *Beckett's Intermedial Ecosystems: Closed Space Environments across the Stage, Prose and Media Works*. Cambridge: Cambridge University Press.

Nixon, M. (2009). '"Writing myself into the ground": textual existence and death in Beckett', in S. Barfield, P. Tew and M. Feldman (eds), *Beckett and Death*. London: Continuum, pp. 22–30.

Nixon, M. (2014). 'Beckett's unpublished canon', in S. E. Gontarski (ed.), *The Edinburgh Companion to Samuel Beckett and the Arts*. Edinburgh: Edinburgh University Press, pp. 282–305.

Nugent-Folan, G. (2021). *The Making of Samuel Beckett's 'Company' / 'Compagnie'*. Brussels and London: University Press Antwerp and Bloomsbury.

O'Reilly, É. M., D. Van Hulle and P. Verhulst (2017). *The Making of Samuel Beckett's 'Molloy'*. Brussels and London: University Press Antwerp and Bloomsbury.

Pilling, J. (2017). 'Changing my tune: Beckett and the BBC Third Programme (1957–1960)', in D. Addyman, M. Feldman and E. Tonning (eds), *Beckett and BBC Radio: A Reassessment*. New York: Palgrave Macmillan, pp. 169–83.

Sanders, J. (2016 [2006]). *Adaptation and Appropriation*. London and New York: Routledge.

Stewart, P. (2017). 'Fitting the prose to radio: the case of *Lessness*', in D. Addyman, M. Feldman and E. Tonning (eds), *Beckett and BBC Radio: A Reassessment*. New York: Palgrave Macmillan, pp. 211–27.

Tonning, E. (2017). 'Mediating modernism: the Third Programme, Samuel Beckett, and mass communication', in D. Addyman, M. Feldman and E. Tonning (eds), *Beckett and BBC Radio: A Reassessment*. New York: Palgrave Macmillan, pp. 59–79.

Tophoven, E. (2015). *Godot hinter Gittern: Eine Hochstaplergeschichte*. Berlin: Verbrecher Verlag.

Van Hulle, D. (2011). *The Making of Samuel Beckett's 'Stirrings Still' / 'Soubresauts' and 'Comment dire' / 'what is the word'*. Brussels: University Press Antwerp.

Van Hulle, D. (2015). *The Making of Samuel Beckett's 'Krapp's Last Tape' / 'La Dernière Bande'*. Brussels and London: University Press Antwerp and Bloomsbury.

Van Hulle, D. (2021). 'Creative concurrence: gearing genetic criticism for the sociology of writing', *Variants*, 15–16, pp. 45–62.

Van Hulle, D., and P. Verhulst (2017a). *The Making of Samuel Beckett's 'En attendant Godot' / 'Waiting for Godot'*. Brussels and London: University Press Antwerp and Bloomsbury.

Van Hulle, D., and P. Verhulst (2017b). *The Making of Samuel Beckett's 'Malone meurt' / 'Malone Dies'*. Brussels and London: University Press Antwerp and Bloomsbury.

Verhulst, P. (2021). 'Beckett's technography: traces of radio in the later prose', in E. Adar, G. Kiryushina and M. Nixon (eds), *Beckett and Technology*. Edinburgh: Edinburgh University Press, pp. 95–108.

Verhulst, P. (2022). 'Beckett's intermedial bodies: remediating theatre through radio', in M. Nixon, B. Rapcsak and P. Schweighauser (eds), *Beckett and Media*. Manchester: Manchester University Press, 107–22.

Verhulst, P. (2023 [forthcoming]). *The Making of Samuel Beckett's Radio Plays*. Brussels and London: University Press Antwerp and Bloomsbury.

Wakeling, C. (2021). *Beckett's Laboratory: Experiments in the Theatre Enclosure*. London: Methuen Drama/Bloomsbury.

Weller, S. (2015). 'The tone of displacement: Samuel Beckett, Robert Pinget and the art of adaptation', in J. Pilling and M. Nixon (eds), *On in their Company: Essays on Beckett, with Tributes and Sketches*. Reading: Beckett International Foundation, pp. 21–41.

Whitelaw, B. (1996 [1995]). *Billie Whitelaw … Who He? An Autobiography*. London: Hodder & Stoughton.

Zilliacus, C. (1976). *Beckett and Broadcasting: A Study of the Works of Samuel Beckett for and in Radio and Television*. Åbo: Åbo Akademi.

2

Adaptation and convergence: *Beckett on Film*

Jonathan Bignell

The *Beckett on Film* project, completed in 2000, originated in the Dublin Gate Theatre's 1991 staging of all nineteen of Beckett's theatre works and led to the adaptations being screened at film festivals and as television broadcasts, sold as DVD box sets and distributed via online video streaming.[1] Because of its scale, *Beckett on Film* is perhaps the most salient ever example of adapting Beckett. This chapter argues that these evolutions of the project are more significant than simply repackaging the content produced in one medium for distribution in another. Rather, they work with and reflect on the borders between mediums, and the ways that creative works fit into new medial environments. By studying these transitions, *Beckett on Film* can be seen not as a fixed text (or collection of texts) but as a mobile and mutable work that changes in relation to medium and audience, with different spatial and temporal specificities across the history of its adaptations. The chapter debates these questions mainly by tracing the British and Irish stories of how its makers, the Blue Angel production company, the Irish broadcaster RTÉ (Raidió Teilifís Éireann) and the British Channel 4 television channel, framed *Beckett on Film*. The chapter addresses its genesis, production, scheduling for cinema and television screenings aimed at specialist, general and then educational audiences. It also considers how the project's adaptation into the 'new' media of DVD and online video framed the DVD as a cultural asset and a prestige collectable, aligning it with discourses of taste and connoisseurship.

The completed films of Beckett's plays are not the primary objects of analysis here. Instead, the focus is on the processes of their production and distribution, and the interstitial and paratextual materials that accompanied them, because these shaped what *Beckett on Film* was perceived to be. A proliferation of press releases, news coverage, product packaging, interviews and behind-the-scenes footage, as well as several associated print publications, framed, targeted and interpreted the *Beckett on Film* productions. The appropriate metaphor, picking up on the Darwinian associations of adaptation, might be that the project was designed to fit a certain niche in the audio-visual ecosystem, and over time it expanded, contracted and was retrospectively modified in order to fit into new, changed environmental conditions. The point is not to critique the ambition and achievement of this expensively mounted, comprehensive series of Beckett adaptations, featuring international stars. It is not perverse that it changed and became something else. Indeed, critical investigation of the genesis and afterlife of the series can shed light on how Beckett's work was renegotiated in the twenty-first century in order to better survive. This chapter argues that *Beckett on Film* has been agile, resilient and adaptable in ways that suited an emergent culture of media convergence.

Adaptation, authorship, text and medium

There are (at least) two axes for the analysis of adaptation. As Sarah Cardwell (2018) has explored, adaptation implies the production of sequential versions based on an original, in a temporal and relatively linear progression. Alternatively, adaptation can describe an intertextual, intermedial, transmedial field in which a work undergoes or results from an expanding, spatial spreading-out where some of its components are reconfigured in different guises but remain recognisably the same. This chapter argues that *Beckett on Film* has aspects of both the linear and the spatial dimensions, which is the secret of its success. Of course, the films are adaptations of prior works: Beckett's plays. The project is also fitted to the spatial axis of media convergence (Jenkins, 2008), in which audio-visual texts are designed for, and consumed via, multiple platforms and devices at the same time. In the era of convergence, hitherto separate media technologies come together, so that a portable phone can play radio or TV, or access an online newspaper, for example. Films and television programmes are available online, and live broadcasts and DVD recordings are supplemented by additional content that can be accessed either via the television set or via the screen of another device like a tablet computer. What made this transformation possible was digitisation, whereby both production and distribution are carried out by digital means, making hitherto different mediums compatible.

Because of its associations with mutability and transformation, convergence implicitly questions ideas of textual identity, self-sufficiency and stability. At the same time as enabling Beckett's plays to shift from medium to medium, convergence might separate them from their origins in, and dependence on, a theatrical provenance. The signalling of theatricality in some of the *Beckett on Film* adaptations, such as *Catastrophe* (directed by David Mamet), shot on location in a dilapidated theatre, can be seen as a recuperative strategy that addresses this issue. Wilton's Music Hall, originally built as a sumptuous palace of entertainment in 1859, had fallen into dereliction by the time it was used for *Catastrophe* ('History', 2021). Its Victorian stage had appeared in films and video to introduce reflexive discourses about performance, including in the biopic *Chaplin* (1992), in Frankie Goes to Hollywood's pop video 'Relax' (1984) and when Deborah Warner directed Fiona Shaw in a staged reading of T. S. Eliot's poem *The Waste Land* (1997). To use Wilton's as a production location was to invoke theatricality in ruins, while also calling on theatre performance's liveness and bodily materiality, whose power relationships *Catastrophe* instantiates and explores on screen. Because convergence means moving across and between forms of expression, a work can be potentially deconstructive and experimental by engaging in dialogue with them. The adaptation of *Play* (directed by Anthony Minghella) in the *Beckett on Film* project does this too, through allusions to the conventions of cinema and visual art as well as theatre (Bignell, 2009: 33–7). A soundstage at Pinewood Studios houses a large set whose design invokes artistic images of hell, the staging of *Play* in the theatre and the mechanical apparatus of filmmaking, all at the same time.

The places where artworks are made condition and enable their meanings, and the properties of specific spaces and diverse locations in *Beckett on Film* are important to its significance. It used convergent facilities that were routinely rented out, short-term, for both cinema and television production, rather than being the established production base of a large institution (such as the BBC's Television Centre or studio backlots in Hollywood). The most-used production base was Ardmore Studios, a major studio site in Ireland ('Ardmore Studios', 2021). RTÉ's most popular TV programme, the soap opera *Fair City* (1989–present), had been shot there until 1994, and previously its studios had been used on big-budget films for the international market.[2] The Dublin-set film *Angela's Ashes* (1999) used the studios for its interior scenes shortly before the large soundstages, equipped with cyclorama backdrops, housed *Beckett on Film*. *Not I* was shot at Shepperton studios near London, where its actor Julianne Moore, director Neil Jordan and producer Stephen Woolley had just made *The End of the Affair* (1999), a romantic drama based on Graham Greene's eponymous novel ('Not I', 2021). The huge studio complex was being used for productions including *102 Dalmatians* (2000), *Gladiator* (2000) and Channel 4's television sitcom *Black Books* (2000–4). In planning how to realise the *Beckett on Film* adaptations in concrete, spatial terms, the production team chose sites that expressed ideas of medium specificity, and also sites that had adapted to the era of media convergence and were used for cinema, television and video projects.

What holds *Beckett on Film* together as an adaptation, signalling it, precisely, as adaptation, is Beckett's name.[3] The very title indicates that

Beckett on Film is authorised by Beckett's authorial brand, and the entire spoken text of each published play is delivered in its film adaptation. This completeness and fidelity were the prime conditions the project's producers had to satisfy to get copyright permission to adapt the plays. The issue of rights invites us to consider creative work as property that can have a persistent identity across time and across different realisations because it is owned by its author (or their estate in this case) (Bignell, 2015). Property rights provide some stability across porous media boundaries in the shifting landscape of convergence.

Since Beckett's spoken text is the basis for the *Beckett on Film* productions, plays that have no dialogue can push at the boundaries of adaptation. These plays' intertextual fields can spread out further when there are no words to which they are bound. For John Frow, the 'identification of an intertext is an act of interpretation. The intertext is not a real and causative source but a theoretical construct formed by and serving the purposes of a reading' (1990: 46). When Damien Hirst placed surgical equipment in the shape of a swastika among the detritus that the camera swoops over in his adaptation of *Breath*, it is an intertextual motif that results from and leads to a whole network of interpretations (Hüser, 2011). In the adaptation of *Act Without Words II*, directed by Enda Hughes, animated actors seem to recreate a 1920s slapstick film short, recalling Beckett's fascination with silent cinema and vaudeville performance. Creators and audiences make intertextual and intermedial connections, and Beckett's audio-visual work was already intermedial from the beginning (Bignell, 2020). The *Beckett on Film* adaptations that are not constrained by the requirement to use Beckett's full text can more actively seize opportunities for rich intertextual allusion. Such exceptions draw greater attention to the strictures that *Beckett on Film* accepts when it proclaims itself an adaptation oriented around authorship and textual fidelity.

From stage to screen

The main originator of the project was Michael Colgan, director of the Gate Theatre between 1983 and 2016. There he mounted classic plays featuring international stars.[4] In October 1991 Colgan produced the Gate's Beckett Festival, nested within a broader Dublin Theatre Festival. It included productions in other media: RTÉ broadcast Beckett's radio dramas, readings from his novel *Malone Dies* and two of his dramas for television, *Eh Joe* and *… but the clouds …*. In subsequent years the theatre productions toured internationally to Beijing, London, Melbourne, New York and Toronto, for example. The Gate productions were a travelling cultural festival, an event which sought to raise the profiles of the Gate, of Beckett and of Ireland and Irish culture in general. *Beckett on Film*, made shortly after the end of the 1999 tour, is not a record of the theatre productions like the videotapes of live performances collected for Britain's National Theatre Archive or the Theatre Archive in London's Victoria & Albert Museum. Nor are the films remountings of stage productions, such as were done by the BBC when actors, designer and stage props for a recent production were set up in a studio to make a television version of one of Beckett's theatre plays (Bignell, 2022). But when the *Beckett on Film* versions were made they were first screened at film festivals, events like the theatre festivals in which cultural value, national canons and international recognition were negotiated. *Beckett on Film* was in some ways a legacy of the Gate's Beckett extravaganza, an adaptation in the sense of a natural progression or successor.

In an interview for the film industry magazine *Netribution*, Colgan's collaborator, the Irish producer Alan Moloney, formerly of Parallel Films, recalled: 'It was slow to get going, in that people laughed at what we were trying to achieve, saying it couldn't be done. Then gradually one by one, word got out, and we got people interested, then attached. That in turn changed the perception of it' (qtd in Wistreich, 2000). The existing relationship between Colgan and the Beckett Estate 'facilitated the deal' but Moloney found that 'one of the difficulties we had with financing it was convincing people that the way to do it was to do all of the plays, that there was no point in just financing some of them' (qtd in Wistreich, 2000). The profitability and practicality of the project were also challenged by the inherent tension between fidelity and artistic freedom: 'Obviously each director/producer team had complete control over casting, art direction, photography and so forth. Interpretation is not the right word, but they were visual interpretations. There was a lot of flexibility within that, but they weren't allowed to rewrite anything' (qtd in Wistreich, 2000). Given the different stagings and locations in *Beckett on Film*, it is not surprising that Wistreich asked Moloney about stylistic consistency. The project adapted the work of one author but 'visually, they could do anything. You can see in each piece the personality of the director, in an acute way. There is a consistency in terms of the shape of the titles that open and close each of the films' (Moloney qtd in Wistreich, 2000). Common branding of the films became crucial as one of the few means to express the project's coherence, even more so later when the films were packaged together as a DVD set.

The project was not financed in the same way as commercial cinema, since the £4.5 million budget excluded actors' and directors' fees: 'all of the directors and the cast worked on a favour-expenses basis, so there was an enormous amount of co-operation and a lot of goodwill that made it happen' (Moloney qtd in Wistreich, 2000). The films were shot intermittently for a full year, then some were shown at festivals in New York, Toronto and Venice before they were all screened in Dublin in February 2001. The launch was covered in RTÉ news bulletins that included extracts from a speech by the Director General of RTÉ, Joe Mulholland, and interviews with Colgan and the actor Michael Gambon (who starred in *Endgame*). The event was also reported internationally: *Irish America* magazine, for example, aimed at émigrés and US citizens claiming Irish ancestry, reported that 'the Irish Film Center's two theaters were filled with fans eager to catch the premieres of cinematic versions of all 19 of Samuel Beckett's stage plays. Nearly every screening sold out well in advance' ('Celebrating', 2001). In September 2001, the London launch was introduced by Harold Pinter at the Barbican, and the directors Conor McPherson and Enda Hughes were interviewed alongside screenings of their respective adaptations of *Endgame* and *Act Without Words II*. For audiences, the launch was an event not so different from Colgan's theatre festival and was oriented around Beckett's profile as an Irish author. Such ambivalences can be seen throughout the project. *Beckett on Film* is both cinema and theatre, it is oriented around Beckett but also the films' different directors, Irish and international, and it is definitively faithful to, yet creatively adaptive of, Beckett's texts. Characteristically, RTÉ News's interview with Gambon was shot with a large photograph of Beckett looming over Gambon's shoulder (see Figure 2.1), and Gambon recalled 'you can't get a comma or a full stop wrong. Have to get it right. If you get it wrong, the estate would complain, so it's got to be very accurate. It was a tough order but I wouldn't have missed it'.[5] Beckett's authorship and his estate's authorisation of the productions provided discourses of coherence and value that legitimated the project's diverse approaches to adaptation and the films' diverse visual styles.

The films were made in collaboration with Tyrone Productions, a company with experience of producing television programmes and DVD video, using facilities in both Belfast and Dublin ('About us', 2021). The company made the video adaptations of the live stage show *Riverdance*, which became an internationally successful DVD showcasing Irish traditional dancing, and they went on to make the similar music and dance spectacular *Heartbeat of Home* (2013). Tyrone Productions is closely connected with Irish broadcasters, making factual programmes, entertainment specials (like *Christmas Carols with The Priests*, 2013) and programmes in the Irish language. Resembling some of Tyrone's other work, *Beckett on Film* was positioned as an audio-visual event expressing Irish identity in a marketable way.

The branding of the *Beckett on Film* productions distinguishes them from conventional film adaptations, since they have a common title sequence, introductory music and graphic style, for example. These paratextual and

Figure 2.1 Michael Gambon at the launch of *Beckett on Film*.

interstitial elements are specific to each film (naming its director, for example) but also similar to the other *Beckett on Film* adaptations. Selected films were grouped together at the Venice and Toronto Film Festivals, emphasising their unity. Film festivals are sales events as much as cultural ones, and *Beckett on Film* was being showcased to distributors for exhibition in different national territories and for television screening, with the implicit invitation to show the films as a series or season of related works. Such seriality is associated much more with television than cinema, however, and a review of the adaptation of *Happy Days* for the cinema industry newspaper *Variety* expressed uncertainty about where the project belonged. This was 'probably an unfilmable play', in which

> Canadian director Patricia Rozema, faced with specifically theatrical material, does her best to open out the piece by filming it in a windswept desert landscape, with middling results. Pic [i.e. the movie] is more suited to the small screen than the large; it's the power of the dialogue and the emotions, and the agonizing truthfulness of the performance, that succeed here. (Stratton, 2000)

There was uncertainty about what *Beckett on Film* is, and *Variety* implicitly advised buyers that it would work better on television than in the cinema.

The legal entity behind the project was Blue Angel Films, a production company set up for the purpose and headed by Colgan and Moloney.[6] Between them, they had extensive contacts with Irish and international actors, directors and production staff. The other partners in the production were solely investors. The Irish Film Board (renamed Screen Ireland in 2018) was a government-funded organisation with a remit to support and promote Irish film and television production. This included bringing outside investment and foreign creative talent to Ireland, as *Beckett on Film* did, for economic as well as cultural reasons. The Board is closely associated with Culture Ireland, which promotes Irish arts within Ireland and worldwide, such as through film festivals or providing Irish films to exhibitors overseas.[7] By investing in *Beckett on Film*, the Irish Film Board and Culture Ireland drew creative personnel and other investors into Ireland but also supported the export of Irish cultural products and promoted the visibility of Ireland as a brand. Many of the directors making *Beckett on Film* already worked in Ireland, and overseas collaborators such as the Canadian Atom Egoyan had links with Ireland. Egoyan had shot his film *Felicia's Journey* (1999) in Cork shortly before he directed *Krapp's Last Tape* for the project. Investment from Channel 4 for *Beckett on Film* followed the channel's policy to both support production of independent films and promote cultural knowledge among its audience (Smith, 2014).[8] The channel had an Independent Film and Video Department to sponsor experimental productions, and funded films intended for theatrical distribution but also television showing on its own Film4 channel (launched in 1998). Channel 4 did not engage with the strong British tradition of commissioning original television drama so much as with the British film industry, financing and screening films by directors such as Stephen Frears or Derek Jarman. *Beckett on Film* was supported by institutions with a cultural mission and money to support experimental projects, though for different reasons.

As an independent production company, Blue Angel owns the films it makes and can sell rights to them. The sale of distribution rights is the major income source for filmmaking and the profitability of a film depends on correctly estimating their commercial value. Another key funding source is the sale of secondary or subsidiary rights, especially television broadcast, DVD sales or streaming of a film, and merchandising rights for film-related products. Both RTÉ and Channel 4 had track records of making television adaptations of Beckett's plays and co-financed the project in exchange for television rights to screen it. Although Beckett on screen in the Anglophone world is most associated with the BBC (Bignell, 2009: 99–111), Channel 4 made *Three Plays by Samuel Beckett* (1990) with director Walter Asmus, for example. Channel 4's original remit, laid down by the 1980 Broadcasting Act, required it to appeal to tastes and interests not generally catered for by Britain's main commercial broadcaster, ITV, to make educational programmes and to encourage innovation in the form and content of programmes. *Beckett on Film* could be seen as realising each of these three imperatives (Bignell, 2019). Channel 4 became involved when the production team approached it for a substantial financial contribution. Michael Jackson, the channel's Chief Executive from 1997 to 2001, recalled: 'As I remember it they needed to make up the budget and had a specific number in mind' (Jackson, 2021). Despite the project's many links to cinema auteurs, its title's incorporation of the word *Film* and its presence on the international film festival circuit, financially the project was structured like a television co-production. Again, *Beckett on Film* straddled distinctions between mediums, taking advantage of convergences between them.

Screening and distribution

When screened on RTÉ and Channel 4 in 2001 the plays achieved low audience ratings but they fitted the remit of the channels to do cultural work for the public good (Bignell, 2019). RTÉ, the main broadcaster in Ireland, is funded both through general taxation and by advertising revenue, and is tasked with offering a broad-based entertainment, education and information service that gives space to domestically produced Irish content and represents Irish life. Since 1999 it had been required by law to commission 20 per cent of its programmes from independent producers and undertook co-productions with Channel 4 to make the most of its shrinking budget (Sheehan, 2004: 47). Channel 4, established in 1982, was required to be distinctively different from the main BBC1 and ITV channels and to represent and serve minorities. It made no programmes of its own and often commissioned or acquired them from small, independent producers with specialist interests. Its dependence on advertising revenue meant Channel 4 also showed popular audience-pleasing programmes like reality shows and US sitcoms, yet its brand was appropriate for Beckett's prestigious but demanding work. By the time of the making of *Beckett on Film* in 2000, Channel 4 had bulging coffers, thanks to profits that had risen from £330 million in 1993 to £650 million (Born, 2003: 778). According to Jackson (2021), *Beckett on Film* was 'not commissioned with profit in mind' but represented a 'classic example of cross subsidy' in which income from commercially successful output was used to fund programmes with perceived public value. This was recognised when the project was awarded the South Bank Show prize for Best Television Drama in 2002, selected by a panel of British industry experts. The prize categorised the plays as a single television work, rather than as a set of cinema films or as multiple television dramas. Accepting the prize, Cathal Goan, RTÉ's Director of Television, described Beckett as 'a giant of Irish literature'. In his view, the project was 'a huge privilege for RTÉ, and as such it belongs to the highest traditions of public service broadcasting' ('Beckett on Film wins', 2002). *Beckett on Film* conflated literature, theatre, film and television to the project's benefit.

Beckett on Film was already a convergent product deriving from both cinema and television cultures. For Channel 4 it was also aligned with a broader move into digital services such as the launch of a digital channel for youth audiences, E4, in 2001. Jackson summarised the position as being

> like the BBC but maybe more so; always a mix of objectives – sometimes, as with C4 news, subsidised, sometimes profit making as with *Big Brother*. Often C4 [is] at its best when it combines 'remit' with noisy and noticed programmes like *Queer as Folk*. Over the years it's been harder for C4 to devote airtime to the kind of programming that defined C4 in its earlier days – like Beckett, things like a Fred Wiseman season or foreign language films. Even [the] Film Four channel now has commercials. To a certain extent the rise of feature length docs and on-line has stood in for this. (2021)

The British television broadcasts of *Beckett on Film* got rather lost in Channel 4's schedules (Bignell, 2019). In Ireland, as Helena Sheehan reports, 'many [viewers] taped them, because they were worthy and should be archived, but never got around to watching them' (2004: 47). The emergent positioning of the project as a multiplatform, convergent work was supported by Channel 4's commissioning of theatre critic Aleks Sierz (2001) to write an accompanying booklet, priced £4.95, as a further supplement to the adaptations. The richly illustrated booklet gives an account of Beckett's life and work, as well as his importance to theatre, and has short features on the *Beckett on Film* adaptations including quotations from their actors and directors. Increasing numbers of paratexts and supplementary texts became attached to the project as its mediums and audiences changed.

There was an economic downturn around the millennium that reduced advertising income, and the internet and multichannel television eroded television audiences (see Channel 4, 2020: 24–8). Channel 4 moved *Beckett on Film* to a daytime slot and targeted the films at schools and colleges under its 4Learning brand, set up in 2000 as a commercial subsidiary. This opportunity to offer Beckett's work to schools came about because the two major providers of curriculum support on television, the BBC and ITV, had withdrawn from educational broadcasting on their main channels, moving such content to specialist channels or online. As Jackson saw it: 'C4 needs to use its limited airtime to fight for attention in a crowded multi-channel – and streamer and on-line – market. Arguably it still provides value – see *Channel 4 News* and Paralympics and *It's a Sin*, for example. C4 has had to change with the cultural and creative context it lives in' (2021). Digital multichannel television allowed big international players like Sky and Disney to launch new services and peel viewers away from the older generalist channels, which regrouped and changed their strategies. Channel 4 stepped into a role left vacant by its competitors, offering public value and commercial educational material in a distinctive way. *Beckett on Film* was part of a strategy to develop programming niches that others had abandoned, and to address specific audiences that were under-served. Teenagers at school were now the audience for *Beckett on Film*, overlapping with Channel 4's address to teenagers in its entertainment programmes and channels. Georgina Born describes 4Learning in this context as 'cross-platform educational output, seen as ripe for both commercial and public service expansion as well as a means of responding to government promotion of broadband educational delivery' (Born, 2003: 784). *Beckett on Film* adapted again, fitting into a complex audio-visual ecosystem that was continually in flux.

DVD, online video and resilience

As a DVD, *Beckett on Film* invites comparison with other box set products and their attractions for a purchaser. It was released in November 2001, at a price of £100, via the website of the films' Irish distributor, Clarence Pictures ('Beckett on Film reaches', 2001), and also through Channel 4's website.[9] By that time about one-third of the British audience was viewing television on digital rather than analogue devices (Born, 2003: 773), and the UK government's Communications White Paper of 2000 had placed the onus on television broadcasters to bring the country into the internet age by driving take-up of digital services. The UK's regulatory bodies for cinema, television, telephony and the internet were subsumed into a single authority, Ofcom. Divisions between media and between public and commercial services were being blurred, and Channel 4 pioneered multiplatform and interactive television in which programme brands were used to invite audiences to migrate from television to DVD, to the internet and back. The channel also needed to monetise programme-related digital resources after it had dropped into deficit due to over-spending on imported popular US series. While the *Beckett on Film* DVD would not have swelled Channel 4's coffers significantly, Beckett's plays were carried along in a larger shift of educational and high-cultural resources from analogue, time-bound mediums towards digital products to be owned and consumed at the user's convenience. The audio-visual landscape was changing, and *Beckett on Film* changed with it.

On DVD the plays have higher image and sound quality than are normally available to viewers of broadcast television, with a picture format (based on the MPEG-2 standard) offering about twice the detail of analogue television, and with Dolby Digital sound (Tryon, 2013: 100). Additional features emphasise the project's curation as well as the attractions of the films themselves, pandering to the cinephile, Beckett fan or educational user. The DVD is, in a sense, a documentary that illustrates how Colgan and Moloney's project of adaptation was done, since, as well as the plays themselves, the box set includes the 'making of' film *Check the Gate*, featuring extracts from interviews with the plays' directors and some behind-the-scenes footage. The DVD package is aligned with the cinephilia associated with box set culture, which Barbara Klinger calls 'a mainstreaming of the educational imperative' in that the purchaser is invited to add *Beckett on Film* to a 'personal library, no longer solely the possession of the eccentric, as both an archive of the past and a signifier of erudite taste' (2008: 26).

The packaging of the box set includes a forty-page booklet, described on its front cover as a 'souvenir book', which briefly introduces the project and has an illustrated layout of one or two pages for each play, incorporating images, production credits and brief quotations from the director or actors. The *Check the Gate* documentary gets its own feature page too, marking the significance of the DVD's 'making of' and behind-the-scenes information in adding value to the plays themselves. These supplementary materials enfold the plays in a rich interpretive context and raise further questions as to what *Beckett on Film* is. Its curation by Colgan and Moloney presented it as the legacy of the Gate's Beckett Festival. Yet the films on the DVD set are largely not versions of the theatre productions and make much of the creative interpretations by international cinema and television directors. As a physical object designed to be owned and repeatedly viewed, the box set invites its viewer to contextualise the plays in relation to the interviews, production history and reference material about Beckett's life and artistic significance provided in its accompanying materials and packaging. The DVD archives the project for posterity and memorialises it, in what John T. Caldwell calls a process of 'aesthetic canonizing' that comprises four activities, each of which has been discussed in this chapter: 'control' of the material, 'virtuosity' in its creation, and the promotion of the project's 'authenticity and cultural influence' (2008: 163–4).

YouTube versions of the *Beckett on Film* plays do not seem to have been uploaded by their copyright owner and their legitimacy is uncertain. They are unlike the cross-media spin-offs and promotional extras commonly produced for YouTube, where streamed video offers limited free content that persistently invites users to intensify and extend their involvement with a creator or a brand by moving across to paid content on parallel platforms or to a DVD product. The free upload of selected or abbreviated works, such as extracts from archive television series or samples of older cinema films, can encourage consumers to buy the original and it may be that the online *Beckett on Film* plays tempt purchasers towards the DVD. The public benefits of *Beckett on Film* last longer when the plays are freely accessible on the internet, while at the same time showcasing the project's achievement. Such a cultural service may be worth the loss of some potential revenue. *Beckett on Film* on YouTube does not offer the opportunity to possess a commodity like a DVD but it does enable users to partially evade the relatively prescriptive discourses of authorisation in the DVD's paratextual materials. Mike Frangos (2012) has analysed unauthorised internet video adaptations of Beckett's plays and, like them, the unauthorised YouTube *Beckett on Film* videos introduce uncertainty about control, authorship, authorisation and authority.

YouTube becomes a channel through which the *Beckett on Film* adaptations pass relatively unchanged, but with greater freedom for users to frame them in their own ways. The user 'Dublin Tales', apparently a group comprising Dublin tour guides, uploaded *Waiting for Godot* from the DVD in 2018, describing the drama as 'one of the most significant plays of the twentieth century' and as 'a masterpiece that draws endless interpretations' (*Waiting for Godot Movie*, 2018). A variety of viewers commented on the play, many of them confirming its emotional impact on them. Other responses noted that the video was useful for university students, that the performance would benefit from some music in the silent passages or that it was a boring waste of time. But in each case what YouTube made possible was a public demonstration of a relationship between user and text. The opportunity to comment publicly on *Godot* is an occasion for self-identification and for taking part in repositioning the adaptation within a new and modifiable context comprising the always-visible users' comments. Online video is another – democratised but disordered – kind of curation and archiving to which *Beckett on Film* adapts.

The tensions at stake in the transitions of *Beckett on Film* between different mediums are displayed not only in the texts but also in the peripheral, paratextual materials around the project. The transposition of Beckett's plays from theatre to film and television, DVD to streamed video, is a movement across audio-visual media which have developed specific historical conventions that are not essential but contingent. 'Film' can mean not only the theatrical exhibition of individual audio-visual works, such as when some of the *Beckett on Film* productions were scheduled at the Venice Film Festival, but also the group of television films funded by and intended for screening on Channel 4 as part of a series of free-to-air broadcasts. A 'film' can equally be one of the items on a menu of works laser-etched on a DVD and packaged in a box for home viewing. It can be a kind of audio-visual content requested and delivered wirelessly over the internet to a smart TV screen. Each of these 'films' might in some sense contain the same material (a production of *Waiting for Godot* comprising the same visual, aural and linguistic materials, for instance) but each is in dialogue with the conventions of the medium in which it is presented.

One of the ways that mediums have adapted to changing historical circumstances has been by changing their position relative to their comparators. By adapting to the changed opportunities and constraints of the present, both the medium and the text it adapts can suit themselves to the demands of the moment. It follows, as cinema theorist André Bazin (2000) has argued, that neither texts nor media are self-sufficient essences. Adapting the concepts of performativity developed in linguistic theory (Austin, 1971) and for Performance Studies (Parker and Sedgwick, 1995), we can consider the identity of a medium to be performative, as mediums jostle amongst each other to find their place, converging and diverging in new ways. Performance is an activity of articulating identity, in which it is continually becoming and being remade, and the intermedial and transmedial adaptations of *Beckett on Film* are an excellent site for studying the resultant complex processes of interaction, circulation and appropriation.

Notes

1 Beckett's first play, *Eleutheria* (written in 1947), was not adapted because performing rights were not available.
2 The film director John Boorman, who lived in Ireland, used the studios for *Excalibur* (1981) and *The Tailor of Panama* (2001).
3 Beckett's first audio-visual work, *Film* (1964), already thematised the relationship between authorship and medium specificity (see Bignell, 1999).
4 Examples include siblings Niamh, Sorcha and Sinéad Cusack in Anton Chekhov's *The Three Sisters* (1990) and Tennessee Williams' *A Streetcar Named Desire* with Frances McDormand (1998).
5 RTÉ News, 5 February 2000. Available at www.rte.ie/archives/2020/0116/1107863-beckett-on-film/ (accessed 15 October 2021).
6 Blue Angel has not been a prolific producer, but also made the Irish-based *Miss Conception* (2007), a comedy romance starring Heather Graham.
7 See www.screenireland.ie (accessed 15 October 2021).
8 For example, Channel 4's first chief executive, Jeremy Isaacs, appointed film critic Leslie Halliwell to acquire television rights to classic films and Derek Hill to secure art films and foreign films for television transmission.
9 The DVD sales web pages, www.clarencepix.ie and www.beckettonfilm.com, no longer exist.

References

'About us' (2021). *Tyrone Productions*, www.tyroneproductions.ie/about-us/ (accessed 15 October 2021).

'Ardmore Studios' (2021). *Fís Éireann / Screen Ireland*, www.screenireland.ie/filming/studios/ardmore-studios (accessed 15 October 2021).
Austin, J. L. (1971). *How to Do Things with Words*. Oxford: Oxford University Press.
Bazin, A. (2000). 'Adaptation, or the cinema as digest', in J. Naremore (ed.), *Film Adaptation*. New Brunswick, NJ: Rutgers University Press, pp. 19–27.
'Beckett on Film reaches the Barbican' (2001). *IFTN*, 13 September, www.iftn.ie/?act1=record&aid=73&rid=3042&sr=1&only=1&hl=scann%E1n&tpl=archnews (accessed 1 May 2022).
'Beckett on Film wins "best TV drama"' (2002). *IFTN*, 8 February, www.iftn.ie/news/?act1=record&only=1&aid=73&rid=303&tpl=archnews&force=1 (accessed 1 May 2022).
Bignell, J. (1999). 'Questions of authorship: Samuel Beckett and *Film*', in J. Bignell (ed.), *Writing and Cinema*. Harlow and New York: Pearson Longman, pp. 29–42.
Bignell, J. (2009). *Beckett on Screen: The Television Plays*. Manchester: Manchester University Press.
Bignell, J. (2015). 'Performing right: legal constraints and Beckett's plays on BBC television', *Samuel Beckett Today / Aujourd'hui*, 27, 129–41.
Bignell, J. (2019). 'When "Beckett on Film" migrated to television', Књижевна историја [*Literary History*], 51.169, 97–108.
Bignell, J. (2020). 'Specially for television? *Eh Joe*, intermediality and Beckett's drama', *Samuel Beckett Today / Aujourd'hui*, 32.1, 41–54.
Bignell, J. (2022). 'Screen and stage space in Beckett's theatre plays on television', in J. Wyver and A. Wrigley (eds), *Screen Plays: Theatre Plays on British Television*. Manchester: Manchester University Press, pp. 226–45.
Born, G. (2003). 'Strategy, positioning and projection in digital television: Channel Four and the commercialization of public service broadcasting in the UK', *Media, Culture & Society*, 25.6, 774–99.
Caldwell, J. T. (2008). 'Prefiguring DVD bonus tracks: making-ofs and behind-the-scenes as historic television programming strategies prototypes', in J. Bennett and T. Brown (eds), *Film and Television After DVD*. New York and London: Routledge, pp. 149–71.
Cardwell, S. (2018). 'Pause, rewind, replay: adaptation, intertextuality and (re)defining adaptation studies', in D. Cutchins, K. Krebs and E. Voigts (eds), *Routledge Companion to Adaptation*. New York and London: Routledge, pp. 7–17.
'Celebrating Beckett on Film' (2001). *Irish America*, April/May, www.irishamerica.com/2001/02/celebrating-beckett-on-film/ (accessed 15 October 2021).
Channel 4 (2020). 'Taking risks, challenging the mainstream'. London: Oliver & Ohlbaum Associates Ltd with Channel 4. www.channel4.com/media/documents/press/news/C4_Risk_Report_Singlepages_FOR_NINA.pdf (accessed 15 October 2021).
Frangos, M. (2012). 'Transmedia Beckett: *Come and Go* and the social media archive', *Adaptation*, 6.2, 215–29.
Frow, J. (1990). 'Intertextuality and ontology', in M. Worton and J. Still (eds), *Intertextuality: Theories and Practices*. Manchester: Manchester University Press, pp. 45–55.

'History' (2021). *Wilton's*, http://wiltons.org.uk/heritage/history (accessed 15 October 2021).
Hüser, R. (2011). 'Großvater's Axt: 2 x *Breath*', in G. Hartel and M. Glasmeier (eds), *The Eye of Prey: Beckett's Film-, Fernseh- und Videoarbeiten*. Berlin: Surkamp, pp. 213–62.
Jackson, M. (2021). Interview with J. Bignell, 26 August. Unpublished.
Jenkins, H. (2008). *Convergence Culture: Where Old and New Media Collide*. New York: NYU Press.
Klinger, B. (2008). 'The DVD cinephile: viewing heritages and home film cultures', in J. Bennett and T. Brown (eds), *Film and Television after DVD*. New York and London: Routledge, pp. 19–44.
'Not I' (2021). *Pinewood*, https://pinewoodgroup.com/pinewood-today/credits/not-i (accessed 15 October 2021).
Parker, A., and E. K. Sedgwick (1995). *Performativity and Performance*. London: Routledge.
Sheehan, H. (2004). *The Continuing Story of Irish Television Drama: Tracking the Tiger*. Dublin: Four Courts.
Sierz, A. (2001). *Beckett on Film*. London: Channel 4.
Smith, J. (2014). 'Channel 4 and the red triangle: a case study in film curation and censorship on television', *Journal of British Cinema and Television*, 11.4, 481–98.
Stratton, D. (2000). 'Happy Days', *Variety*, 9 October, https://variety.com/2000/film/reviews/happy-days-3-1200464913/ (accessed 15 October 2021).
Tryon, C. (2013). *On-Demand Culture: Digital Delivery and the Future of Movies*. New Brunswick, NJ: Rutgers University Press.
Waiting for Godot Movie (2018). Upload by Dublin Tales, 18 December, www.youtube.com/watch?v=YuxISg9tjHk (accessed 12 January 2022).
Wistreich, N. (2000). 'Alan Moloney. Beckett on Film', *Netribution*, www.netribution.co.uk/features/interviews/2000/alan_maloney/1.html (accessed 15 October 2021).

3

'Imprecations from the Brighton Road to Foxrock Station': the effect of place on Mouth on Fire's stagings of *All That Fall*

Feargal Whelan

The frequently quoted letter which Beckett wrote to Barney Rosset on 27 August 1957 regarding the staging of *All That Fall* suggests that he seems to have believed any visual intrusion necessitated by the mere fact of transposing the play from radio to stage altered it so much by interfering with the quality of it as 'coming out of the dark' that he could not see any merit in the process, despite agreeing to a number of requests to do so (2014: 63). By assessing two productions of the radio play by Mouth on Fire from 2019, performed to a wholly blindfolded audience at Tullow parish church in Beckett's native Foxrock and Áras an Uachtaráin, the official residence of Irish president Michael D. Higgins, I argue that the effect of transposition is not merely confined to visually distracting an audience from the dialogue and soundscape. Rather, the effect of where it was performed, and the necessary setting of its transposition, demanded that the play inevitably formed part of a broader event beyond its original intent. As a consequence, the two performances, which embraced the idea of using the play as the centrepiece of a commemorative event, amplified both the subject matter of the play (a meditation on Beckett's childhood community) and a revisiting of the play's production history (Beckett's unilateral withdrawal of permission to perform his work in Ireland in the 1950s). The dialogue between audience and performance ultimately enabled local acknowledgement of Beckett as an Irish writer and member of the community which he described in the play, and also allowed for a reappraisal of his central concerns about what might be lost in transferral from radio to stage in comparison to what might be gained. In addition, I will situate these productions against the background of two earlier stagings by Out of Joint and Jermyn Street.

Boghill/Foxrock

All That Fall, which describes the journey of Maddy Rooney to collect her husband from the local station, depicts moments in the largely Church of Ireland community in the fictional village of Boghill on the Saturday of a race meeting. It draws heavily on Beckett's memory of his childhood, as he made explicit in a letter to Aidan Higgins on 5 July 1956 discussing the play's origins:

> Have been asked to write a radio play for BBC and am tempted, feet dragging and breath short and cart wheels and imprecations from the Brighton Road to Foxrock Station and back, insentient old mares in foal being welted by the cottagers and the devil tattered in the ditch – boyhood memories. (2011: 632)

In his youth, Foxrock was an isolated commuter suburb of substantial detached houses outside of Dublin. Originally a rural hamlet, it was expanded with the arrival of the railway in the 1850s (Shepherd and Beesley, 1998: 18) so that by the time Beckett's father built his home there in 1900, Foxrock was a well-located *rus in urbe* benefitting from a frequent commuter connection attracting a community of well-off, mostly Protestant professionals and tradespeople (Daly, 1984: 201). Beckett's house, Cooldrinagh, was one kilometre from the train station and two hundred metres from the parish church of Tullow, which served the vast majority of the mostly Church of Ireland inhabitants. Community life was triangulated by the railway station, the church and the substantial grocer's, Connolly's Stores, a further two kilometres north of Cooldrinagh in Stillorgan. Underpinning local life was Leopardstown racecourse, which provided the meetings that punctuated the Foxrock year. The effect of the horse racing on the otherwise isolated community was enormous, as it sustained the economy of the village and provided entertainment for the residents through its sense of occasion. So important were the meetings that the railway station required the addition of a special platform allowing direct access to the course through a turnstile (Mac Aongusa, 2003: 16–17).

The geography of 'Boghill' is a critical component in *All That Fall*. The opening sounds of farmyard animals initially suggest a rural setting but, as the radio play progresses, the appearance of the train and the information that one of its passengers, Dan Rooney, is commuting from work in a nearby unnamed city more precisely locate the scene to a semi-rural suburban village. It is exactly in this quality of being a space semi-detached from both the city, for which it is a satellite, and the rural landscape, from which it is partly divorced, that Boghill's appearance so fundamentally resembles Foxrock. Like the actual village, what dominates the life of its fictional counterpart are the church, the railway and the racecourse. Dan Rooney's journey is the reason for Maddy's trip to the station, and his regular commute seems to be his 'season ticket' which costs him 'twelve pounds a year' (Beckett, 2009: 25). The central event of the day in Boghill is the race meeting – Beckett titled an early draft of *All That Fall* 'Lovely Day for the Races' (Lake, 1984: 93) – and the clerk of the course, Mr Slocum, is one of the most significant characters to interact with Maddy on her way to the station. Finally, the church and its liturgy pervade the text through Maddy's hymn singing to accompany Miss Fitt's humming (Beckett, 2009: 15–16), Maddy's discussions of Bible text and Maddy and Dan's final mocking of the theme of the following day's sermon (2009: 29–30).

Present-day Foxrock is no longer a geographically isolated suburb, as it had been in Beckett's youth, although it retains its status as a comfortable neighbourhood with median house prices ranking among the top three areas of the country's residential property price index ('Residential Property', 2021). While the railway station closed when the line was abandoned in 1959 (Mac Aongusa, 2003: 71), the racecourse still thrives and is now the only functioning track in the Dublin area, hosting twenty-two meetings in the 2019 season ('Fixture List', 2019). Much in the same way that the community was portrayed by Beckett in the mid-1950s, the decline of the Church of Ireland population continues, even though the parish of Tullow remains as active and central to the community as the church in which Miss Fitt and Maddy pray.

The Beckett family connection with the Tullow Church is strong, although William Beckett, the author's father, did not attend, preferring either to undertake long walks on a Sunday or, when he 'would condescend to go to church', attend a service in Monkstown, where the parson was a friend of his, as Beckett told James Knowlson (1996: 24). Beckett himself attended Sunday school at Tullow and was awarded a Bible there, by the Reverend G. W. Clark on 13 December 1912, 'for diligence and attendance' according to the flyleaf, which he kept with him until at least his university years (Van Hulle and Nixon, 2013: 173–6).[1] Whenever he visited from Paris after the war, he would accompany his mother to worship in Tullow, 'singing the hymns in his quavering voice but staying silent as the credo was recited' (Knowlson, 1996: 344). A parish anecdote relates that as Tullow's bell was audible from the nearby Cooldrinagh, May Beckett would set off from home on the first stroke and take her seat on exactly the final stroke, giving the impression that it was she who was giving the celebrant the imprimatur to begin the service. It was also said that if you were on your way to church and were behind the Becketts you were certainly going to be late, but if you were ahead of them you were early.[2]

It was against this setting that *All That Fall* was performed on 23 March 2019 as part of the annual event 'Beckett in Foxrock', begun in 2016 by members of the parish with the intention of celebrating the author in his boyhood church. At the original event, a plaque was unveiled at the pew where the Beckett family had habitually sat, bearing the inscription 'Samuel Beckett (1906–1989) / Nobel Laureate for Literature / Worshipped Here'. Following that ceremony, and on each occasion since, one of Beckett's works is performed, usually preceded by an introductory talk on the author and the text at hand. Given the strong local resonances of the setting of *All That Fall*, Mouth on Fire director Cathal Quinn had been particularly eager to perform the play in the church, although this was not its first off-radio production.

Staging precursors

Attending all non-radio performances of *All That Fall* is Beckett's direct and often-quoted caveat that it should be avoided. In his earlier mentioned letter to Barney Rosset outlining his scruples about any staging of the play, Beckett is adamant, stating 'I am opposed to any form of adaptation with a view to its conversion into "theatre"', despite leaving the door slightly ajar by adding that a 'perfectly straight reading before an audience seems to me just barely legitimate' (2014: 63). Yet in his correspondence with Alan Simpson, of Dublin's Pike Theatre, Beckett is more equivocal, eventually relenting to the director's request for permission, and he also provides an insight into the particular qualities he felt radio drama had offered him with regard to executing the play. In answer to Simpson's suggestion that he might stage the work with 'little more than a few props', Beckett replied on 28 January 1958:

> no props or make up or action of any kind, simply the players standing reading the text. The ideal for me would be a stage in darkness with a spot picking out the faces as required. It is a text written to come out of the dark and I suppose that is the nearest one could get to that with a stage reading. There could be a preliminary presentation of the characters, with lights on, by a speaker, who should also read the indications given in the text with regard to sounds, movements, etc., many of which I think could be omitted. No sound effects. In New York I am told they used a lectern from which the actors read as their turns came. I don't think this is a good idea. Don't think I'm imposing this form of presentation. Do it your own way. All I want you to observe is the strict limits of a reading. (2014: 102)

Here, Beckett emphatically indicates that the primary quality of the (radio) play must be an aural one, specifically a vocal one, completely avoiding both visual interference *and* sound effects. Although this is frequently interpreted as Beckett's plain demand for a rigid respect of genre in his work, it is worth remembering that he did allow staged readings to take place, and since his death a number of performances have been sanctioned by his estate. Mouth on Fire's version adhered to the requirement of minimal visual content in performance by having the audience blindfolded, but it strongly emphasised a naturalistic soundscape, so that it fell short of what Beckett seems to have intended. To examine the effect of such choices on the production, it is useful to look briefly at two previous versions transposed to the stage.[3]

Jermyn Street

In October 2012, Trevor Nunn directed a production at Jermyn Street Theatre in London in which the audience could observe the actors through the conceit of attending the recording of a radio play. As Ben Brantley notes in his *New York Times* review, the play was 'presented as if it were taking place in a radio studio, sort of. A phalanx of microphones hangs from the ceiling, there's a red "on air" light above a door and the performers hold scripts' (2013). In addition, however, the visual design of the performance was as important to the narrative as the aural dimension, since the actors

> wear clothes appropriate to the play's time and setting. And while vintage radio-style sound effects provide much of the atmosphere, the cast members match their movements, more or less, to the noise of recorded footfalls. A few moments, including the struggles of getting Mrs. Rooney in and out of a car, and of helping her up a hill, are given fairly detailed physical life. (2013)

It is quite clear from this report that there was a profoundly visual element at play in this production, as Maddy's movements (seen rather than heard) provided much of the focus. Wholly in contradiction to Beckett's indications, the production actually seemed to demand the intrusion of the visual, as can be gleaned from Michael Billington's favourable review, which 'in the case of Eileen Atkins as Beckett's heroine, ... allows us not merely to hear but also to see a great piece of acting' (2012). The demands of a fully realised performance visible to an audience may also, in this case, have altered certain points of the mystery within the play. As Everett Frost notes, the need to serve the visual seemed to influence particular directorial choices, as elements of the plot which Beckett had left vague were made explicit. Illustrating the point, Frost cites the example of the 'visual nods [which] indicated that Dan Rooney was actually responsible for the young boy's death on the train, something which Nunn deliberately inserted to clear up any ambiguity' (2013: 251). In essence, therefore, Nunn's choice of adding the framing device of a radio play studio may have led to a more familiar experience for a live theatre audience, one that also respected some of

Beckett's wishes regarding a 'straight reading', but seems to have transformed the play through transposition.

Out of Joint

For the next production, directed by Max Stafford-Clark for Out of Joint and which debuted in August 2015 at the Happy Days Enniskillen International Beckett Festival in Northern Ireland, the company were required to eliminate any visual element in order to secure the rights to perform the play. The actor Adrian Dunbar, who had been heavily involved in the festival, recalled the discussions around finding a solution to satisfy the requirements of the rights while producing a viable performance:

> I began to have some thoughts on our possible production and thought of the audience in darkness but ultimately suggested the idea of masks. This I suggested to Edward [Beckett] as a way the play might remain true to its inception as a radio or 'listened to' play, and this he agreed to. The play, then under Max's direction, occupied the theatre auditorium making it a quadraphonic experience further enhanced by a wonderful soundscape [by Dyfan Jones] and of course his casting of a company of great Irish actors. Audiences were remarkably compliant to the idea of wearing the masks and let their imagination run riot as Beckett would have wanted, I believe, given the dark twist the play has in its tail. (2020)[4]

Stafford-Clark added succinctly that 'when we sought permission from the Beckett estate to stage *All That Fall* and they asked me what was my vision for the play, I knew the correct answer was that there was no vision at all' (2016). On entry to the auditorium, each audience member was handed a mask of the type normally used as a sleep-aid on long-haul air flights, to be worn from the beginning of the performance. Chairs were arranged on the flat surface of the auditorium into rows facing each other and in a triangular arrangement, allowing for a continuous pathway on which the actors promenaded. At certain intervals, chairs were deliberately left vacant so that actors could stop and deliver lines from within the audience. The raised stage acted as the site of Boghill railway station. As a result of the visual deprivation, the effect seems to have been a greater concentration by the audience on the text and a more nuanced appreciation, as Michael Billington noted: 'Wearing blindfolds forces us to listen more intently. I was especially struck not just by the tenacity of Beckett's Protestantism but by his evocation of a past where the rural poor were steeped in books' (2016).[5] The two Dublin performances by Mouth on Fire at Tullow Church and Áras an Uachtaráin emphasised Beckett's religious upbringing, in addition to his Irish background, even more.

Mouth on Fire's relocations of *All That Fall*

The productions by Out of Joint and Jermyn Street differed greatly in their choice of emphasis, with the former privileging the aural while the latter's addition of movement encouraged an audience response to a previously absent visual aesthetic. Despite these differences, both shared the experience of being performed in a traditional theatrical space, albeit one that was used for the performance of a radio play. Conversely, Mouth on Fire's two productions took place within a context that celebrated the author, and in untraditional venues which carried added significance: Beckett's childhood church, and the official residence of the President of Ireland.

Tullow Church

All That Fall was performed in Tullow parish church on Saturday 29 March 2019, before a sold-out audience of 217 that included President of Ireland Michael D. Higgins and the author's niece, Caroline Murphy. For this production, director Cathal Quinn states that his overriding concern from the outset was, like Stafford-Clark's, an avoidance of any visual reference: 'I was aware of the other versions and I was strongly convinced that there should be no visuals ... that it should be a radio play. I gathered together experienced radio actors [with the intention of] producing a fully realized "live" radio performance ... following the norms of the discipline' (2020). As in the Jermyn Street production, actors used scripts and delivered their lines from lecterns, but a particular emphasis was placed on the elimination of page-turning and extraneous background noises, as would be the case in a radio broadcasting or recording environment.

The design of the performance was intended to enhance the experience of *All That Fall* as a radio play by consciously drawing attention to its genre from the beginning. A 1950s valve radio was set on the centre of the stage area at the foot of the altar and lit by a single spotlight, making it the focus of attention before the audience was masked (see Figure 3.1). Following the request to mask themselves, the audience heard indistinct sounds of a radio being tuned, referencing the old set which they had just seen. Quinn's voice, affecting the authoritative intimacy of a BBC continuity announcer, introduced them to a 'broadcast' of '*All that Fall*, by Samuel Beckett', setting the conceit of communal listening to a transmitted performance. At the conclusion, Quinn once again affected the style of a radio announcer beginning 'you have been listening to ...', before listing the cast and technical crew details, after which the audience were invited to take off their masks and observe a traditional live theatre curtain-call.

Mouth on Fire's stagings of All That Fall   57

Figure 3.1 Audience at Tullow Church for *All That Fall*, 23 March 2019.

Perhaps the most important choice to be made in every production is how the environmental sounds in the background should be reproduced and how realistic they should be. This question exercised Beckett, as gleaned from his correspondence with Donald McWhinnie, the play's first producer, in preparation for the broadcast premiere on the BBC Third Programme. McWhinnie decided that all animal noises should be made by the actors because he felt it would 'get real style and shape into the thing', thus overcoming the problems – as he saw them – of obtaining 'the right sort of timing and balance with the realistic effects' (qtd in Beckett, 2011: 689n1). By contrast, Beckett felt they should be real sounds, albeit with an 'unreal quality', which he suggested might be achieved through 'distortion by some technical means' (2011: 688).[6] Mouth on Fire paid significant attention to sound, recorded and designed by Paul Doran, which was as full and naturalistic as possible, with the intention of creating a wholly realistic soundscape. Quinn explains: 'I wanted people to listen to the sound of the train pulling into the station, not merely as a sound "effect", so that the sounds were another character in the piece. Each train had a different sound to note the difference between each' (2020). In addition, the human sounds, such as the footsteps and the tapping of Dan's stick, were made by the actors on mats or, in the case of the steps of Boghill railway station, on the steps of the altar. This contrasts both with Beckett's wish to have no sound effects at all in staged readings, as he explained to Simpson, and his desire for them to be heavily stylised in radio productions.

Particular care was also devoted to the accents assigned to each character, with Quinn insisting that they should be recognisable to the audience in Tullow. Although the original BBC broadcast had been careful to choose a wholly Irish cast, there was little cohesion in relation to the social or environmental background in their voices, at least to an Irish ear. All are rural in intonation, with perhaps the exception of Sheila Ward's Miss Fitt, and the only depiction of a higher-class enunciation is found in J. G. Devlin's Dan, while Patrick Magee as Mr Slocum uses his native and distinctive Armagh accent. Cathal Quinn observed that the original recording seemed to have 'shoved in every Irish accent they could find … no matter where they were from. For the English ear that was fine but for [the Irish] ear it didn't quite work' (2020). As a result, Quinn aimed for cohesion across the production, although he felt that it should not be so strict as to interfere with the clarity of the performance. He was adamant that Donncha Crowley (Dan) should have no trace of his own Cork accent. In the case of Geraldine Plunkett, he felt that her speaking voice was already 'distinctive and refined' and was therefore left untouched, avoiding the impulse to impose 'anything Anglo-Irish' on her intonation (2020). As a consequence, it is likely that Maddy may not have sounded 'Protestant', or certainly not as much as Miss Fitt, but in this case she emphasised the theory proposed convincingly by Terence Brown that the disruptive force of Maddy is partly a result of her also being, in reality, a Roman Catholic convert to Protestantism (see Brown, 1988: 124).[7] Elsewhere in Quinn's production, the accents of the figures involved mirrored what would be expected from local inhabitants and were modulated according to their class, with Mr Tyler and Mr Slocum appearing middle-class and privately schooled, while Mr Barrell and Tommy were noticeably working-class Dublin. The one exception was the role of Christy, played by Paul Marron, who employed his native Cavan accent. This was a specific choice for 'comedic' effect, according to Quinn (2020), and it is true that for some reason the accent and character of the Cavan native are frequently the butt of jokes in Ireland. The result of such attention to detail in the choice of accents was possibly only noticeable to an Irish ear, but it had the particular effect of resituating the play in a semi-rural, suburban setting, highlighting the layers of social class distinction apparent in the text, flattened out of the original BBC recording. As such, it stayed true to Quinn's idea of a natural soundscape, so that how the characters sounded – no less than how the animals or trains sounded – was a coherent representation of the lived environment outside the venue's door.

From their entrance to the building to the details surrounding the play's performance, the event presented the Foxrock audience with a communal experience reminiscent of a service of worship. The public came in by the main church door and were guided to whichever seating was available in the pews, as might be expected at a religious service. The church was lit inside by minimal artificial lighting enhanced by the positioning of large candle lanterns; the stained-glass windows facing the pews were illuminated from outside the building, and the altar was lit from below with artificial red light. Preceding the performance, an introductory talk detailing Beckett's links with the church and outlining the connections between the setting of *All That Fall* and the locale was delivered by Feargal Whelan from the pulpit, at which point the cast entered from the sacristy, taking their place on the choir pews surrounding the altar before the performance began. Three microphones and music stands were placed in front of the altar, at which the actors took their places when required to deliver their lines. What was ultimately achieved was the immediacy of a live performance but with the maintenance of the strange quality conferred on its emerging from the dark. In addition, the uniqueness of the venue and its overabundance of Beckett resonances, made explicit in the introduction, demanded that the author's relationship to the play became an unavoidable presence, which is not usually the case, as a comparison between his fictionalised evocation of the surrounding environment and the contemporary reality was strongly encouraged.

Áras an Uachtaráin

Mouth on Fire's second performance took place at Áras an Uachtaráin, the official residence of the President of Ireland, on 20 September 2019, as part of the countrywide festival Culture Night. While the cast and crew remained the same as that in Foxrock, as did the requirement for the audience to be masked, the soundscape was further enhanced by Doran through a manipulation of the stereo effect to provide an even more realistic sense of movement in the trains. This had been impossible to achieve in Tullow because of the shape of the church, thus further widening the contrast with the artificiality of the original BBC recording. This added naturalistic detail provided Quinn with a more precise rendition of what he had had in mind, despite its contravention of Beckett's original thoughts on the matter, much like it added to the sense of place created by the deeply resonant venue, which had also been present in Tullow. The audience consisted of a list of invitees and others whose names had been drawn by lot following an open application. Among the audience were, again, the author's niece, Caroline Murphy, as well as his nephew, Edward Beckett, and their immediate families. As in

Tullow Church, the specific homage being paid to Beckett as an Irishman was highlighted in the opening introductory talk and in the president's closing remarks, which were followed by a presidential reception. In many respects, this might be regarded as echoing the sense of official honouring of Beckett which had been witnessed by the state-sponsored week-long celebrations for the author's birth that took place in 2006.

There was a sense of commemoration underpinning both performances, divorced from the actuality of the play but exerting a subtle effect on each night. Foregrounded in the introductory lecture was the point that in 2019 two important anniversaries in Beckett's life were to be celebrated: the fiftieth anniversary of the awarding of the Nobel Prize for literature and the thirtieth anniversary of his death. These commemorations added significance to both performances, but apparently in very separate and distinct ways. For the parishioners and audience in Tullow, the celebration of the 'local boy made good' was obvious, but the additional resonance drawn from the radio play came from listening to a description of their shrinking community withering on the vine, which had been presented seventy years earlier and was now being re-presented to that very same community who had survived through their own resilience. In Áras an Uachtaráin, the sense of shared national pride in the international acclamation of Beckett was apparent, an upscaling of the 'local boy made good' effect, chiming with the recent practice of naming public entities in his honour, such as the naval patrol ship LÉ. Samuel Beckett and Dublin's Samuel Beckett Bridge over the River Liffey. But within the president's remarks there was also a sense of acknowledgement of the Protestant community's resilience in a sometimes hostile environment, highlighting its frequently awkward negotiation of life in an independent Ireland through modes of 'acceptance, obedience and participation', as Ian d'Alton has described it (2019: 20). In many respects, the official celebration of Beckett as a Dublin Protestant in the company of his descendants and those of his parish drew attention to a central concern of the play, namely the perseverance of the community in adversity and under wider social pressure.

This national acclamation of Beckett was not the state's first attempt, but it may have been its most sincere to date. It is true that he received, and accepted in person, an honorary doctorate from his alma mater, Trinity College Dublin, in 1959, but this can hardly be seen as a national acknowledgement given that institution's fiercely held view of its independence within the nation. In 1984 he had also been elected as the first Saoi (literally translated as 'sage') by Aosdána, the state-sponsored gathering of artists – similar to the Académie Française in gravitas but devoid of actual academics ('Annual Report', 1984). While he accepted the honour, it was presented *in absentia* to his niece at a reception on the author's eightieth birthday which, despite an address by the Prime Minister Garret FitzGerald, was a rather low-key event held over lunch in a Dublin hotel ('Beckett greets Aosdana', 1986; 'Minutes', 2019). In 2006, the state also funded a comprehensive festival to commemorate the centenary of Beckett's birth, but the intimacy of the performance and presidential eulogy at Áras an Uachtaráin – dedicated to the great radio play about his community, resonating with their enduring history within the state – increased the sense of an official recognition, if not of a rapprochement on the part of the state. The paradox of the nation's embrace of Beckett, whose work they had previously banned and whose presence they frequently ignored, is reciprocated by his own sense of ambivalence towards the state, most eloquently summed up in a letter to Adam Tarn on 9 April 1968, following his last visit to the country: 'The short stay in Ireland was very moving. ... I understood even better than before, the need to stay the need to return, and was glad to get out' (2016: 123n3). Much later, in 1987 and approaching his death, in his reply to the then Lord Mayor of Dublin, Bertie Ahern, Beckett expressed a need for some sort of recognition of his work by the Irish people, writing: 'It is indeed with pleasure that I note the growth of interest in my work among the younger generation of my countrymen and women and with gratitude for the contacts it affords me of which I have so long felt the want' (2016: 686). In a real sense, Beckett here recalls the intervention of a censorious Ireland in 1957, which had precipitated the unilateral withdrawal of his work from the country, perhaps even hinting at the personal hurt it had caused him.

The process through which he granted permission to Simpson and the subsequent events which led to his banning all performances of his work in Ireland inadvertently make *All That Fall* a significant work by which his wider relationship with the country might be examined, I suggest. The subject matter born explicitly out of Beckett's experience, which includes the depiction of a suburban Irish Protestant community persevering while in decline, was obviously attractive to Simpson and was enormously important to Quinn. The play both celebrates the Protestant community's resilience and mocks their hypocrisy while ridiculing the independent Free State and at the same time lamenting the loss of its language so that a fierce ambivalence is maintained which reflects Beckett's own ongoing engagement with the country. Simpson received the right to perform the play from the author on 15 January 1958, with the intention of staging it in that year's Dublin Theatre Festival. However, following the withdrawal of Sean O'Casey's latest play from the event, and also of a dramatised version of Joyce's *Ulysses* following a circuitous intervention by the Catholic Archbishop of Dublin, John Charles McQuaid, Beckett reacted by retracting his consent, stating to Barney Rosset: 'The Roman Catholic bastards in Ireland yelped Joyce and O'Casey out of their "Festival", so I withdrew my mimes and the reading of All That Fall to be given at the Pike' (2014: 107n1).[8] He made clear that this action covered all of his works for the whole country, as he remarked in a letter to Carolyn Swift, stating that he did not want his work performed there '[a]s long as such conditions prevail in Ireland' (2014: 112). Although he withdrew the embargo again in 1960 (2014: 332–3), it is worth bearing in mind for any future productions in Ireland just how central a role this singularly Irish play had in triggering such a serious action in regard to Beckett's working relationship with the state.

Conclusion

Beckett's insistence on not staging *All That Fall* may simply have been his belief that its potency lay in the reproduction of the play's disembodied voices, but it is also true that the effect of its transposition in the cases examined here added an extra layer to the setting of the play in order that it might work as a piece of live theatre. This is most obvious in the case of Jermyn Street, as the production embracing actors' visibility foregrounded their bodily participation and movement so that a separate locale (a radio studio in which the recording of the play took place) was added to the original text. Even in the cases of Out of Joint and Mouth on Fire, where all visual interference was removed during the production, a frame was created for the performances. In Mouth on Fire's case, this comprised the introductory talk and the broader events of both the Foxrock festival and the Áras an Uachtaráin celebration. Even Out of Joint's eschewing of the visual was contextualised for the audience by the highly unusual act of being given face masks and by being told when they must don them or when they could remove them. If the natural consequence of transposition is some sort of framing device, then it would appear that the one adopted in Tullow actually drew attention to the play rather than interfered with it. Situated within a local festival celebration of Beckett's work, with its explicit guiding of *All That Fall*'s resonances of the local environment and population in the opening remarks, the context demanded a dialogue between the audience and the performance as they experienced it, and by extension a dialogue with Beckett himself. Separately, the setting of the presidential residence demanded a similar response, albeit with a different emphasis. In this case, the complexity of Beckett's relationship to his home country rather than to his home village/suburb recast the dialogue with the audience, while implicitly invoking his own response to the issue in 1958 as a result of the Dublin Theatre Festival controversy. *All That Fall* thus provided a particularly apt vehicle for a meditation on Beckett's unresolved feelings towards Ireland

and also, in the settings which were adopted for its 'transmission', allowed for local public acknowledgement and appreciation, perhaps fulfilling the 'want' he expressed to the Lord Mayor in 1987. Mouth on Fire's *All That Fall* demonstrated that the need to create an added frame for its performance, demanded by any stage transposition, could overcome the scruples which Beckett expressed about its adaptation by using the unique venues to invite a communion between the audience and the subject matter of the play, which would be unavailable to a traditional radio listener.

Notes

1 This Bible is held at the City of Dublin Public Library, Pearse Street, and can be consulted online in the *Beckett Digital Library* (as part of the Beckett Digital Manuscript Project) at www.beckettarchive.org/library/HOL-BIB-1.html (accessed 26 August 2021).
2 I am grateful to the Rev. John Tanner of Tullow Church for this information.
3 One recent production not discussed here is Pan Pan Theatre's 'stage' rendition from 2013, which created a synaesthetic audio-visual experience. See, for example, Wilkinson (2014), Tubridy (2018) and Johnson and Heron (2020).
4 I am grateful to Adrian Dunbar for providing a longer detailed account of the production from which this excerpt is taken.
5 Max Stafford-Clark's Enniskillen Festival production of *All That Fall*, using the same sound design by Dyfan Jones, was afterwards broadcast by BBC Radio 4, on 26 March 2016, in a production by Catherine Bailey. This was no doubt helped by the fact that it anticipated a blindfolded audience and foregrounded the act of listening. See www.bbc.co.uk/programmes/b074vrpd (accessed 26 August 2021).
6 For more information on how McWhinnie and sound designer Desmond Briscoe realised the effects for *All That Fall* within the contours of Beckett's advice, see McWhinnie (1959: 133–50) and Briscoe and Curtis-Bramwell (1983: 18–27).
7 Brown points out that Maddy sings 'Lead Kindly Light', the hymn with words by Saint John Henry Cardinal Newman, regarded as initiating the conversion of the song's author from Anglicanism to Catholicism. For more on the representation of Protestantism in the radio play, see Kennedy (2003) and Boyce (2009).
8 See also Moran (2013: 30) and Cronin (1997: 493).

References

'Annual Report' (1984). *An Chomhairle Ealaíon / The Arts Council*, www.artscouncil.ie/uploadedFiles/An_Chomhairle_Ealaion_1984.pdf#page=11 (accessed 26 August 2021).
'Beckett greets Aosdana honour "with a shy nod"' (1986). *Irish Times*, 14 April, 9.

Beckett, S. (2009). *All That Fall and Other Plays for Radio and Screen*. Pref. E. Frost. London: Faber and Faber.

Beckett, S. (2011). *The Letters of Samuel Beckett, Volume II: 1941–1956*. Ed. G. Craig, M. Dow Fehsenfeld, D. Gunn and L. More Overbeck. Cambridge: Cambridge University Press.

Beckett, S. (2014). *The Letters of Samuel Beckett, Volume III: 1967–1965*. Ed. G. Craig, M. Dow Fehsenfeld, D. Gunn and L. More Overbeck. Cambridge: Cambridge University Press.

Beckett, S. (2016). *The Letters of Samuel Beckett, Volume IV: 1966–1989*. Ed. G. Craig, M. Dow Fehsenfeld, D. Gunn and L. More Overbeck. Cambridge: Cambridge University Press.

Billington, M. (2012). 'All That Fall – review', *Guardian*, 12 October, www.theguardian.com/culture/2012/oct/12/samuel-beckett-all-that-fall-michael-billington-review (accessed 15 March 2021).

Billington, M. (2016). 'All That Fall review – Beckett's best play brought to life for blindfolded audience', *Guardian*, 24 March, www.theguardian.com/stage/2016/mar/24/all-that-fall-review-samuel-beckett-out-of-joint-wiltons-music-hall (accessed 15 March 2021).

Boyce, B. (2009). 'Pismires and Protestants: the "lingering dissolution" of Samuel Beckett's *All That Fall*', *Irish Studies Review*, 17.4, 499–511.

Brantley, B. (2013). 'Funny, how gravity pulls us, and the safety net is an illusion', *New York Times*, 8 December, www.nytimes.com/2013/11/13/theater/reviews/michael-gambon-and-eileen-atkins-in-all-that-fall.html (accessed 16 March 2021).

Briscoe, D., and R. Curtis-Bramwell (1983). *The BBC Radiophonic Workshop: The First 25 Years*. London: British Broadcasting Corporation.

Brown, T. (1988). 'Some young doom', in *Ireland's Literature: Selected Essays*. Mullingar: Lilliput Press, pp. 117–26.

Cronin, A. (1997). *Samuel Beckett: The Last Modernist*. New York: Da Capo.

d'Alton, I. (2018). '"No country"? Protestant "belongings" in independent Ireland, 1922–49', in I. d'Alton and I. Milne (eds), *Protestant* and *Irish: The Minority's Search for Place in Independent Ireland*. Cork: Cork University Press, pp. 19–33.

Daly, M. (1984). *Dublin: The Deposed Capital*. Cork: Cork University Press.

Dunbar, A. (2020). Interview with F. Whelan, 23 March. Unpublished.

'Fixture List' (2019). *Horse Racing Ireland*, www.hri.ie/hri/2018/2019%20Fixtures%20List%20A4%20(Weekly).pdf (accessed 16 March 2021).

Frost, E. (2013). 'Performing the Jermyn Street Theatre's staging of *All That Fall*: a review essay', *Journal of Beckett Studies*, 22.2, pp. 245–54.

Johnson, N. E., and J. Heron (2020). *Experimental Beckett: Contemporary Performance Practices*. Cambridge: Cambridge University Press.

Kennedy, S. (2003). '"A lingering dissolution": *All That Fall* and Protestant fears of engulfment in the Irish Free State', in L. Ben-Zvi (ed.), *Drawing on Beckett*. Tel Aviv: Assaph Books, pp. 247–62.

Knowlson, J. (1996). *Damned to Fame: The Life of Samuel Beckett*. London: Bloomsbury.

Lake, C. (1984). *No Symbols Where None Intended*. Austin: Humanities Research Center, University of Texas at Austin.

Mac Aongusa, B. (2003). *The Harcourt Street Line: Back on Track*. Dublin: Currach Press.
McWhinnie, D. (1959). *The Art of Radio*. London: Faber and Faber.
'Minutes' (2019). *Aosdána*, http://aosdana.artscouncil.ie/wp-content/uploads/2014/11/7-Feb-2019.pdf (accessed 26 August 2021).
Moran, J. (2013). *The Theatre of Seán O'Casey*. London: Bloomsbury.
Quinn, C. (2020). Interview with F. Whelan, 30 March. Unpublished.
'Residential Property Price Index January' (2021). *An Phríomh-Oifig Staidrimh / Central Statistics Office*, www.cso.ie/en/releasesandpublications/ep/p-rppi/residentialpropertypriceindexjanuary2021/housepricesbyeircode/ (accessed 26 August 2021).
Shepherd, E., and G. Beesley (1998). *Dublin & South Eastern Railway*. Leicester: Midland Publishing.
Stafford-Clark, M. (2016). 'I had no vision for this play at all', *What's on Stage*, www.whatsonstage.com/london-theatre/news/max-stafford-clark-on-all-that-fall_40048.html (accessed 16 March 2021).
Tubridy, D. (2018). 'Installing Beckett: Pan Pan Theatre and Company SJ', *Contemporary Theatre Review*, 28.1, pp. 68–81.
Van Hulle, D., and M. Nixon (2013). *Samuel Beckett's Library*. Cambridge: Cambridge University Press.
Wilkinson, J. (2014). 'Theatre in an expanded field? *All That Fall* and *Embers* reimagined by Pan Pan', *Journal of Beckett Studies*, 23.1, pp. 128–36.

4

Engines of reverence? Beckett, festivals and adaptation

Trish McTighe and Kurt Taroff

Festivals are quite often the scenes through which ideas of nation, cultural value and the literary canon are negotiated, as Brian Singleton has remarked about Irish festival practices (2004: 259), and these factors can heavily influence the festival's capacity or appetite for adaptation. The festivals we examine in this chapter demonstrate the tensions that exist between reverence for and the preservation of canonical or classical work of highly regarded authors on the one hand, and the need to continually breathe life into such work on the other. The first part of the chapter will explore these issues in general, placing concerns for the canon, audience expectation, national identity and cultural capital within the broad context of festival cultures. The latter parts trace adaptation practices within specific Beckett festivals in Ireland. The festivalisation of Beckett in this context provides fertile ground for an examination of the relationship between the festival form and adaptation, and shows how notions of identity, authority and institutional power play a role in what it becomes possible to 'do' with canonical work.

A glance at the evolution of theatre festivals since the 1950s suggests a negotiation between celebrations of the local for a local audience, on the one hand, and an attempt to advertise a place to a global artistic audience, on the other. The ways in which such festivals approach the treatment of the canon is more than just a question of programming choices, but rather a statement of where the festival (and its location) stands on the question of reverence for an author and, frequently, their (supposed) intentions. When we focus this same question on the 1990s in Ireland, the festival might be seen as a key mode via which Beckett's work was celebrated and his Irishness confirmed. Lately, the festival might be understood as a way of negotiating a more complex identification between author and place – a trend that brings new perspectives on Beckettian adaptation. Through comparing several Irish festivals – the Gate Theatre's 1991 Dublin festival, the 2006 Centenary Festival (which also involved the Gate and took place in Dublin) and the Happy Days Enniskillen Beckett Festival (in Northern Ireland) – we will identify several differing approaches to adapted work that appear within these festival events. At first glance, Happy Days would seem to contain significantly more adapted work than earlier festival events. This chapter will examine some of the reasons for this, assessing why it is that festivals may make room for experiments with genre. At the very least, we suggest that festivals' concentration of multiple artworks into specific times and places offers a glimpse of broader trends in cultural production and so may offer a unique window onto shifting attitudes towards adapting Beckett's work.

While festivals are the focus of this chapter, the number of genre-transgressive Beckett performances in Ireland is notable (Johnson, 2016: 185) and perhaps reflects a wider international trend. Just as Ireland's performance culture contains a rich and long tradition of festivals, it also holds a long history of intermedial recompositions of Beckett's work, beginning with Jack MacGowran's reworking of Beckett's prose in *End of Day* (1962) and *Beginning to End* (1965). For Nicholas Johnson and Jonathan Heron this is indicative of how Beckett's work is 'already a terrain for experimental practice' (2020: 2). The narrative of Beckett's contentious history with adaptation and its history in Ireland may be reconsidered in light of the broader arguments concerning adaptation and canonicity, particularly in the wider festival context, to which we now turn.

Festivalised experiments

The relationship between a theatre festival and its content is conditioned by a number of complex and interconnected factors. The festival's aim, remit and target audience are variables that help to determine the tolerance for experimental approaches to canonical works. Added to this also is the connection drawn between author and place or nation, as well as the festival's use of local spaces and institutions. It is perhaps unsurprising that the largest and broadest festivals exhibit the most experimental approaches to the presentation of canonical work. A survey of the two best-known theatrical festivals in the Western world – the Edinburgh International Festival (EIF) and the Festival d'Avignon – suggests that relatively few works from the canon make it into the main festival programmes today, and that when they do, the productions are generally anything but standard versions of those plays.[1]

While Avignon and Edinburgh both began with relatively conservative programmes, their founding concepts are telling. Jen Harvie argues that the EIF arose after the Second World War, at least in part, 'to bolster a badly damaged sense of European identity by supporting the post-war revival of European arts and culture' (2003: 14). The roots of Avignon, on the other hand, appear more local and grounded in 'the strong post-war impetus to break the conservative Parisian monopoly on artistic and theatre practices' (Wehle, 1984: 52). But while the EIF may arguably have utilised the founding works of European culture as a means of re-establishing the concept of a shared European cultural heritage (the pedigree of which was, unquestionably, established by an elite culture), Jean Vilar instead believed that 'a genuinely democratic public was essential to Avignon's success' (qtd in Wehle, 1984: 55).

The perception of these divergent aims is paradoxical in light of the extent to which both festivals would later largely jettison conventional stagings of canonical work. Harvie notes that 'in its commitment to commissioning new work ... the [EIF] avoided producing strictly canonical plays from as early as 1949' (2003: 16). This is not to say that canonical work is not produced but, when it is, it is given a thorough makeover. Announcing their 2016 homage in honour of the 400th anniversary of Shakespeare's death, the festival blog announced that he was to be celebrated 'in truly international style with three unique productions – none of them in English'.[2] This insistence seems to be intended to reassure audiences that these were not to be conventional Shakespeare productions. Similarly, with regard to Avignon, by the 1980s it was clear that while occasional classical productions might appear in the festival, they were likely to undergo a similar process of reimagination (Wehle, 1984: 58–9). Edward Baron Turk (a nearly annual reviewer of the festival in the pages of *The French Review* in the 2000s–2010s) noted in 2011 that 'the 2010 Festival's one major attempt at classic *théâtre de repertoire*' was *Richard II*, directed by Jean-Baptiste Sastre. It was not well received, with one reviewer, René Solis, calling the piece 'static and declamatory, totally resistant to modernity'.[3] This reception undoubtedly reflects the commitment of the festival to presenting '*un art du présent*' (Turk, 2011: 30–1). One might conclude that these sorts of international festivals are ripe with possibility for adaptation and that they see themselves as leaders in the field in terms of breathing new life into old work.

The phenomenon of the single-author festival would appear, at first glance, to be fundamentally different from mega-festivals such as Edinburgh or Avignon. But examples of such festivals, from the Shakespeare Festival of Stratford, Ontario, to the various single-author festivals in Ireland, suggest that these festivals, when programming their events, are confronted with similar choices regarding the figuration of the author, prestige and national identity, as well as audience composition.

Festivalisation and adaptation: Ireland as case study

Alongside picturesque landscapes, literature in Ireland became an important national 'product' and tourist draw (Johnson, 2004: 96). Ireland was by no means alone in embracing festivals as a means to package cultural products and regenerate certain areas in order to play out narratives of national identity. Yet it offers an important case study of the ways in which processes of commemoration and festivalisation are linked to the formation of the national canon and national identity. Remarking on large-scale celebrations in the 1990s of both Beckett and Brian Friel, Singleton suggests: 'Perhaps the simplest way of determining the canonical in Irish theatre is to isolate writers whose work has been "festivalized", embraced by the trend of single-author marketing which recognizes that great theatre writers are the mainstay of Irish cultural capital' (2004: 259). When it comes to canonical writers such as Yeats and Joyce, the relationship between author and place is all-important. The annual Yeats Summer School and Festival in Sligo has been attracting both scholars and tourists since 1959. The playful animations of Joyce's *Ulysses* in Dublin's annual Bloomsday celebrations began in 1954.

When it comes to Beckett, the equation of author and place – and therefore the canon – is more complex due to his self-exile in Paris. The somewhat belated Irish engagement with Beckett and the tensions around his relationship with Ireland necessarily influenced the programming choices made at the Gate Theatre's 1991 festival. Coming just two years after the author's death, the festival might be seen as necessarily reverential and commemorative. As we explore below, it does not reflect the earlier prose performances by Barry McGovern at the Gate but rather focuses on orthodox renderings of the work which articulate a sense of pride in the association between Beckett and Ireland (Wolf, 1991). By 'doing' Beckett with as much respect for authorial intentions as possible, the festival implicitly argued for the naturalness of the connection between Ireland (or maybe more so, Dublin) and Beckett, and for its authority as an institution to do so.

Elsewhere McTighe has discussed the Gate Theatre's significance in 'articulat[ing] the material roots of Beckett's often dislocated corpus' (2018a: 313). The Gate's 1991 Beckett Festival helped to 'process ideas about Beckett and Ireland' (Harrington, 2008: 136), even if the urgency of the concern over his national affiliation dissipated somewhat after the festival's successful tours to the Lincoln Center in New York in 1996 and the Barbican, London in 1999 (2008: 138). As Patrick Lonergan has suggested, the 1990s in Ireland was an era of newfound national confidence that had much to do with Ireland's status abroad (2009: 52–3). An underlying ideology of national prestige and homage permeated the work and so genres were kept more or less 'distinct' at this festival, to adapt Beckett's oft-quoted letter (2014: 63–4). This approach fitted with the tendency of the time for reverence towards authors and authorship and reflects the sort of authority that longstanding cultural institutions like the Gate hold in Ireland.

The Gate Festival was shaped across three such significant Irish institutions – the Gate Theatre itself,[4] Trinity College Dublin (Beckett's alma mater) and RTÉ (Raidió Teilifís Éireann, Ireland's national broadcaster) – and ran for the first three weeks of October 1991. It was nested within two broader festival events: the Dublin Theatre Festival, which listed the productions within its programme,[5] and the Dublin City of Culture celebration, for which Claudia Harris frames the Beckett Festival as a signature event connecting the national with the international (1992: 405). The Gate staged faithful versions of nineteen of Beckett's dramas for the stage, barring *Eleutheria* (for which no performance rights have been granted). RTÉ broadcast both the radio dramas and two of the television dramas (*Eh Joe* and *... but the clouds ...*) on its television networks on two Mondays during the festival at 23.15. *Malone Dies*, read by Barry McGovern, aired as a book at bedtime nightly at 23.10. Trinity College Dublin functioned as a space of mediation for the work, with exhibitions and academic events running throughout. The university also functioned as a performance space staging *Cette fois* and *Solo* in a production by David Warrilow and including a staged version of the prose piece *Company* by Julian Curry. For his performance, Warrilow added an unscheduled reading of *Stirrings Still* (White, 1991: 8). Altogether, it might be inferred that the space provided by the university offered somewhat more leeway for experimental work, a fact that continues to be lived out in The Beckett Laboratory at the Samuel Beckett Summer School.[6]

Then Gate Director Michael Colgan's approach to audiences involved what he termed 'Eventing' (2001: 82), an approach that packages a work so that audiences understand and experience it as an 'Event' and will therefore 'tolerate' the less traditionally dramatic aspects of Beckett's later dramas. For the festival this meant programming multiple billings of the shorter work. While many of the productions were exemplary in quality and style, performed to packed houses (see Harris, 1992; Colgan, 1991a and 1991b), this is indicative of the ways in which Beckett's work was arranged to fit within the above institutions and cater to their audience profiles. The 1991 festival did not contain the same range of genre 'transgressions' as later festivals – proximity to the author might of course have been a significant reason for this. Colgan had met with Beckett in Paris and been granted his imprimatur to go ahead with the project several years beforehand. This was to be the first time that a significant number of Beckett's works were staged in Ireland in this way, a far cry from 1958 when the author withdrew permission for the staging of any of his works at the Dublin Theatre Festival (see

Knowlson, 1996: 447–8). There is a sense, then, that the festival bore the weight of its duty to the author carefully while also offering a space to reconsider the place of the author and his work within Irish culture.

As noted above, events of this festival did not reflect the longer history of prose adaptation connected with the Gate in the work of Barry McGovern. For Johnson, the fact that such work had been openly embraced hitherto by the theatre is a sign of the 'cultural authority of the Gate in the Beckett sphere, in which they are well placed to get broader forms of permission' (2016: 189).[7] That said, in its homage to Beckett and its articulation of his identity with Ireland, this festival can be perceived as closer to the preservation end of the spectrum, or at the very least as faithful as possible to the author's intentions.

Comparable to the EIF's 400th anniversary of Shakespeare's death, the 2006 Beckett Centenary Festival in Dublin shifted somewhat towards medial experimentation. In many ways this event also had a great deal in common with the commemorative aspects of Bloomsday 2004, which was set within a four-month-long season of celebration to mark the 100th year since the fictional day on which Joyce's novel takes place. The 2006 Centenary was also a multi-arts one, with institutions such as the National Gallery, the National Concert Hall and Dublin City Libraries hosting events and exhibitions. With the addition of a version of *Eh Joe* for the stage by film director Atom Egoyan to the Gate Theatre programme and a very rich range of visual art inspired by Beckett,[8] this festival took on a slightly more fluid aspect than the Gate 1991 event. It certainly reflected a growing awareness of the visual in Beckett, in terms of film, painting and installation, reflected also in the academic work that Trinity College facilitated. Previous medially transgressive approaches can be observed at the Gate and in the work of Gare St Lazare Ireland, who have been performing the prose since 1996, yet the centenary festival marks a growing sense of medial flexibility around Beckett's work. The ways in which Dublin itself formed the canvas for the Bloomsday and Beckett centenaries are significant. The sorts of public visual art installations that populated the city during these festivals are indicative of an attempt to engage an audience wider than the theatre-going crowd alone as well as produce an image of Dublin to the world as a vibrant, cultural and creative city. While these impulses are by no means absent from the earlier Beckett Festival and the City of Culture celebration of which it was part, these events emerge here as part of the more sophisticated cultural branding that has come to dominate the conceptualisation of postindustrial urban locales relative to the arts (see Florida, 2002; Landry, 2000).

It is worth noting though that even if these festivals begin to mark a certain loosening of attitudes towards Beckettian adaptation, they all, including the more recent Happy Days as discussed below, tend to shy away from the sorts of choices guaranteed to receive shut-down orders and loss of good relations with the estate: e.g. textual changes, cross-gender casting or significant design changes to the major plays, except when those alterations come with some prior seal of approval – for example, Robert Wilson's version of *Krapp's Last Tape* at the 2012 Happy Days Festival. The 'genre-unruliness' of this festival, if it can be called such, lies elsewhere: space, site and the fluid temporality afforded by the festival form become the means by which its adaptations take place.

Spatiality, temporality and adaptation

The Happy Days Enniskillen Beckett Festival might, at first glance at least, appear significantly more unruly than previous events when it comes to adaptation.[9] Firstly, the profiles of the directors who manage these events and their relationships with specific institutions are very different. In shifting from Colgan to Seán Doran we see a shift from a director immersed in the world of the theatre (Colgan was director at the Gate from 1984 to 2016) to someone with stronger connections to opera and a background in classical music, although they both have experiences with large-scale arts festival management. Prior to his appointment at the Gate, Colgan was heavily involved in the Dublin Theatre Festival, while Doran's previous roles included directorship of the English National Opera and of the Perth International Arts Festival. Colgan's rootedness in and long commitment to the Gate Theatre in Dublin contrasts with Doran's relative lack of permanent attachment to a specific institution.

With only one major theatre, the Ardhowen, it would seem Enniskillen presents some challenges for a festival director. Doran, however, sees this as a driver of creativity. If institutions offer festivals (and indeed any art practice in general) conceptual and material frames for the production of work, they also, even implicitly, influence how the work is done, and how is it read and received. Happy Days has increasingly combined commissioning with receiving, yet even in its work of receiving it performs adaptive gestures. Note, for instance, Doran's siting of Lisa Dwan's touring production of *Not I* (otherwise presented in traditional theatre spaces) in the Marble Arch Caves, an underground cave system not far from Enniskillen. The caves inspired that year's theme, the work of Dante. Doran comments that in

> bringing together Beckett, Dante and Virgil, for example, it was the caves that inspired the event rather than the other way round. ... I also remembered Beckett's wish to have the darkest of all possible spaces for *Not I* and there's no darkness greater than underearth. All this came about because I went down to see these special Marble Arch caves. (2015; see also Doran, 2018)

Site drives the festival content, both in relation to its commissioned work (Adrian Dunbar's productions of *Catastrophe* in a ruined church and *Ohio Impromptu* on Devenish Island are examples of this) and the work received.[10] Many of the works form what can be termed a site-sympathetic or site-generic relationship with the locale. This means that they resonate meaningfully with the place of performance but are not created out of or for a particular site, as is the case with site-specific work (Wilkie, 2002: 150). The many churches of the town provide acoustically rich sites for musical concerts, and apart from these the festival utilises any spaces it can.

The location itself complicates any identitarian questions around Beckett and nation. Enniskillen is in Northern Ireland, a part of the island that has remained under British rule since Ireland's independence in 1922 where identity is contested and national affiliation politically fraught. Although Beckett attended high school there, it is not reflected in his writings in any significant way.[11] All this means that identity, and identification between author and local place, is much more 'in play' at this festival than was the case in Dublin, even if Beckett's exilic status makes nationalising him a fraught project overall. This means also, however, that some funding sources are not as readily available for Happy Days as for the more institutionally connected work in Dublin. Drawing inspiration annually from another author that had some influence on or connection with Beckett was also a way for Doran to enrich funding streams. He has been able to attract funding from various societies or trusts based on the connections being drawn. For instance, the festival put T. S. Eliot in dialogue with Beckett in 2015 and Eliot's estate contributed money to events that year.

What are the implications of all this for adaptation practices? A brief survey indicates the range of adapted work being done at the festival. Pan Pan's touring staged version of *All That Fall* was programmed in 2012 and another staged version of the radio play was shown in 2014 (Out of Joint Company, directed by Max Stafford Clark). Subsequent years saw a significant number of such medially transgressive versions of works. Netia Jones curated a stage production of *Words and Music* in 2014 and directed a sited (secret location) production of *Stirrings Still* in 2015 with actor Ian McElhinney. Annually, there are a number of works inspired by Beckett: 2013 had two dance pieces inspired by *Godot* (by Finnish company Tero Saarinen and French company 2nd Act). That year also had a dance work by Dylan Quinn Dance Theatre inspired by *Catastrophe* and 2015 saw a revival of Maguy Marin's *May B* (first performed in 1981). Festival work spilled beyond its medial boundaries into installations in 2012 with Atom Egoyan's *Steenbeckett*, Joseph Kosuth's *Texts (Waiting for-) for Nothing*, alongside Antony Gormley's *Tree for Waiting for Godot*. In 2013 art installations appeared from Tomoko Mukaiyama and Jean Kalman, and

Robert Wilson. This short account cannot do justice to the diversity of the festival's annual programme. What can be inferred, however, is that there are two general routes to adaptation that this festival allows: one involves the site-sympathetic work mentioned above, the other concerns the transgression of the boundaries of genre and is frequently interwoven with sited aesthetics. A significant number of Beckett's prose works have been 'performed' each year, whether fully adapted for performance or read aloud, often in early morning sessions at secret and remote locations. The more playful elements of the festival, such as Beckett-inspired sandwiches or haircuts, show Doran's willingness to utilise Enniskillen itself as a canvas, in a similar way to the centenary celebrations mentioned above. This festival makes space for adaptation and is in itself a work of adaptation, painting Enniskillen with a Beckettian brush at the same time as moulding itself to the landscape of the region. Certain external factors contribute to this also: the emergent softening of the estate's attitudes towards some cross-genre work, revisionist readings of Beckett's own attitude to such work and the exploration of site as a means to 'do' Beckett already being practised by artists such as Sarah Jane Scaife.[12] In some ways, as a partly receiving festival, Enniskillen is simply reflecting national and international work being done on Beckett. But perhaps there is a uniqueness to this festival, in terms of both vision and geography, that warrants its consideration as a particular space for Beckettian adaptation. The geographic distance from centralised arts institutions contributes to this in no small measure, leading to a context in which genre permeability (but not necessarily erasure) becomes a potent possibility.

Drawing on the discourses which have emerged in the wake of site-specific work over the last twenty to thirty years (Kaye, 2000; Kwon, 2002; Birch and Tompkins, 2012) and the turn to questions of place and architecture in theatre studies (Carlson, 1989; Turner, 2015), as well as the materiality of theatre (Knowles, 2004), we might begin to think usefully about festival adaptation in this light. As Nick Kaye puts it, reading, understood from a semiotic perspective, is an act of location in which the sign is recognised within its semiotic system; site-specific work 'might articulate and define itself through properties, qualities or meanings produced in specific relationships between an "object" or "event" and a position that it occupies' (2000: 1–2). Sited work allows Beckett practitioners the space – as with the work of Sarah Jane Scaife – to reconfigure meaning within the text without, crucially, making alterations to the printed version. Scaife's 2021 project for the Galway Arts Festival is a fine example of this. She directed an outdoor production of *Laethanta Sona* (an Irish language version of *Happy Days*) on the Gaelic-speaking Aran Islands, off the west coast of Ireland. Winnie's mound was constructed out of the fabric of the landscape, grey limestone, and her bodice was the colour of a rare flower that grows between the island's rocks. As the *Irish Times* critic Éilis Ní Anluain points out, this production puts text in dialogue with place in fascinating ways, demonstrating the potency of site as a resource for theatre production: 'The play's theme, the need for everyone's voice to be heard, takes on a new meaning when a major work is heard in the language of the people where it is performed' (2021).

Director and designer Netia Jones speaks fascinatingly about the elements of the Happy Days Festival (and festivals in general) that allow her creative freedom. Jones, whose expertise is in digital design and who works primarily in opera, says that reading Beckett's prose in her early years has had a significant influence on her visual style. Her monochromatic design for the 2016 production of Beckett's late prose piece *Stirrings Still* evidences this.[13] She also observes how working on a prose text offers a degree of visual freedom, as it presents a text not dominated by the sorts of instructions contained in a dramatic text (Jones, 2020). This understanding of the text is akin to what Martin Puchner sees as an emergent feature in modern drama, a 'text that has withdrawn from any instrumental relation to the stage' (2011: 295). Although Beckett's prose is not to be thought of as 'dramatic' in this sense, work at the Happy Days Festival adds yet another chapter to the sorts of medial boundary-crossing that the work inspires, particularly when it comes to the prose. A text with no directions for staging is difficult to police, so the high number of prose performances at this festival is perhaps no accident. The situation is helped in no small way by the fact that artists at the festival do not have to negotiate directly with the estate; this is handled by Doran himself, whose careful curation, as evidenced above, steers a course between reverence and mutation of meaning through site. Jones's *Stirrings Still*, set in a secret location – a ruined barn an hour's bus ride from the town – exemplifies the adaptive practices of this festival as both spatialised and genre-crossing. The text remains complete and unaltered, yet the site and Jones's visual design illuminate it in arresting ways.

Furthermore, Jones finds it liberating to be relieved of the pressure to work towards an arbitrary equation of time and value in theatre, in order to produce work of appropriate length to satisfy audiences' expectations (2020). Doran chooses to 'solve' the challenge of Beckett's brevity through the use of site and the creation of a journey, sometimes of up to an hour, between the centre of Enniskillen and the site of the performance. Theatremakers like Jones are then free to create a work of shorter length than would normally be acceptable, and this applies to festivals in general, not only Beckett ones. Festival events open up the horizon of audience expectations. As Jones puts it, they 'obliterate' a normal schedule, allowing festivalgoers to step out of normal time, to choose their own path through the festival offerings and perhaps suspend judgement and attend performances that they would not otherwise countenance (2020), including ones of unusual duration, or involving experimental aesthetics. What might be concluded is that there is a certain temporality to festivals in general, a carnival chronotope in Mikhail Bakhtin's terms, in which festivals provide the space for the suspension of temporal and behavioural norms. This aspect of festivals offers immense potential for experimental and adaptive work. The temporality of this festival, interwoven with the festival's spatialised performance practices, engenders continuous and fluid (re)production of new meanings around old texts or new meanings out of old sites. What is interesting about *Stirrings Still*, and indeed about many of the adaptive 'journey' works that happen at the festival, is how site is utilised as a means of illuminating the text and vice versa. But site also becomes the means by which a certain set of temporalities is generated, ones that are part of the festival form in general but have implications for how we think of adaptation in festival contexts. Creating a performance out of prose engenders a different form of temporal engagement with the work than reading allows, and such cross-genre work becomes possible in and through the festival.

Furthermore, Beckett's work, perhaps more than any other artist, benefits greatly from the opportunity to contemplate what one has just witnessed. And yet, in the overwhelming majority of cases, economics, convention and expectations of theatre audiences mean that Beckett's shorter plays have been presented in double or triple bills, intended to provide an evening of theatre for a paying audience. Regardless of the rationale, producing these plays together, usually with only a short gap between them, forces the audience to draw a line under their processing of the first play before the next begins. And while the spectator is of course free to think through each play after the entire performance is over, the very density of these works, combined with natural human tendencies and frailties, raises the risk of confusing aspects of the different plays, or simply forgetting the earlier ones in favour of the more recent. The format certainly does not lend itself to poring over detail or meaning in works that arguably demand just that.

Multiple billing is in itself a form of adaptation, with the bill often organised around a theme. The Happy Days Festival's temporality and logic of consumption offer a unique opportunity for the non-adaptation of the shorter plays. Attendees at the Enniskillen Festival (as with many festivals) generally attend a number of works over several days, rather than a single show on a single evening. One might even suggest that the festival becomes a sort of interactive work of art as a whole, rather than simply being a collection of discrete works. This structure allows for the presentation of the shorter plays on their own. And not only does the festival allow for a period of contemplation following a single short play but it even in some cases forces that opportunity for contemplation, as in the bus or boat rides returning the playgoers to town from their sites. While the spectator may well go on to see another performance an hour or two later, there can be little doubt that this length is far more conducive to careful consideration than fifteen minutes or less. Thus, for all its playfulness, the festival may be seen to offer a more engaged and incisive means of viewing many of Beckett's most complex plays.

Conclusion

While this chapter cannot provide a comprehensive overview of the vast number of festivals that include adapted or experimental work, by way of tentative conclusion we can identify several emergent strands. The size of a festival, as well as its prestige and cultural value, greatly influence the sorts of work that it programmes. While mega-festivals like EIF and Avignon are beholden to audiences who attend in part because of the reputation for cutting-edge work these events have carefully cultivated, the lack of institutional shaping and relative obscurity of Enniskillen allow Doran and the artists he curates a sense of freedom, both from audience expectations and, to a lesser degree, from the Beckett Estate. But festivals also find themselves a product of a dialogue (concocted or not) between an author and a place, and operate at the nexus of culture and tourism. Beckett in Ireland is not immune to such forces, as festivals are fundamentally interlinked there with tourist marketing. We can see quite readily the tensions around the preservation of authorial vision and intentions mapping onto the Gate and Happy Days festivals.

We might conclude also that festivals are somewhat unruly in themselves. They have the capacity, even if directors and programmers do not always exploit it, to suspend normal time and offer uniquely concentrated dialogues between authors and places. These aspects of festival time and festival space are exemplified by Happy Days in particular in its unruly approach to boundaries – spatial, institutional, national and, especially, boundaries between genre and between media. That said, the festival form in general terms does not automatically produce the conditions for adaptation, especially when the festival is one caught up with notions of authorship and cultural identity. Furthermore, it is perhaps not possible to separate the festival form from the individual vision of its creative team or artistic director – these are other forms of authority influencing programming and aesthetic choices. Yet what this survey of festival practices indicates is that festivals have the capacity to create certain spatial and temporal conditions under which permissions can be granted, institutional authority manipulated and audiences' judgement suspended. On the one hand, the concentration of such work allows us to map and trace broader trends in arts production and, specifically to do with Beckett, these festivals seem to reflect an increasing tolerance for adaptations of the work. On the other hand, festival practices allow us to see with clarity under what conditions Beckettian adaptation might take place at all, what it looks like to steer a careful course between reverence and the perhaps necessary evolution of art through adaptation and experimentation.

Notes

1. It is worth noting Beckett's own experience with Avignon. In 1982 he was horrified by the 'creative' directorial liberties taken with *Catastrophe*, the play he submitted for a special event in support of Václav Havel at that year's festival: 'the Protagonist all trussed up with screaming white bonds to facilitate comprehension' (Beckett, 2016: 584–5).
2. See www.eif.co.uk/festival-guide/news-and-blogs/shakespeare-2016-edinburgh-international-festival (accessed 1 May 2020).
3. 'statique et déclamatoire, tout à fait réfractaire à la modernité' (qtd in Turk, 2011: 30; our translation).
4. See www.gatetheatre.ie/ (accessed 1 May 2022).
5. Dublin Theatre Festival online archive, https://dublintheatrefestival.ie/about/archive (accessed 1 May 2022).
6. See https://beckettsummerschool.wordpress.com/beckettlab/ (accessed 1 May 2022).
7. McGovern's one-man show *I'll Go On*, it might be noted, was among the few Irish works running in conjunction with (though not officially part of) Beckett's 1986 Paris birthday celebration (see Siggins, 1986).
8. For instance: Cian O' Loughlin's large-scale portraits inspired by Beckett's plays exhibited at the Office of Public Works, and light projections on landmarks of Dublin city centre were created by Jennie Holzer.
9. The festival was unruly in other ways in its early days. Peter Crawley concludes that the 2014 festival was 'oddly, endlessly consoling' while acknowledging the unevenness in organisation: 'dialogues of contradiction, dispossession and persistence became a mainstay; not a day passes without discovering that an event or an exhibition had either been mislabelled, relocated, cancelled, or, more appropriately, delayed' (2014).
10. For a more detailed consideration of landscape and of the touristic aspects of the festival, see McTighe (2018b).
11. Beckett was educated at Portora Royal School in Enniskillen. For more background on Enniskillen, see Knowlson (1996: 25) and Kennedy (2009: 55).
12. See www.company-sj.com/ (accessed 1 May 2022).

13 Productions shots, including of the ruined building, can be found on Jones's website: https://netiajones.com/project/stirrings-still/#&gid=1&pid=5 (accessed 1 May 2022). Other works by her documented here illustrate her commitment to a strikingly austere, monochromatic and minimalistic visual style.

References

Beckett, S. (2014). *The Letters of Samuel Beckett Volume III: 1957–1965*. Ed. G. Craig, M. Dow Fehsenfeld, D. Gunn and L. More Overbeck. Cambridge: Cambridge University Press.
Birch, A., and J. Tompkins. (2012). *Performing Site-Specific Place: Politics, Place, Practice*. Basingstoke: Palgrave Macmillan.
Carlson, M. (1989). *Places of Performance: The Semiotics of Theatre Architecture*. Ithaca, NY and London: Cornell University Press.
Colgan, G. (1991a). 'Beckett brought home in radiant darkness', *Irish Times*, 22 October, 8.
Colgan, G. (1991b). 'Three more Beckett pieces at the Gate', *Irish Times*, 15 October, 8.
Colgan, M. (2001). 'Michael Colgan in conversation with Jeananne Crowley', in L. Chambers, G. Fitzgibbon and E. Jordan (eds), *Theatre Talk: Voices of Irish Practitioners*. Dublin: Carysfort, pp. 76–89.
Crawley, P. (2014). 'Passing the time at Enniskillen's Happy Days Festival', *Irish Times*, 4 August, www.irishtimes.com/culture/stage/passing-the-time-at-enniskillen-s-happy-days-festival-1.1887208 (accessed 8 February 2021).
Doran, S. (2015). Interview with T. McTighe, 26 July. Unpublished.
Doran, S. (2018). 'Interview with Trish McTighe', *Contemporary Theatre Review*, 28.1, 150–60.
Florida, R. (2002). *The Rise of the Creative Class*. New York: Basic Books.
Harrington, J. (2008). 'Festivals national and international: the Beckett Festival', in N. Grene, P. Lonergan and L. Chambers (eds), *Interactions: Dublin Theatre Festival 1957–2007*. Dublin: Carysfort, pp. 131–42.
Harris, C. W. (1992). 'The Beckett Festival by Samuel Beckett: review', *Theatre Journal*, 44.3, 405–7.
Harvie, J. (2003). 'Cultural effects of the Edinburgh International Festival: elitism, identities, industries', *Contemporary Theatre Review*, 13.4, 12–26.
Johnson, N. (2004). 'Fictional journeys: paper landscapes, tourist trails and Dublin's literary texts', *Social & Cultural Geography*, 5.1, 91–107.
Johnson, N. (2016). '"The neatness of identifications": transgressing Beckett's genres in Ireland and Northern Ireland, 2000–2015', in T. McTighe and D. Tucker (eds), *Staging Beckett in Ireland and Northern Ireland*. London and New York: Bloomsbury/Methuen, pp. 185–202.
Johnson, N. E., and J. Heron (2020). *Experimental Beckett: Contemporary Performance Practices*. Cambridge: Cambridge University Press.
Jones, N. (2020). Interview with T. McTighe, 20 April. Unpublished.

Kaye, N. (2000). *Site-Specific Art: Performance, Place and Documentation*. London: Routledge.
Kennedy, S. (2009). 'Samuel Beckett's reception in Ireland', in M. Nixon and M. Feldman (eds), *The International Reception of Samuel Beckett*. London: Continuum, pp. 55–74.
Knowles, R. (2004). *Reading the Material Theatre*. Cambridge: Cambridge University Press.
Knowlson, J. (1996). *Damned to Fame: The Life of Samuel Beckett*. London: Bloomsbury.
Kwon, M. (2002). *One Place after Another: Site-Specific Art and Locational Identity*. London and Cambridge, MA: MIT Press.
Landry, C. (2000). *The Creative City: A Toolkit for Urban Innovator*. London and Sterling, VA: Earthscan.
Lonergan, P. (2009). *Theatre and Globalisation: Irish Drama in the Celtic Tiger Era*. London and New York: Palgrave Macmillan.
McTighe, T. (2018a). '"Be again, be again": the Gate's Beckett country', in D. Clare, D. Lally and P. Lonergan (eds), *The Gate Theatre, Dublin: Inspiration and Craft*. Dublin: Carysfort Press, pp. 299–313.
McTighe, T. (2018b). 'In caves, in ruins: place as archive at the Happy Days Beckett Festival', *Contemporary Theatre Review*, 28.1, 27–38.
Ní Anluain, É. (2021). '*Laethanta Sona / Happy Days*: a daring, bold vision, brilliantly realised', *Irish Times*, 3 September, https://www.irishtimes.com/culture/stage/laethanta-sona-happy-days-a-daring-bold-vision-brilliantly-realised-1.4664170 (accessed 8 November 2022).
Puchner, M. (2011). 'Drama and performance: toward a theory of adaptation', *Common Knowledge*, 17.2, 292–305.
Siggins, L. (1986). 'A Paris weekend of Beckett goings-on', *Irish Times*, 28 April.
Singleton, B. (2004). 'The revival revised', in S. Richards (ed.), *The Cambridge Companion to Twentieth-Century Irish Drama*. Cambridge: Cambridge University Press, pp. 258–70.
Turk, E. B. (2011). 'Avignon 2010: celebrating the body – singular and collective', *The French Review*, 85.1, 30–41.
Turner, C. (2015). *Dramaturgy and Architecture: Theatre, Utopia and the Built Environment*. Basingstoke: Palgrave Macmillan.
Wehle, P. (1984). 'A history of the Avignon Festival', *The Drama Review: TDR*, 28.1, 52–61.
White, V. (1991). '*Cette fois* and *Solo* at TCD', *Irish Times*, 16 October, 8.
Wilkie, F. (2002). 'Mapping the terrain: a survey of site-specific performance in Britain', *New Theatre Quarterly*, 18.2, 140–60.
Wolf, M. (1991). 'Just how Irish is Samuel Beckett?', *American Theatre*, 8.9, 56–7.

5

Passing by, gazing upon: gendered agency in adaptations of *Come and Go* and *Happy Days*

Katherine Weiss

In *Happy Days*, Beckett's protagonist, Winnie, appears to be terminally optimistic until she recalls a crude passer-by, gawking at her. Like Winnie, many of Beckett's characters, including Flo, Vi and Ru in *Come and Go*, are exposed to the cruelty of being seen. The eyes bearing down on his characters are recalled in the stories they tell as well as in the technology used to create the work. In Winnie's tale of Mr Shower, or Mr Cooker (she does not remember the name of the man who gazes at her as if she is an object) (Beckett, 2010: 24, 34), she struggles to regain agency each time she tells the story of when she had little to no control over how others saw her. In *Play*, the characters confront the torturous eye of the spotlight. The technological device is transformed into an eye that they attempt to placate and evade. Likewise, in *Film* Beckett identifies E as the camera – a mechanical eye that is in pursuit of O, the man who fears being turned into an object by the camera. Beckett includes in the treatment of the film a section called 'General' in which he quotes Bishop George Berkeley's '*Esse est percipi*' (2009a: 97). Being seen is essential to existence for Berkeley as well as for the existence of theatre productions. Self-reflective and meta-theatrical, Beckett's plays comment on the audience's necessary presence and their potential scrutiny.

It is no wonder, then, that adaptations of Beckett's plays, particularly of *Happy Days* and *Come and Go*, have built upon his fascination with Berkeley's credo and the numerous instances in which characters remember being seen. Some experimental directors and artists have adapted Beckett's plays to draw on the anxiety and agony of being looked at and the way in which the patriarchal gaze positions women as objects. This chapter will look at adaptations of *Come and Go* and *Happy Days*, exploring the ways in which directors and artists have used casting and spatial location to turn the gaze onto the audience. The legendary director Peter Brook and actor-director Marie-Hélène Estienne employed cross-gender casting and camp humour in their 2015 *Come and Go*, which was part of an evening of Beckett one-acts. Roughly forty-five years earlier Mabou Mines staged a site-specific *Come and Go* which the company readapted for an off-off-Broadway auditorium. Like Lee Breuer of Mabou Mines, Patricia Rozema's film from 2001 and Arlene Shechet's performance art of 2018 produced and staged their *Happy Days* in site-specific locations. These adaptations manage to blur the borders of what is Beckett and what is theatre by exploring the gaze in his work, and in doing so the audience finds themselves looking at the way they look at Beckett's women.

Beckett scholar and director Nicholas Johnson has stated that theatre is a way to cross different kinds of borders. For Johnson, this happens because theatre 'has the capacity and responsibility to amplify voices that are muted, to expose difficult and unsavoury histories, to elevate thoughts and opinions that fall outside those easily affirmed, and to work to engage conflicting philosophies – first and foremost by bringing people together' (2018: 38). The actor Wendy Salkind, like Johnson, noted that, for her, Beckett staged 'the voice that is not heard' (qtd in Weiss, 2013: 197). In bringing people together to witness a theatrical event, Johnson sees the potential for making the audience acutely aware of and empathetic towards the once silent and silenced voices. Beckett's plays written for women are sensitive to the lack of agency they may experience. It is no wonder, then, that *Come and Go* and *Happy Days* have energised theatre companies and artists alike.

Mabou Mines' *Come and Go*

The avant-garde theatre collective Mabou Mines became known in the mid-1960s and through the 1970s for their radical adaptations of classical theatre in addition to Beckett's prose and drama. With Beckett's permission, the group staged, among other works, *Play*, *The Lost Ones* and *Come and Go*. David Warrilow of Mabou Mines was praised for his rendition of *The Lost Ones*, and the adaptation of the short prose fiction work has become, at least in Beckett studies, synonymous with Mabou Mines, David Warrilow and Lee Breuer. Despite its success and that of their subsequent Beckett adaptations, the company's production of *Come and Go* has received little attention from scholars. Rather, the focus lies either on Warrilow's *The Lost Ones* or JoAnne Akalaitis's failed *Endgame*. Akalaitis, one of the founding members of Mabou Mines cast as an actor in *Play* and *Come and Go*, has been forever remembered for her troubled *Endgame*. It is important to note that her production of *Endgame* was not part of Mabou Mines' repertoire, and thus the controversy should not be aligned with the company. This is not to say, however, that Mabou Mines created faithful versions of Beckett's work. Rather, the company, inspired by Beckett and Bertolt Brecht, strove towards a theatre with a 'conceptualizing actor' who 'makes visible the "texts" of all the artists involved in the work' (Fischer, 2012: 18).

In 1970 Mabou Mines first developed *Come and Go* for The Brooklyn Bridge Festival. Ruby Cohn recalls that Breuer was interested in the 'spatial manipulation' (1999: 220) the festival's outdoor location offered up: 'He positioned the three actors and the audiences on two different piers separated by a considerable distance. The three women (Akalaitis, Maleczech and McElduff) wore body mikes, so that the audience heard these small faraway figures as though they were close by. The disturbing words of Beckett's text also disturbed the audience's sense of space' (1999: 220). Four years later, a slightly altered version of the play was produced alongside *Play* and *The Lost Ones*, during an evening of shorts by Beckett, which was praised in *Newsweek*, among other important publications (Fischer, 2012: 101). Despite having moved the play into the Theater for the New City (an off-off-Broadway venue), Breuer's production maintained the spatial manipulation by creating two spaces which effectively 'divorced' voice and body (Cohn, 1999: 221). Audiences of Breuer's New York *Come and Go* saw the performance reflected on mirrors while sitting in the comfort and safety of the theatre. Iris Smith Fischer, one of the few scholars to pay much attention to Mabou Mines' production, interviewed the actors and described the event as follows:

> The actors performed behind the audience at a spot from which their image would be visible in the mirror. It was as though the audience was 'spying through a telescope, or down Alice's rabbit hole, at a shimmering trio clustered on a park bench'. Just as *Play* used a spotlight (run by Breuer) to compel speech from each figure, *Come and Go* constrained and distanced the movement of the three figures by framing them in the rectangle formed by the mirror, as though they were 'birds on a branch'. (2012: 106)[1]

Although Fischer draws a parallel between the spotlight in *Play* and the framing of Ru, Vi and Flo in *Come and Go*, it is very much an external interrogator, the fourth player Beckett identified in the work. It attacks each of the characters, male and female alike, attempting to pull their stories out of them. In *Come and Go*, the female characters of Ru, Flo and Vi are not enclosed or confined by any object but rather they sit on a bench which they periodically leave. Nonetheless, Breuer's staging drew attention to the audience's experience of looking at these three women.

In Beckett's play, the viewers look upon the women as though they are sitting or standing in front of them. In Mabou Mines' adaptation, Breuer moved the women offstage. The gaze of the audience was thrown off kilter by positioning the actors in the Brooklyn Bridge Festival at a distance, and, in the later New York production, behind the audience. The audience was placed in the role of a peeping Tom, peering into the mirror situated in front of the seat. The mirrors served as windows to discover what remains ultimately unknown. The desire to penetrate the unknown, the Victorian world that Breuer created in the costuming of the characters, comments on the audience's desire to know the secrets shared between Ru, Vi and Flo. While it is possible to piece together a story of friendship and unfulfilled dreams about the three women in the fragmented sentences they share, the gossip and secrets whispered between two characters, when one of them leaves for a brief spell, are left unknown. The costuming, which reflected the rigid social codes of the Victorians, added to the secrecy which the viewing audience struggled to penetrate. The audience, as Ruth Maleczech (who was cast as Vi in the production) noted, found itself, like Alice in Lewis Carroll's Victorian-era children's story *Alice's Adventures in Wonderland*, peering into a rabbit hole in which it discovered a world of mystery and wonder.

The desire to peer into forbidden spaces and listen to secrets, or metaphorically peeping through keyholes, is often depicted as a gendered action. Fischer reminds us that Mabou Mines recognised 'the constructedness of gender' early in the company's formation (2012: 19). The peeper, for the theatre company, would nearly always be patriarchal. The mirror the audience peered into reflected the manner in which the audience gazed. As such, the audience became the object on display, witnessing its own gaze with the hope that it would question its role as onlooker. The mirror is also an object in which women have judged themselves, as is evident in fairy tales such as *Snow White*. Shari Benstock reminds us that 'the mirror into which every woman peers for confirmation of her beauty, her worth, her identity, is not a mirror that reflects woman's own image but rather a mirror that reflects the patriarchal simulacrum of that mirror' (1992: 175).[2] What is thus fascinating about the metamorphosis of Breuer's *Come and Go* is that the later rendition puts the spotlight on the audience. What they see in the mirror are the three women but what is also reflected in that image is their own gendered gaze.[3] For Breuer, the audience hears the women clearly but struggles to see them in both productions: first on the pier opposite them, then later in the mirrors in front of their seats. The spatial distance, voice and body displacement, together with the mirrors, create an exploration of an audience's gaze as patriarchal – wanting to know and see all, but being unable to.

Peter Brook and Marie-Hélène Estienne's *Come and Go*

Like Mabou Mines' *Come and Go*, Peter Brook and Marie-Hélène Estienne's 2015 version of the play explores gender as a patriarchal construction, and in doing so drives the audience to see that their reactions cannot be separated from the patriarchal and heteronormative gaze. To achieve this, Brook and Estienne do away with Beckett's stage and casting notes. Brook firmly believes that fidelity to Beckett is to move beyond being faithful to his written word.[4] In a 2015 interview recorded along with *Fragments* for Arte Concert, Brook (as summarised by Dominic Glynn) explains that 'Beckett's stage directions are marked by the time in which he was writing. Now, it is possible to move away from his directions to find the "essential" part. It is this gesture that thus is more faithful to the text by not being subservient to it' (Glynn, 2020: 68). In distancing himself from Beckett's stage and casting directions, Brook echoes the author's own aim to abuse language to distance himself from stylistic and formal writing. By abusing language, Beckett, like Brook, believed that he could reach the essential 'something or nothing' beyond the words, as stated in his famous Axel Kaun letter (Beckett, 2009c: 518). Brook's openness about his 'abusive fidelity' to Beckett to tap into the play's essential core may have been the key that made this adaptation of *Come and Go* possible. He and Estienne were granted permission by the Beckett Estate to cast the short one-act for three women with male actors.[5] With a mixed cast of two male actors and one female actor, the production travelled from London to New York and Paris, where it met with great success.[6]

Brook and Estienne's production certainly challenges the audience as Ru and Flo are barely disguised as women. In the video made for Arte Concert of the 2015 staging at Brook's Théâtre des Bouffes du Nord in Paris, *Come and Go*, the last of Beckett's shorts in *Fragments*, is met with laughter and applause from the audience. Playing with gender's constructedness, Brook and Estienne's *Come and Go* is strikingly different from Beckett's own conception. His is a quiet and subtle play that resembles ghostly chamber music. Audiences are invited to peer into the secrets the mysterious elderly women share with one another. They listen intensely to Beckett's Ru, Flo and Vi as the women remember longingly their desire for love and friendship. Brook and Estienne's adaptation destabilises Beckett's original text through casting choices and cross-dressing. The male actors, Marcello Magni and Jos Houben, cast as Ru and Flo respectively, play *Come and Go* as if in drag, which causes Vi, played by Kathryn Hunter, to respond with exaggerated expressions of disbelief. The audience is quick to pick up on Hunter's expression, registering that this is an adaptation which invites laughter.[7]

In Beckett's original, the 'dull' (2009b: 75) yellow, violet and red coats worn by Flo, Ru and Vi define them as faded flowers, dimmed by their inability to make their dreams of love come true. In most productions, the coats and hats are elegantly cut, suggesting that these women once belonged to the privileged class. It is worth noting that the coats and hats in Brook and Estienne's adaptation appear drabber and are not elegant or sophisticated; they are, however, not shabby either. The effect of the dowdy wool coats is to heighten the impossibility of mistaking Ru and Flo for women. The cross-dressing and exaggerated facial expressions that mock dread and enjoy gossip make up the 'stylistic exaggeration' and 'excessive theatricality' that through humour 'disrupts normative notions of gender and sexuality … as well as any given pretext's status as "original" or "natural"' (Horn, 2017: 21).

Even before Magni and Houben begin hamming up their performance with exaggerated facial expressions, the audience starts to teeter. Those familiar with the play expect to see three women, who should appear to be as similar as possible with the exception of their coat colours; that is, they expect the original text. What they find are two men dressed as women who dwarf the petite Vi. Men in women's clothing and men performing the roles of women in Western civilisation are sites of humour as they challenge what is considered normal and natural by the dominant heteronormative audience. What the cross-dressing in Brook and Estienne's *Come and Go* strives to achieve is to disrupt the way the audience responds to the gossip Ru, Flo and Vi share. In Beckett's play, the audience seeks to know what the secrets are, a desire that functions like the gaze by constructing she who is spoken about as data, an item of information the audience wants to possess. Beckett's women, along with the audience, indulge in gossip which ultimately colours how the absent women are viewed. In Brook and Estienne's adaptation, the act of gossip and the desire to know become secondary to the exaggerated facial expressions and vocal inflections of the actors. Through the excessive mocking of the shock and judgement each character expresses, the audience taps into Brook and Estienne's playful exploration of Beckett's *Come and Go* and the constructions of gender in his text. Ironically, the audience's laughter throughout the performance helps to construct, but also disrupt, heteronormative gender norms.

Patricia Rozema's *Happy Days*

In the opening stage directions to *Happy Days*, Beckett writes that Winnie is '*well-preserved*' (2010: 5). Indeed, the audience sees Winnie, an ageing but attractive woman, continue to do what she can to maintain her feminine physical attractiveness and composure, despite the harsh environment she cannot flee. Perhaps because Beckett situates the women in *Come and Go* and *Happy Days* outside the refuge of their home, many of these experimental adaptations occur outside conventional theatres. Site-specific productions emphasise 'how contexts collide, shift, blur, merge, and are reimagined, revealing power embedded in the moment of performance' (Cole, 2019: 92). Canadian director Patricia Rozema filmed *Happy Days* for the *Beckett on Film* project. Rather than create a desert landscape within a film studio,

Rozema sets her *Happy Days* in the Tenerife desert. Shot on location, her Winnie, played by Rosaleen Linehan, is in a vast stony desert and windy landscape which prove to be, like the gawking Mr Shower/Cooker, a hostile environment that she must fight through, straining her voice to be heard. Despite the desire to see *Happy Days* as 'genderless', as one reviewer claims Rozema's adaptation attempts ('True to Beckett', 2001), it is very much about a woman under the male gaze. The film opens with a shot from above and slightly from behind, as though Winnie was being looked down upon without her knowledge. This opening shot very much reminds the viewer of Winnie's examination of the emmet which she peers at with a magnifying glass. The camera angle is one that diminishes Winnie as object. She is also objectified when the camera is positioned slightly below her. Rather than a shot of power (that is, an image towering above the eye looking up), the angle makes it appear as though Winnie is on display, an oddity presented to the viewer on a plinth. In fact, Rozema's many jump cuts, showing Winnie from various angles and distances, have a scientific, almost clinical resonance; she is being gawked at from every angle.

Most interesting is what Rozema does during the instances when Winnie recalls the conversation shared between the passers-by she presumably heard. During the first recollection of Mr Shower/Cooker, the camera jump cuts, capturing Winnie at different angles each time she alters her voice to recreate the dialogue. This technique provides a sense of movement and comedy. However, after Winnie is buried up to her neck and the memory resurfaces, the camera moves in closer to Linehan's face. The extreme close-up and the absence of mockery in Winnie's voice change the relationship the viewer has with her. No longer an oddity that we want to scrutinise, Winnie deserves our compassion. We notice the redness around her eyes, the sweat on her face and the moisture building up around her nostrils. She becomes human in these last moments of the film. The viewers now see how they are guilty of objectifying Winnie. Rozema's *Happy Days* is still very traditional in its approach to Beckett, unlike the adaptations of *Come and Go* by Breuer of Mabou Mines or Brook and Estienne. Still, like sculptor Arlene Shechet's approach to *Happy Days* discussed below, all have created adaptations of Beckett's plays for women that have gone beyond exploring the gaze in the text; they have asked the audience to reflect on its act of seeing and for them the audience too is being seen.

Arlene Shechet's *Passing By*

Outdoor productions help to blur the boundaries between performance and lived spaces, as well as complicate the role of the onlooker as a passive viewer to complicit passer-by. Such outdoor productions also ask the audience to question gender boundaries. They, essentially, invite spectators to cross physical and mental borders. Arlene Shechet draws on this border crossing in her adaptation of *Happy Days*, aptly renamed *Passing By*. For Shechet the gaze is a construction which needs to be reconstructed or even deconstructed. In a short video for New York City's Pace Gallery, Shechet reveals that she hopes her viewers will recognise that looking is an attempt to piece together how we want to be seen and what we want to see (Pace Gallery, 2019). *Passing By* was only one piece of her larger installation project, *Full Steam Ahead*, which took over a large area of Madison Square Park from 25 September 2018 to 28 April 2019, aimed at creating a public space where individuals could look at and talk to one another – even engage with strangers. *Passing By* was essentially an edited-down version of the Theatre for New Audiences and Yale Repertory Theatre production of *Happy Days*, which starred Dianne Wiest and began its run at the Brooklyn-based theatre. *Happy Days*, which normally runs roughly 90 to 115 minutes with intermission, was reduced by Wiest for Shechet's installation to 45 minutes. Performed for five consecutive days from 22 to 26 October 2018 during lunchtime, *Passing By* made headlines and drew thousands of individuals to see the work.

The performance was free and open to the public, blurring the borders between theatre and an event. Except for the Madison Square Park website, the performance was not advertised ahead of time. Jonathan Kalb confirms on his blog *Theater Matters* that '[t]his event has arrived totally under everyone's radar. The Park has dropped the ball on publicity. But maybe that's okay' (2018). Shechet aimed to reach individuals who unsuspectingly found themselves amid Winnie's world. She was less concerned about reaching theatregoers or Beckett scholars, instead bringing art and theatre to an audience not expecting to cross the border into a theatrical event when they took their lunch break, in the hopes of having those passing by listen and look at Winnie. The viewing audience was encouraged to come together to witness something unexpected and extraordinary. While risky, since Beckett is often cast as high culture that is impenetrable, the popularity of the performance was evident in that the audience organically grew from roughly thirty witnesses to over a thousand within its run.

Shechet revealed in a telephone conversation in June 2019 that the question she was eager to explore was 'how does one create a place in the park for people to come together, to look at one another while simultaneously transforming the space into a place where the onlookers are seen?' By staging *Passing By* inside the park's reflection pond when it was drained for winter, she transformed a barren space into one where viewers sat and stood all around its edges (despite there being no markers that kept them from entering the dried-up area), looking inward at Winnie and across the space at one another. In *Passing By*, then, Winnie is surrounded by an audience gawking at her, eager to hear her words and discover something that might make sense of what they see.

Being surrounded by the audience is also reflected in Shechet's stone sculpture which Winnie is embedded in – a double entrapment. Like Breuer's Victorian costuming for *Come and Go*, Shechet's costuming speaks to how these female characters become objects to be looked at. By creating a costume and set which give the impression that Winnie is encapsulated in stone, Shechet reimages Winnie's imprisonment and the experience of the passers-by. Shechet's sculpture, which doubly serves as costume and set, is a capsule that resembles piled stone masonry. The unnatural shape of the sculpted stones, moreover, suggests that Winnie, now in the midst of Manhattan, is trapped in a mound of urban debris. Of *Passing By*, Kalb asserts: 'This is environmental Beckett. Beckett as a condition of urban life' (2018).[8] Environmental theatre 'erases the divide between performers and viewers' (Cole, 2019: 92). Shechet's adaptation indeed manages to bring together performer and park guests, erasing the boundaries that separate them and the boundaries that separate the passer-by from the theatregoer. During the performance, the sounds of people walking by, as well as the sounds of sirens and traffic, could be heard. These sounds, however, did not distract the viewers; the sounds became part of the rich soundscape, perhaps even the cries that Beckett's characters hear in their minds, beating down on Winnie in the same manner that the harsh stage lighting does in theatre productions of the play.

The urban wilderness offers a vast landscape of stones, like Rozema's film which provides clear shots of the stony landscape and the small pebbles swallowing Winnie. Shechet's sculpture takes on an additional level of importance when the viewers hear Winnie recall being gawked at by Mr Shower/Cooker, who wonders crudely what she has on underneath the sculpture. In creating the juxtaposition between the stones surrounding Winnie and the memory of Mr Shower/Cooker (kept intact in both acts), Shechet asks that the gaze of the passers-by does not resemble the threatening gaze of Mr Shower/Cooker, who metaphorically casts stones at Winnie through his crude remarks. The stone structure takes on new significance during the performance, moving from an image of entrapment to one that monumentalises Winnie, a woman calling out into the vast metropolis to be heard and seen by a compassionate passer-by.

Shechet's Winnie is not in an isolated desert space fighting the scorching sun, as the text calls for and Rozema's production attempts to recreate, but rather she is exposed to the cold late October air in a public city park. Visitors, rather than paying audiences, stopped to witness the strange image of a woman in stone in one of New York City's most frequented public spaces. As such, *Passing By* attempts to awaken the viewer not just to the hungry gaze that seeks to get closer and know more, as Breuer's *Come and Go* does with its spatial manipulation. Rather, it awakens the observer to the hostility of the gaze that resides all around us – that has crossed boundaries and challenged the borders that made us feel safe – and, in doing so, Shechet calls for empathy.

While Shechet's adaptation stays true to the structure of the two-act play, it is important to discuss what she has left out. In *Passing By*, Winnie's bag – crucial to the play – is strikingly absent. Despite Winnie referring to the object and the items in it, she has nothing to keep her hands occupied. Steven Connor, in his book *Paraphernalia*, provides an intriguing philosophical jaunt on the significance of bags. He notes that they are not just the containers of our stuff but more importantly bags and their contents 'are memory, the weight of all we have been' (2011: 15) and as such they weigh us down and keep us up. Because bags are usually associated with the feminine, for Connor they additionally represent the female body and its ability to generate life. They 'irresistibly suggest wombs, bellies and breasts' (2011: 19). Despite the erasure of the handbag in *Passing By*, Shechet's sculpture itself becomes a bag that contains Winnie. Wiest is enclosed in the round container, as is Winnie in the mound. In Shechet's sculpture, Winnie's memories surface; the enclosure that embodies her memories simultaneously weighs her down and keeps her going.

In *Passing By*, Willie, too, is missing; there is no actor cast as the silent husband. Instead, Wiest, according to Shechet, imagined Willie in the pieces of mirrored glass that were placed in the pond as part of *Full Steam Ahead*. These mirrors were collectively called *Ghost of the Water*. Interestingly, Willie is reduced in this adaptation to a reflection, a mere ghost of himself. Writing about *Happy Days*, Benstock offers a feminist reading of Beckett, arguing that 'Winnie does not consult her mirror for reassurance of her place in the signifying chain or for patriarchal approval', and as such the play does not repeat the 'traditional patriarchal script' (1992: 176). This is because Beckett does not reinforce a patriarchal view of the gaze; instead, according to Benstock, he asks his audience to challenge it. Directors like Breuer of Mabou Mines and artists like Shechet recognise this quality in Beckett's work. And, yet, despite the desire to minimise Willie's presence, as Shechet attempts to do, Willie nevertheless is always present in the very mirrors (the reflective pieces of glass in *Passing By* and the handheld mirror in *Happy Days*) that Winnie gazes into. In Beckett's text, Willie's silence, neglect and refusal to admit whether he once loved her mirror Winnie's vulnerability in the world outside the domestic sphere. The fact that Beckett wants us to empathise with Winnie, so that we shake our heads at her memories of being crudely looked at and spoken about by Mr Shower/

Cooker, does not take away from the presence of that cruel gaze. In Shechet's adaptation, the onlookers are cast as Willie while simultaneously being encouraged to resist the objectifying gaze.

Although *Happy Days* does not provide Winnie with relief or compassion, Shechet's adaptation moves to free her from intrusive peepers. She does this by veering from Beckett's tableaux in which productions forgo the curtain-call; instead, Shechet inserts herself into the performance between the acts and at the play's conclusion to model for the onlookers an act of compassion. In *Passing By*, the viewer's exposure to the transitions is a powerful element of the artist's work. Shechet was clearly seen walking Wiest to the sculpture at the beginning of the piece and helping her inside it. Roughly ten minutes in, she brought Wiest an additional piece of costuming, a felt cape to hide her arms and bury Winnie up to her neck. In addition to draping her with this costuming, Shechet applied to Wiest what appeared to be lip balm. These transitions were watched eagerly by the audience, wondering what would happen next. Once Shechet moved away, Wiest began again until the end of the performance, which was roughly another twenty-five minutes. At the conclusion, as captured by the Pace Gallery video crew, the onlookers heartily applauded while Shechet re-entered the scene to help Wiest out of the sculpture and walk her towards the park's green. Not only does the performance ask the passers-by to witness with empathy but the artist's friendship with the actor also reveals the compassion that Beckett's Winnie is never afforded. What is more, Shechet allows the viewers to see all transitions as part of her artistic vision for the installation. Like the monologue Winnie delivers, the transitions are not smooth. Winnie breaks off in mid-thought and she changes in mid-stream. To truly empathise with Winnie, Shechet seems to be saying that the rough edges must be seen and felt. The fragmentary nature of Shechet's work is meant to heighten the viewer's awareness of Winnie's fragility and strength – both, according to Shechet in a phone conversation we had, are present in Beckett at all times.

Conclusion

Adaptations of Samuel Beckett's work have been the subject of controversy among Beckett scholars and the Beckett Estate, sometimes even resulting in the closure of productions and legal battles. However, it is crucial that theatre companies and artists keep working to reimagine Beckett and further the questions raised in the original works. Even projects that never reach a viewing audience, such as those shut down by the estate or university experiments, nonetheless are important to challenge the boundaries that the audience may need help crossing. A particular sore spot for Beckett studies has been gender rigidity. Many theatre companies and university departments of theatre have attempted to stretch the limits in cross-gender casting. Theatre professionals who cross these borders, as Peter Brook and Marie-Hélène Estienne have done with *Come and Go*, help to keep questions regarding the patriarchal and controlled gaze in the public sphere. The adaptations of *Happy Days* and *Come and Go* discussed in this chapter are vibrant works that turn the gaze from the characters onto the audience. The onlookers are put in positions where they reflect upon their act of looking, hopefully to reimagine the role of the audience. It is the aspiration of artists such as Shechet, and directors like Estienne and Brook or Breuer and Rozema, that one day the audience will see themselves not as passive onlookers but as active agents who question their own values, seek answers from unjust institutional borders and aid in the change.

Notes

1 Fischer, here, is drawing on Ruth Maleczech's description of the event, quoting at times directly from the actor.
2 As will be discussed later in this chapter, in casting male actors in the roles of two of the three women in *Come and Go*, Brook and Estienne remind the audience that Ru, Vi and Flo are created in man's (i.e. Beckett's and Brook's) image.
3 Similarly, Brook and Estienne's 2015 production of *Come and Go* comments on the gaze of the liberal audience who find humour in cross-dressing but who are also reminded through the cross-dressing of the characters that for centuries women had been excluded from performing on stage.
4 It is important to note that, despite Brook's revisioning of Beckett's plays, his interest in and admiration for the author's theatre is long-standing. In 'Beckett by Brook or Theatre Uplifted by Abusive Fidelity', Dominic Glynn reminds us that in 1964 Brook had written to Beckett with an invitation to collaborate on an adaptation of Pedro Calderón de la Barca's 1635 play *La vida es sueño* (*Life Is a Dream*), but the collaboration never came to fruition (2020: 60; see also Beckett, 2014: 640). However, Brook continued to turn to Beckett in his own work. In 1965 he published an essay titled '*Endgame* as *King Lear*; or how to stop worrying about Beckett' as a response to his own awareness of how much the Royal Shakespeare Company production of *Endgame* seeped into his production of Shakespeare's classic. More recently, Brook had been applauded by the *Guardian* for his 1995 production of *Oh les beaux jours* (*Happy Days*) as being 'musically phrased and emotionally exact' (Glynn, 2020: 65).
5 Several theatre companies have attempted to produce Beckett's plays with cross-gender casting. The desire to stage Beckett's *Waiting for Godot* with women in the roles of the tramps is perhaps the most common of such experiments. While theatre companies often make it through rehearsals, these productions rarely make it to the stage. The Beckett Estate has stopped productions such as the Edinburgh

Fringe Festival's 1998 *Waiting for Godot* by a Manchester theatre company and forced the cancellation of Oberlin College and Conservatory's 2019 production of an all-female *Waiting for Godot*. Beckett's reasoning, repeated by his estate, is inherently gendered: he is quoted as saying that women do not have prostates and, as James Knowlson explained when interviewed regarding the Edinburgh Fringe Festival controversy, Beckett 'always took the attitude that *Waiting for Godot* was a play for four male figures and one boy and he did actually feel quite strongly about that. There are reference [sic] to prostate problems and he just felt that it did not make sense to have the play acted out by women' ('Two women', 1998). In our age of gender fluidity, it is not surprising that the Manchester-based group's counterargument pointed to the plight of survival and waiting as gender neutral ('Two women', 1998), while Oberlin's managing director of Theatre, Dance and Opera, Eric Steggal, and director of the production, Tlaloc Rivas, pointed to the demographics of their auditioning actors, adding that excluding females was sexist (Fogel, 2019; Simakis, 2019). Although Beckett and his estate have successfully stopped cross-gendered productions, some theatre companies have won the battle over casting in court. The judge in the lawsuit against the Dutch theatre company De Haarlemse Toneelschuur ruled that, since the play focused on the human condition, the restrictions regarding casting were unwarranted (Wright, 2016: 7). A court in Italy ruled in favour of the Pontedera Theatre when they changed the casting of Gogo and Didi to women in their 2006 production of *Waiting for Godot*, although it is important to add that the women cast as Gogo and Didi in the Italian production played the parts as men. The director of the theatre company, Robert Bacci, triumphed over the ruling that took in consideration the clause in the contract that casting could change and noted that in Italy men and women have equal rights and opportunities. The theatre company's lawyer 'hailed the decision as a victory for civil liberties' (McMahon, 2006). While these examples are not, strictly speaking, adaptations of Beckett's work, nonetheless in challenging his casting choices they deviate from Beckett's text enough to be considered here as experiments that help to contextualise Brook and Estienne's project.

6 Andrew Dickson of the *Guardian* applauded Brook and Estienne's *Come and Go*, along with the other four Beckett shorts featured in the 55-minute show called *Fragments*, as 'beautifully maudlin' (2008).

7 See https://youtube/Bq3AmbbRg0I?t=3115 (accessed 3 September 2021).

8 Beckett's work has resonance for urban and distressed environments. Paul Chan's 2007 *Waiting for Godot* set in the aftermath of post-Hurricane Katrina is one such example. Chan's production blurred racial and historical borders in both its setting and casting by asking audiences to see themselves as inhabitants of New Orleans' ruined Ninth Ward while watching *Waiting for Godot* performed on the streets of the city's most affected area. Those from the neighbourhood surely saw their plight given a voice and those who travelled to see the show would find in the production ways to further empathise, and perhaps even become socially engaged, to right the wrongs of the racial disparity in New Orleans (see Duerfahrd, 2013: 63–111; Collins, 2017).

References

Beckett, S. (2009a). *All That Fall and Other Plays for Radio and Screen*. Pref. E. Frost. London: Faber and Faber.

Beckett, S. (2009b). *Krapp's Last Tape and Other Shorter Plays*. Pref. S. E. Gontarski. London: Faber and Faber.

Beckett, S. (2009c). *The Letters of Samuel Beckett Volume I: 1929–1940*. Ed. M. Dow Fehsenfeld and L. More Overbeck. Cambridge: Cambridge University Press.

Beckett, S. (2010). *Happy Days*. Pref. J. Knowlson. London: Faber and Faber.

Beckett, S. (2014). *The Letters of Samuel Beckett Volume III: 1957–1965*. Ed. G. Craig, M. Dow Fehsenfeld, D. Gunn and L. More Overbeck. Cambridge: Cambridge University Press.

Benstock, S. (1992). 'The transformational grammar of gender in Beckett's dramas', in L. Ben-Zvi (ed.), *Women in Beckett: Performance and Critical Perspectives*. Urbana and Chicago: University of Illinois Press, pp. 172–86.

Cohn, R. (1999). 'The Becketts of Mabou Mines', in L. Oppenheim (ed.), *Samuel Beckett and the Arts: Music, Visual Arts, and Non-Print Media*. New York: Garland Publishing, pp. 217–36.

Cole, P. (2019). 'Site-based theatre: the beginning', *Theatre History Studies*, 38, 91–103.

Collins, S. (2017). 'The tragic romance of language: Paul Chan and Samuel Beckett', in R. Reginio, D. Houston Jones and K. Weiss (eds), *Samuel Beckett and Contemporary Art*. Stuttgart: Ibidem, pp. 293–314.

Connor, S. (2011). *Paraphernalia: The Curious Lives of Magical Things*. London: Profile Books.

Dickson, A. (2008). 'Fragments', *Guardian*, 29 August, www.theguardian.com/stage/2008/aug/29/theatre.beckett.fragments (accessed 2 February 2021).

Duerfahrd, L. (2013). *The Work of Poverty: Samuel Beckett's Vagabonds and the Theater of Crisis*. Columbus: Ohio State University Press.

Fischer, I. S. (2012). *Mabou Mines: Making Avant-Garde Theater in the 1970s*. Ann Arbor: University of Michigan Press.

Fogel, A. (2019). 'All-female "Waiting for Godot" cancellation sparks "collective rage"', *The Oberlin Review*, 15 November, https://oberlinreview.org/19883/arts/all-female-waiting-for-godot-cancellation-sparks-collective-rage/ (accessed 2 February 2021).

Glynn, D. (2020). 'Beckett by Brook or theatre uplifted by abusive fidelity', *Francosphères*, 9.1, 55–69.

Horn, K. (2017). *Women, Camp, and Popular Culture: Serious Excess*. London: Palgrave Macmillan.

Johnson, N. (2018). 'Rethinking borders in Beckett studies and beyond', *Trinity College Dublin: Research Case Studies*, 4.8, 38–9, www.tcd.ie/provost/review/2018/04.8.TCD_Research_Case_Studies_Nicholas_Johnson.pdf (accessed 2 February 2021).

Kalb, J. (2018). 'Dianne Wiest's Winnie in Madison Square Park', *Theater Matters*, 23 October, www.jonathankalb.com/post/2018/10/23/dianne-wiests-winnie-in-madison-square-park (accessed 2 February 2021).

McMahon, B. (2006). 'Beckett estate fails to stop women *Waiting for Godot*', *Guardian*, 4 February, www.theguardian.com/world/2006/feb/04/arts.italy (accessed 2 February 2021).

Pace Gallery (2019). '"Arlene Shechet: Full Steam Ahead" at Madison Square Park', 19 February, www.youtube.com/watch?v=HCQebjb9LOI (accessed 2 February 2021).

Simakis, A. (2019). 'It's 2019 and women still can't wait for Godot, even in Oberlin', *Cleveland.com*, 17 November, www.cleveland.com/news/2019/11/even-in-oberlin-in-2019-women-still-cant-wait-for-godot-andrea-simakis.html (accessed 2 February 2021).

'True to Beckett' (2001). *The Internet Movie Database (IMDb)*, 3 March, https://m.imdb.com/title/tt0263422/ (accessed 2 February 2021).

'Two women must wait some time longer for Godot' (1998). *Irish Times*, 27 July, www.irishtimes.com/news/two-women-must-wait-some-time-longer-for-godot-1.177183 (accessed 2 February 2021).

Weiss, K. (2013). *The Plays of Samuel Beckett*. London: Methuen.

Wright, R. (2016). 'Gender and power in *Waiting for Godot*', *The Oswald Review*, 18.1, 7–28.

6

'last state last version': adaptation and performance in Gare St Lazare Ireland's *How It Is*

Dúnlaith Bird

'This is not a play, this is a novel', director Judy Hegarty Lovett tells the audience at the world premiere of *How It Is* (Part 1) in January 2018. Gare St Lazare Ireland's adaptation at the Everyman Theatre in Cork flips the theatre: the audience remains on stage for the duration of the performance along with the technical crew, while the performers lay claim to the auditorium, stage and light box. From the opening soundscape of near-white noise to the weaving of recorded and live voices, to the shadowy doublings of the cast, the production eschews the traps of a 'direct' adaptation, instead attempting to make mud in the mind. Out of this disconcerting and at times disturbing sump of voices and visions, the occasional flash of sublimity emerges: 'life life the other above in the light' (Beckett, 2009: 4).

This chapter will examine the Gare St Lazare Ireland (GSLI) productions of *How It Is* (Part 1 and Part 2) as groundbreaking examples of intermedial adaptations of Beckett's prose work. After exploring the concepts of adaptation, performance and intermediality, as well as Beckett's own ideas regarding adaptations, this chapter will use the GSLI productions as case studies to analyse the specific challenges of adapting his prose for the stage. It will argue that, as in the original text of *How It Is*, there is no 'last state last version' (Beckett, 2009: 3), no 'resting place' (2009: 36) that can or should be achieved in adaptation.

Adaptation, performance and intermediality

As Corinne Lhermitte notes in her historical overview of adaptation, it was originally seen as a creative act. The term 'was associated with a particular type of translation involving a certain degree of creativity', meaning that 'adaptation carried the idea of transformation, adjustment and appropriation when it first appeared during the 13th century' (Lhermitte, 2004: para. 3). A shift in perception in Europe from the sixteenth century onwards meant that creative translation was increasingly seen not as originality but rather as infidelity or even, from the eighteenth century, as an act of plagiarism. This in turn contributed to the modern conception of adaptation as a derivative iteration of the source material, rather than part of an artistic continuum (2004: para. 20). In *A Theory of Adaptation*, Linda Hutcheon similarly acknowledges the ongoing and 'constant critical denigration of the general phenomenon of adaptation', ascribing it in part to the ubiquity of adaptations and their varying quality (2013: xiii–xiv). She identifies a pervasive tendency to compare adaptations to the 'original', despite the lessons taught by 'Kristevan intertextuality theory and Derridean deconstruction and by Foucauldian challenges to unified subjectivity', noting that 'disparaging opinions on adaptation as a secondary mode – belated and therefore derivative – persist' (2013: xv).

Hutcheon reminds her readers, however, that 'to be second is not to be secondary or inferior; likewise, to be first is not to be originary or authoritative' (2013: xv). In the context of *How It Is* this perspective is particularly pertinent, with the text questioning notions of source, origin and authority from its opening line: 'how it was I quote before Pim with Pim after Pim how it is three parts I say it as I hear it' (Beckett, 2009: 3). The authority of the first three words, 'how it was', is visually undermined for the reader by the absence of a capital letter. The temporal disjunction with the title, a sudden shift from present to past, also puts the reader on their guard against the speaker, all the more so as this is not their own statement but reported speech – 'I quote' – or even a recording or repetition: 'I say it as I hear it'. The original protagonist, 'I', becomes a mouthpiece for someone else's words, as their authority and even their identity as narrator is undermined.

Given Beckett's own textual testing of authority and origins, as well as his wider predilection for genre-hopping, adaptation and innovation, it seems unhelpful to consider adaptations of his work purely in terms of respect for the 'original'. Adaptation theory has largely moved on from questions of fidelity, where 'adaptations were being judged in terms of quality by how close or far they were from their "original" or "source" texts' (Hutcheon, 2013: xxvi). Rather, Hutcheon suggests that adaptations may be more fruitfully considered 'in terms of successful replication and change' (2013: xxvi). Mark Brokenshire also follows this more rhizomatic and organic vision of adaptation, arguing that, when successful, an adaptation 'both evokes and is amplified by a user's experience of the original, while also taking on distinct qualities of its own … not only carrying the aura with it, but contributing to its continual expansion' (2020). In analysing the adaptations of *How It Is*, we can thus more fruitfully ask if they carry on the essence or 'aura' of Beckett's text while generating distinct artistic qualities of their own.[1]

In many ways 'performance' is a more problematic term in relation to Beckett's text than 'adaptation'. Etymologically, a performance is completed: 'that which is accomplished, a thing performed' ('Performance', n.d.). Accomplishment and completion are alien to *How It Is*, a text in which the 'present formulation' (Beckett, 2009: 39) repeatedly fails as the 'wrong' words multiply on the page: 'two and two twice two and so on' (2009: 39). This may be one reason why Hegarty Lovett and the GSLI company avoid conventional theatrical terms such as 'performance' and 'character' in discussing *How It Is* (Part 1 and Part 2), as for example during the *How It Is* Symposiums in Paris (2018), in Cork (2019) and fully online (2021), not wishing to offer any sense of completion to such protean prose, nor to render their adaptation definitive. As in the case of Sarah Jane Scaife's productions of *Company*, in 1990 and again in 2018, the act of adaptation is an ongoing dialogue with the work, less a performance than a 'staging' as GSLI describe it on their website ('How It Is', n.d.). Rather than seeing performance as a finished product, the end result of a process, GSLI seem to have taken it as a process in itself, movement without a fixed destination, reflecting on the content and form of the text.

Intermediality, as Chapple and Kattenbelt state in their introduction to *Intermediality in Theatre and Performance*, 'is associated with the blurring of generic boundaries, crossover and hybrid performances, intertextuality, intermediality, hypermediality and a self-conscious reflexivity that displays the devices of performance in performance' (2006: 11). In *How It Is* (Part 1 and Part 2), we are shown the tape recorders, sound desk and microphones, the lighting effects and theatrical tricks. With the 'curtains parted' (Beckett, 2009: 45), the company is free to find 'new ways of structuring and staging words, images, and sounds', according to Chapple and Kattenbelt (2006: 11). Therefore, 'intermediality becomes a process of transformation of thoughts and processes where something different is formed through performance' (2006: 12). They claim that 'intermediality leads us to an arena and mental space that may best be described as *in-between realities*' (2006: 11). The disorientation, the sound and lightscapes, and the polyvocal nature of the GSLI productions are designed, I would argue, to bring the audience to this space.

Beckett and adaptation

On 14 October 1961, at the same time as Beckett was translating *Comment c'est* into English as *How It Is*, he also appeared to be setting his mind against adaptations. An enquiry by his German editor Stefani Hunzinger regarding a possible television production of *Endspiel* provoked a short reply rejecting the offer. Beckett justified his refusal by claiming: 'I would have to adapt it profoundly, something for which I have neither the time nor the desire' (2014: 437). The term 'profoundly' – 'profondément' in the original French (2014: 436) – gives some insight into Beckett's understanding of the process of adaptation, conditioned perhaps by his previous experience of preparing other texts for television. Rather than a translation across media, Beckett envisaged adaptation as a digging downwards into the text, requiring both time and effort. The playwright went further, telling his editor: 'More generally, I am going to be obliged from now on to hold out against any adaptations of this kind, so that only in the theatre will there be performances of plays for theatre, only on radio of those for radio' (2014: 437). In reality, the author was both unable to 'hold out' against all of the requests he received for adaptations and intrigued enough by the increasing availability of new media to develop his own adaptations. 'As media develop and mix', the editors of his letters point out, 'Beckett finds himself both seduced and repelled' (2014: lxxviii). The fact that the Beckett Estate has seen fit to grant the rights for theatrical productions, not just of *How It Is* (Part 1 and Part 2) but of a number of other prose texts, indicates a recognition of Beckett's increasing openness to adaptation and intermediality during his lifetime.

Initially, Beckett's comments to George Duthuit regarding the painter Nicolas de Staël's contributions to the theatre suggest a similarly implacable rejection of intermediality: 'I do not believe in collaboration between the arts' (2011: 218). His use of the term 'collaboration', given its specific post-Second World War associations of treason, underlines the strength of his conviction. Rather, he demanded 'a theatre reduced to its own means, speech and acting, without painting, without music, without embellishments' (2011: 218). He offhandedly ascribed this pared-back aesthetic to his Protestantism – 'we are what we are' – before more seriously asserting that 'the setting has to come out of the text, without adding to it' (2011: 218). His fear appears to be that in adding, for example, a painted set by Bram van Velde to *En attendant Godot*, the audience would hear nothing and see nothing but the paintings (2011: 218). The risks in creating an intermedial adaptation of *How It Is* are therefore high. It requires an intermediality that deprives spectators of certainty and 'visual convenience' (2011: 218), not adding to the text but delving into it, leading the audience into the dark.

How It Is: composition and adaptability

On 17 December 1958, Beckett began a preliminary text entitled 'Pim', published in 1961 as *Comment c'est* and in English as *How It Is*, translated by himself, in 1964. The composition appears tortuous; Beckett spent a large amount of time writing to his friends to complain about the writing that he should be doing. 'Struggling on with new work' (2014: 229), he told Barney Rosset on 5 May 1959, which was proving 'horribly difficult I needn't say' (2014: 230). The process as Beckett describes it is one of piecemeal writing followed by furious editing: 'I rely a lot on demolishing process to come later and content myself more or less with getting down elements and rhythms to be knocked hell out of when I'm ready' (2014: 230). Distance, approximation and the staving off of failure were integral elements of this formative phase, as they are in the final text: 'I see fairly well what I have to do but so far can't get very near it, only near enough to keep me from giving up in disgust' (2014: 230). Somewhat problematically in terms of a theatrical adaptation of *How It Is*, Beckett claimed that the new work 'has nothing to do with theatre or radio' (2014: 229–30).

He also described the premise of *How It Is* in his letter to Rosset: 'It all "takes place" in the pitch dark and the mud, first part "man" alone, second with another, third alone again. All a problem of rhythm and syntax and weakening of form, nothing more difficult' (2014: 230). His use of scare quotes suggests a contestation of the traditional narrative conventions of location and a fixed protagonist, contributing to the 'weakening of form'. By November 1959, the process had become considerably more difficult, with Beckett telling Barbara Bray that he had 'written about 6 pages of Part III, can't see how I'll ever do the 25 or 30 I need. Dark as 5th Canto of Hell' (2014: 250). The challenge of 'demolishing' the text, of breaking apart units of sense into 'elements and rhythms', was persistent: 'trying to break up into short units the continuum contrived with such difficulty. Apart from that nothing' (2014: 282). Having finally dug himself out of the dark with the publication of *Comment c'est*, on 15 July 1961 Beckett began the English translation, telling Barbara Bray: 'I'm afraid I must do it myself or – as I'm more and more tempted – leave it untranslated' (2014: 432). He completed a draft of the translation on 31 January 1962 (2014: 465), telling Ruby Cohn: 'I have finished first draft of *HOW IT IS*. Very unsatisfactory' (2014: 466).

In the text, a man lies in the 'impenetrable dark', recounting his life, or *a* life, in three parts, as he hears it uttered by another voice: 'scraps of an ancient voice in me not mine' (Beckett, 2009: 3). The fragmentation of self and of syntax explored in *The Unnamable* is pushed to the extreme here: 'my life last state last version ill-said ill-heard ill-recaptured ill-murmured in the mud brief movements of the lower face losses everywhere' (2009: 3). The unpunctuated paragraphs of text and repeated phrases construct a methodical and almost mathematical collage, which when read resembles the desperate panting of a disturbed mind. As Édouard Magessa O'Reilly states in his preface: 'Rather than units of meaning, these fragments reconfigure the narrative as units of breath' (Beckett, 2009: ix). Its orality is evident, 'close to everyday, informal speech, and many commentators have pointed out how much *How It Is* benefits from reading aloud' (2009: xi). Beckett fills this breath-timed text with body parts and organic machinery, making it an embodied experience. In this sense, the GSLI production can be seen as part of the 'natural order more or less' (2009: 3), speech on the page becoming speech on the stage.

How It Is (Part 1)

Over the past twenty-one years, GSLI have built up a repertory including eighteen Beckett titles, and they are particularly known for their productions of his prose texts, including *Molloy* and *First Love*. From 2015–18 the company were Artists in Residence at the Cork Everyman Theatre, having obtained permission from the Beckett Estate to stage *How It Is* (Part 1) and later *How It Is* (Part 2) and *How It Is* (Part 3). As Anna McMullan notes in the *How It Is* (Part 1) programme for the Everyman premiere in 2018: 'When staging prose texts, decisions have to be made about the environment in which the dramatization will take place: what will be embodied or rendered visible and present on stage? The live actor constitutes a physical anchor on stage, whereas the shapeshifting of Beckett's fictional narrators can produce unlimited identities, locations and bodies'. She also questions whether the same 'sense of sharing the intimate inner consciousness of the narrator or characters, of being inside the head' can be equalled by 'watching or hearing the character speak' (2018). A theatrical adaptation of the text must also convey the text's lexicon of light and dark, of cinematic visions and sadistic torturers, without falling into painfully literal representation, with props and accessories – or worse, actors rolling around on stage in a pool of mud.

At the rehearsals of *How It Is* (Part 1) at the Everyman in November 2017, which I was invited to attend, the GSLI performers and technical crew were attempting to address some of those questions. The process was collaborative, with the lighting, sound, stage manager, director and performers all on the same level. Conor Lovett paced as he practised his lines, while the technical crew ran experiments using sugar glass and catgut, trying to shatter the glass in the control booth. We heard them wondering whether the natural sound of splintering glass would be sufficient or require augmentation with a recording so that the audience would gain a sensory experience of the boundaries of theatre being broken, and the similar shattering of their own expectations. They were still grappling with some of the practical questions posed by the text, including how to make a lightscape of 'impenetrable dark' (Beckett, 2009: 7). In one of the more glorious moments during the rehearsal, Lovett walked into the parterre, suspended in the mist and the darkness at an impossible height and distance. The members of the technical team made a note that the surface of the walkway must have enough grip to not send him sliding headfirst into the seats during a performance. From our seats on the stage there was a sense that we were participating in an evolving act of theatre, rather than a performance, a quality retained for the premiere.

How It Is (Part 1) premiered at the Everyman Theatre in Cork from 30 January to 3 February 2018. An audience of around fifty people entering via the stage door are invited to take their seats on stage. The safety curtain has been used to create a new proscenium arch, deliberately limiting and framing the audience's perspective, making them active participants in the production rather than complacent consumers. As though to underline this refusal of a traditional performance, Hegarty Lovett strolls out with two actors, Conor Lovett and Stephen Dillane, and the sound engineer, Mel Mercier, to remind us that 'this is not a play, this is a novel'. Such insistence on intermediality is carried through into the staging; a copy of the novel pokes out of Dillane's pocket throughout the performance and Mercier appears to read from his, though this turns out to have been 'recorded' (2009: 3). Given that the text, in particular in the English translation, is a layering of recorded words, imperfect copies and remixes that seem to anticipate the technological act of recording, GSLI's insistence on it illustrates again their commitment to plumbing the depths of the text. At one point Mercier even hands Dillane a tape recorder, in an apparent intertextual nod to *Krapp's Last Tape*.[2]

There is no fourth wall and no fixed boundary between the performance space and our own, and the actors regularly approach the audience to speak directly to them, just as there is no clear division between technical crew and performers. Mercier remains on stage for large parts of the performance, running the sound desk and even acting at certain points. As the play opens, his soundscape buries us in a landslide of not-quite-white noise. The initial visual and aural cacophony was described by Marjorie Brennan in her review for the *Irish Examiner* as an 'assault', designed to 'discombobulate' (2018). Eventually, the cacophony of sound and voices eases away, and yet we are still lost in eddies of repetitions and snatches of sense. Similarly, sounds from outside the theatre are integrated into the staging, church bells and ambulance sirens, the wash of water and the screech of gulls, resembling the half-familiar literary references that surface in the text.[3] It is impossible to determine, at times, what is natural and what is amplified, what is accidental and what design. The audience have already been brought to the mental state Chapple and Kattenbelt refer to as '*in-between realities*' (2006: 11), where new creative forms and insights emerge.

In *How It Is* the narration is filled with backtracking and caveats: 'ill-said ill-recaptured when the panting stops ill-murmured to the mud' (Beckett, 2009: 15). In the GLSI production of *How It Is* (Part 1), each of the performers interrupts and overlaps the other with the repeated phrase 'something wrong there' (2009: 19). There is no fixed idea as to what is wrong, only that it must be articulated, as pressing as the need for narration. It is difficult, in the face of so much wrong-footing, to trust our own perceptions. Is the moment when an actor gestures for a light to come up a mistake in the lighting cue or a deliberate drawing of the audience's attention to the presence of the technician on stage? Has the actor forgotten his lines or is the company using uncertainty as a tool to undermine the audience's expectations? Lhermitte underlines the inherent flexibility in adaptation, 'both viewed as a state and a process of transformation' (2004: para. 6). Such an experiential and experimental definition of adaptation requires agility on the part of the company, from the Latin *agere*, 'to set in motion, keep in movement' ('Agility', n.d.). The agility of this production, with all of its moving parts and echoed voices, its sense of fracturing and faltering and its apparent improvisations, means that, rather than a fixed and final product, what the audience experiences is the process of adaptation, the feeling of a text as it shifts form and shape, constantly adapting to its new environment.

Confounding the audience's desire for 'physical anchors' and fixed references, as McMullan notes in the programme, it is made impossible to judge where the voice or voices are coming from, or from whom, just as it is unclear which parts of the text are recorded in the production and which are spoken *viva voce*. There are even recorded fragments of the French text, drifting like flotsam through the soundscape. The auditorium, where the audience conventionally sits and listens, becomes a voice box of echoing sounds, with even the coughing and shifting of the audience becoming part of the soundscape, eliciting slight reactions from the performers. The lighting and sound design work together to reinforce our sense of disorientation: an actor speaks into a microphone, only for the lighting to reveal the owner of the voice sitting in the parterre. At one point we see four shadowy figures following Lovett as he walks along the upper circle, doubled into eight by the lighting. This 'shadow cast', consisting of students from Cork School of Music, serves to heighten the sense of uncertainty and of endless refractions so central to Beckett's text, and to this staging.

In the opening moments of the production our eyes are drawn to the control booth, where, as the sound crescendoes, the window smashes and splinters outwards. The booth, designed to limit the leakage of sound and light, and to ensure the smooth running of the performance, is broken open. Shards of glass and splinters of sound are propelled outwards, linearity and control giving way to fragmentation and refraction. Yet the lighting is not simply an assault. It can also be delicate and intimate, as when a close spot reveals the brief movements of Lovett's lower face. The lighting is sharp enough for the audience to see the tiny movements of his jaw and unconsciously mimic them, rereading the text from his lips. Similarly, while we are distracted by a close-up of one of the actors, the theatre fills with smoke. When the house lights tone up to grey, the theatre is awash with a sea of mist curling between the seats, with only a single pale column rising into the light. The 'house' becomes completely other, an uncanny vision, a *coup de théâtre* in an auditorium transformed.

One of the potential problems with the production, outlined by McMullan in her concern over 'anchoring' and 'embodiment' of the voices in the text, was borne out in the reviews. Rather than the 'shapeshifting' infinity of narrators conjured by the text, the staging offered a few named actors. Brennan clearly distinguishes between them: 'Where Lovett appears to turn inward in his torment, imbuing his performance with a sense of heartbreaking humanity, Dillane preens with mischief and humour, in an utterly compelling performance' (2018). Her repetition of the word 'performance' confirms that, in speaking the text on stage, there is a risk of anchoring it to a performer and in turn of solidifying the text into a finished performance. Largely, however, the agility of the performers and the intermedial approach taken to the production result in an immersive, destabilising, invigorating experience.

How It Is (Part 2)

The production *How It Is* (Part 1) met with near-universal acclaim, including rave reviews from critics such as Mary Leland of the *Irish Times*, who described it as 'a flawless conjunction of lighting, music, acting and, probably pre-eminently, setting' (2018). It also received a number of nominations for the Irish Times Irish Theatre Awards, with Kris Stone and Mel Mercier winning for lighting and sound design respectively. *How It Is* (Part 2) was inevitably a more complicated prospect, both in terms of the methodical torture enacted by the narrator on Pim and in terms of audience expectations after Part 1, anticipated in the text itself: 'at last part two' (Beckett, 2009: 43). During the brief preview of Part 2 offered by GSLI during the Beckett Summer School in 2019, Stephen Dillane's authority and ease were particularly compelling, his comic timing pitch-perfect and his sadistic pleasure contagious. How then to avoid anchoring or embodying the 'character' of the torturer in a single actor or repeating the same intermedial tactics used to such effect in *How It Is* (Part 1)?

One enters the Cork Everyman Theatre via the upper circle for the performance on 5 September 2019. After having been trapped on a claustrophobia-inducing stage for Part 1, the seating for Part 2 induces a relative sense of vertigo. A new stage has been constructed by the company, extending from the balcony into the auditorium and half-obscuring the original stage below, in the first of many doublings. Even more disconcertingly, this stage is covered by a Persian rug and filled with gleaming bronze instruments. It becomes clear that GSLI has indeed enlisted the Irish Gamelan Orchestra for their production of *How It Is* (Part 2). In comparison with the stripped-back staging of Part 1, the ornate abundance is jarring and incongruous.

While the house lights remain up and the audience are still talking amongst themselves, Mel Mercier walks on stage and sits with his back turned to us, followed by the other members of the orchestra, clearly at ease in the environment. For the spectator, however, the effect is highly disconcerting, both because sound engineer and performer Mercier has metamorphosed in Part 2 into a musician-conductor and because the Gamelan instruments, including gongs and metallophones, are largely unfamiliar to this audience. At the same time, a certain continuity is maintained: Judy Hegarty Lovett notes afterwards that Part 1 ended on the sound of bells, and Mercier begins Part 2 with them. The spatial dynamics in Part 2 are rendered particularly interesting by the fact that the orchestra occupies almost all of the available performance space, leaving the performers on the edges, forced to adapt to 'the anatomy the geometry' of Part 2 (Beckett, 2009: 47).

The question of soundscape, in what is explicitly a silent, panting text, 'without motion or sound of any kind were it but breath' (2009: 46), is fundamental to the success of the adaptation. This time the orchestra, with its burnished bronze instruments and players, sets a more organic tone than the cool, almost industrial recordings of Part 1. They also offer an intermedial reflection of the text. In the absence of any physical contact between the actors, GSLI evokes the search for connection and human love in Part 2 through the warm, breathing bodies of the orchestra. Just as the narrator seeks to know if Pim loves him by torturing him to provoke howls, the music of the Gamelan is created by people hitting their instruments. Some of the Gamelan players get up and leave at certain points during the performance, while others switch between instruments, as though, like the metallophones and like Pim, they are different yet almost indistinguishable, merely the means by which sounds are made.

Along with the orchestra, the production also introduces Mark Padmore who walks and sings a Schubert lied, 'Der Leiermann' from *Die Winterreise*, about a ragged old hurdy-gurdy man on the outskirts of a village, and the dogs that bite: 'Keiner mag ihn hören / Keiner sieht ihn an' (No one wants to hear him / No one looks at him; my translation). In the case of both the orchestra and, to a lesser extent, the singer, rather than experiencing them as self-evident expressions of the text in other forms, I find myself trying to justify their presence by recourse to the old trope of fidelity to the 'original' text. The explanation for the presence of the singer comes as the narrator comments on Pim's singing: 'perhaps he's singing a lied' (2009: 48). The orchestra also appears in vague flashes in the text, as when the speaker notes 'orchestra-drowned a faint flageolet of pleasure' (2009: 44), the 'eastern sage', or the 'white dhotis' (2009: 45), traditionally worn by men in Indonesia. Yet there is a sense, both in my own experience and judging from the overheard reactions of audience members afterwards, that the inclusion of the orchestra at times seemed more a curiosity than a coup, their presence leaving some people bemused rather than disoriented, the incongruity of the music in relation to the text potentially preventing us from fully accessing the altered state of *'in-between realities'* described by Chapple and Kattenbelt (2006: 11).

The tricks of double vision and ventriloquism used so effectively in Part 1 are evident again, as the audience is disturbed by a latecomer, the stairs creaking as he takes his seat in the shadows a few rows up. Our surprise as the man begins to speak is compounded by the fact that this actor turns out to be not Conor Lovett but rather Stephen Dillane, who has shaved his head for the production. Lovett and Dillane interchange the role of torturer, so that the audience is not quite sure who is speaking nor when the switch occurred: 'I talk like him Bom will talk like me only one kind of talk here one after another' (Beckett, 2009: 66). It is hard at times to hear them over the interruptions of the gongs of the Gamelan, their voices so closely following each other that they seem to eat each other's words, breathing each other in and out: 'the opener the opener soon Pim will speak' (2009: 57). Lovett seems to speak louder and enunciate more here, lacking some of the compelling uncertainty and introspection of Part 1. Dillane's voice, by contrast, is more lilting and less self-consciously dramatic than in Part 1, as though he has felt his way into the role: 'firm and even with a touch of ownership' (2009: 43). There is a febrility to his delivery, so that one believes when he stumbles or repeats that he might have forgotten his lines: 'my hand recoils hangs a moment it's vague' (2009: 43).

In his tone, one can hear the pleasure of a job well done, and Dillane is careful to share that pleasure with the audience, laughing with them, implicating them in the torture: 'there's nothing better' (2009: 44). Later he takes his shoes off and pushes them to the side, while Lovett sits among the orchestra to watch. Softly, kneeling, Dillane mimes as he 'carves my Roman capitals' (2009: 60), his quiet voice contrasting with the plosive violence of his words: 'proof I need proof so stab him in a certain way' (2009: 61). As he gives the line 'he was a bad pupil I a bad master' (2009: 62), Dillane moves back towards us, writing on an invisible board like a teacher, as though we too had become his pupils, suffering in this endless succession of phrases without progression, teased by the promises of darkness and an end: 'leave it vague leave it dark end of part two part one is ended leaving only part three and last' (2009: 64).

In Part 2, as in Part 1, it is difficult, despite the fact that the house lights remain up, to keep track of the performers. They seem to disappear while one's attention is drawn elsewhere, a theatrical sleight of hand which leads to some perfect moments of intermedial interaction. At one point, as Dillane says, 'it is required therefore that I sing what if I were he' (2009: 54), the audience becomes aware of the singer, now standing beside the gongs in the half-light, who provokingly remains silent. The lightscape in Part 2 is just as skilfully constructed, and perhaps even more subtle, than in Part 1. As Dillane returns from a celestial contemplation of the human race – 'billions of us crawling and shitting in their shit' – to the pressing business of torture – 'now my nails' – his left hand holding the banister is casually lit, serving as a focal point for the embodiment of the text (2009: 44). Everyone is watching everyone else here, the audience, the singer and the performers, unsure who will make the next move and what comes next, bound together in mounting tension: 'even beasts observe each other' (2009: 47).

The lighting also distorts the relationship between staging and text: just before the narrator says, 'you see right hand left hand', the singer raises his right hand with the palm lit (2009: 66). Temporal linearity breaks down, the adaptation instead pre-empting and almost prompting the original text. Inevitably, some visual jokes are lost in the transference from text to stage. The image of a paragraph desperately crying out for punctuation, for a full stop, cannot be replicated in a stage production: 'one can't go on one can't stop put a stop' (2009: 78). Largely resisting the temptation to add elements in order to compensate for such losses, the staging instead echoes reality in the flattest way possible, with words. This echoes what Beckett suggested in his dismissal of 'collaboration between the arts' in relation to *En attendant Godot* and discussed above, with words acting as 'labels, or better still ... by announcements: "Well, it seems this is the sky, all this, and that thing over there is a tree, apparently"' (2011: 218–19). GSLI appear to play with Beckett's idea that 'the setting has to come out of the text without adding to it' (2011: 218). As the performers give the line 'my lamps are going out', they are lit by two spots and an artfully positioned reading lamp on the balcony (2009: 72).

Conclusion

Towards the end of the performance, Lovett, Dillane and Padmore together on the lower stage intone the line 'new methods a necessity' (2009: 70), reminding us in Beckett's own words why such adaptations are essential to the ongoing life of the text. Rather than existing in a vertical or hierarchal relationship, they inform and engage with each other, providing faint flashes of illumination. The orchestra rises again, and all of the gongs are set to ringing as we see the suffering of the interrogator searching for questions, the actor spitting out the words: 'if he talks to himself no thinks no believes in God yes every day no wishes to die yes but doesn't expect to no he expects to stay where he is yes' (2009: 84). Finally, we are released from the interrogation into 'how it is' and the blessed relief of darkness, as the lights go down.

Beckett's text is made of leftovers and remainders: 'only two or three last scraps and then the end end of part one leaving only part two leaving only part three and last something missing there' (2009, 38). When we think of leftovers, i.e. the 'last scraps', we tend to think of the plenitude left behind, with an accompanying sense of loss. With Beckett, however, the art of leftovers is not in looking back but in moving forward, however slowly and painfully; a remainder, a 'last scrap', is enough of an impetus to continue. In 'leaving' we also hear heaving; heaving the body forward through the mud, heaving in enough breath to continue since no 'end end' is possible. The form of adaptation envisaged by GSLI does not hold the text as sacrosanct, a frozen religiosity to be reproduced word for word, but rather makes something of the leavings, continuing the heaving forward of the work. Something will always be 'missing there'; this is the inscribed nature of the text, its endless 'on-ness'.

As mentioned in the introduction, adaptation was originally associated with creative translation and transformation (Lhermitte, 2004: para. 3). Beckett's self-translation of *Comment c'est* into English as *How It Is* introduces the resonant phrase 'last state last version' (2009: 3). It is as though the author wished to underline the irony of a translated text claiming a definitive status rather than acknowledging its part in a creative continuity (Van Hulle, 2006/2007: 100). The English translation is by design a text in flux, itself an adaptation of language, a fact GSLI recognises by using ghostly recordings of snippets of the French text through *How It Is* (Part 1). The GSLI productions become, as Walter Benjamin has it in 'The Task of the Translator', part of the text's 'continued life' (1968: 71). Their productions present '*a* version', not '*the* version', paying homage to Beckett's poetics of incompletion and helping to ensure that there will be no 'last state last version' (2009: 3).

Notes

1 Brokenshire's reference to 'aura' is an engagement with Walter Benjamin's discussion of artistic reproduction, authenticity and uniqueness in 'The Work of Art in the Age of Mechanical Reproduction' (1935).
2 For more in-depth analyses of the intermedial references in the prose text, see Albright (2003: 120), Sinoimeri (2012), Baroghel (2017) and Verhulst (2021). Johnson (2020) also discusses Gare St Lazare's *How It Is* in light of other adaptations for diverse media.
3 For more details on these references, see Cordingley (2018).

References

'Agility' (n.d.). *Online Etymology Dictionary*, www.etymonline.com/search?q=agility (accessed 20 March 2020).
Albright, D. (2003). *Beckett and Aesthetics*. Cambridge: Cambridge University Press.
Baroghel, E. (2017). '"My god to have to murmur that": *Comment c'est* / *How It Is* and the issue of performance', in. D. Addyman, E. Tonning and M. Feldman (eds), *Beckett and BBC Radio: A Reassessment*. New York: Palgrave Macmillan, pp. 185–209.
Beckett, S. (2009). *How It Is*. Ed. Édouard Magessa O'Reilly. London: Faber and Faber.
Beckett, S. (2011). *The Letters of Samuel Beckett Volume II: 1941–1956*. Ed. G. Craig, M. Dow Fehsenfeld, D. Gunn and L. More Overbeck. Cambridge: Cambridge University Press.
Beckett, S. (2014). *The Letters of Samuel Beckett Volume III: 1957–1965*. Eds. G. Craig, M. Dow Fehsenfeld, D. Gunn and L. More Overbeck. Cambridge: Cambridge University Press.
Benjamin, W. (1968). 'The task of the translator', in *Illuminations*. Trans. Harry Zohn. New York: Brace and World, pp. 69–82.
Brennan, M. (2018). 'Theatre review: How It Is (Part I) at the Everyman Palace Theatre, Cork', *The Irish Examiner*, 2 February, www.irishexaminer.com/breakingnews/lifestyle/culture/theatre-review-how-it-is-part-1-at-the-everyman-palace-theatre-cork-826092.html (accessed 25 February 2020).
Brokenshire, M. (2020). 'Adaptation', *The Chicago School of Media Theory*, https://lucian.uchicago.edu/blogs/mediatheory/keywords/adaptation/#_ftn16 (accessed 10 April 2020).
Chapple F., and C. Kattenbelt (2006). *Intermediality in Theatre and Performance*. Amsterdam: Rodopi.

Cordingley, A. (2018). *Samuel Beckett's 'How It Is': Philosophy in Translation*. Edinburgh: Edinburgh University Press.

'How It Is' (n.d.). *Gare St Lazare Ireland*, http://garestlazareireland.com/how-it-is (accessed 10 April 2020).

Hutcheon, L. (2013 [2006]). *A Theory of Adaptation*. New York: Routledge.

Johnson, N. (2020). '*How It Is*: intermedial prose performance and the "unperformable"', *Samuel Beckett Today / Aujourd'hui*, 32.1, 86–103.

Leland, M. (2018). 'How It Is review', *Irish Times*, 2 February, www.irishtimes.com/culture/stage/theatre/how-it-is-review-a-flawless-conjunction-of-acting-and-staging-1.3377880 (accessed 25 February 2020).

Lhermitte, C. (2004). 'Adaptation as rewriting: evolution of a concept', *Revue Lisa: Littératures, histoire des idées, Images et Sociétés du monde Anglophone*, 2:5, 26–44. https://journals.openedition.org/lisa/2897#ftn7 (accessed 18 March 2020).

McMullan, A. (2018), 'Performing Beckett's prose', programme note for premiere of *How It Is* (Part 1), Cork Everyman Theatre.

'Performance' (n.d.). *Online Etymology Dictionary*, www.etymonline.com/search?q=performance (accessed 20 March 2020).

Sinoimeri, L. (2012). '"Ill-told, ill-heard": aurality and reading in *Comment c'est / How It Is*', *Samuel Beckett Today / Aujourd'hui*, 24, 321–33.

Van Hulle, D. (2006/2007). 'Bilingual decomposition: the "perilous zones" in the life of Beckett's texts', *Journal of Beckett Studies*, 16.1–2, 97–109.

Verhulst, P. (2021). 'Beckett's technography: traces of radio in the later prose', in G. Kiryushina, E. Adar and M. Nixon (eds), *Samuel Beckett and Technology*. Edinburgh: Edinburgh University Press, pp. 95–108.

7

Intermedial embodiments: Company SJ's staging of Beckett's *Company*

Anna McMullan

Theatrical adaptations of works created in a different medium are proliferating in the new millennium. Frances Babbage argues that '[t]he contemporary theatre's appetite for prose texts has engendered significant expansion of performance vocabularies' (2018: 2). This certainly applies to stage adaptations of Beckett's prose, which offer a rich arena for theatre-makers to expand the Beckett repertoire for performance. Though performances of Beckett's prose are also subject to licensing by the estate, there are no stage directions to negotiate, allowing theatre-makers greater scope for their own interpretation of a Beckettian performance aesthetic inspired by the published prose text and by Beckett's own theatrical experimentation. Such a 're-invention' of Beckettian theatre (Gontarski, 2006) in the case of performances of the author's prose texts is at least partly enabled by the intermedial exchange between the writing and reception conventions of prose and theatre, the latter being a multi-sensory medium, relying (usually) on the embodied presence of the actor.

There is a long history of stage adaptations of Beckett's prose, going back to Jack MacGowran's one-man show *Beginning to End* in the 1960s.[1] Contemporary adaptations for the theatre are increasingly incorporating other media and digital technologies: for example, Gare St Lazare Ireland's *How It Is* in three parts (2018–22) employed a range of audio and lighting technologies and an innovative use of theatre architecture to forge a theatrical equivalent of the deconstruction of traditional narrative conventions in Beckett's novel.[2] Because of the ways in which Beckett's late prose presents time, space and bodies as unstable and always mediated by language, stage adaptations of this work potentially challenge the association of live performance with the presence of the actor and the material space of the stage, forging new performance languages that address our contemporary digital age.

This chapter will analyse the performance of Beckett's novel *Company* directed by Sarah Jane Scaife with Company SJ, as part of the 2018 Dublin Theatre Festival.[3] This production is particularly interesting in relation to adaptation for performance, as it created an intermedial dialogue between the original textual medium of the work and its theatrical performance through voice-over and the projection of phrases from the novel onto the back of the stage. This dialogue also helped to translate into theatrical language the layers of narrative creation inherent in the novel, as the text repeatedly invites us to imagine a figure on his back in the dark listening to a voice recounting scenes from a life attributed to him, but which he fails to recognise as his: the origin of the voice becomes lost in a series of devisers devised. In Company SJ's staging, the live actor, Raymond Keane, was doubled not only by a voice-over but also by a sculptural figure, which enabled the ontological blurring and layers of creature/creator in the text to be presented onstage. Company SJ's *Company* is therefore an apt case study for exploring intermedial adaptation and digital scenography.

From material to virtual bodies: Company SJ

Company SJ was founded by Irish actor, choreographer and director Sarah Jane Scaife in 2009, as she began a multi-year project on Beckett in the City which presented his work at site-specific locations in Dublin and elsewhere. The marginal or dilapidated sites chosen recontextualised Beckett's dispossessed figures within the contemporary conditions of inequality and deprivation in the surrounding urban landscapes (Scaife, 2016). Scaife has been working for many years on staging Beckett since presenting a season of his mimes at the Peacock Theatre Dublin in the early 1990s. Her recent work brings together a concern with intensely focused corporeal movement (she trained in Polish physical theatre and Butoh[4]), with the intermedial effects of projecting filmed sequences onto a historical site. *The Women Speak* (2015), including *Not I*, *Footfalls*, *Rockaby* and *Come and Go*, was part of the Beckett in the City project, and was presented in numbers 20 and 21 Parnell Square, Dublin, the derelict site of the former national ballroom, evoking layers of time and history. The sense of the material bodies of the actors in the here and now of performance being doubled and reframed as ghosts of other marginalised women within the history of the Irish state was highlighted through the projection of filmed sequences in the foyer and in corridors and stairways between performance areas. These had been shot in a hexagonal room in Coláiste Mhuire,[5] the original choice of site, with light slanting in from the dust-covered windows, and featured the three female performers of the programme (Joan Davis, Michèle Forbes and Bríd Ní Neachtain) wandering aimlessly in this enclosed space between windows and doors, as if they had been incarcerated there for years. *Fizzles* (2014) was adapted from a selection of Beckett's short prose texts and used projection and recorded sound to continually re-envision and re-embody the textual narration through the intersections between the live and the mediatised. The body of performer Raymond Keane, who slowly moved along the rooms of a dilapidated Georgian townhouse in inner-city Dublin (Henrietta Street) before the seated audience, was doubled by his virtual self, filmed in the vast space of the equally derelict former power station, the Pigeon House, and projected onto the walls of the performance site which seemed to open up, creating an alternative sense of space, time and embodiment, somewhere between the material and the virtual (McMullan, 2020).

With her 2018 adaptation of *Company*, Scaife returned to the black box of the stage but continued her exploration of how digital technologies and intermedial scenography can translate the ontological instabilities of Beckett's late prose work into the medium of live performance. She had previously staged *Company* in 1990, and again at the Project Arts Centre in 2004, remounted at the Samuel Beckett Theatre, Trinity College Dublin, in 2006. The 2006 version I saw featured a male performer (Jack Walsh) in a loincloth lit against a dark stage as in many of Beckett's late plays, with the text spoken as voice-over by Scaife herself. At times, when the voice-over evoked a life scene, a fragment or shadow of the scene appeared in the darkness, as when, returning home from the local shops hand in hand with his mother, the little boy asks about how far away the sky seems, indicated on stage by the appearance of a maternal hand (that of Flo McSweeney), which suddenly shook off that of the performer, following the mother's 'cutting retort' in the text (Beckett, 2009a: 6). This moment recalled Beckett's television play *Nacht und Träume*, where a hand appears from the top of the televisual frame, with no visible body, and clasps that of the figure in the dream. The production therefore referenced Beckett's prose, dramatic and televisual work in its focused lighting framed against undefined darkness, its use of textual voice-over and its focus on micro-movements of the actor's body. Scaife's 2018 staging of *Company* was a revisiting and reinvention of this earlier production,[6] informed by intervening work and new digital technologies, which enabled a more complex set of intermedial exchanges and kinetic, choreographic and audio-visual layering.

Staging intermediality

André Gaudreault and Philippe Marion have discussed the interconnections between the fields of adaptation and intermediality in terms of an encounter between different media materialities: 'any process of adaptation has to take into account the kinds of "incarnations" inherent in this encounter in terms of the materiality of media'. They emphasize that 'the encounter, or better the profound interaction, with the resistant opacity of the chosen matter of expression is itself generative, even decisive, within the process of creation' (2004: 61, 65).[7] Such encounters may produce new, hybrid or liminal 'incarnations'. Ágnes Pethö has argued that '[i]ntermediality appears as a *border zone* across which media transgressions take place, or an instable "place" of "*in-between*" ("*Zwischenraum*"), a *passageway* from one media towards another' (2011: 42–3).[8] My interest here is in how theatrical adaptations can present an unstable sense of materiality, agency and embodiment through their intermedial encounters.

It has often been argued that theatre's association with the here and now of the stage limits its capacity for presenting ontological, spatial or temporal instability or uncertainty because, as Dean Wilcox notes, it tends to ground 'place' and 'time': 'As the body of the performer enters the performance location, the assumption is that its mere presence, defined by [phenomenologist Edward] Casey as a quality of placeness, grounds undifferentiated space within the narrative action, thereby limiting the potential for space to escape representation' (2003: 546). However, Wilcox states that in the case of Beckett, and other experimental practitioners such as Oscar Schlemmer or Richard Foreman, 'an architectural, absent, repetitive or otherwise "unrealistic" use of the body of the performer(s) (which can be extended to other manifest theatrical elements like objects, settings, and costumes) can disrupt not only the mimetic exchange between stage and audience, but have an effect on the occupation and location of the stage space' (2003: 544). Wilcox further argues that Beckett focuses on formal stage space rather than on fictional location, place or representation. Indeed: 'By manipulating the appearance of the performer in the same sense that Schlemmer's work at the Bauhaus manipulated the form, Beckett's lack of a body, like Schlemmer's ambulant architecture, helps limit mimesis and redistribute focus onto the space present in performance' (2003: 551).

The space of the stage can therefore become a formal space of composition rather than representation and can foreground or frame different modes of composition inherent to different media, whether words, live performance or audio-visual recording. This has been described not only as intermediality but more specifically as 'metamediality' by Claudia Georgi:

> Metamediality is no inherent function of intermediality, but it presupposes 'meta-aesthetic' or 'metamedial self-reflexivity' (Wolf 1999: 48 f.). By reflecting on their own mediality and particularities, the involved media simultaneously comment on their mutual relations, similarities or differences. In doing so they not only self-reflexively cast light on their own mediality, but they also comment on the other media that form part of the combination. (2014: 43)

Moreover, Georgi argues that this metamediality can also highlight the mediated nature of what we call 'reality', either because our access to much of the external world is in fact mediated, increasingly through electronic devices and social media, or because all reality is constructed through language or other conventions: 'By juxtaposing or fusing distinct media and their corresponding modes of presenting reality, media combination may thus reflect on the ontological status of reality per se and explicitly or implicitly comment on the questions of whether an immediate access to reality is possible and whether or to what extent media shape reality' (2014: 44).

It is precisely this juxtaposition of different media and modes of presenting reality, resulting in a complex undermining of any stable sense of body, space, time or place, that I want to analyse in Company SJ's *Company*. However, it is worth examining the already intermedial echoes in Beckett's text, to appreciate the ways in which Company SJ's staging of it re-presented the novel's multiple layers of textual narrative, identities and spaces.

Beckett's *Company*: 'Devised deviser devising it all for company'[9]

Company was published in 1979, and it is, on one level, an attempt to construct an autobiography: the text narrates vivid scenes which evoke places from Beckett's childhood and youth, such as the Forty Foot 'bathing place' (Beckett, 2009a: 11) in south Dublin, and specifically invokes the date of his own birthday on Good Friday: 'You first saw the light and cried at the close of the day when in darkness Christ at the ninth hour cried and died' (2009a: 36).[10] However, *Company* radically deconstructs the assumptions of autobiography as a chronology or history of the self, as identity is fractured between the figure on his back in the dark referred to as 'he', the persona in the life scenes addressed as 'you', and the narrating voice, wherever it issues from. The text states that 'He speaks of himself as of another' (2009a: 16). This 'he' is initially portrayed as a creator figure W, who devises a self, M, 'for company': 'So W reminds himself of his creature as so far created' (2009a: 30). Yet any identity in this text is provisional and hypothetical as 'W too is creature. Figment' (2009a: 30). Both narrative voice and listening figure are posited as invented or created by another deviser, who may in turn be devised by yet another: 'Deviser devised devising it all for company' (2009a: 30). The proliferation of creators and creatures increasingly erodes the identity and authority of any one creator-origin or self.

In addition to the instability of origin or identity, *Company*, like much of Beckett's late prose, destabilises media boundaries, as Steven Connor has noted:

> The close attention to details of space and position in the related texts *The Lost Ones*, *Ping*, *Imagination Dead Imagine* and *All Strange Away*, as well as the theatrical language often used in these works, suggests a certain variability or doubling of medium, as though the texts included within themselves the possibility of their staging in some other form. Among the most striking of these is *Company*. The voice which 'comes to one in the dark' throughout this text has many of the qualities of the voices 'coming out of the dark' of radio drama and the details of the listener's position remind us remarkably of the listening face of *That Time*, a stage play that itself uses some of the properties of radio drama. The careful attention to the physical space of the listening, and the division of this physical space from the imaginary spaces of quotation/remembering, suggests the simple insistent physicality of some of Beckett's late drama, while the use of intercutting and flashback, as well as the close visual attention paid to certain items in the narrative, such as the watch face, suggests continuities with visual media. (1988: 166)[11]

Sarah West discusses *Company* in relation to the 'performative' voice in Beckett's late prose as well as his stage works, which has the dual function of 'voice as a dramatic entity and voice as a performer of language' (2010: 14). The text of *Company* begins, 'A voice comes to one in the dark. Imagine' (Beckett, 2009a: 3), which mentally conjures up the performative voice in something like a black box. The scenario therefore recalls many of Beckett's late theatre plays, where a subject who may be represented by an isolated body or body part on stage (as in the spotlit faces of *Play* or the rocking figure in *Rockaby*) listens, as does the audience, to scenes from their past life spoken by recorded voices. As Steven Connor notes, 'the actual space of what we see in the theatre has been turned into a mental, potential space, for which we must supply the action' (1988: 163), as when reading fiction or listening to the radio.

However, in fiction the body and the space evoked are not material, breathing bodies in three-dimensional space shared by the audience as in theatre, but may dissolve back into words at any point. This returns to the question of the presence of the actor in the concrete space of the stage, in the same auditorium as the audience. Yet Beckett also undermines the status of the body on stage in his late theatre through the use of recording and lighting technologies, so that the body appears missing, apart from an isolated mouth (*Not I*) or head (*That Time*), or seems hardly there, suspended between being and non-being, like the ghostly figure of May in *Footfalls*. Therefore, theatre's ontology of presence may be undermined through exploiting exactly the intermedial and technological strategies that Beckett's own theatre employs, conflating material with imagined spaces and bodies in a way that can begin to adapt or translate the ontological in-betweenness or instability of a prose text such as *Company*.

Company SJ's performance of *Company*

In Scaife's direction of *Company*, the fracturing of identity, voice and space was produced through different layers of embodiment and digital mediation: the live performer, Raymond Keane, the sculptural figure of an old man, a voice-over (Keane's recorded voice) and lines of text projected at the back of the stage at particular moments. This fracturing also invoked an intermedial dialogue between live performance, sculptural figure and forms of textuality, whether via the reading of the text in the voice-over or the projection of the words. The rest of this chapter will tease out these different layers of performance, identity and text in order to evaluate how this production of *Company* created an innovative performative model of intermedial adaptation.

Company SJ's *Company* initially seemed to establish a clear distinction between Keane as subject-creator and the sculptural figure as creature. The figure designed by Roman Paska was to scale, about 4 feet (or 1.2 metres) in length. When we first see him, he is stretched out on a black table which almost disappears because of the general darkness, except for the very focused lighting on both figure and actor. Keane is dressed in black with bare hands and feet. The performance opens with Keane directly addressing the audience as he stands over the figure, referring to the latter as 'he'. During the description of the figure crawling in the dark or falling, or hunched or prone, the actor gently manipulates him, not in any detailed mimesis of the text but in patterned minimalist movements which accompany the text, juxtaposing the heard and the seen, where they sometimes, but not completely, overlap. Keane's manipulation of the figure obeys its own stylised rhythm and pattern, lifting him in a certain way and always ending with pointing the feet together, as Dúnlaith Bird has noted: 'At the end of each interaction Keane returns the figure to the rest position on his back in the dark, and the feet are carefully turned up, like the full stops at the end of a paragraph' (2018).

During the voiced-over life scenes, especially at the beginning, Keane also moves the figure. Sarah West notes that '[f]or the drama of listening to be effective in the theatre, it must also be visual' (2010: 50), as the image directs the ear as well as the eye. But the visual in Company SJ's production is kept to a minimum, so that the audience is assisted with, but not distracted from, listening.[12] My own experience combined or layered the interior eye of the mind or imagination with physiological vision, what Beckett referred to in *The Lost Ones* as the 'eye of flesh' (Beckett, 2010: 109),[13] I mentally envisaged the scenes from the voice-over while, at the same time, watching a figure on stage evoking or paralleling the narrated movement or scene. This balance maintained a somewhat uncanny sense of medial instability:

118   *Beckett's afterlives*

we are watching a performance but also listening collectively as if to a radio drama or audiobook.

Keane therefore seems at first to be in control of the creature who moves at certain moments in the narrative, walking, lying or crawling. However, as the text unfolds, and the sense of the creator as also creature builds, the choreography plays with different registers of relationship between Keane and the figure. From manipulating the figure as creator, Keane becomes the figure in the dark or the persona in the life scenes, doubling the figure, as when he lies supine on the forestage, mirroring the pose of the sculptural figure on the table (see Figure 7.1). The actor seems to be projected into being by his voice(-over), mirroring the generation of creator and creature in and by the text, thereby destabilising the ontology of live presence.[14] As in the prose text of *Company*, no stable origin of identity, voice or text can be established. Stephen Dodd's lighting plays a part in this: it illuminates the figure from different angles so that it appears dynamic with different moods and expressions. But the lighting also picks out features of Keane in a similar way, especially when static, so that the two bodies echo each other, with Keane lying parallel to the figure on the forestage, curled up under the table or slowly walking as he had guided the steps of the sculptural

Figure 7.1 Raymond Keane in Company SJ's *Company*. Sculptural figure by Roman Paska.

figure. The location of any creator via voice-over or projected text becomes obscured in this interplay of fractured and multiple elements and perspectives. The visual evocation of the author Beckett in Keane's aquiline profile, tall lean figure and shock of white hair is a playful incorporation of the figure of the author caught up in his own fictions.

As in several of Beckett's late stage plays, the live body of the actor is juxtaposed with the materiality of an object with which it becomes identified in a strange organic-inorganic osmosis, as the rocking chair curves around the body of W in *Rockaby*: 'those arms at last' (Beckett, 2009b: 133, 134). The use of the sculptural figure recalls Beckett's oft-noted interest in Heinrich von Kleist's theories of the *Übermarionnette*. As James Knowlson (1979), Anthony Paraskeva (2013), David Tucker (2015) and Anthony Uhlmann (2005) have noted, Kleist attributes a more graceful movement to animals or puppets because they are not imbued with self-consciousness. Knowlson notes that Beckett specifically mentioned Kleist in rehearsals of *Happy Days* in 1971 at the Schiller Theater, recommending that the actor aim for precision and economy of movement in order to achieve 'grace in the Kleistian sense' (1996: 584).[15] The concept is reprised in the text of *Company*: 'From time to time with unexpected grace you lie' (Beckett, 2009a: 41).

Scaife has a long interest in Asian forms of performance such as Butoh (hence the very focused, slow movements). The sculptural figure also recalls the Japanese performance genre of Bunraku, where a figure similar to the proportions of the figure in *Company* is visibly manipulated by three performers clad in black: an unmasked chief puppeteer and two masked supporters who often merge into the darkness. In addition to the grace of the figure's movements, the experience and theorisation of Bunraku emphasise the viewer's affective investment in the material figure of the marionette. Yuji Sone argues that this affective charge derives from the stylisation or patterning of emotions: 'The audience of Bunraku is drawn into a drama portrayed on the stage through patterned gestures (*furi* and *kata*) and vocal expressions' (2005: 54). These gestures are distilled 'indices of the intangible emotions or empathies they reference …. Pattern provides a framework and legitimation for, and expectation of, audience affect' (2005: 54). Sone also argues that the impact of Bunraku depends on the audience responding to both the discrete elements involved and their interaction: 'the contextual environment of Bunraku simultaneously disperses and reassembles the audience's attention' (2005: 53). The emotion is not directly expressed by any one of the elements but by how they interact, so that 'the theatrical space performs as an embodied whole' (2005: 53).

These arguments link back to Beckett's interest in Kleist's theories and their relevance to how both affect and perceptual impact operate in a performance where the scenography as a whole is foregrounded, rather than an individual actor's expressive delivery. As Anthony Uhlmann argues: 'The emotions that the actor brings to bear in performing can behave as a kind of interference to this process. They are interference because they do not relate to the affects which the work itself is seeking to convey' (2005: 60). In other words, echoing Wilcox's argument above, Beckett 'was attempting to stage a space: the gestures, the qualities of light and voice as well as words and presence. The performance is no longer textualised by the actors and a director, the text extends to the limits of the stage and involves the development of a univocal externalised expression' (2005: 69).

Beckett's stage plays incorporate schisms as an inherent part of their dramaturgy and scenographic aesthetic, but the argument of a *mise en scène* which operates in its entirety as a compositional space where the 'expression' is subject to formal rhythms and patterns is certainly true of Beckett's late plays, his staging of them and of Company SJ's *Company*. As Uhlmann stresses, this approach does not lack affective impact, but the affects arise from the overall scenography of the performance rather than from the actor's delivery. While this was true of most of the performance of *Company*, Keane's delivery became more expressly emotive towards the end. This conveyed the hearer's utter frustration and desire to end, and yet this 'naked emotion', as Bird suggests, was 'perhaps too easy a release' (2018), leaving less space for the audience's own emotional responses, which the earlier scenes had done very effectively.

'Who exclaims thus?'[16]

In addition to the schisms between the live actor, the sculptural figure and the voice-over, the performance of *Company* added a further scenographic layer: words from the text of the novel were projected onto the back of the stage. The visual appearance of the words referenced the prose medium of the original novel, but the projection of the text was spatialised – it appeared unexpectedly in different areas at the back of the stage and in different fonts and formats. At times it seemed to be in dialogue with Keane or the voice-over, textually declaiming 'No' or qualifying the spoken statements: 'Up to a Point'. The projected text therefore evokes an agency whose origin remains unclear, disorienting the viewer; it seems to have some kind of authority, as if it was conjuring the whole world of the performance. While the words derived from the actual text of the novel, they also seemed to be generated by the stage apparatus, as if the *mise en scène* had a posthuman life of its own. It teased, dancing across the back of the stage, falling like rain or dropping like a curtain or a blind. The text functioned as interpretable language like that of the novel, but also as materiality, shape, formation or agency, constituting another layer in the overall spatialised stage composition and echoing visually the rhythmic syntax of the prose.

Sone's essay cited above argues for the concept of 'intermediated embodiment', derived from the idea of the encounter between disparate elements in Bunraku, to account for the hybrid modes of sensory encounter and perceptual experience in mediatised performance: 'Traditional forms of sensory engagement are often overlapped, integrated and confounded in media-based work' (2005: 60). Certainly, in Scaife's staging of *Company*, the reading experience of the text is translated into a multi-sensory kinetic and intermedial experience, where watching, listening and reading are all part of the synaesthetic perceptual encounter with the performance. In fact, this combination of layering with minimalism – there are not, in fact, many stage elements – means that audiences can focus intensely on the interaction between them and on the different sensory engagement of each as they combine and also interrupt each other. The sound design by Scaife's late husband, Tim Martin, also enhanced the aurality of the performance and the clarity of Keane's recorded voice-over. He is now well immersed in the aural landscape of Beckett's texts, having previously collaborated with Scaife on many stagings of his prose, theatre and mimes. Keane spoke the text with precision, lyricism, humour, irritation or frustration as the relentless drive to imagine will not give rest. However, Martin also mediated the recording so that every detail of the rhythmic score is enhanced. I heard the text anew and was surprised by some passages, especially the mental measuring of the crawling figure, continually changing, reverting, contradicting itself, interspersed with moments of vividly evoked scenes of memory, so that the frames of fiction, observation, abstract calculation and memory are continually intersecting.

Conclusion

Company SJ's staging of *Company* presented diverse layers of embodiment, identity and composition. The different elements of the staging, where the live body, the voice-over and the projected text all 'speak', placed the body of the actor as an element in the composition, not as the origin of the text or as the secure central subject position. The minimalism and slow pace of the performance created, in my experience, what Carl Lavery has described as the alternative 'spatio-temporal rhythm' (2019: 17) of Beckett's work, which 'slows perception down to the point where things and experiences that ordinarily go unnoticed are allowed to impress themselves upon us' (2019: 19). The different layers of the performance never cohered into a single perspective or subject position, conveying the schisms of the prose text. This sense of layering and instability was created through the intermedial encounter between the prose text, spatialised in projected words; performance, with its specific materiality and multi-sensory modes of perception and encounter; and the digital, where technology sharpened visual and aural perception, and the projected text seemed to take on a life and agency of its own. The diminution of audio-visual elements encouraged a micro-intense focus on every element of scenography and performance, including sound and lighting design and choreography, and on the journey from text to embodiment in all its lived, material and technologically mediated complexity. This is one of the sources of the excitement and energy of contemporary stagings of Beckett's prose: they enable a re-engagement with and reimagining of Beckett's aesthetic for the twenty-first century. As Gontarski has argued, such 're-imaginings' or re-visionings of Beckett are 'necessary to a living art' (2006: 448).

Notes

1 MacGowran's performance was initially entitled *End of Day* and premiered at the Dublin Theatre Festival in 1962. However, Beckett was unhappy with the presentation and choice of texts, so when the show was reprised in 1965, he worked with MacGowran on a considerably modified version, retitled *Beginning to End* (see Young, 1987).
2 Gare St Lazare Ireland's *How It Is (Part 1)* premiered at the Everyman Theatre in Cork in February 2018.
3 I saw the 2.30 p.m. performance at the Project Arts Centre, Dublin, on 7 October 2018.
4 Butoh is a form of dance theatre that emerged in post-World War II Japan. It was founded by Tatsumi Hijikata and Kazuo Ohno and is characterised by slow movement, stillness and the whitened face and body of the performer.
5 Coláiste Mhuire, an Irish language school in Dublin, was founded by the Christian Brothers and occupied number 23, Parnell Square, close to the National Ballroom, until the buildings fell into disrepair. The site was unavailable for performances of *Beckett in the City: The Women Speak* because of Health and Safety concerns (Scaife, 2016).
6 See www.company-sj.com/samuel-becketts-prose-piece-company (accessed 12 August 2021). Scaife writes there that it was during her first staging of *Company* that she worked with sound designer Tim Martin, who became her husband and who also worked on this 2018 production, but tragically died before it premiered. She draws attention to the 'father's shade' that initially accompanies

the narrated persona on his walks in *Company*, having also recently lost her own father.
7 See also Elleström (2017) and Voigts-Virchow (2009).
8 See also Chapple and Kattenbelt: '[T]he intermedial is a space where the boundaries soften – and we are in-between and within a mixing of spaces, media and realities' (2006: 12).
9 Beckett (2009a: 30).
10 See Knowlson (1996) and O'Brien (1986) for such autobiographical details.
11 See also Verhulst for the impact of Beckett's experience with radio on *Company* and on the concept of 'media confluence' in his later work: 'the experience [Beckett] had accumulated in audio-visual media over the preceding decades flowed back into his prose' (2021: 106).
12 Several reviews note the 'understated theatricality' (O'Rourke, 2018) of the production, which created a 'liminal space between the inertia of the page and the action of the stage' (Anton, 2018) while focusing attention on the 'mesmerising' and 'exquisitely articulated physicality' of Keane's performance (O'Rourke, 2018).
13 The phrase also occurs in *Ill Seen Ill Said* (Beckett, 2009a: 51).
14 See Auslander (1999) for a detailed discussion of liveness and mediation.
15 Beckett also mentioned von Kleist's concept of grace to Ronald Pickup when rehearsing the television play *Ghost Trio*, broadcast by the BBC in 1977 (Knowlson, 1986: 197).
16 Beckett (2009a: 39).

References

Anton, S. (2018). Review of Company SJ's *Company*, *The Reviews Hub*, 5 October, www.thereviewshub.com/dublin-theatre-festival-company-project-arts-centre-dublin/ (accessed 12 August 2021).

Auslander, P. (1999). *Liveness: Performance in a Mediatized Culture*. London and New York: Routledge.

Babbage, F. (2018). *Adaptation in Contemporary Theatre: Performing Literature*. London: Bloomsbury Methuen Drama.

Beckett, S. (2009a). *Company, Ill Seen Ill Said, Worstward Ho, Stirrings Still*. Ed. Dirk Van Hulle. London: Faber and Faber.

Beckett, S. (2009b). *Krapp's Last Tape and Other Shorter Plays*. Pref. S. E. Gontarski. London: Faber and Faber.

Beckett, S. (2010). *Texts for Nothing and Other Shorter Prose, 1950–1976*. Ed. Mark Nixon. London: Faber and Faber.

Bird, D. (2018). '*Company*, Project Arts Centre, Dublin, directed by Sarah Jane Scaife, featuring Raymond Keane (and sculptural figure), October 5th, 2018, *company sj*, www.company-sj.com/dunlaith-bird (accessed 12 August 2021).

Chapple F., and C. Kattenbelt (2006). *Intermediality in Theatre and Performance*. Amsterdam: Rodopi.

Connor, S. (1988). *Samuel Beckett: Repetition Theory and Text*. Oxford: Blackwell.
Elleström, L. (2017). 'Adaptation and intermediality', in T. Leitch (ed.), *The Oxford Handbook of Adaptation Studies*. Oxford: Oxford University Press, pp. 509–26.
Gaudreault A., and P. Marion (2004). 'Transécriture and narrative mediatics: the stakes of intermediality', in R. Stam and A. Raengo (eds), *A Companion to Literature and Film*. Malden, MA: Blackwell, pp. 58–70.
Georgi, C. (2014). *Liveness on Stage: Intermedial Challenges in Contemporary British Theatre and Performance*. Berlin: De Gruyter.
Gontarski, S. E. (2006). 'Re-inventing Beckett', *Modern Drama*, 49.4, 428–51.
Knowlson, J. (1979). 'Beckett and Kleist's essay "On the Marionette Theatre"', in J. Knowlson and J. Pilling (eds), *Frescoes of the Skull*. London: Calder, pp. 277–85.
Knowlson, J. (1986). '*Ghost Trio / Geister Trio*', in E. Brater (ed.), *Beckett at 80 / Beckett in Context*. Oxford and New York: Oxford University Press, pp. 193–207.
Knowlson, J. (1996). *Damned to Fame: The Life of Samuel Beckett*. London: Bloomsbury.
Lavery, C. (2019). 'Ecology in Beckett's theatre garden: or how to cultivate the *oikos*', *Contemporary Theatre Review*, 28.1, 10–26.
McMullan, A. (2020). 'Samuel Beckett and intermedial performance: "passing between"', *Samuel Beckett Today / Aujourd'hui*, 32.1, 71–85.
O'Brien, E. (1986). *The Beckett Country*. Dublin and London: The Black Cat Press and Faber and Faber.
O'Rourke, C. (2018). 'Dublin Theatre Festival 2018: *Company*', *The Arts Review*, www.theartsreview.com/posts/Dublin-Theatre-Festival-2018%3A-Company (accessed 12 August 2021).
Paraskeva, A. (2013). 'Beckett, biomechanics and Eisenstein's reading of Kleist's marionettes', *Journal of Beckett Studies*, 22.2, 161–79.
Pethö, A. (2011). *Cinema and Intermediality: The Passion for the In-Between*. Newcastle upon Tyne: Cambridge Scholars Publishing.
Scaife, S. J. (2016). 'Practice in focus: Beckett in the city', in T. McTighe and D. Tucker (eds), *Staging Beckett in Ireland and Northern Ireland*. London and New York, Bloomsbury/Methuen, pp. 153–67.
Sone, Y. (2005). 'East meets west: *Bunraku*, intermediation and Australian institutional concepts of interdisciplinarity', *Performance Paradigm*, 1, 47–68.
Tucker, D. (2015). '"Beckett's Guignol Worlds": Arnold Geulincx and Heinrich von Kleist', in M. Feldman and K. Mamdani (eds), *Beckett / Philosophy*. Stuttgart: Ibidem, pp. 235–60.
Uhlmann, A. (2005). 'Expression and affect in Kleist, Beckett and Deleuze', in L. Cull and I. Buchanan (eds), *Deleuze and Performance*. Edinburgh: Edinburgh University Press, pp. 54–70.
Verhulst, P. (2021). 'Beckett's technography: traces of radio in the later prose', in G. Kiryushina, E. Adar and M. Nixon (eds), *Samuel Beckett and Technology*. Edinburgh: Edinburgh University Press, pp. 95–108.
Voigts-Virchow, E. (2009). 'Metadaptation: adaptation and intermediality – cock and bull', *Journal of Adaptation in Film & Performance*, 2.2, 137–52.
West, S. (2010). *Say It: The Performative Voice in the Dramatic Works of Samuel Beckett*. Amsterdam and New York: Rodopi.

Wilcox, D. (2003). 'Ambient space in twentieth-century theatre: the space of silence', *Modern Drama*, 46.4, 542–57.

Wolf, W. (1999). *The Musicalization of Fiction: A Study in the Theory and History of Intermediality*. Amsterdam and Atlanta, GA: Rodopi.

Young, J. (1987). *The Beckett Actor: Jack MacGowran, Beginning to End*. Beverley Hills, CA: Moonstone Press.

8

Beckett, neurodiversity and the prosthetic: the posthuman turn in contemporary art

Derval Tubridy

This chapter argues that the posthuman in Beckett provides the most fertile ground for intermedial adaptation of his work in the contemporary arts. It focuses on the intersections between Beckett and posthumanism by analysing examples of how selected contemporary artists in different media draw on his work in order to expand and explore normative categories of human embodiment and subjectivity, such as the interface between the machinic, the prosthetic and the corporeal in work by Rebecca Horn (1970s–2010s) and neurodiverse theatre performance that reconfigures modalities of subjectivity and agency in Jess Thom's Touretteshero production of *Not I* (2017).[1] The chapter draws into the discussion an exploration of how ideas of silence, recalibrated by neurodiversity, are rendered somatic through Anne Niemetz and Andrew Pelling's sound work *Dark Side of the Cell* (2004).[2]

On the posthuman

In her landmark study on *The Posthuman*, Rosi Braidotti maps out the 'historical decline' of humanism and the Enlightenment ideal of the self, proposing instead 'alternative ways of conceptualizing the human subject' (2013: 37). She outlines three models of posthumanism. The first is reactionary posthumanism, which derives from moral philosophy and retains 'universalistic human values' (2013: 39) and a humanist concept of the individual subject. The second, analytic posthumanism, like the concept of transhumanism, turns to science and technology to extend the limits of human corporeality and expand human agency, prising open post-Enlightenment ideas of the human in order to reframe 'crucial ethical and conceptual questions about the status of the human' (2013: 39). However, according to Braidotti, analytic posthumanism fails to fully engage with the social and moral consequences of unequal access to advanced technologies, or to tackle the contested notion of subjectivity. The third model of posthumanism is critical posthumanism (where Braidotti situates herself), which integrates new materialities of the human with a refiguration of subjectivity as it engages with the discursive, affective and environmental to forge, as Braidotti explains, a 'reintegrated posthuman theory that includes both scientific and technological complexity and its implications for political subjectivity' (2013: 42).

It is crucial to our understanding of the importance of Beckett's work for twenty-first-century artists, and the role of adaptation and remediation in that exchange, that we develop our thinking of Beckett in terms of the posthuman, counterpointing the transhumanism of analytic posthumanism, defined by a valorisation of technological engagements with embodiment and consciousness, with the materialist and relational subjectivity of critical posthumanism. Beckett articulates the crisis of the '*anthropos*' through two distinct forms of posthumanism. In his early to middle work, in prose as well as theatre, the dissolution or disablement of the body, framed by its engagement with the prosthetic and the machinic (the bicycle, the stick, the tape recorder, the megaphone) can be identified as a search towards a transhuman subject characteristic of analytic posthumanism. This corporeal and machinic nostalgia, I contend, gives way in Beckett's later work to a more complex and mobile vision of the human characterised by critical posthumanism in which corporeality is no longer framed within the mensurated form of the body and its engagement with objects, but is disarticulated and re-formed among contested elements of subjectivity framed within an environment that does not adhere to a fixed, embodied materiality.

Jonathan Boulter configures posthuman Beckett as a 'diminishing of the material, phenomenal body' and a concomitant 'distance from discourse', arguing that 'to be posthuman is to be in a space where it is impossible to locate oneself within discourse' (2008: 124, 129). Elizabeth Effinger underlines the fluid nature of posthuman Beckett in her reading of *The Unnamable* as 'a subjectivity without a subject, and yet a subjectivity that has corporeality and spatiality that are equally and contingently metamorphous' (2011: 370). Alys Moody examines the interplay between the human body and the machine in her reading of the 'mechanised affect' generated by the language of Beckett's prose text *Ping*, arguing that the 'cyborg affect' attributable to his writing has 'a very specific temporality, staging an imagined future in the infinitely prolonged present of performance' (2017: 99). In these configurations of the posthuman Beckett, we see a tension between the body and the machine, informed by a focus on the discursive condition of his contested subjectivity.

Tracing the history of the critical reception of Beckett as either a 'transcendental writer who subscribed to a Cartesian dualism' or one who created a 'discursively produced body at the expense of the material fleshly one', Ulrika Maude argues that the 'material body forms the ultimate foundation of identity, by constituting that self that is both singular and, in its perpetual complexity and mutability, always plural and indecipherable' (2009: 1–2). She underlines how technologies such as the microscope, stereoscope, chronophotography and x-ray transformed perceptions of the body and opened up the possibility of virtualisation and adaptation (2009: 127). Indeed, to return to Moody's argument, we might note Dan O'Hara's suggestion that Beckett's experience of an ECG or electrocardiograph machine led to the distinctive prose of *Ping* as 'a closed circuit between man and machine' (2010: 442). In *Samuel Beckett and the Prosthetic Body*, Yoshiki Tajiri points out that the distinction between body and machine has become increasingly complicated since 'the clear-cut distinction between the body (considered internal and organic) and technology (considered external and inorganic) is being rendered obsolete by advanced medical technologies including genetic engineering' (2007: 2). Tajiri retains a nostalgia for the boundaries characteristic of dualistic thought as he argues that Beckett's is a prosthetic body 'that harbours the outside or the alien within it, thereby becoming the locus of interactions between the inside and the outside' (2007: 167).[3]

In his study *Prosthesis*, David Wills affirms the necessary supplementarity of the prosthetic, arguing that prosthesis is 'inevitably caught in a complex play of displacements; prosthesis being about nothing if not placement, displacement, replacement, standing, dislodging, substituting, setting, amputating, supplementing' (2021: 9). This research on the interdependence between body and machine in Beckett's work (and in the experiences that informed his writing) underscores what for Donna Haraway is a fundamental condition of the late twentieth century, a period she describes as the 'era of techno-biopolitics' (2013: 249n7). In *Simians, Cyborgs, and Women: The Reinvention of Nature*, Haraway argues that the prosthetic is not simply a conjunction of bodies and machines, but a relational exchange predicated on power and communication: 'Prosthesis becomes a fundamental category for understanding our most intimate selves. Prosthesis is semiosis, the making of meanings and bodies, not for transcendence but for power-charged communication' (2013: 249n7).

In order to explore further these posthuman interchanges between body and prosthetics, I turn to Rebecca Horn's work, including her more recent engagement with Beckett's prose text *The Lost Ones*, and to Jess Thom's neurodiverse performance of the play *Not I*.

On Rebecca Horn

Rebecca Horn's prosthetic artworks or 'body modifications' – such as *Finger Gloves* (*Handschuhfinger*, 1972) and *Pencil Mask* (*Bleistiftmaske*, 1972)

– were born out of physical disability and confinement, and they seek to stretch the body beyond itself while retaining a constraining nostalgia for habitual gesture and form.[4] Poisoned by the fibreglass materials that she was using for her sculptures, Horn damaged her lungs and was hospitalised for months: 'that's when I began to make my first body-sculptures. I could sew lying in bed' (qtd in Winterson, 2005). Katharina Schmidt notes that Horn's works of the 1970s, and particularly her 'hospital drawings', are informed by 'the objects that so starkly resemble prostheses, surgical equipment, bandages, straps and body trusses' (2005: 50). In these works Horn explores the limits of the body in space and the role of the prosthetic in embodied agency and interrelations. Constructed out of cloth and balsa wood, Horn's *Finger Gloves* enable the wearer to extend the parameters of their reach by over a metre, reaching down to touch the floor with only a slight bend of the torso. Long, thin black forms extend from the tip of the fingers, elongating the body and reconfiguring its balance and reach. Horn describes the haptic experience of wearing 'finger gloves' as one which creates intimacy, yet reaffirms distance:

> The finger gloves are made from such a light material, that I can move my fingers without effort. I feel, touch, grasp with them, yet keep a certain distance from the objects that I touch. The lever action of the lengthened fingers intensifies the sense of touch in the hand. I feel myself touching, see myself grasping, and control the distance between myself and the objects. (qtd in Haenlein, 1997: 58)

Finger Gloves forms part of a series of prosthetic extensions that were filmed on site-specific performances as part of a moving image work called *Performances II* (1973), in which Horn examines the possibilities of extending her body into space.[5] In *Performances II*, Horn is filmed touching the floor with her extended fingers and tracing the back and hair of a person lying prone in an intimate gesture of exploration. *Finger Gloves* developed into a work that Horn called *Touching the Walls with Both Hands Simultaneously* (*Mit beiden Händen gleichzeitig die Wände berühren*, 1974–5), in which she recreated the body extension to fit a particular space, so that, when extended, the wearer's hands could touch both sides of a space simultaneously, leveraging the body to form an integral part of its own environment, achieving what Hamm fails to do in *Endgame* when he seeks to navigate the circumference of his room in his chair and then return to the centre: 'Hug the walls, then back to the centre again' (Beckett, 2009a: 18).

While *Finger Gloves* extends the facility of the hands as haptic forms, *Pencil Mask* subverts the Levinasian idea of the face as a direct and defenceless place of engagement with the Other (Levinas and Kearney, 1986: 24). Horn's *Pencil Mask* hides and protects the face while also allowing it a mode of expression normally associated with the hand. Fashioned out of a grid of green strips of cloth that is strapped around the whole head, the mask holds a series of pencils at the intersection of each strip. Facing outwards from the face, these pencils allow the wearer to express through drawing, obscuring the nuances of facial expression and substituting them with an expressive gesture both awkward and abrupt. Horn explains the work thus: 'All the pencils are about two inches long and produce the profile of my face in three dimensions ... I move my body rhythmically from left to right in front of the white wall. The pencils make marks on the wall the image of which corresponds to the rhythm of my movements'.[6] The head approaches the wall with caution. Slowly, with the eyes fixed on the wall, the head turns sideways to the right. Moving forward imperceptibly, the pencils of the mask make contact with the wall and slowly swing to the left. The soft scratch of graphite on surface sounds the gesture, its silence signalling a pause, before the head turns to draw again, from left to right.

In these works the prosthetic element enhances the impaired body, extending the reach and actions of the body as it negotiates its relations with others and adapts to its environment. Power and agency underpin the transhuman impulse in Beckett's and Horn's work, recognising both the limitations and exigencies of the body, and the circumscription of the environment in which it operates. As Beckett's work drives towards configurations of prose and theatre in which the corporeal cogito is sidelined, fragmented and undone, bodies become words and selves become signifiers. Commenting on Horn's later development of larger drawing machines such as *The Little Painting School Performs a Waterfall* (1988), Armin Zweite notes that the 'ritualised turning of the masked head' of Horn's *Pencil Mask* has a 'robotic undertone' and 'could be performed not only with greater stamina but also far more effectively with an actual machine' (2005: 15–16). Horn's prosthetic body-works, engineered and controlled by human agency, give way in later works to self-contained performance machines that respond (sometimes) to the interaction of the viewer, yet are still considered by the artist as spectres of a self. 'I like my machines to tire', the artist notes: 'They are more than objects. These are not cars or washing machines. They rest, they reflect, they wait' (qtd in Winterson, 2005).

Horn shares with Beckett an abiding interest in the work of Buster Keaton, the comic performer who stars in *Film*. Keaton ghosts Horn's only feature film, *Buster's Bedroom* (1991), which is set in Nirvana House, the place where the ageing actor recuperated from alcoholism. The film follows a young woman, Misha, who is obsessed with Keaton, and it depicts the assorted idiosyncrasies of the inhabitants of Nirvana House that she encounters there. In its obscure metaphysics Nirvana House is reminiscent of Mr Knott's house in Beckett's novel *Watt* and bears more than a passing resemblance (the uniformed nurses, the doctor, the wheelchair) to the sanitorium where Horn recuperated from lung damage.

Horn engages with Beckett's work directly in her 2015 piece *The Lost Ones, Samuel Beckett*.[7] A steel cuboid, walled with glass, holds a series of objects. Like the accidental jerk of a pen, three wires scribe down from the roof of the vitreous space, each suspending an object: a brass wire coil (reminiscent of Robert Smithson's *Spiral Jetty* (1970) in miniature), a fragment of wood and a feather. A small glass funnel pierces the lower right wall, a conduit for sound or substance (echoing a complementary piece from the same year, *Musical Funnel*). Above, attached to the top front of the cuboid, is a small steel circular blade, suspended as if waiting to slice the space below. Obliquely, fire scorches a dark mark of carbon across the glass. On this flaming is scratched the words 'The Lost Ones', which are then partially erased by two transverse lines.[8] Horn's *The Lost Ones, Samuel Beckett* is not a translation of the cylinders and ladders of Beckett's prose text *The Lost Ones* but rather an adaptation that evokes the closed space of the constrained environment, and the idea of the quest for a relationality that is traced between the iconographic signifiers of elements such as the feather, wire and wood that form the language of Horn's *oeuvre*. The human presence evoked by the prosthetic object in Horn's earlier work gives way to an associative environment animated by the machine (Horn's spinning circular saw) and witnessed by botanical, mineral and zoological traces (wood, wire and feather).

On Jess Thom

The lens of posthumanism reveals both the corporeal sites of embodiment that intersect with prosthetic objects and machines in the work of Beckett and Rebecca Horn, and a fluid and recursive subjectivity that mutates in its relations with language, materialities and space, as in Jess Thom's performance of Samuel Beckett's *Not I*. Thom recognises the radical neurological environment of Mouth and extends the parameters of performance in three ways: by drawing out the corporeal and linguistic implications of neurological diversity, by making manifest the intersection between agency and intention in the speaking body and by embedding corporeal translation of the voiced text at the heart of performance.

Thom, who plays Mouth in Beckett's play, has Tourette's Syndrome. She makes involuntary, repetitive movements and vocalisations that are sometimes coprolaliac. Writing in her blog, Thom explains that it was collaborator and co-founder of Touretteshero Matthew Pountney who introduced her to Beckett's play at a time when her tics were intensifying and she was 'struggling to recognise them' as part of herself (2017). In reading *Not I* she found a play that resonated with her: 'I was stunned to find line after line that spoke deeply to my lived experience. So much of what Mouth describes I can relate to, and there are lines in the text that cut right to the heart of some of the struggles, challenges and joys of having a brain and a body that work differently from other people's expectations' (2017).

Thom's performance of *Not I* embraces her tics: the involuntary utterances of the performer interjected into Beckett's text in ways that deepen the lived experience of the play. Writing in the *New York Times*, Jesse Green agrees that 'far from masking Beckett's brilliance or diluting the play's power, Thom's speech patterns make uncanny sense of "Not I," in the process making it more overwhelming' (2020). Over a three-year period, Touretteshero toured with *Not I* playing at the Edinburgh Fringe Festival (2017); the Battersea Arts Centre, London; the Staatstheater in Mainz, as part of the Grenzenlos Kultur Festival; Sophiensaele, Berlin (2018); and BRIC House, Brooklyn (2019). Touretteshero's production of *Not I* is divided into four parts. The members of the audience are welcomed into the auditorium by Thom and her sign language interpreter. In London, Charmaine Wombwell signed in British Sign Language (BSL); in Germany, Julia Cramer signed in Deutsche Gebärdensprache (DGS); and in New York, Lindsey Snyder signed in American Sign Language (ASL). Thom gives a visual introduction of herself and her interpreter for those with sight impairments and explains what will happen during the performance. Thom, who uses a wheelchair, is then elevated to a point eight feet above the stage. There is a brief pause, and then Thom begins to speak: '...out...into this world...this world...tiny little thing...before its time...in a godfor–...what?...girl?...yes...tiny little girl...into this...out into this...before her time...godforsaken hole called...' (Beckett, 2009b: 85).

The play is followed by a short film that explores the rehearsal process, the challenges of the text for a neurodiverse performer and how Beckett's exploration of the agonistic relation between body, voice and self in the play relate to Thom's own experience with Tourette's Syndrome. The performance closes with a discussion with Thom, her interpreter and the audience in which we are encouraged to exchange views with our neighbours, and concludes with a moment of collective release as we are invited to collectively shout, speak or make some noise. As Thom is a long-standing activist for the inclusion of disabled artists and audiences in theatre and performance spaces, each of Touretteshero's performances of *Not I* is relaxed, meaning that the theatre conventions of silence and stasis no longer apply and audience members are welcome to move about, come in and out, and make noise as they wish. Thom explains that, by playing Mouth in *Not I*, she also wanted 'to change some of the academic discourse on the text itself. I want to show that the character of Mouth is only as isolated as her community makes her. We've re-interpreted the stage directions in a way that works for my body and agreed with the Beckett Estate that my performance will come with extra "biscuits!"' (Thom and Hambrook, 2018).

Key elements of the staging of *Not I* are adapted into 'body modifications' – to borrow Rebecca Horn's term – that enable Thom's neurodiverse body to perform Beckett's exacting text. The frame-like structures that constrained the bodies of Jessica Tandy, Billie Whitelaw and Lisa Dwan (to name but a few of the actors who have played the role), in order to enable the spotlight to illuminate Mouth, are of no use to Thom for whom staying still is never a question of doing nothing but rather a highly volitional condition. Instead of forcing her to adopt a fixed position (which, as we will see shortly, is an impossibility), the light is incorporated into a hooded garment that Thom wears, obscuring the upper part of her head from the audience's gaze and illuminating her mouth. The hood grafts onto Mouth the garb of the second figure of the play, the silent standing figure of the Auditor who, in Beckett's stage directions is described as follows: '*downstage audience left, tall standing figure, sex undeterminable, enveloped from head to foot in loose black djellaba, with hood, fully faintly lit*' (2009b: 85). Responding to Beckett's direction that Mouth be '*faintly lit from close-up and below, rest of face in shadow*' (2009b: 85), designer Maria Almena of Kimatica Studio worked within the parameters of Thom's neurodiversity, devising a body-sculpture that is part prosthesis and part scenography. Now, the actor is in charge. No longer a passive, constrained, disembodied voice centred by the objectifying light of the spot, Thom's Mouth controls her own light. Here body and technology interact to reframe and reinterpret Beckett's directorial vision to include non-normative human agency and embodiment.

Thom has worked to examine and reconfigure normative ideas of the individual as an independent agent, proposing through her theatre, installation and collaborative performances a relational idea of the self as inherently connected to peoples, communities and technologies. Independence is always interdependence. Speaking of her decision to use a wheelchair when her physical tics intensified, orchestrating an unexpected series of trajectories that rendered walking difficult if not dangerous, Thom emphasises the affordances of technology. In a report for the BBC's Freedom2014 season, a series of events that explored what freedom means in contemporary society, Thom explains that it is not her tics or her wheelchair that disable her but rather the inaccessible environments that she encounters (2014). Thom's wheelchair is an integral part of Touretteshero's neurodiverse production of *Not I*. Beckett requires that the actor's mouth be placed '*about 8 feet above stage level*' (2009b: 85), a direction that further decorporealises the actor in the eyes of the audience since that height is not within the normal range of a standing person. Working with designers Ben Pacey and Will Datson, Thom and Pountney commissioned a manually operated 'see-saw' structure calibrated by counterweights to raise Thom's wheelchair from stage level to eight feet above, in order to facilitate the performance while maintaining the security of the actor.[9] The machine is not only a means to fulfil the stage directions (a static structure would suffice in that case) but also facilitates the inclusive nature of the performance where audience participation is key. Additionally, the structure serves to spatially connect Mouth with her Auditor, in this case the sign language interpreters who stand adjacent to Thom, *'facing diagonally across stage intent on MOUTH'* (2009b: 85). Yet, rather than standing immobile and silent as Beckett's stage directions propose – *'dead still throughout but for four brief movements'* (2009b: 85) – the interpreters are live, with movement, translating a dual discourse of Beckett's text and Thom's tics, the one interweaving with the other in a fluid gestural semiosis that foregrounds the multiple interdependencies of bodies, voices, selves and machines that are integral to Touretteshero's *Not I*.

In 2015, just as the Touretteshero production of Beckett's play was being considered, Thom and Pountney explored key elements of *Not I* (the relation between movement and agency and the impossibility of stasis and silence) in a performance piece called *10 Minutes of Nothing* at the South London Gallery. Working in collaboration with artist Will Renel (whose research examines involuntary performance from a human-centred perspective), Thom and Pountney devised a work that challenged normative ideas of 'nothing'. The ten-minute performance begins as Thom leaves her wheelchair to kneel on the floor of the Clore Studio of the Gallery. Those who assist her are nearby in case her tics intensify and she injures herself. For a moment, nothing happens. Then, with compellingly deliberate yet anarchic movement, Thom begins to swoop and turn from the waist, her head crashing directly towards the concrete floor before swerving and soaring, in a near miss that leaves the audience stunned. The energy and force of her body are palpable. As the performance develops it is clear that the narrative logic through which we are trained to understand movement has no place here. Yet we are drawn to an affective engagement with this urgent choreography that demands a response even as it refutes expectations. And then, it is over. Thom returns to her seat. In the post-performance discussion she explains how appearing to do nothing requires enormous physical and mental control on her part, and what we just witnessed was her doing nothing: a performance that undercuts the idea of the human as *homo agere*.

Touretteshero's *Not I* and *10 Minutes of Nothing* alter the debate about intention, volition and agency, shifting the parameters of that debate away from the epistemology of what Gilbert Ryle discredited as a category mistake (the distinction between mind and body) towards a pragmatics of agency and access (2002: 16). Deborah Barnbaum asserts the importance of cognitive pluralism in terms of both fact and value and, drawing on Joyce Davidson (2008), underlines that (as she writes), 'these different sets of neurological traits can, and do, comprise individual's identity and potentially provide a basis for culture' (2013: 143). Andrew Fenton and Tim Krahn point out that neurodiverse communities 'contest the default pathologizing of differences in brain circuitry that are revealed in behavioural deviances from the standard norm' and seek (as they emphasise) 'a recognition that, though they are neurologically, cognitively and behaviourally different, they do not necessarily suffer from being neurodiverse nor do they need to be cured' (2007: 1). At the heart of these debates lie issues of power and the dynamics of social inequality that cut across communities to include long-standing debates concerning gender and ethnicity. Touretteshero's *Not I* challenges the pathologisation of neurodiversity and breaks new ground in theatre performance to include the neurodiverse body as a central agent and a vital audience.

Touretteshero's adaptations of Beckett's work also reconfigure the silence that marks the ellipses and pauses of the text of *Not I* and underscore so much of Beckett's writing. In *Not I*, narrative, performance and enactment fuse in a taut trajectory of sound. The rigours of Beckett's text play out on Thom's neurodiverse body in ways different to previous productions of *Not I*. Voluntary and involuntary speech contest within an agonistics of agency. The silences that punctuate Beckett's play during the brief moments when Mouth stops speaking become the points at which Thom's own body gives voice. The sounds that Mouth hears but does not recognise as her own voice – 'the buzzing?…yes…all the time the buzzing' (Beckett, 2009b: 86) – are rendered material through Thom's neurodiversity. *Not I* interleaves the voluntary and the involuntary. The first, the performed script about a woman's intermittent aphasia, traumatic affective experiences and logorrhea, is intercut by the second, the involuntary utterances or tics of the actor's body creating for the audience a multi-layered experience of Beckett's script in which ideas integral to the play are enacted within the performance.

Jess Thom's tics operate on a continuum with, rather than in contradistinction to, the voicings and sounds of the neurotypical body. What differs, here, is the question of agency understood in terms of the interaction between linguistic structures, neurological systems and intentionality. Neurodiverse activists have taken to task twentieth-century philosophers of language such as Donald Davidson, Paul Grice and David Lewis, who ascribe a common set of propositional attitudes to language users that are predicated on a theory of mind based on the neurotypical body. Davidson's idea of linguistic communication, for example, is based on what he terms 'prior' and 'passing' theories – whereby interlocutors enter into conversation with assumptions about what might be construed, assumptions that are then modified as the conversation develops (1986: 436, 442–3). Davidson's theory of radical interpretation is challenged by Barnbaum, who argues that the neurodiverse and the neurotypical are 'speaking different languages' (2013: 134).

However, new technologies can also alter our assumptions about agency and the corporeal production of sound. Is visceral silence a phenomenological impossibility, as in *10 Minutes of Nothing*? Composer John Cage wrote about experiencing the sounds of his own body within the putative silence of an anechoic chamber (as the anecdote goes, the high pitch he could hear was that of his nervous system, the low pitch that of his circulation system). While it is unlikely that Cage could indeed hear his circulatory or neurological systems, the visceral sonoscape is accessible through technology. Haraway notes in 'A Cyborg Manifesto' that 'by the late twentieth century, our time, a mythic time, we are all chimeras, theorized and fabricated hybrids of machine and organism' (2000: 70). Haraway's idea of the machine is not a constraining metal contraption or carapace but rather interrelated economies of information: machines are 'nothing but signals, electromagnetic waves, a section of a spectrum', 'floating signifiers' (2000: 73). Indeed, microelectronic devices radically alter scale and perception, 'the silicon chip is a surface for writing: it is etched in molecular scales disturbed only by atomic noise, the ultimate interference for nuclear scores' (2000: 73). Artist Anne Niemetz and nanoscientist Andrew Pelling's collaborative sound work *The Dark Side of the Cell* enables us to hear the sounds created by the oscillation of living cells through the nanotechnology of an Atomic Force Microscope (AFM). Transforming the local oscillating motion of Saccharomyces cerevisiae cells into sound, Pelling's work with James Gimzewski on sonocytology renders the condition of an individual cell audible, reminding us that silence and stasis are corporeal impossibilities. As the narrator of Beckett's novel *The Unnamable* notes, 'it is all very fine to keep silence, but one has also to consider the kind of silence one keeps' (2010: 19).

Conclusion

The conceptual frameworks through which we understand human corporeality and agency are under stress and need now to be reconfigured. Haraway argues presciently that 'biological organisms have become biotic systems, communication devices like others. There is no fundamental, ontological separation in our formal knowledge of machine and organism, of technical and organic' (2000: 82). Similarly, in *How We Became Posthuman*, N. Katherine Hayles argues that the posthuman subject 'is an amalgam, a collection of heterogeneous components, a material-informational entity whose boundaries undergo continuous construction and reconstruction' (1999: 3). Through the remediative and appropriative strategies of the contemporary art and performance under discussion here – in which Beckett's work forms the mode and material for new constructions and behaviours – Braidotti's vision of a 'refiguration of subjectivity' that interrogates the ethical and conceptual frameworks of the human is realised (2013: 42).

This chapter has focused on how contemporary art and performance respond to the condition of the posthuman evident in Beckett's writing. By tracing his use of the prosthetic through the work of Rebecca Horn and the refiguring of subjectivity and embodiment in neurodiverse performances by Touretteshero, we affirm the importance of the transhuman in recent key adaptations of Beckett's work. By counterpointing *Not I*, the disembodied but utterly material articulation of differential subject positions, with the sound work *Dark Side of the Cell*, we explore how artists generate new forms of intersubjective relationality and consider how the mutability of contemporary art is an essential experimental space for adaptation within the posthuman.

Notes

1 Touretteshero is a disabled-led multi-disciplinary arts organisation; see www.touretteshero.com/ (accessed 8 September 2021).
2 See www.darksideofcell.info/about.html (accessed 8 September 2021).
3 For more recent work on Beckett and the posthuman, see Rabaté (2016), Boulter (2018) and the special issue of *Samuel Beckett Today / Aujourd'hui* on 'Samuel Beckett and the Nonhuman / Samuel Beckett et le non-humain' (32.2, 2020), guest edited by Amanda Dennis, Thomas Thoelen, Douglas Atkinson and Sjef Houppermans.
4 For more information about Rebecca Horn's work, see https://rebecca-horn.de/index_eng.html (accessed 7 October 2021).
5 Horn's body extension work also includes *Unicorn* (*Einhorn*), *Head Extension* (*Kopf-Extension*), *White Body Fan* (*Weißer Körperfächer*), *My Hand Can Fly* (*Meine Hand kann fliegen*), *Gavin*, *Cockfeather Mask* (*Hahnenmaske*) and *Cockatoo Mask* (*Kakadu-Maske*).
6 Rebecca Horn cited in the display caption for '*Pencil Mask*, 1972' (2004).
7 Rebecca Horn (2015), *The Lost Ones, Samuel Beckett*. Steel, glass vitrine, writing on the glass treated with flaming, glass funnel, brush, saw blade, feather, wood, electronic device, brass, wire. Dimensions: 45 7/10 x 30 3/10 x 12 1/5 in / 116 x 77 x 31 cm. For an image, see www.studiotrisorio.com/rebecca-horn (accessed 13 June 2022).
8 Although the words appear crossed out rather than erased, since they are still legible, the etymology of 'erase' – Latin $ērās$- participial stem of $ērādĕre$, < $ē$ out

+ *rādĕre* to scrape or scratch – works well with the way the writing is treated in Horn's art piece. This procedure evokes Beckett's own use of 'textual scars', coined by Dirk Van Hulle (2014), i.e. passages omitted from the drafts whose erasure is still foregrounded in the published texts rather than completely effaced. A famous example is Molloy's comment 'What then was the source of Ballyba's prosperity? I'll tell you. No, I'll tell you nothing. Nothing' (Beckett, 2009c: 170), his refusal pointing to a deleted section in the manuscript and typescript where the source of that prosperity was still explained at length (see O'Reilly et al., 2017: 63–8, 262–76, 380–7).

9 For more information, see https://benpacey.wordpress.com/portfolio/not-i/ (accessed 14 September 2021).

References

Barnbaum, D. R. (2013). 'The neurodiverse and the neurotypical: still talking across an ethical divide', in C. D. Herrera and A. Perry (eds), *Ethics and Neurodiversity*. Newcastle upon Tyne: Cambridge Scholars Press, pp. 131–45.
Beckett, S. (2009a). *Endgame*. Pref. R. McDonald. London: Faber and Faber.
Beckett, S. (2009b). *Krapp's Last Tape and Other Shorter Plays*. Pref. S. E. Gontarski. London: Faber and Faber.
Beckett, S. (2009c). *Molloy*. Ed. S. Weller. London: Faber and Faber.
Beckett, S. (2010). *The Unnamable*. Ed. S. Connor. London: Faber and Faber.
Boulter, J. (2008). *Beckett: A Guide for the Perplexed*. London: Continuum.
Boulter, J. (2018). *Posthuman Space in Samuel Beckett's Short Prose*. Edinburgh: Edinburgh University Press.
Braidotti, R. (2013). *The Posthuman*. Cambridge: Polity Press.
Davidson, D. (1986). 'A nice derangement of epitaphs', in E. LePore (ed.), *Truth and Interpretation: Perspectives on the Philosophy of Donald Davidson*. Oxford and New York: Basil Blackwell, pp. 433–46.
Davidson, J. (2008). 'Autistic culture online: virtual communication and cultural expression on the spectrum', *Social and Cultural Geography*, 9.7, 791–806.
Effinger. E. (2011). 'The ontopology of *The Unnamable*', *Samuel Beckett Today / Aujourd'hui*, 23, 369–81.
Fenton, A., and T. Krahn (2007). 'Autism, neurodiversity and equality beyond the "normal"', *Journal of Ethics in Mental Health*, 2.2, 1–6.
Green, J. (2020). 'When disability isn't a special need but a special skill', *New York Times*, 13 January, www.nytimes.com/2020/01/13/theater/under-the-radar-festival-neurodiversity.html (accessed 19 February 2021).
Haenlein, C. (ed.) (1997). *Rebecca Horn: The Glance of Infinity*. New York: Scalo.
Haraway, D. (2000). 'A cyborg manifesto: science, technology, and socialist feminism in the late twentieth century', in N. Badmington (ed.), *Posthumanism*. London: Palgrave, pp. 69–84.
Haraway, D. (2013). *Simians, Cyborgs and Women: The Reinvention of Nature*. London: Routledge.

Hayles, N. K. (1999). *How We Became Posthuman: Virtual Bodies in Cybernetics, Literature, and Informatics*. Chicago: University of Chicago Press.
Horn, R. (2004). '*Pencil Mask*, 1972', *Tate*, www.tate.org.uk/art/artworks/horn-pencil-mask-t07847 (accessed 19 February 2021).
Levinas, E., and R. Kearney (1986). 'Dialogue with Emmanuel Levinas', in R. Cohen (ed.), *Face to Face with Levinas*. New York: State University of New York, pp. 13–33.
Maude, U. (2009). *Beckett, Technology and the Body*. Cambridge: Cambridge University Press.
Moody, A. (2017). 'A machine for feeling: *Ping*'s posthuman affect', *Journal of Beckett Studies*, 26.1, 87–102.
O'Hara, D. (2010). 'The metronome of consciousness', *Samuel Beckett Today / Aujourd'hui*, 22, 435–47.
O'Reilly, É. M., D. Van Hulle and P. Verhulst (2017). *The Making of Samuel Beckett's 'Molloy'*. Brussels and London: University Press Antwerp and Bloomsbury.
Rabaté, J.-M. (2016). *Think Pig! Beckett at the Limit of the Human*. New York: Fordham University Press.
Ryle, G. (2002). *The Concept of Mind*. Chicago: Chicago University Press.
Schmidt, K. (2005). 'Rebecca Horn: drawings from 1964–2004', in R. Horn, *Bodylandscapes*. London: Hayward Gallery, pp. 45–62.
Tajiri, Y. (2007). *Samuel Beckett and the Prosthetic Body*. London: Palgrave Macmillan.
Thom, J. (2014), 'Jess Thom: what does freedom look like?', *BBC News*, 24 January, www.bbc.com/news/av/magazine-25847734 (accessed 19 February 2021).
Thom, J. (2017), '*Not I* and me', *Touretteshero* blog, 26 May, www.touretteshero.com/2017/05/26/not-i-and-me/ (accessed 19 February 2021).
Thom, J., and C. Hambrook (2018), 'Jess Thom on Touretteshero's production of Beckett's "Not I" and the irrepressible character "Mouth"', *Disability Arts Online*, 23 February, https://disabilityarts.online/magazine/opinion/jess-thom-on-touretteshero-production-of-becketts-not-i/ (accessed 19 February 2021).
Van Hulle, D. (2014). 'Textual scars: Beckett, genetic criticism and textual scholarship', in S. E. Gontarski (ed.), *The Edinburgh Companion to Samuel Beckett and the Arts*. Edinburgh: Edinburgh University Press, pp. 306–19.
Wills, D. (2021). *Prosthesis*. Minneapolis: University of Minnesota Press.
Winterson, J. (2005). 'The bionic woman', *Guardian*, 23 May, www.theguardian.com/artanddesign/2005/may/23/art (accessed 19 February 2021).
Zweite, A. (2005). 'Rebecca Horn's Bodylandscapes' in R. Horn, *Bodylandscapes*. London: Hayward Gallery, pp. 13–43.

9

Beckett and new media adaptation: from the literary corpus to the transmedia archive

David Houston Jones

This chapter considers the presence of 'borderline' forms of Beckettian adaptation in new media. In particular, it examines the productive but critical engagement of those forms with key tenets of Linda Hutcheon's classic *A Theory of Adaptation* (2006), especially the constraints which Hutcheon's theory imposes upon adaptation where scope is concerned. Although Hutcheon's understanding of adaptation is broad, considering video games and interactive art, 'brief echoes' of works are excluded because they 'recontextualise only short fragments' (2006: 9). Adaptation, by contrast, must involve an 'extended, deliberate, announced revisitation of a particular work of art' (2006: 170). The resulting understanding poses crucial problems in the remediations I am concerned with, and those problems stem in part from Beckett's works themselves. How, in thinking about adaptation, are we to deal with a body of work in which fragmentation is itself a structural principle? Many of Beckett's works are self-consciously fragmentary and deliberately create brief echoes of other works within the canon. Indeed, the 'extended, deliberate' notion of adaptation seems in some respects fantastically ill-suited to a corpus characterised by the recurring Beckettian dilemmas of reflexivity, fragmentation and ending, and to cry out for a model which might accommodate those dilemmas.

The desire in adaptation to 'retell the same story over and over in different ways' (Hutcheon, 2006: 9) is always anticipated in a body of work whose narrators are sentenced to 'keep on saying the same old thing' (Beckett, 2010c: 108). The moment in which they 'shall be able to go silent, and make an end' (2010c: 12) famously represents both salvation and extinction, and the paradoxical 'search for the means to put an end to things, an end to speech, is what enables the discourse to continue' (2010c: 10). Such an implosive narrative premise poses unique problems when it comes to theorising Beckettian adaptation, which is always pre-emptively ironised. It is itself deeply embedded in Beckett's literary corpus as an *adaptive* principle: the expression of the impossible narrative imperative is reworked intertextually (between prose works, for example) and between genres. *The Unnamable*, in which the problem attains particularly acute form, refers back to earlier distillations in the first two volumes of the trilogy and in Beckett's earlier prose: 'all these Murphys, Molloys and Malones do not fool me. They have made me waste my time, suffer for nothing, speak of them when, in order to stop speaking, I should have spoken of me and me alone' (2010c: 14). The notion of 'intra-intertextuality', described in Brian T. Fitch's classic account as 'the multiple relationships between texts by the same author' (1988: 23), is one of the tools by which the overarching problem is endlessly redeployed and reimagined, as narrators refer to other works in which the issue has already been aired.

These two interrelated dilemmas, of ending and narratorial reflexivity, are significantly revisited in recent games and simulations. The present chapter considers, firstly, John Gerrard's *Exercise (Djibouti)* (2012), in which ending is pitted against seemingly endless duration; secondly, Gerrard's *Exercise (Dunhuang)* (2014), in which the intertextual and intermedial engagement with ending is further complicated; and, finally, James Meek's *Beckett* (2018), in which the Beckettian ironies of voice and narration are recontextualised in gameplay characterised by a searching enquiry into media.[1] New media forms complicate storytelling (one of the key preoccupations of many theories of adaptation) with a reflexive attention to the target medium, and sometimes they elaborate a vast secondary architecture based on fragmentary reference to source material. The seemingly infinite scale of the game world is matched by an impression of endless duration, as the simulation unfolds according to multiple variables, and of a potentially infinite number of iterations. 'Beckett', here, can operate as anything from a strict citational matrix to a generic, inherited paradigm. In Gerrard and Meek, the works' relation to Beckett is variously indicated by citational titles or, more broadly, in the exploitation of a universe or 'heterocosm' which is recognisably 'Beckettian'. I analyse the construction of a Beckettian heterocosm in the light of the notion of the transmedia archive, in which 'adaptations' are reconceived not as versions of a pre-existing essence but rather as instances in the iterative, diachronic elaboration of the work.

The Beckettian body, performance affect and computer simulation

In order to bring these perspectives clearly into view, I turn now to two comments on Beckett by British cultural critic and blogger Mark Fisher. The first is concerned with the ironies inherent in any encounter between Beckett's work and the imperative, in adaptation, to 'repetition without replication' (Hutcheon, 2006: 7). The second, meanwhile, sees Fisher return to Beckett's work in the context of installation art, and of the simulations of John Gerrard. The first comment, posted on Fisher's *k-punk* blog in 2006, concerns a panel discussion held at the Barbican as part of the Beckett Centenary Festival, which also included a series of Beckett productions by the Gate Theatre.[2] After praising the interventions of Nina Power (to whom he refers via the alias Infinite Thought or I.T.) in a conversation otherwise marked by an insistence on 'seeing Beckett in the terms that had been established in the 1950s', Fisher turns to the performance of *Rockaby* and *Ohio Impromptu* which followed the panel discussion. He suggests that there was 'altogether *too much* expression' in vocal delivery (2006; original emphasis):

> Here, 'live' theatre regains its power precisely by subtracting the 'living' and the 'theatrical' – the shrill mugging of theatre acting is replaced by the stasis of bodies assuming the unvitality of the catatonic. Yet, as I.T. complained, the actors and the director could not seem to prevent themselves from interpreting Beckett's notoriously precise instructions. (Hence Beckett's famous exasperation with actors). (2006)[3]

Fisher's comments engage the view of expression and the actor's body which has arisen from Beckett's famous comments on Billie Whitelaw's early preparations for *Not I*: 'too much colour, no no, too much colour' (qtd in Whitelaw, 1995: 120). Whitelaw's account of rehearsing the play refers too to Jocelyn Herbert's contentious claim, in *A Theatre Workbook*, 'that what Sam was after was to find out how far you can remove the body altogether from the stage, yet still end up with an intensely dramatic situation' (1995: 123).

The problem of performance affect, I suggest, has a significant bearing on the adaptation of theatre works for other forms and genres, some of which have the potential to neutralise the inevitable 'colour' of human performance and even to replace the physical body with a virtual avatar. In Herbert's argument, fidelity to Beckett logically engenders a commitment to removing the body from the stage: to be faithful to Beckett's theatre is to adapt it, to begin to move outside of the theatre. For Fisher, too, the way out of the impasse of performance is paradoxically through forms of adaptation which are anticipated and signposted in Beckett's work itself, in particular an appeal to installation art: 'these stark tableaux, where bodies sit in near-catatonic near-stillness while sparse, recited text (sometimes spoken by them, sometimes by an offstage voice) is subjected to micro-varied repetition, are closer to installations than to traditional drama' (2006). Fisher, in fact, ponders two solutions to the problem of performance, namely installation and artificial intelligence:

The productions inevitably prompted the question: can any actor do justice to Beckett's austerity? Is the temptation to expression and interpretation always too much for any actor to resist? What is required is the catatone of a meat puppet, and I wondered if Beckett's scripts hadn't posed a problem that only AI imagineers or CGI animators can solve. Perhaps only an artificial life form can adequately give body and voice to Beckett's human unlife. (2006)

The problem of performance, in this reading, is the driver of an ever-more radical process of adaptation: the problem of excessive expression can only be resolved by recourse to installation or computer simulation. I want to retain Fisher's point of view, in what follows, for its provocative vision of a progressive evacuation of theatre into other forms and for the specific reference which Fisher makes both to simulation and to John Gerrard. At the same time, though, I reserve judgement as to Fisher's argument on expression. For all that new media forms cater to the possibility of eliminating the various expressive acts carried out onstage by the human actor, such forms can certainly not be straightforwardly understood as inexpressive and have much more ambiguous implications.

John Gerrard's *Exercise (Djibouti)* and perpetual permutation

Fisher returns to concerns such as these during a round table discussion held at the University of Oxford in 2012 as part of an event entitled 'Simulation, Exercise, Operations'. The event was dedicated not to Beckett but to John Gerrard's work, coinciding with the installation of Gerrard's *Exercise (Djibouti)* at the Old Power Station in Oxford, and yet Beckett loomed large here once more. Although Gerrard's art is usually displayed in installation, *Exercise (Djibouti)*, like most of his work, is a simulation. It shows two groups of athletes, one dressed in blue and one in red, going through an endless series of formalised movements against the backdrop of the vast desert landscapes of Djibouti. The movements of the avatars in the installation originate in a series of routines carried out by a group of athletes training for the London 2012 Olympics and recorded using motion capture technology.

Exercise (Djibouti) is not obviously an adaptation of Beckett, and certainly not a titular adaptation, but it nevertheless displays an extraordinary crystallisation of recognisably Beckettian concerns. The use of computer simulation allows Beckettian duration to be expressed more fully than in prose or drama, running through permutations of bodies as long as the hardware can operate, potentially for many years. In the round table discussion that was part of the 'Simulation' event, Fisher explicitly links this 'purgatorial' aspect to Beckett in a remark in which he also comments on the work's elimination of the expressive dilemmas of the human actor:

> I certainly see the relation to Beckett, and I've written before that there is something unsatisfactory about any actor playing Beckett; that actually, in order to get Beckett done properly, in order to get the correct degree of choreography and the right kind of flatness of affect, you'd really need a simulation to do it. And maybe we can see John's work as the beginning of the construction of this Beckett Engine which ultimately can perform his work better than any actor has so far managed to do it. (qtd in Mackay, 2015: 69)

The comment is part of a round table exchange in which Fisher rejects Shane Brighton's notion of a tradition of 'tragic witnessing' seen in Beckett and Gerrard. For Brighton, Gerrard's work is situated within 'a specifically Irish tradition, that of Samuel Beckett. In Beckett we find characters whose tragic experience is radically trapped within particular spaces from which they have no way of moving' (2015: 46). Fisher, meanwhile, rejects the paradigm of the tragic, instead linking Gerrard's work to the problems of the human actor and of purgatorial duration, concerns which are aired, too, in the 2006 blog post. Both problems, he argues, demand an evacuation of dramatic form and an embracing of the possibilities of simulation.

The idea of getting 'Beckett done properly' once more intersects with the omnipresent problem of ending, shackling the prospect of getting the work done and completing it to a form of virtual performance in which it can continue indefinitely. The structural ironies of the bilingual corpus, meanwhile, implicitly suggest 'pour en finir avec Beckett' as the logical translation of Fisher's phrase. The translation immediately recalls the existing collection *Pour finir encore et autres foirades* (Beckett, 1976), so that even the most innovative attempts to conceptualise Beckettian adaptation are anticipated within the corpus proper. To get Beckett done properly, then, may also imply to 'have done with Beckett', a fantasy of completion which is perpetually postponed. The English counterpart to *Pour finir encore*, meanwhile, is *For to End Yet Again* (Beckett, 2010b: 151–3), which might in turn suggest 'to get Beckett done *yet again*' as a gloss on Fisher's original statement. Such an unstable literary corpus, in which the 'grey canon' (see below) is constantly flexing its muscles, has the potential to significantly redefine Beckettian adaptation and even to threaten the stable notion of the literary work upon which much adaptation theory depends.

The prospect of perpetual permutation in Gerrard's work acts as an uncanny future counterpart to that of Beckett, recalling his glee at a test viewing of the colour print of *Quad* on a black-and-white monitor, an effect which he described as 'marvellous, it's 100,000 years later' (qtd in Brater, 1990: 109). *Exercise*, moreover, constitutes a dramatic amplification of the combinatorial dilemma of *Quad*, 'the art or science of exhausting the possible, through inclusive disjunctions' (Deleuze, 1995: 5), as Gilles Deleuze puts it in his preface to the French edition of Beckett's television plays (Beckett, 1992). Where *Quad* stipulates four players, 'as alike in build as possible' and 'gowns reaching to ground, cowls hiding faces' (Beckett, 2009a: 145), Gerrard's software renders facial features indistinct and dresses all of the actors in the same virtual clothing. If individuality is maintained through sound in Beckett (as each player is identified with a particular sound), Gerrard's simulation is silent. The central action of the exploration of the space through movement receives a closely analogous treatment, as Beckett's text specifies all of the possible routes through the square and all of the possible combinations of actors: 'Four possible solos all given. Six possible duos all given (two twice). Four possible trios all given twice' (2009a: 144).

The central ambiguity of *Quad*, though, concerns the work's own textual and generic status. *Quad II*, accidentally created during work towards the 1982 Süddeutscher Rundfunk broadcast, consists of a mere two-line note in the English published text: 'No colour, all four in identical white gowns, no percussion, footsteps only sound, slow tempo, series 1 only' (Beckett, 2009a: 146). If *Quad II* is in a sense an adaptation of *Quad*, the printed text of *Quad* itself serves as little more than a gloss on the diagram which describes the movement of the actors across the playing space (2009a: 146). At the origin of the multiple adaptations of the work we find not a text but a formal blueprint. For Graley Herren, *Quad* is more 'a set of assembly instructions than a play proper' (2007: 124), or even, in Piotr Woycicki's analysis, 'a repetition of two vector movements, one along a side of the square and the other one across the diagonal. These two vectors form a core path for each player. Once the path is completed, it is turned 90° clockwise and repeated again' (2012: 140). *Quad*, then, is always already an adaptation of this minimal schematic, as it is variously translated into prose, theatre and television.

John Gerrard's *Exercise (Dunhuang)* and the transmedia archive

If Gerrard's work pursues such a line, his *Exercise (Dunhuang)* draws still closer parallels with *Quad*. The piece presents 'a mysterious structure in the heart of the Chinese desert, a precise system of roadways the size of a small town' (Gerrard, n.d.). Human figures explore the vast network of roads, and once again the duration of the piece is potentially infinite. The 'danger zone' (Beckett: 2009a: 145) referred to as point E in the *Quad* diagram (2009a: 146), and which Beckett's actors instinctively avoid, has a counterpart here not in a fixed location but in the moment at which two actors meet: 'when two participants meet, the actor closest to their goal continues walking, while the other must sit or lie on the landscape and rest. After a period lasting between 24 and 36 hours, only one remains standing' (Mackay, 2014: 13). As Robin Mackay notes, the piece recalls 'Beckett's minimal theatre of exhaustion' (2014: 5); in fact, though, that theatre is expanded from the limited permutations of *Quad* to a network of dozens of pathways. At the end of the iteration, when only one participant remains, like the last searcher of *The Lost Ones*, the scenario initiates another run, so that, as in Beckett, 'all begins again' (2010b: 101). In a further parallel to the mathematical undergirding of *Quad*, the workers' movements across the grid are calculated by the A* search algorithm, one of whose principal applications is pathfinding. It works by comparing a given location on a map, typically a two-dimensional grid, to a predefined goal and calculating the optimal route to that goal (see Wenderlich, 2011).

The encounter between Gerrard and Beckett begs the question of just what their works are adaptations *of*: if *Quad* is always already an adaptation, stemming from the inscrutable diagram or principle of movement at the heart of the printed text, and the archival antecedent 'J. M. Mime' (TCD MS 4664), *Exercise (Dunhuang)* originates in a Google Earth satellite image circulated by Reza Negarestani.[4] In a 2013 article where he specifically mentions *Quad*, Mike Frangos comments on the presence of diagrams and instructions in late Beckett: 'Beckett's late works for film, theatre and television have often been compared to installation pieces, minimalistic and iterative texts that resemble instruction manuals more than theatre' (2013: 217). The inclusion of 'diagrams, maps and charts indicating a set of instructions to be executed rather than the text of a traditional play' (2013: 221) may stem from the emphasis on medium-specificity which Frangos sees in late Beckett, and in particular from a desire to rigorously control theatrical performance. In fact, though, it may facilitate the evacuation of theatre and the move into other forms such as installation and new media, while responding to Fisher's questions: 'What do we look like from cyberspace? What do we look like to cyberspace? Surely we resemble a Beckettian assemblage of abstracted functions more than we do a wholistic organism connected to a great chain of being' (2006).

Frangos links Beckett's reflexive investment in media to theories of remediation and above all *transmedia*, in which, following an article from 1948 by André Bazin and, later, Henry Jenkins' *Convergence Culture* (2006), 'a novel, a play and a film all based on the same source need not be seen as adaptations but as a "single work reflected through three art forms"' (Bazin, 1948: 26; Frangos, 2013: 216). As a result, Frangos argues, even contemporary social media versions of Beckett should be understood as part of the author's own body of work: 'in such a media ecology, not only can any singular "work" be seen as an archive of iterations spanning media but the concept of the "author" must also be extended to include content generated by a crowd of amateur producers' (2013: 216). Frangos' argument, I suggest, extrapolates from the discussion of the 'grey canon' which has periodically taken place since Beckett's death and S. E. Gontarski's 2006 essay 'Greying the Canon: Beckett and Performance', in which he foregrounds the capacity of ancillary or paratextual material to reconfigure the primary corpus:

> As the Beckett canon is extended into the palimpsest that Gerard [sic] Genette calls 'paratexts,' that is, as more of the peripheral, secondary, or what we might call the ghost or grey canon comes to light and is made public (letters, notebooks, manuscripts, and the like), it inevitably interacts with and reshapes, redefines, even from the margins (or especially from the margins), the white canon (or the traditional canon), and the more apparent it becomes that Beckett's voice was aporetic, as plural if not contradictory as that of his (other) characters. The voice of Beckett we hear as a commentator on his work might best be read as fictive, the creation of his own ideal reader or spectator. As the grey canon expands, it offers additional authoritative voices. (2006: 143)

While Gontarski is largely concerned with Beckett's reluctance to offer interpretation of his works, coupled with an attention to performance verging on the dictatorial, Frangos applies Gontarski's model of authorship to areas of production which significantly expand definitions of the literary corpus: amateur productions and versions recorded on YouTube. Whereas Gontarski's grey canon is essentially concerned with authorial material, Frangos' enquiry, too, extends significantly beyond the authorial signature. Focusing on the production of *Come and Go* by two amateur practitioners using the name Offshore Drama Club, Frangos notes that YouTube has now become a 'community archive through which anyone can submit individual performances corresponding to each of the three women in the play' (2013: 216). Such a situation sidesteps cardinal precepts of Beckettian performance like the ban on cross-gender casting, which emanates from Beckett's own comments on the issue, as social media effectively exist outside of the estate's regulatory power. Most radically, perhaps, for Frangos, 'all media projects are imagined as archives' and their activity is essentially iterative (2013: 217). The 'archival' nature of the work thus means that latter-day adaptations are to be understood as integral to it: the Offshore Drama Club piece is now part of *Come and Go* by Samuel Beckett, which subsists within an ever-evolving and expanding media ecology.

The notion of the transmedia archive has further implications for Beckettian adaptation: medium-specificity is replaced by endless intermedial transfer and individual performances are relativised. Authorship, too, is demoted in an ever-growing corpus whose constitutive elements are no longer limited to the range of works produced in a given individual's lifetime. If, as Frangos argues, Beckett must now be understood 'in the context of a transmedia culture where the status of the archive has already been remediated by that of the database' (2013: 218), the author's name is simply one amongst the immense 'list of items' by which the database represents the world in Lev Manovich's account (2002: 225). Beckett's work is predisposed to such a logic: 'posthumous' acts of expression are explicitly highlighted within it, and narrators deny their own authority over their utterances. Just as the notion of authorship now stretches to accommodate an endless vista of posthumous contributions, the grey canon is already threatening the fixity of the corpus proper, as the category of the 'work' is underwritten with contrasting, or even conflictual, bilingual counterparts.

Simon Meek's *Beckett* and the video game 'heterocosm'

I turn now to an example with very particular implications for transmedial Beckett adaptation: *Beckett*, a 2018 video game created by developer and designer Simon Meek ('Beckett', 2018). *Beckett* is situated at the heart of the transmedial situation described by Frangos: like Gerrard's simulations, it is literally made up of algorithms, and the presence of the human actor within it is more tenuous still. *Beckett* belongs both to the posthumous domain of Beckettian production and to a genre which would have been unambiguously situated outside of the literary canon during Beckett's lifetime, that of computer games. Its peculiarity, though, is that it is, or appears to be, a titular Beckett adaptation. The game combines explicit titular reference to Beckett with a broad-based invocation of a 'Beckettian' world, or what Hutcheon refers to as the 'heterocosm':

> What gets adapted here is a heterocosm, literally an 'other world' or cosmos, complete, of course, with the stuff of a story – settings, characters, events and situations. To be more precise, it is the 'res extensa' – to use Descartes' terminology – of that world, its material, physical dimension, which is transposed and then experienced through multisensorial interactivity. (2006: 14)

Hutcheon's argument here is concerned with computer games: she refers to *Zelda*, *The Godfather* and to the account of virtuality in Oliver Grau's *Virtual Art*, in which he analyses the promise of 'immersing oneself in the image space, moving and interacting there in "real time", and intervening creatively' (2003: 3). Her conception of the heterocosm, though, is highly literary and arguably originates in M. H. Abrams' discussion of 'The Poem as Heterocosm' in *The Mirror and the Lamp*, in which the 'second nature' of the fictional world is cast as an 'act analogous to God's creation of the world'. Key to Abrams' account is the distinction, which he roots in eighteenth-century literary criticism, between earlier views of the poem as imitation and the later conception of an *other* world (1971: 272).

Beckett extends the promise of immersion to a broadly Beckettian world, largely monochrome in appearance and preoccupied with waiting and forgetting: 'We all forget. We're all forgotten. It's just a matter of time'. The player takes the part of Beckett, an ageing private investigator, although instead of first-person, the graphics are largely 2D and seen from a top-down perspective. The character of Beckett occupies a circular marker and is frequently represented by a grainy photograph of an older man's face seen in profile, his vaguely Beckettian features obscured by thick glasses with heavy dark frames. Beckett, it is strongly implied, has seen better days and laments Amy, his dead wife and an intimation of *Footfalls*, with whom he associates a time when he 'still saw hope in the world'. Beckett's central task, to track down the missing boy Peregrine Starlight, also has shades of *Molloy*: like Moran, his identity seems to fuse with that of his quarry in the latter stages of the game, where Starlight taunts him with his failure to understand the double-edged nature of the quest.

The final scenes on the beach, another archetypal Beckettian setting, in which the abandoned Peregrine washes up amongst the city's rubbish, tap into the central theme of 'the things we leave behind'. The phrase, made explicit in the game narrative here, points to Beckett's own imminent transition to detritus: although he is useful to the city authorities, 'for now', he too will soon be cast off. Beckett lives largely in his memories: 'Amy saw life in what was left behind', he reminisces earlier on and, paradoxically, 'it's what we leave behind, she would say. That's all we'll be remembered by, when the memories fade'. Despite his preoccupation with the past, Beckett appears to be losing his memory. This is a hard-drinking, partly amnesiac protagonist, and the textual admonition we periodically receive – 'Beckett you'll be late' – is both a prompt to gameplay and the marker of an uncontextualised voice. As so often, the comment is *almost* citational, invoking a key Beckett topos while failing to quote the specifics of Beckett's work. Upon leaving the game (switching off, perhaps, as in *What Where*, but only until the next purgatorial instance of play), we are confronted with two apparently typewritten messages: 'lights out' and, doubling Beckett with *Macbeth*, 'what's done can't be undone'. If, as Sonya Freeman Loftis puts it in *Shakespeare's Surrogates*, the deteriorating tissue of quotations in so many of Beckett's works functions as something 'to be rebelled against and forgotten' (2013: 80), in *Beckett* the Beckett corpus itself becomes an ambivalent object, both revered and hated, a residual but half-forgotten presence. Like the classics of which only 'a part remains' in *Happy Days* (Beckett, 2010a: 34), Beckett's work here is invoked in its residuality, its surrogate evocation of works which are always already partially lost.

Beckett, despite its explicit referentiality, then, takes up a problematic standpoint on Beckettian adaptation. Despite the titular announcement, the game does not amount, in Hutcheon's terms, to a deliberate revisitation of 'a particular *work*'. Instead, it offers a tortured quasi-citational model in tandem with the generalised evocation of a 'Beckettian' world derived in part from his works and in part from biographically inflected marginalia. The glimpses of the Beckett character, features deliberately rendered slightly generic, are infused with the aesthetic of black-and-white photographs of Beckett like those of Jane Bown and John Haynes. In this, Meek's work taps into the increasingly prevalent creation of authorly heterocosms, worlds derived from authors' works and supplemented by details taken from authors' lives. Prominent amongst recent examples is Wes Anderson's *The Grand Budapest Hotel* (2014), in which an early twentieth-century central European setting inspired by the works of Stefan Zweig is complemented by the 'Zweig-esque' (Seitz, 2015: 177) device of a frame narrative in which an elderly author recalling Zweig reflects on a pre-1939 world like that in Zweig's autobiographical *Die Welt von Gestern* (1942) (Zweig, 2009).

Anderson's film, too, enjoys an extended media afterlife, producing later surrogates such as *Maquisard* (2015), 'a charming game of snooping and investigation' ('Maquisard', 2015). This game is set in a large central European hotel based on Anderson's *The Grand Budapest Hotel* and recognisable, above all, in a pastel-dominated palette derived from Anderson's research into the Photochrom Print Collection, the US Library of Congress archive of Photochrom images dating from 1895 to 1910 which Anderson acknowledges as a 'great inspiration' for his film (Seitz, 2015: 101). Anderson's deep investment in the Photochrom archive and in the antique form of the photolithograph is only vestigially present in *Maquisard*, however, which simply attaches a diluted version of the film's aesthetic to highly conventional gameplay. More remarkable is the 2014 Pushkin Press volume *The Society of the Crossed Keys*, a Zweig anthology announced as 'Wes Anderson's selections from the writings of the great Austrian author Stefan Zweig, whose life and work inspired *The Grand Budapest Hotel*' (Zweig, 2014: cover text). The book, its cover characterised by the pastel shades of the film and a hand-written title superimposed on what appears to be an early twentieth-century notebook, represents an intervention in the Zweig corpus itself and, as in *Beckett*, that intervention takes place by means of the authorly heterocosm. It is the transposition of Zweig's 'actual life into the dream life of his stories' (Zweig, 2014: 9) in Anderson's film that ultimately produces *The Society of the Crossed Keys*, a posthumous addition to the Zweig corpus which is announced under the sign of Anderson's belated, idiosyncratic cinematic aesthetic.

Conclusion

It is to this model of intervention that I wish to draw attention as I conclude. Building on the arguments I have made so far, we might say firstly that the author's body of work is forever modified, posthumously or 'preposterously' (i.e. paradoxically positioning what came first as an after-effect and what came later as pre-text), by its adaptations (see Bal, 1999). The work of Zweig and Beckett is forever altered by Anderson's film or the simulations of Gerrard and Meek. In the uses of the heterocosm, however, a deeper, more fundamental challenge to existing models of adaptation lies. Hutcheon's consideration of the heterocosm evaluates both 'truth-of-coherence', or internal consistency, and 'truth-of-correspondence' (2006: 14). The latter is an external quality and is located by Hutcheon in relation to 'the universe of a particular adapted text' (2006: 14). It is here that problems arise in the case studies which I have considered and that their borderline status in relation to existing models of adaptation becomes clear. Because the case studies do not refer to a single text but to increasingly diffuse notions of Beckett drawn from various works and paratextual matter, they inevitably violate Hutcheon's truth-of-correspondence. Engaging with a vast textual repertoire, there is no stable referent against which they can be evaluated. While an adaptation of *Molloy* might be analysed in terms of its portrayal of the characters Moran and Molloy and the much more complex question of their relation to the text's narration, such an operation becomes quite simply impossible in Meek and Gerrard. *Beckett* knowingly enters into an unstable textual matrix, invoking the Beckett canon both explicitly and through implicit, sub-citational means. Gerrard's simulations, meanwhile, do not amount to deliberate, announced engagements with Beckett's works but display a logic of potentially infinite duration and repetition which nevertheless resonates deeply with Beckett's poetics. Gerrard's *Exercise* works, as we have seen, to exploit the logic of iteration which is at the heart of *Quad*, suggesting a revised conception of the work as a principle or set of instructions rather than a text. Such a conception is closely allied to that of the transmedial, in which any work is understood as an archive of iterations.

As a result, Hutcheon's truth-of-coherence must also be redefined. In *Beckett*, a 'time of pen and ink' is evoked via simulated paper files, ticket machines and the chatter of television, radio and typewriters, self-consciously rooting the black-and-white aesthetic in a pre-digital world. Coherent as this world is, its purpose is not necessarily related to verisimilitude or to the invocation of the Beckett corpus. The minutely detailed simulation of analogue media, in the clicking of typewriters or the rustle of paper, in fact taps into the ambivalent media archive in Beckett's own work. An important source for such a heterocosm is *Krapp's Last Tape*, in which the central prop of the tape recorder seems to offer stable grounding in mid-twentieth-century media and technology. Recent iterations of the play in performance have come up against the problem of how to accommodate the obsolete device, but the play's setting during '*a late evening in the future*' (Beckett, 2009b: 3) embeds obsolescence in a disorientating futurity. Whatever the future iterations of the play, the corpus seems to tell us, they will always be embedded in a mid-twentieth-century past which is somehow simultaneously situated in the future. Some of the most compelling responses to the problem, such as Atom Egoyan's *Steenbeckett* (2002), transpose the play's preoccupation with archival media to an installation environment. The juxtaposition of digital and analogue copies of *Krapp's Last Tape* in the installation space foregrounds the physical deterioration of the film, both making the viewer painfully aware of the material consequences of remembering and conjuring a vision of the archive which is not limited by them (see Jones, 2016: 21–6). Such an ambivalent standpoint to the work's material support is bound up, once more, with the unstable subject at the heart of adaptation studies, as Beckett's work is comprehensively remade outside the theatre.

To play *Beckett*, meanwhile, is to enter into a space of archival mediation in which the experience of analogue materiality is inescapably mediated by the digital. Meek's *Beckett* takes up a typically complex position within the transmedia archive: as a game, a set of algorithms deployed in the course of an interactive experience, it belongs to the transmedia landscape, and yet the analogue insistently resurfaces, perhaps most notably in the game's 'Physical Remix', as a set of story cards made for V&A Dundee ('Make Works: Simon Meek', 2020). Meek's *Beckett* nevertheless contains a further complication: for all that it productively undermines truth-of-coherence, in its titular appeal to Beckett it nonetheless invokes the literary corpus. In other words, this is an appeal to the 'traditional archive', guaranteed by literary canons, of which the transmedial aspect of Beckett's late work, according to Frangos, is a critique (2013: 218). The transmedia archive, in which the authority of the author is devolved to an endless stream of posthumous iterations, is paradoxically shackled to the age of literary canons indexed by the name of the author and irrevocably called into question by late modernism. What is striking here is not that the transmedia archive comes to dominate, but that it inexplicably fails to do away with its traditional counterpart and associated literary historical baggage. New media, then, underwrite established models of adaptation with a deeply problematic hinterland, a blind spot in which its essential precepts are radically redefined, and yet, in its residual, nostalgic invocation of the author, its address remains ambivalent.

Notes

1 See also my discussion of Gerrard's use of 'human' viewpoints as part of a forensic vision of landscape (Jones, 2022: chapter 3).
2 The performances took place simultaneously at the Gate Theatre, Dublin, and at the Barbican as part of BITE'06 (Barbican International Theatre Events); see 'Barbican Centre Annual Review 2006/07' (2007: 10, 28).
3 See also Fisher (2018). The posthumously published *k-punk* volume does not include Fisher's 'Cartesianism' blog post.
4 John Gerrard in a telephone conversation with the author (May 2019).

References

Abrams, M. H. (1971). *The Mirror and the Lamp: Romantic Theory and the Critical Tradition*. Oxford and New York: Oxford University Press.
Bal, M. (1999). *Quoting Caravaggio: Contemporary Art, Preposterous History*. Chicago: University of Chicago Press.
'Barbican Centre Annual Review 2006/07' (2007). *Barbican*, www.barbican.org.uk/sites/default/files/documents/2017-08/488Annual_Report_06-07.pdf (accessed 17 September 2021).
Bazin, A. (2000 [1948]). 'Adaptation, or the cinema as digest', in J. Naremore (ed.), *Film Adaptation*. New Brunswick: Rutgers University Press, pp. 19–27.
'Beckett' (2018). *The Secret Experiment*, https://thesecretexperiment.co.uk/ (accessed 3 February 2021).
Beckett, S. (1976). *Pour finir encore et autres foirades*. Paris: Les Éditions de Minuit.
Beckett, S. (1992). *Quad et autres pièces pour la télévision, suivi de L'Épuisé par Gilles Deleuze*. Paris: Les Éditions de Minuit.
Beckett, S. (2009a). *All That Fall and Other Plays for Radio and Screen*. Pref. E. Frost. London: Faber and Faber.
Beckett, S. (2009b). *Krapp's Last Tape and Other Shorter Plays*. Pref. S. E. Gontarski. London: Faber and Faber.
Beckett, S. (2010a). *Happy Days*. Pref. J. Knowlson. London: Faber and Faber.
Beckett, S. (2010b). *Texts for Nothing and Other Shorter Prose, 1950–1976*. Ed. M. Nixon. London: Faber and Faber.
Beckett, S. (2010c). *The Unnamable*. Ed. S. Connor. London: Faber and Faber.
Brater, E. (1990). *Beyond Minimalism: Beckett's Late Style in the Theatre*. New York: Oxford University Press.
Brighton, S. (2015). 'Tragic witnessing', in R. Mackay (ed.), *Simulation, Exercise, Operations*. Falmouth: Urbanomic, pp. 41–6.
Deleuze, G. (1995). 'The exhausted', trans. A. Uhlmann, *SubStance*, 24.3, 3–28.
Fisher, M. (2006). 'Cartesianism, continuum, catatonia: Beckett', *k-punk*, http://k-punk.abstractdynamics.org/archives/007587.html (accessed 17 September 2021).
Fisher, M. (2018). *K-Punk: The Collected and Unpublished Writings of Mark Fisher*. Ed. D. Ambrose. London: Repeater.

Fitch, B. T. (1988). *Beckett and Babel: An Investigation into the Status of the Bilingual Work*. Toronto and London: University of Toronto Press.

Frangos, M. (2013). 'Transmedia Beckett: *Come and Go* and the social media archive', *Adaptation*, 6.2, 215–29.

Gerrard, J. (n.d.). 'Resources', www.johngerrard.net/resources/ (accessed 10 March 2020).

Gontarski, S. E. (2006). 'Greying the canon: Beckett in performance', in S. E. Gontarski and A. Uhlmann (eds), *Beckett after Beckett*. Tallahassee: University Press of Florida, pp. 141–57.

Grau, O. (2003). *Virtual Art: From Illusion to Immersion*. Cambridge, MA: MIT Press.

Herren, G. (2007). *Samuel Beckett's Plays on Film and Television*. Houndmills: Palgrave.

Hutcheon, L. (2006). *A Theory of Adaptation*. London and New York: Routledge.

Jones, D. H. (2016). *Installation Art and the Practices of Archivalism*. London and New York: Routledge.

Jones, D. H. (2022). *Visual Culture and the Forensic: Culture, Memory, Ethics*. London and New York: Routledge.

Loftis, S. F. (2013). *Shakespeare's Surrogates: Rewriting Renaissance Drama*. Houndmills: Palgrave Macmillan.

Mackay, R. (ed.) (2014). *Exercise, John Gerrard*. Istanbul: Borusan Contemporary.

Mackay, R. (ed.) (2015). *Simulation, Exercise, Operations*. Falmouth: Urbanomic.

'Make Works: Simon Meek' (2020). *V&A Dundee*, www.vam.ac.uk/dundee/articles/make-works-simon-meek (accessed 17 September 2021).

Manovich, L. (2002). *The Language of New Media*. Cambridge, MA: MIT Press.

'Maquisard' (2015). *Itch.Io*, https://maquisard.itch.io/maquisard (accessed 17 September 2021).

Seitz, M. Z. (2015). *The Wes Anderson Collection: The Grand Budapest Hotel*. New York: Abrams.

Wenderlich, R. (2011). 'Introduction to A* Pathfinding', *raywenderlich.com*, www.raywenderlich.com/3016-introduction-to-a-pathfinding (accessed 17 September 2021).

Whitelaw, B. (1995). *Billie Whitelaw ... Who He? An Autobiography*. London: Hodder & Stoughton.

Woycicki, P. (2012). '"Mathematical aesthetic" as a strategy for performance: a vector analysis of Samuel Beckett's *Quad*', *Journal of Beckett Studies*, 21.2, 135–56.

Zweig, S. (2009). *The World of Yesterday: Memoirs of a European*. Trans. A. Bell. London: Pushkin Press.

Zweig, S. (2014). *The Society of the Crossed Keys*. Trans. A. Bell. London: Pushkin Press.

10

Opera as adaptation: György Kurtág's *Samuel Beckett: Fin de partie, scènes et monologues*

Olga Beloborodova

Much has been written on Beckett's relationship to music. Most of the critical literature can be roughly broken down into two strands: 1) the way music features in his work, and 2) the musicality of his own texts. Two of the seminal book-length studies on the subject – Mary Bryden's *Beckett and Music* (1998) and Catherine Laws's *Headache among the Overtones* (2013) – combine the two topics, and the general consensus is that Beckett, a great lover of music, both drew inspiration from and used that art form extensively in his own work.[1]

The present chapter is not an addition to the already copious literature on the subject of Beckett and music. Instead, I will examine György Kurtág's 2018 opera *Samuel Beckett: Fin de partie, scènes et monologues* as a particularly interesting case study to delve into the broader issues of the relationship between the original and the adaptation. To investigate this general issue, I will zoom in on Kurtág's intention to remain faithful to the text as much as possible, despite the obvious need to transpose the play into a completely different genre. In particular, the chapter will take issue with John Bryant's 'fluid text' principle (2002; 2013), which argues for the inclusion of all forms of adaptation (whether authorial or not) in the work's genesis.[2] The question the chapter attempts to answer is whether there are compelling arguments to consider Kurtág's opera a 'fluid text' and thus to implicitly treat Samuel Beckett as a posthumous co-author of his play's transgeneric and transmedial adaptation.

John Bryant's fluid text and adaptation

In 2002, John Bryant, a distinguished textual scholar and editor of Herman Melville's works, came up with the notion of the 'fluid text', which posits that '[l]iterary works invariably exist in more than one version, either in early manuscript forms, subsequent print editions, or even adaptations in other media *with or without the author's consent*' (2002: 1; emphasis added). In other words, the fluid text subsumes not only pre-publication and post-publication revisions by the original author but also those made by any other creative agent, including adapters of the original work. Bryant distinguishes three kinds of revision: those 'performed by originating writers, by their editors and publishers, or by readers and audiences, who reshape the originating work to reflect their own desires for the text, themselves, their culture' (2013: 48). The latter category, called 'cultural revision' (2002: 75), is where (non-authorial) adaptations belong.

Such a high degree of textual fluidity inevitably raises a number of questions, most notably on the authorship of the original source and the revised text. As Bryant himself acknowledges, 'to suggest that the adaptor is in some way extending a work or collaborating with the originating author might seem a stretch, especially if we hold authorial intentions to be sacrosanct' (2013: 49). The 'stretch' is especially long in cases of posthumous adaptations, since the fluid text principle posits that 'fluidity extends into numerous kinds of cultural revision, beyond the writer's death and "will." Thus, from a fluid-text perspective, genesis can be both authorized and nonauthorized' (2002: 75–6). In other words, Bryant's inclusive theory suggests that the adaptation is another version of the original and hence the original author remains the (co-)author of this new version as well, in some cases from beyond the grave (see the discussion of the opera's title below).

In her discussion of Bryant's concept of adaptation as fluid text, Linda Hutcheon emphasises 'a continuum of fluid relationships' between the production and the reception side of the adaptation story (2013: 171). She notes Bryant's focus on the production-oriented elements (whether textual or performance ones, such as the production of a Beckett play following Beckett's playtext or possibly even directed by Beckett himself) and devotes her own attention to the reception side, which is a spectrum in its own right. This spectrum ranges from the more literal modes, such as translations, to '(re-)interpretations and (re-) creations' (2013: 171–2), where Hutcheon places adaptations, thus emphasising their difference from, rather than likeness to, the original. By contrast, the question that this chapter sets out to investigate – whether the posthumous opera adaptation of *Fin de partie* can be classified as a version of the original work – is grounded in Kurtág's outspoken drive to remain faithful to Beckett's original text. The matter is further complicated by the fact that most transmedial and transgeneric adaptations are collaborative endeavours, and this certainly applies to the opera genre, 'the collaborative medium par excellence' (Halliwell qtd in Hutcheon and Hutcheon, 2017: 305).

Beckett and opera

It is a critical commonplace that Beckett did not appreciate opera. As James Knowlson mentions in his biography, he 'simply never liked opera, perhaps because it was such a mixture of music, singing and acting, but also because for him it was too grandiose and unsuggestive an art form' (1996: 194). Knowlson's widely shared view is largely based on Beckett's own denigrating appraisal of the genre in *Proust*, in turn heavily influenced by Schopenhauer's antagonism towards it, where he claims that 'opera is a hideous corruption of this most immaterial of all arts: the words of a libretto are to the musical phrase that they particularize what the Vendôme Column, for example, is to the ideal perpendicular' (1965: 92). Beckett rejected the idea of a *Gesamtkunstwerk*, which opera invariably is, by referring to it slightingly as 'Wagnerism' in a letter to Georges Duthuit of 3 January 1951: 'I do not believe in collaboration between the arts, I want a theatre reduced to its own means, speech and acting, without painting, without music, without embellishments' (2011: 218). At the same time, Beckett apparently enjoyed Debussy's *Pelléas et Mélisande* (1898) and 'had an enormous admiration for Alban Berg's ... *Wozzeck*, which he regarded as a masterpiece of the twentieth century' (Knowlson, 1996: 194).[3] So, perhaps it would be more accurate to say that, although Beckett did not like the more traditional strands of the genre, he did appreciate the modernist, expressionist variety, marked by less grandeur and a more subjective, fragmented form of composition.

Apart from his aversion to the idea of a *Gesamtkunstwerk*, Beckett is famous for his reluctance to 'mix media', even though his letters reveal a much less straightforward attitude than generally assumed. When asked by composer Edouard Coester in 1954 whether he could set *Waiting for Godot* to music (for voice and orchestra), Beckett adamantly rejected the possibility: 'I have already publicly expressed my opposition to any stage music. ... For me that would be an awful mistake. A very different case would be music inspired by the play and I would be greatly flattered by any venture in that direction. But, in saying that, I have in mind instrumental music, no voices' (2011: 475–6). What Beckett apparently had in mind was 'pure music', probably interspersed heavily with 'silence', which was 'still waiting for its musician' (2011: 476). As is well known, he would later attempt to implement this aesthetic in his *Words and Music* and *Cascando*, which he appropriately referred to as 'text-music tandems' (qtd in Zilliacus, 1976: 99). In those radio plays, music does not have a subservient part that 'carries' the text; instead, both are on equal terms with each other, taking turns and avoiding synthesis as much as possible.

All the more surprising in the light of the above was Beckett's decision in 1959, by way of his English publisher John Calder, to allow Marc Wilkinson to set a part of Lucky's speech (renamed *Voices*) to music for soprano and chamber orchestra (Beckett, 2014: 262–3),[4] and around the same time he gave Marcel Mihalovici permission to transpose one of his stage plays – *Krapp's Last Tape* – into an opera, their close friendship no doubt contributing to the decision. The opera was very much a collaborative effort between the author and the composer, to which the draft material kept at the University of Reading (MS 1227-7-10-2) testifies. Like Kurtág later on, Mihalovici also aspired from the very start to maintain strict fidelity to Beckett's original text. For his part, Beckett made suggestions for the score and showed remarkable flexibility in adapting his original text as well as the French and German translations in order to suit the music (see Van Hulle, 2015: 126–7; Knowlson, 1996: 466–8).

Despite his direct involvement in the opera's composition process, Beckett's imperative of avoiding the 'Wagnerism' inherent in the opera genre did not seem to come to fruition in the end result: as he confessed to Barbara Bray on 17 February 1961, after seeing the performance, the text was 'rather obliterated' (2014: 399). Nonetheless, given the close collaboration between the original author and the adapter, it seems only logical to consider Beckett as the co-author of Mihalovici's opera, following Bryant's 'fluid text' principle, and to include the opera in the (epi)genesis of the work called *Krapp's Last Tape*. For obvious reasons, Kurtág's posthumous adaptation of *Fin de partie* is a different story altogether.

György Kurtág's *Samuel Beckett: Fin de partie – scènes et monologues* (2018)

On the surface, Kurtág's opera adaptation of *Fin de partie* is the most unlikely of projects.[5] To begin with, turning Beckett's favourite play (by his own admission; qtd in Beckett, 1992: xv) into a specimen of his least favourite genre was always going to be a challenge, to say the least. As one reviewer noted, 'Samuel Beckett's plays seem ill-suited to operatic adaptation. Their philosophical rather than dramatic character works against the form's strengths, and their intricately woven texts risk being hampered by music' (Imam, 2018).[6] Besides, this was going to be Kurtág's first ever completed opera, a genre that seems an unlikely fit for his trademark minimalist style. A closer look at Kurtág's career and aesthetics may, however, help us to see that the *Fin de partie* opera project as a crowning glory of the great composer's long life is not as inconceivable as it initially appears to be. First of all, Kurtág is an admirer of Beckett's work, and he has set a number of his texts to music in the past.⁷ Laws also notes several similarities between Beckett and Kurtág as creative artists: their characteristic minimalist style, long periods of creative struggle, their reluctance to 'explain' their work and their habit of recycling older work in later pieces (2005: 242–3).

The connection between Kurtág and *Fin de partie* goes a long way back to the composer's time in Paris, when his close friend György Ligeti took him to see the play in 1957 (shortly after it premiered). According to Kurtág, in conversation with critic Jeremy Eichler, it was one of the strongest experiences in his life (see Ross, 2018). Both works also have long and complicated composition histories. It took Beckett over six years to write *Fin de partie* (if one includes early abandoned fragments as precursors of the play; see Van Hulle and Weller, 2018: 131), and Kurtág needed seven years to complete the opera in its present state (the score indicates 2010–17 as its composition date). The fact that Kurtág refused to sign a contract with La Scala or accept money for the work (Karasz, 2018) speaks volumes about his insecurity as to whether he would ever be able to finish the project. This reluctance to commit is similar to Beckett's own attitude to working on commission; although he did, at times, he thought the idea to be paralysing to his creativity.⁸

Approaching the same phenomenon – the relationship between words and music – from two different angles, Beckett (in his radio plays) and Kurtág both aspired to reach an equilibrium between the two art forms. Drawing inspiration from Debussy's *Pelléas et Mélisande* (which Beckett also liked) and Monteverdi's *Orfeo* (1607), Kurtág tried to make sure that 'the text doesn't move to the background in favor of the music' (Karasz, 2018), as it did in Mihalovici's opera adaptation of *Krapp*. It seems that Kurtág's efforts in this direction had the desired effect: in his review, Alex Ross notes that '[t]he music hovers around Beckett's language without ever obscuring or upstaging it'. He commends Kurtág's 'vocal writing of [great] radical transparency: every wounded word strikes home' (2018). Kurtág himself explains that his composition process was primarily driven by Beckett's original play: 'I almost obsessively want to remain faithful to his text and his initial concept', adding that 'he had spent two years just on studying the playwright's word choices' (qtd in Karasz, 2018).⁹ Elsewhere, he confessed his 'intention of translating each moment of the text in musical gestures, the harmonies and the semantics accurately responding to the situation of the text itself' (Temeş, 2019: 274).

My discussion of Kurtág's opera as an adaptation of Beckett's play focuses on the textual and performance elements (libretto and scenography), leaving music largely beyond inspection. It should be noted that virtually all reviewers agree that Kurtág's music is as 'Beckettian' as an opera score can be. In particular, Rachel Beckles Willson comments on the restraint Kurtág seems to exercise with the musical component, in order to avoid 'giving dramatic direction to a work intending to shun precisely that' (2019: 92). Catherine Fahy notes 'the granular mimesis of voice and orchestra' and 'Kurtág's adept use of a veritable toy box of music instruments, employed ... for their comic and dramatic potential to highlight the distinction between the vaudeville of imbedded narratives and the chronic action of the play' (2019).[10] The reason for largely disregarding the music derives from the fluid text principle: if the opera *Fin de partie* (2018) is the continuation of the original play's genesis, as Bryant's concept suggests, then it makes sense to compare those elements that Beckett himself could have had a say in as a playwright and director, i.e. the text and the staging. In other words, the discussion aims to answer the question of whether the opera is a case of 'posthumous collaboration' between Beckett and Kurtág (as one reviewer put it)[11] or whether we are looking at an adaptation that is located at the far end of the reception part of Linda Hutcheon's continuum discussed above.

In this connection, the opera's full title deserves some attention. Although often abbreviated as *Fin de partie – scènes et monologues*, it is actually called *Samuel Beckett: Fin de partie – scènes et monologues*. The fact that Beckett's name 'dominates the opera's title' (Beckles Willson, 2019) is remarkable and can indicate a number of things. Apart from possible commercial motives (which, however unappealing, should perhaps not be entirely discarded), it is a direct reference to the 'secondary' nature of the adaptation and an homage to the original author. At the same time, it could also create the misleading impression that this is *Beckett's* (rather than Kurtág's) *Fin de partie*. Conversely, including Beckett's name in the title (and thus implicitly lifting him from the position of the author) could also be a way of foregrounding Kurtág's authorship of the opera and help to situate it as a separate, non-derivative work of art. This impression is strengthened by the fact that Kurtág is also the author of the libretto, however bound he was by the strict fidelity standards of the Beckett Estate.

Libretto

As Hutcheon and Hutcheon note, the libretto is almost always an adaptation in its own right of the original text to the opera format, which typically entails 'drastic selection and compression' (2017: 308–9). What is atypical in the case of *Fin de partie* is that Kurtág had to use Beckett's text almost verbatim: as the opera's production director Pierre Audi noted, Kurtág in fact used the play as a libretto, which – according to Audi – is very unusual and has hardly ever happened in the history of music (see Lockwood, 2021).[12] However, even though he was not in the position to change the wording, Kurtág was free to choose which parts to keep or which ones to cut, and his choice is an interesting one.

All in all, Kurtág has kept about 60 per cent of Beckett's original text (Fahy, 2019). He excised almost all the dialogues between Hamm and Clov, most probably to emphasise the disconnectedness and isolation of the two protagonists; as Beckles Willson notes, 'most of the scenes are shaped by solipsistic monologues' (2019: 92). The question is whether this decision, no doubt in part motivated by operatic conventions (possibly to reduce the share of recitatives in favour of arias), chimes well with Beckett's 'initial concept' that Kurtág so wished to implement: the original play is deeply rooted in conversation and in the interaction, however unproductive, between Hamm and Clov.[13] Besides, taking out most of the dialogues has resulted in the absence of some of the play's central themes, such as Hamm's position in the centre of his universe (Beckett, 2009a: 18–19) and his insistence that Clov kill the flea he found on his body, since 'humanity might start from there all over again' (2009a: 22). Only one (longer) dialogue between the master and his servant is retained – i.e. the parting scene ('Scene 9: DIALOGUE de Hamm et CLOV'; Kurtág, 2018: 31–2). An even more drastic intervention is Kurtág's division of the text into twelve scenes, each given a title and clearly separated by a curtain drop – the added parts, 'Prologue' and 'Epilogue', do not belong to the playtext proper and will be discussed below. The curtain drop after each scene is another means of foregrounding the motif of disconnection and fragmentation that marks Beckett's play. While the Hamm/Clov sections are significantly reduced, the Nagg/Nell parts are largely left untouched, creating a better balance between the two pairs of characters and thus enhancing the lyrical element that Nell represents – a perfectly understandable choice from the point of view of staging an opera.

Kurtág did not just cut the text; he added sections at the beginning and the end as well. Surprisingly, the traditional overture – a staple feature of the genre – does not open the opera but is part of the second scene ('PANTOMIME de CLOV'). Instead, there is an unexpected prologue, which contains Nell's rendition of 'Roundelay', one of Beckett's poems (written in English in 1976). Not immediately related to Fin de partie, the poem is 'enigmatic but similarly prescient: we are entering a time-space in which the sound of words is as important as their meaning, and where lonely characters attempt to cope with their sense of imminent end, mysteriously near and yet also bafflingly unreachable' (Beckles Willson, 2019: 91). The poem's inherent circularity, with the opening lines repeated at the end, alludes to the play's own repetitive and circular structure. Catherine Fahy suggests that the composer may have been 'drawn to its inherent sonic properties: the word "sound" returns six times and the sibilant qualities of the text are exploited with staccato, shortened and detached articulation to animate the footfalls evoked in the poem' (2019). Besides, the very choice of an English poem that is also sung in English could be interpreted as Kurtág's homage to Beckett's bilingual *oeuvre* (de Ruyter, 2020: 323).

Although the use of 'Roundelay' in the prologue is perhaps the most conspicuous addition, it is certainly not the only one: throughout the libretto, Kurtág has inserted lines of text both in the stage directions and in the arias. Some of those are necessitated by the process of transposition to a different medium (for instance, instructions for vocals, see below), but others are less evident and deserve more attention. It is important to bear in mind that, unlike a production notebook, a libretto is a published text that is meant to be read by the audience (Hutcheon and Hutcheon, 2017: 312), so any additions to Beckett's original are significant. The opening monologue by Clov is indicative of Kurtág's minor and subtle yet not insignificant additions to the speeches:[14]

> Clov: *(regard fixe, voix blanche)* Fini, c'est fini, ça va finir, ... **peut-être ça va peut-être finir. Ça va bientôt finir.** Les grains s'ajoutent aux grains, un à un, et un jour, soudain, **un beau jour soudain**, c'est un tas, un petit tas, l'impossible tas. On ne peut plus me punir. **Non, plus jamais!** Je m'en vais dans ma cuisine, *(respiration rapide, agitée; audible)* trois mètres sur trois mètres sur trois mètres, attendre qu'il me sifffffle... **trois, sur trois, sur trois...** sur *(presque muet)* trois. Ce sont de jolies dimensions, je m'appuierai à la table, je regarderai le mur, en attendant qu'il me siffle. (Kurtág, 2018: 9)

The addition 'Ça va *bientôt* finir' seems to undo the rising degree of tentativeness in Clov's successive statements about the impending end. The added phrase 'Non, plus jamais!', along with the subsequent stage direction, inject an emotional element into a speech that is otherwise devoid of emotion. The other, more neutral, additions either serve to adapt the text to the music or to enhance the repetition effect.

Kurtág's additions are most frequent in the stage directions. A good example is the dialogue between Nagg and Nell ('Scene 5: La Poubelle'), which is interspersed with numerous added indications of the characters' emotional states:

> Nell *(un peu embarrassée)* C'est pour la bagatelle?
>
> Nell *(fatiguée)* Oh non!
>
> Nell *(avec dégoût)* Pourquoi cette comédie, tous les jours [hein]?
>
> Nagg *(avec gravité)* Notre vue a baissé.
>
> Nell *(nuance désagréable, agressive, voix perçante)* Notre quoi?
>
> Nagg *(recroquevillé, rétréci, comme un chien battu)* Notre ouïe. (2018: 11–13)

Elsewhere, both Hamm and Clov receive similar emotional colouring:

Hamm *(en jouant le rôle de la Providence)* Ça avance. (2018: 11)

Hamm ... *(wie ein Urteil)* c'est sans remède! (2018: 26)

Hamm *(bouche mince, dents serrées; avec joie maligne, sadique)* Il n'y a plus de dragées. (2018: 28)

Clov *(avec ironie et amertume)* Ton cœur! (2018: 33)

Hamm *(très timidement, avec une nostalgie douloureuse)* Clov! (2018: 35)

This kind of over-interpretation and over-explication, however subtle, is profoundly un-Beckettian, especially if we recall that his own instructions to his actors were typically not to (over)act.[15]

Another notable move away from Beckettian aesthetics is the foregrounding in the libretto of originally covert intertextual allusions. For instance, Beckett translated Hamm's line 'Finie la rigolade' by a quote from *The Tempest* (uttered in Shakespeare's play by Prospero): 'Our revels now are ended' (Beckett, 2009a: 35). In what seems to be a nod to *Endgame*'s bilingual nature, Kurtág has decided to bring the Shakespearian reference to the surface by adding (after 'Finie la rigolade') 'Mon bisaïeul Prospero l'a dit: "Our revels now are ended"'. Apart from alluding to some ancestral link between Prospero and Hamm (which is more than Beckett ever did in his original text), this addition makes explicit the intertextual underground that the original author would typically obscure during the writing process. Similarly, Kurtág mentions the name of Baudelaire in Hamm's last monologue ('Scene 13'):

Un peu... un peu... *(hommage à Baudelaire)* Un peu de poésie. *(un temps)* Tu appelais... Non! non-non... *(un temps. Il se corrige)* Tu RÉCLAMAIS le soir; il vient... non! Il DESCEND: le voici. *(il reprend, très chantant; comme une mélodie de Debussy)* Tu réclamais le soir; il descend: le voici. *(un temps; petit mouvement d'approbation avec la tête, même avec la main)* Joli çççça. Et puis? (2018: 36)

Baudelaire is clearly present in the monologue, as Hamm 'quotes – with hitches – the second line of the sonnet 'Recueillement', addressed to pain and suffering ("Douleur")' (Van Hulle and Weller, 2018: 251). Kurtág was probably driven by the desire to make sure that his audience did not miss the reference; nonetheless, such an explicit pointer does not quite resonate with Beckett's habitual reluctance to explain his work.

In some cases, the composer infuses Beckett's original text with intertextuality and historical context that it did not originally contain. The most striking case is the insertion '**SONG – Le monde et le pantalon [Poldy Bloom singing a Jewish-Irish-Scottish ballad]**' (Kurtág, 2018: 19) before Nagg's rendering of the tailor joke. The author's lifelong connection to Joyce is of course well known even outside Beckett studies, but its relevance to *Fin de partie* (be it the original or the adaptation) is not very clear. The overt emphasis on the Jewishness of the joke in the libretto (no doubt enhanced by both Bloom's and Kurtág's partly Jewish roots) is an element that steers the interpretation of the story in a certain direction. As Ross notes, 'these intertwined allusions ... make one wonder if the composer thinks of "Endgame" as a post-Holocaust work' (2018). One could also wonder if this is the direction that the original work suggests – it seems that straightforward nods at historical events or figures were instead to be avoided, as the next example will demonstrate.

In the libretto, Hamm's penultimate monologue ('Scene 8') contains a seemingly unexpected element:

> Mais réfléchissez, réfléchissez, vous êtes sur ter-re, c'est sans remède!
>
> *(un temps. Avec violence)* Allez-vous en et **(voce distorta)** aimez-vous! Léchez-vous les uns les autres! *(un temps. Plus calme)* Quand ce n'était pas du pain **(hommage à Marie-Antoinette)** c'était du mille-feuille. *(un temps. Avec violence)* Foutez-moi le camp! Retour... Retournez à vos partouzes! (Kurtág, 2018: 30)

A brief look into the original text's genesis makes the mention of Marie-Antoinette slightly less surprising and points to Kurtág's familiarity with the play's draft material kept at the University of Reading (as indicated above). The original line by Hamm read as follows: 'Quand ce n'était pas du pain c'était de la brioche' (BDMP7, FT5, 31r).[16] As is well known, the phrase 'Qu'ils mangent de la brioche' ('Let them eat cake') is allegedly attributed to Marie-Antoinette and has come to embody the arrogance of the ruling elites and their indifference to the plight of the poor. Beckett revised 'brioche' to 'mille-feuille' by hand in the same typescript, probably in an effort to obscure this (all too explicit?) reference to a certain historical person and event. It is therefore possible that Kurtág spotted the connection by looking at earlier versions of the monologue and decided to reintroduce it by writing Marie-Antoinette into the libretto. Whatever his motivation was, this decision – along with the others discussed in this section – seems to be at odds with Beckett's aesthetic principle of 'vaguening' (Pountney, 1988) with regard to overt historical or intertextual references and arguably fails to convey the Beckettian spirit that the composer was so keen on retaining.

Scenography

Just like Kurtág's less-than-straightforward translation of Beckett's text into the opera's libretto, the production itself is an interesting case of fluidity between the original and its 'cultural revision' (Bryant, 2002: 75; 2013: 48). As a courageously unorthodox stage set solution, which at first sight may seem like 'a fatal mistake' (Maprayil, 2020: 144), the production director Pierre Audi has placed the four protagonists ostensibly *outside* their dwelling, announcing a seemingly radical departure from Beckett's own stage directions – '*Bare interior*' being the opening line of the play (2009a: 5). The bewildered audience, having endured their first surprise in the form of 'Roundelay' sung in the 'Prologue' by a spotlit female face shrouded in complete darkness, no doubt gasped in disbelief when the opening tableau was revealed to them. At the very least, the large number of Beckett fans among them were probably expecting to see something like 'the inside of an immense skull', as Hugh Kenner famously described the stage setting of *Endgame* (1973: 155). On the other hand, those not familiar with Beckett's work in general, and the original play in particular, may have thought that what they were seeing onstage was the author's own design all along. However, as Pierre Audi himself explains in an interview with Alan Lockwood, this first impression is indeed deceptive, and the idea of placing the house so explicitly onstage has a different meaning altogether:

> [A]ctually the exterior of the house is like in a Russian doll: it's inside another one that's inside another one. … It's three houses. They're fit into each other. If [Clov] goes out, he's still in the house. *I needed to preserve the integrity of the intention of Beckett*, that there is no way out. They're in a bunker, and they are not leaving. So that somehow needed to be projected. (Audi qtd in Lockwood, 2021: 208; emphasis added)

Audi's reference to Beckett's intention echoes Kurtág's own sentiment, and his staging solution is ingenious in its audacity and simplicity.[17] Audi's insistence on staging a 'bunker' that nobody can leave echoes Beckett's appeal to the actors in the 1967 Schiller Theater production of *Endspiel* that he directed to uphold the fourth wall (Van Hulle and Weller, 2018: 237), thus enhancing the play's already strong sense of confinement to an almost claustrophobic degree. Audi's translation of Beckett's artistic objective into a different medium and by different means is an excellent example of a successful adaptation – to such an extent that the adapter may have even surpassed the original author in enacting the 'skullscape' (Ben-Zvi, 1986: 4) onstage. Indeed, his 'Russian doll' construction is reminiscent of what Daniel Dennett labelled 'Cartesian Theatre' (1991) – the representation of the Cartesian homunculus model of the little man inside a head who manages all brain activity and who would logically need another little man inside *his* head, and so on *ad infinitum*. Although Beckett's alleged devotion to Cartesianism has been revisited and reassessed in more recent scholarship, his predilection for evocative dualist imagery is palpable in his work across his long career: from Murphy's 'little world' (2009c: 112–13) in his mind, or the doodle of the homunculus in the first draft of *L'Innommable* (BDMP2, FN2, 21r) to 'That head in that head' in *Worstward Ho* (2009b: 89), to name but a few. It thus seems that Audi's solution of 'that house in that house in that house' for Kurtág's opera has turned out to be more Beckettian than he himself may have intended in his adaptation of the playwright's staging instructions.

Conclusion

This chapter has investigated the tension between the adapter's wish to retain utmost fidelity to the original and the challenges of retaining such fidelity in a transgeneric and transmedial adaptation. In the case of Kurtág's *Fin de partie*, the adaptation was driven willingly and to an extreme degree by the original text: not only did Kurtág spend two years studying Beckett's play (including draft material) but he was also bound to strict fidelity to the original text by the Beckett Estate. Nonetheless, as we have seen above, despite this self-proclaimed intention to remain faithful to the original, Kurtág's choice to cut most of the dialogues and to foreground covert intertextual as well as cultural references is a decision that deviates from Beckett's 'initial concept' (to use Kurtág's own words) and places the opera on the relatively far end of Hutcheon's reception continuum of textual fluidity. The very fact that Beckett's name is included in the title of Kurtág's opera can be read as a comment on Bryant's 'fluid text' theory, which includes such adaptations in the so-called 'non-authorized' genesis of the work.

Admittedly, Bryant does make an important caveat by emphasising that 'adaptation need not be exclusively derivative; it has its own genius and reason for being' (2013: 51). That being said, the fluid text principle treats Kurtág's opera as another version of the work called *Fin de partie*, which in turn implies that Beckett willy-nilly remains the author of this (and any other) adaptation. By contrast, the inclusion of Beckett's name in the title, and therefore inside the text, is a gesture – however subtle and ambiguous – that shifts its status and function: from naming the author to naming the work. Although it pays homage to the original author of the play *Fin de partie*, the gesture does not contain the presumption that this new version of the work's fluid text is automatically authorised by Beckett or that, more generally, the act of adaptation forces the original author to – *nolens volens* – remain the author of any adaptation of their works.

Notes

1 For more recent book-length studies on the subject, see Bailes and Till (2014) and McGrath (2018), among others.

2 Although Bryant himself uses the word 'genesis' (2002: 76), the more precise term would be 'epigenesis', which denotes 'the continuation of the genesis after publication' (Van Hulle, 2014: 14).
3 Reportedly, *Pelléas* is one of the models that Kurtág examined during his long period of preparation for *Fin de partie* (Ross, 2018).
4 He later authorised another musical setting based on *Godot*, entitled *Credentials, or 'Think, think Lucky'*, for voice and eight players, the composer Roman Haubenstock-Ramati sending him a score and a tape recording of it in 1963 (Beckett, 2014: 563–4).
5 *Samuel Beckett: Fin de partie – scènes et monologues, opéra en un acte* was commissioned by the La Scala Opera Theatre in Milan and premiered there on 15 November 2018.
6 In 1989, Beckett had also contacted director Gildas Bourdet about his *Fin de partie* for the Comédie-Française to 'object formally to aspects of the production, in particular the use of music' (Beckett, 2016: 720n2).
7 These are *what is the word* (in Hungarian; 1990 and 1991) and *…pas à pas – nulle part…* (1993–8), in which Kurtág uses a number of Beckett's early and late poems in French and English (Laws, 2005: 242).
8 In a letter to Alan Schneider of 6 February 1958, Beckett declared: 'I can't write to commission' (1998: 37). See also Verhulst (2017).
9 From early on in the composition process, Kurtág also showed interest in the manuscript material of the play, kept at the University of Reading. According to Anita Rákóczy, who helped the Kurtágs liaise with the Reading Archive, the composer received photocopies of the draft material in 2013–14 and was especially fascinated by the early drafts – the so-called 'Avant *Fin de partie*' (MS-UoR-1227-7-16-7; FT1 in BDMP7) and the first two-act version of *Fin de partie* (MS-UoR-1660; FT2 in BDMP7). He also read 'Mime du rêveur A' (which is in turn connected to Shakespeare's quotation in the play/libretto; see Van Hulle and Weller, 2018: 240), and the Ernest and Alice fragment (MS-UoR-1227-7-16-2; AS4 in BDMP7). Before he had access to the draft material, Kurtág carefully studied the *Theatrical Notebooks* for the play. I owe a debt of gratitude to Mark Nixon for alerting me to the Kurtág-Reading connection, and to Anita Rákóczy for her generous help with this information (personal communication). For more details, see Rákóczy (2019).
10 For more information on the music in the opera, see Fahy (2019).
11 According to Alex Ross, '[t]he opera is less a translation of literature into music than a kind of posthumous collaboration' (2018).
12 For his 1961 opera adaptation of *Krapp's Last Tape*, Marcel Mihalovici did exactly the same. In 2011, Kurtág asked for and received a copy of the opera's score, because he wanted to know what Beckett allowed in relation to music. In any case, Kurtág was obligated by the Beckett Estate to follow the text verbatim, so it is unclear whether he would have made that choice if he had been given the freedom to do otherwise. I thank Anita Rákóczy for the information on Kurtág's interest in Mihalovici's score (personal communication). For more information, see Rákóczy (2019).

13 In this connection, the following exchange is illustrative: 'CLOV: I'll leave you. HAMM: No! CLOV: What is there to keep me here? HAMM: The dialogue' (Beckett 2009a, 36).
14 In all quotes from the score, additions by Kurtág to Beckett's original text of the play are indicated in bold.
15 See, for instance, Billie Whitelaw's recollection of her acting experience with Beckett: 'I can still hear him saying "Too much colour, Billie, too much colour." That was his way of saying "Don't act"' (qtd in McTighe, 2014).
16 BDMP refers to the Beckett Digital Manuscript Project, www.beckettarchive.org (accessed 14 September 2021).
17 The house also rotates each time the curtain goes down, and this change of perspective was much easier to achieve than if the characters had been in a room (Audi qtd in Lockwood, 2021: 208–9).

References

Bailes, S. J., and N. Till (eds) (2014). *Beckett and Musicality*. Ashgate: Farnham.
Beckett, S. (1965). *Proust and Three Dialogues with Georges Duthuit*. London: John Calder.
Beckett, S. (1992). *The Theatrical Notebooks of Samuel Beckett, Volume II: Endgame*. Ed. S. E. Gontarski. London: Faber and Faber.
Beckett, S. (1998). *No Author Better Served: The Correspondence of Samuel Beckett & Alan Schneider*. Ed. M. Harmon. Cambridge, MA: Harvard University Press.
Beckett, S. (2009a). *Endgame*. Pref. R. McDonald. London: Faber and Faber.
Beckett, S. (2009b). *Company, Ill Seen Ill Said, Worstward Ho, Stirrings Still*. Ed. D. Van Hulle. London: Faber and Faber.
Beckett, S. (2009c). *Murphy*. Ed. J. C. C. Mays. London: Faber and Faber.
Beckett, S. (2011). *The Letters of Samuel Beckett, Volume II: 1941–1956*. Ed. D. Gunn, L. More Overbeck, G. Craig and M. Dow Fehsenfeld. Cambridge: Cambridge University Press.
Beckett, S. (2014). *The Letters of Samuel Beckett, Volume III: 1957–1967*. Ed. D. Gunn, L. More Overbeck, G. Craig and M. Dow Fehsenfeld. Cambridge: Cambridge University Press.
Beckett, S. (2016). *The Letters of Samuel Beckett, Volume IV: 1966–1989*. Ed. G. Craig, M. Dow Fehsenfeld, D. Gunn and L. More Overbeck. Cambridge: Cambridge University Press.
Beckles Willson, R. (2019). 'György Kurtág, Samuel Beckett: Fin de partie – scènes et monologues, opéra en un acte', *Tempo*, 73.288, 91–2.
Ben-Zvi, L. (1986). *Samuel Beckett*. Boston: Twaine.
Bryant, J. (2002). *The Fluid Text: A Theory of Revision and Editing for Book and Screen*. Ann Arbor: University of Michigan Press.
Bryant, J. (2013). 'Textual identity and adaptive revision: editing adaptation as a fluid text', in J. Bruhn, A. Gjelsvik and E. Frisvold Hanssen (eds), *Adaptation Studies: New Challenges, New Directions*. London: Bloomsbury, pp. 47–68.

Bryden, M. (1998). *Samuel Beckett and Music*. Oxford: Clarendon Press.
Dennett, D. (1991). *Consciousness Explained*. London: Penguin.
De Ruyter, D. (2020). 'FIN DE PARTIE, György Kurtág / Samuel Beckett: la recherche de l'ailleurs et du silence', *Samuel Beckett Today / Aujourd'hui*, 32, 321–36.
Fahy, C. (2019). 'György Kurtág's *Endgame*', *The Beckett Circle*, https://thebeckettcircle.org/2019/05/02/gyorgy-kurtags-endgame/ (accessed 1 March 2021).
Hutcheon, L. (2013 [2006]). *A Theory of Adaptation*. London: Routledge.
Hutcheon, L., and M. Hutcheon (2017). 'Adaptation and opera', in T. Leitch (ed.), *The Oxford Handbook of Adaptation Studies*. New York: Oxford University Press, pp. 305–23.
Imam, J. (2018). 'Fin de partie: György Kurtág delivers Beckett opera at last', *Financial Times*, 20 November, www.ft.com/content/2f032eb0-ebe6-11e8-89c8-d36339d835c0 (accessed 1 February 2021).
Karasz, P. (2018). 'A 92-year-old composer's first opera is his "Endgame"', *New York Times*, 7 November, www.nytimes.com/2018/11/07/arts/music/gyorgy-Kurtág-opera.html (accessed 1 March 2021).
Kenner, H. (1973 [1961]). *Samuel Beckett: A Critical Study*. Berkeley: University of California Press.
Knowlson, J. (1996). *Damned to Fame: The Life of Samuel Beckett*. London: Bloomsbury.
Kurtág, G. (2018). *Samuel Beckett: Fin de partie, scènes et monologues. Opéra en un acte*. Libretto. Milan: Edizioni del Teatro alla Scala.
Laws, C. (2005). 'Beckett and Kurtág', *Samuel Beckett Today / Aujourd'hui*, 15, 241–56.
Laws, C. (2013). *Headaches Among the Overtones*. New York: Rodopi
Lockwood, A. (2021). 'Interview with Pierre Audi', *Journal of Beckett Studies*, 31.2, 205–18.
Maprayil, R. (2020). 'Review: György Kurtág's *Fin de partie*', *Journal of Beckett Studies* 29.1, 142–52.
McGrath, J. (2018). *Samuel Beckett, Repetition and Modern Music*. London: Routledge.
McTighe, T. (2014). 'Billie Whitelaw was one of Beckett's greatest actors – she suffered for her art', *The Conversation*, 22 December, https://theconversation.com/billie-whitelaw-was-one-of-becketts-greatest-actors-she-suffered-for-her-art-35776 (accessed 1 March 2021).
Pountney, R. (1988). *Theatre of Shadows: Samuel Beckett's Drama 1956–1976*. Gerrards Cross: Colin Smythe.
Rákóczy, A. (2019). 'Kurtág György és Beckett. Úton a Fin de partie opera felé', *Színház Journal*, 6, 36–8.
Ross, A. (2018). 'György Kurtág, with his opera of "Endgame," proves to be Beckett's equal', *New Yorker*, 17 December, www.newyorker.com/magazine/2018/12/24/gyorgy-kurtag-with-his-opera-of-endgame-proves-to-be-becketts-equal (accessed 1 March 2021).
Temeş, B. T. (2019). 'Dead draw? An encounter between Kurtág and Beckett: the opera *Fin de Partie*', *Musica*, 1.64, 269–76.

Van Hulle, D. (2014). *Modern Manuscripts*. London: Bloomsbury.
Van Hulle, D. (2015). *The Making of Samuel Beckett's 'Krapp's Last Tape' / 'La Derniere Bande'*. Brussels and London: University Press Antwerp and Bloomsbury.
Van Hulle, D., and S. Weller (2018). *The Making of Samuel Beckett's 'Fin de Partie' / 'Endgame'*. Brussels and London: University Press Antwerp and Bloomsbury.
Verhulst, P. (2017). 'The BBC as "commissioner" of Beckett's radio plays', in D. Addyman, M. Feldman and E. Tonning (eds), *Beckett and BBC Radio: A Reassessment*. New York: Palgrave Macmillan, pp. 81–102.
Zilliacus, C. (1976). *Beckett and Broadcasting: A Study of the Works of Samuel Beckett for and in Radio and Television*. Åbo: Åbo Akademi.

11

Questioning norms in three Beckettian choreographic projections: Maguy Marin, Dominique Dupuy, Joanna Czajkowska

Evelyne Clavier

The works of Samuel Beckett have been both influenced by dance and transformed by it (see Jones, 2013; Clavier, 2018). They have also long inspired choreographers. In an article entitled 'Projections chorégraphiques beckettiennes, pour un corpus en danse', published in 2015, Stefano Genetti counted no less than fifty choreographic productions, while pointing out that his list was not exhaustive. Faced with such a diverse corpus, Genetti prefers the term 'projection' to 'adaptation' or 'transposition', as theorised by Gérard Genette (1982). In Genetti's view, such traditional concepts are not quite suitable for dance performances that transform Beckett's works so profoundly that they are not always immediately recognisable. The term 'projection', as Genetti defines it, 'désigne des mises en mouvement provenant des textes et des images scéniques beckettiens, traversant les arts et indiquant des trajectoires dans l'espace chorégraphique' (2015: 11) (refers to the setting into motion that originates in Beckett's texts and their scenic images, which crosses the arts to suggest trajectories in the choreographic space).[1] Such choreographic projections are rather to be understood as 'de prolongements, de mises en mouvement et de transfigurations, d'échos kinesthésiques et d'irradiations performatives' (2015: 2) (extensions, movements and transfigurations, kinesthetic echoes and performative irradiations), and less as one-to-one correspondences or relationships that we perhaps more typically associate with adaptation or (intermedial) transposition. From this perspective, I will examine how three choreographers from different generations as well as countries – Maguy Marin with *May B* (1981) and Dominique Dupuy with *La petite dame* (2002) in France; Joanna Czajkowska (Sopot Dance Theatre Company) with *All This This Here* (2015) in Poland – have re-enacted Beckett's works for theatre and television through dance gestures, engaging in a creative dialogue with them.

These three choreographers are similar in that their encounter with Beckett's work was very important for their own artistic careers. It urged them to question norms, to dance differently. It changed their aesthetics, creating new possibilities of gesturing for dancers and choreographers. In this chapter, I will examine how Beckett has transformed dance and, in turn, to what extent choreographic art transforms our conception and reception of his work.

Maguy Marin and 'the writer of joyful resistance'[2]

Maguy Marin, (b.1951), a French choreographer with a classical dance background, met Beckett during the gestation of *May B* (1981).[3] This choreography, mainly inspired by Beckett's early plays, made Marin a leading figure of La Nouvelle danse française, which emerged in the 1970s. The French New Dance movement promoted a revaluation of the choreographer as a creator, and 'theatrality' (*théâtralité*) as a response to abstract American Postmodern Dance.[4] From 1981, La Nouvelle danse française was supported by the left-wing political powers then in place with the creation of the Centre chorégraphique national (CCN). Even if, in its early days, *May B* was not that well received in France, this Beckettian choreographic projection has brought Marin international fame and the piece is now a 'classic' of contemporary dance, performed all around the world.[5]

Before meeting Beckett in person at his country house in Ussy-sur-Marne, Marin first encountered the Irish author's plays. After he received the Nobel Prize in 1969, Beckett's fame grew considerably, and the first play Marin read as a result of this was *Fin de partie* in 1973. She was then a young twenty-two-year-old dancer at the Mudra School of Maurice Béjart, and that reading left her 'bouleversée, ... sens dessus et dessous' (qtd in Mambouch, 2018: 09' 01"–09' 14") (upset, ... turned upside down). Here is what she says with hindsight about reading Beckett's play:

> La lecture de Beckett m'a transformée par rapport au corps. Je viens de la danse classique où il y a un rapport très fort à la jeunesse, à la beauté, à la force physique et à la performance. Ce rapport existe encore dans la danse contemporaine même si quelques chorégraphes ont travaillé avec des personnes plus âgées, moins minces. Mais dans les années où j'ai rencontré l'écriture de Beckett, c'était encore très peu courant. Je me suis dit alors: qu'est-ce qu'on fait alors des autres corps? Les gros, les petits, les maigres, les handicapés, les vieux? Avec *May B*, c'était une façon de jeter tout ça, les passe-droits, la tradition, les esthétiques convenues. (Marin, 2015)
>
> (Reading Beckett transformed me in relation to the body. I come from ballet, where there is a very strong connection to youth, beauty, physical strength and performance. This relationship still exists in contemporary dance, even though some choreographers have worked with older, less slender people. But in the years when I came across Beckett's writing, it was still very unusual. I

thought: what do we do with other bodies? The fat ones, the small ones, the skinny ones, the disabled ones, the old ones? *May B* was a way of getting rid of all that, the privileges, the tradition, the agreed aesthetics.)

Her reading of Beckett thus led Marin to broaden her representation of dancing bodies and to distance herself from the then dominant choreographic aesthetics. As Ann Cooper Albright explains in *Choreographing Difference*, these dominant aesthetics existed well before the 1970s. She asserts that '[a]s an expressive discourse comprised of physical movement, dance has traditionally privileged the able body' (1997: 56), and that 'professional dance has traditionally been structured by an exclusionary mindset that projects a very narrow vision of a dancer as white, female, thin, long-limbed, flexible, able bodied' (1997: 57). Similarly, in an interview during a round table discussion at the Centre Georges Pompidou on Beckett and the other arts in 1993, Marin stated that she wanted to bring to the choreographic stage the limited gestures of Beckett's disabled characters. In *May B*, which was inspired by *Fin de partie*, Marin shows more vulnerability than virtuosity in dance.

In the second part called 'L'anniversaire' (The Birthday), the reference to Beckett's fictional universe is very explicit. Through an aesthetic of collage, Marin stages together Flo, Vi and Ru from *Come and Go* sitting on the floor and going mad, the muted Lucky and the rope that ties him to Pozzo from *Waiting for Godot*, the blind Mr Rooney and his imposing wife Mrs Rooney from *All That Fall*, Hamm the paralytic in his wheelchair with his servant Clov from *Endgame* and May from *Footfalls*, who goes from group to group carrying a birthday cake she cannot prevent from being shared unfairly. Following in Beckett's theatrical footsteps, Marin achieves with *May B* what Jacques Rancière (2004) has called a new 'distribution of the sensible', making visible and audible in dance those whom society would sometimes prefer not to see and hear: people with disabilities, those individuals without fixed borders, the excluded, the defeated of history. Marin thus shares with Beckett a 'political imagination' close to that of the Left (see Morin, 2017), which is characterised by a great attention and consideration for those who are despised and rejected, and whom certain authoritarian regimes tend to believe are superfluous.

However, *May B* is not a mere illustration of the Beckettian fictional universe. During their two-hour meeting in his country house in Ussy-sur-Marne, the Irish artist encouraged Marin to make a personal piece in relation to everyday life, representing 'the man in the street' (Marin, 2012). Beckett, who is generally considered to be uncompromising about adaptations of his work, wanted Marin to emancipate herself from his text, encouraging her 'à le mordre, à le digérer, à le mâcher de façon très libre et très animale'

(Marin, 1994: 77) (to bite it, to digest it, to chew it up in a very free and animalistic way). Of the text of *Fin de partie* only the opening sentence – 'Fini, c'est fini, ça va finir, ça va peut-être finir' (Beckett, 2007: 13) – remains, uttered by the ten characters in the first part, called 'Les Gilles',[6] and by a single character on stage at the end of the last part, called 'Le voyage' (The Journey). Beckett granted Marin permission to do *May B* and to resort to the choreographic art that he himself was about to experiment with in *Quad*. Because she had choreographed Franz Schubert's 'Death and the Maiden' two years earlier,[7] he also suggested that she use two Schubert lieder which, as Beckett told her, 'portent la douleur' (Marin, 2012) (carry the pain). These are 'Der Doppelgänger' and 'Der Leiermann' ('The Hurdy-Gurdy Man'), the lied that closes *Winterreise* and opens *May B*.[8] 'Der Leiermann' speaks of the loneliness and failure of the artist,[9] but also of the possibility of dialogue between the arts and artists. After listening to this lied in the dark,[10] the ten performers begin to dance *May B* with the 'stiff, staggering walk' (Beckett, 2009c: 89) of Clov in *Endgame*. Below are the lyrics of the lied translated into English:

> There, beyond the village,
> stands a hurdy-gurdy player;
> with numb fingers
> he plays as best he can.
>
> Barefoot on the ice
> he totters to and fro,
> and his little plate
> remains forever empty.
>
> No one wants to listen,
> no one looks at him,
> and dogs growl
> around the old man.
>
> And he lets everything go on
> as it will;
> he plays, and his hurdy-gurdy
> never stops.
>
> Strange old man,
> shall I go with you?
> Would you turn your hurdy-gurdy
> to my songs?[11]

Marin heard Beckett and the pain that his work carries. She also sensed his tenderness, which she has channelled into *May B*. As a collective art form, dance allowed Marin to question our 'capacités d'agir' (2002: 76) (capacities to act). In her work, the group rather than the couple is what enables the survival of and the resistance to what she calls 'la catastrophe des corps et des relations' (2015) (the catastrophe of bodies and relationships), a catastrophe she perceives in *Waiting for Godot* and *Endgame*. In these two plays, the bodies are old, sick and disabled. All relationships are based on dominance and subjugation, marked by egotism. In *May B*, the moment when the ten dancers take their shoes off and carry them to the front of the stage, much like Estragon in *Waiting for Godot*, is an example of mutual support to one another.[12] Each of the five women leans on the shoulder of one of the five men to raise their legs and take off their two shoes, one after the other. Symmetrically, the five men repeat their movements, recalling the scene from *Come and Go* where Vi, Ru and Flo '*hold hands*' (Beckett, 2009b: 74) to form a sort of Celtic knot. Again, the gestures also point to *Waiting for Godot*, when in the second act Didi and Gogo try to help Pozzo and Lucky but end up entangled in each other on the ground.

Marin understood the humour inherent in Beckett's work, a humour she presents as 'une fissure dans la catastrophe des corps et des relations' (2015) (a fissure in the catastrophe of bodies and relationships). She has a personal vision of the Irish artist that is close to Alain Badiou's. The French philosopher explains that the concept of 'increvable désir' ('tireless desire') took shape when he was able to stop typecasting Beckett as a writer 'convaincu qu'en dehors de l'obstination des mots, il n'y a que le noir et le vide' (Badiou, 1995: 9) ('convinced that beyond the obstinacy of words, there is only darkness and void'; Badiou, 2003: 40). He was able to discern in Beckett 'un amour puissant pour l'obstination humaine, pour l'increvable désir, pour l'humanité réduite à sa malignité et à son entêtement' (Badiou, 1995: 74–5) ('a powerful love for human obstinacy, for tireless desire, for humanity reduced to its stubbornness and malice'; Badiou, 2003: 75).

For Marin, he is 'l'écrivain de la résistance joyeuse' (2012) (the writer of joyful resistance), a point of view that deviates from the tragic productions of Beckett's work which have long prevailed in France. With *May B*, she allows the French public to experience Beckett's humour. This 'humour kinesthésique' (Bolens, 2016) (kinesthetic humour) that arises in *May B* from the interaction of body tempo and tone as well as their variations puts the spectator in a state of receptivity that frees them from their initial feeling of unease when faced with the disabled characters' 'gestuelle rétrécie' (Marin, 1994: 77) (restricted gesture), as they appear on the choreographic stage. These interacting gestures and body dynamics then demonstrate a kinetic style of resistance to hindrance. The tonal and rhythmic intensification of this first part called 'Les Gilles' brings the spectator closer to those on stage whose lives might be considered tiny, even superfluous. This 'kinesthetic humour' acts on the spectators, offering them the opportunity to free themselves from prejudices relating to 'handicaps' and to reconsider 'disability' in terms of agency rather than deficiency. Through this modified vision, *May B* embodies both Beckett's and Marin's political imaginations, which, in addition to reshaping French dance practice, encourages the spectators to envisage a more inclusive society.

Dominique Dupuy and 'dancing old'

Like Marin, the choreographer Dominique Dupuy (b.1931) frees Beckett from the category of the absurd, to which he has long been assigned against his will (see Juliet, 1999; Bernold, 2006) and which still persists today, particularly in French secondary education. Whereas Marin evokes 'the joyful resistance' that runs through Beckett's works, Dupuy speaks of 'le miracle de l'encore' (2016: 331) (the miracle of the still-happening), the French word *miracle* being understood in its etymological sense of 'amazement' and the French word *encore* in its sense of 'continuation' and 'endurance'. For the elderly choreographer, dancing with Beckett also means 'danser vieux' (dancing old), that is still being able to dance at an advanced age. For him, all of Beckett's theatrical works contain 'une danse latente' (Dupuy, 2007) (a latent dance),[13] which eventually led the Irish author to *Quad*, seen by Dupuy as 'une chorégraphie majeure du XXe siècle' (2014b: 20) (a major choreography of the twentieth century). By developing Beckett's work in the direction of dance, Dupuy similarly paves the way for innovative, less pessimistic approaches.

The French dancer and choreographer, who has been instrumental for the recognition and development of modern and contemporary dance in France after the Second World War,[14] attended the premiere of *En attendant Godot* at the Théâtre de Babylone in 1953. Living in Paris, he also attended a performance of *Oh les beaux jours* with Madeleine Renaud as Winnie and Jean-Louis Barrault as Willie in 1963, in addition to the many revivals of the play that followed. Much later, in 2002, Dupuy condensed *Oh les beaux jours* into a short nine-minute choreography which he entitled *La petite dame*.[15] He danced it as Willie, together with his partner Françoise Dupuy (1930–2022) as Winnie, when they were both over seventy years old, transforming Beckett's play to such an extent that it was almost unrecognisable. Genetti was the first to analyse what he considered to be a 'filiation chorégraphique' (2011) (choreographic filiation) between *La petite dame* and *Oh les beaux jours*, before using the term 'projection' later on.

Unlike Marin, Dupuy never met Beckett in person, yet he might have. In 1953, with his partner Françoise Dupuy, he was also on stage at the Théâtre de Babylone in Paris, where *En attendant Godot* was first performed on 5 January. They were giving a recital entitled 'Dominique et Françoise' on 2, 3 and 4 February of that year, while there was a break in performances of *En attendant Godot* (Dupuy, 2014a). The Dupuys knew the actor and director Roger Blin well. Françoise Dupuy worked with him before joining Jean Weidt, a German expressionist dancer exiled in Paris, with whom Blin also trained. For Dominique and Françoise Dupuy, Blin is one of those theatre practitioners who helped introduce German modern dance to French audiences during the interwar period and were themselves influenced by it. In *Une danse à l'œuvre*, Françoise Dupuy evokes the 'transcendance poétique' (Dupuy and Dupuy, 2002: 211) (poetic transcendence) that marks Blin's productions of *En attendant Godot* and *Oh les beaux jours*. She and her partner were susceptible to Blin's directorial approach, which helped free them from realistic and psychological acting styles and allowed poetry to penetrate theatre, which thus became infused with the abstract qualities usually associated with dance.

There is a convergence between Dupuy's choreographic research and Blin's work as a director, who, thanks to his experience in modern dance with Weidt, freed theatre from its mimetic legacy. Through Blin, Dupuy became interested in Beckett and saw some of the Parisian theatre performances that shaped his own views, writing: 'Garde-toi de la danse! Il y a quelque chose de beckettien dans l'exercice de la danse contemporaine telle que je la conçois' (2010: 30) (Watch out for dance! There is something Beckettian about contemporary dance as I see it). He also added that his research led him to dance 'l'indansable' (2010: 30) (the undanceable), a term inspired by Beckett's own pursuit of the 'unnamable' or 'ineffable', i.e. that which cannot be expressed in language.[16] Dupuy explored the undanceable in *La petite dame*. At first glance, Beckett's play seems the exact opposite of dance because it brings the undanceable to its paroxysm: 'No movement possible in the first act except of Oberleib [upper body], no movement of any kind possible in the second' (2014: 383), as he wrote to American director Alan Schneider on 9 December 1960. The link between *Oh les beaux jours* and *La petite dame* seems flimsy. Not much appears to be left of Beckett's two-act play that is centred on speech and a bag with items. In *La petite dame*, Françoise Dupuy transforms Winnie, who is described as '[a]bout fifty, well preserved, blond for preference, plump, arms and shoulders bare, low bodice, big bosom* (Beckett, 2010: 271), and never stops talking, into a very old, seated dancer who does not speak. Also, the scenic device of the mound with a hole containing the body in *Oh les beaux jours* has been replaced with a small Plexiglas table, an everyday object that is not particularly Beckettian. This Plexiglas table represents a kind of 'armure légère' (Dupuy, 2011: 43) (light armour),[17] one that prevents any 'gesticulations outrancières, insensées' (2011: 43) (outrageous, senseless gesticulations) and accentuates the weight of presence, which consists in doing nothing and just being there.[18] The scenic device thus keeps Dupuy from dancing by putting her in an uncomfortable position that is not conducive to ample gesturing. The position of the dancer, seated on the floor without any support for her back, legs stretched out in front of her at right angles, is tiring, especially for an elderly woman. At the same time, it implies an economy of gesture that is typical of old age and meets the 'subtracting' poetics of Beckett (qtd in Knowlson, 1996: 352). Animated by her partner's gaze, the old woman succeeds in mobilising herself again and inventing, with the invisible objects in the bag, a minimalist dance of the eyes, head and arms.

In *La petite dame*, Dominique and Françoise Dupuy together reconstruct Winnie and Willie as a couple, a unity broken up in *Oh les beaux jours*. They accentuate the persistence of tenderness and love by removing objects that are charged with death and eroticism – the Old Brownie and the obscene postcard – as well as through the gestures of old age and dance. By reconceptualising *Oh les beaux jours* in such a way, *La petite dame* is basically exploring the potentialities of old age in order to propose an innovative form of dance. Performing *Oh les beaux jours* at over seventy years of age also represents for the Dupuys a chance to show their obstinate love of dance, to which they have both devoted their lives. Their choreography testifies to the 'hard desire to last'[19] as a couple of old dancers and subverts stereotypical representations of old age that often consider it as a time of inactivity and waiting for death. This imbues the ageing body with an alternative sense of agency, one that is perhaps un-Beckettian in spirit but at the same time foregrounds minimalistic movements that are.

Joanna Czajkowska: liberating the four ghosts of *Quad*

Joanna Czajkowska (b.1974), a forty-six-year-old Polish dancer, choreographer and pedagogue from a younger generation, did not meet the author either. She discovered *Waiting for Godot* in high school and later encountered other works by him through Professor Tomasz Wiśniewski.[20] Czajkowska became particularly fascinated with *Quad*, '[a] piece for four players, light, and percussion' (Beckett, 2010: 141), which notes that for actors '[s]ome ballet training [is] desirable' (2010: 145). In 2005, more than twenty years after the production of *Quad* for the Süddeutscher Rundfunk (*Quadrat 1+2*, 1982),[21] Czajkowska performed *Quad version 6*,[22] a choreographic rewriting of 'a crazy invention for TV', as Beckett called the piece (2016: 522), which earned her company some renown. In 2015, she performed *Quad* again in a dance video whose Polish title, *To wszystko tutaj*, was translated as *All This This Here* in the credits (18' 21").²³ The title comes from a line in 'what is the word' (Beckett, 2009b: 133), Beckett's last poem and his own English self-translation of 'Comment dire'. Together with the performance *All Seen. OHIO*, this dance video is one of two parts in a project called *Beckett Poruszenie*, which Czajkowska translated as *Beckett – Moves Me*, the term 'move' being understood as both motional and emotional (Clavier and Czajkowska, 2020: 7).

Czajkowska has chosen Beckett's works many times for the dance theatre productions she leads with her company in the city of Sopot. She explains her choice as follows:

> Nous frotter à Samuel Beckett a résulté à chaque fois d'un besoin intérieur de parler de l'existence, de notre existence. *Quad version 6* a été conçu à un moment où nous étions assez désespérés et où notre travail artistique nous semblait dans une impasse. C'est à la première de *Quad version 6* que nous nous sommes aperçus que cette pièce sur l'enfermement parlait de notre propre sensation de claustrophobie en de notre profond désespoir intérieur. (Clavier and Czajkowska, 2020: 3)

> (We got closer to Samuel Beckett every time we had an inner need to talk about existence, about our existence. *Quad version 6* was conceived at a time when we were quite desperate and our artistic work seemed to have reached an impasse. It was at the premiere of *Quad version 6* that we realised this piece about confinement spoke to our own sense of claustrophobia and deep inner despair.)

The confinement in *Quad* is obvious, as the four ghostly characters follow the same route pre-traced by an external authority. During their journey, they carefully avoid the centre, so as to never meet, and they also move around without seeing or hearing the others or what is happening around them. The originality of this 'spectrovision'²⁴ consists in not situating the ghostly in the beyond but in mental and social life. In her *Plea for a Measure of Abnormality*, first published in France in 1978 as *Plaidoyer pour une certaine anormalité*, psychoanalyst Joyce MacDougall evoked 'the spectre of *normative normality*' which hovers over mental and social life (1998: 18; original emphasis). For MacDougall, '*normative normality*' or 'pathological normality' is 'an *overadaptation* to external reality' (1998: 18; original emphasis) where 'everything is likely to happen in a closed circuit' (1998: 224). The subject is distanced both from itself and from others, and by dint of wanting to conform. He or she cannot engage in a process of individuation and develop creativity, whether individually or socially. This is how the ghosts of *Quad* appear, reproducing the same path and the same gestures over and over again, those of bowing one's head and moving one's hips slightly to the left in a strategy of avoidance. *Quad* stages what, in his 1963 book *Stigma*, Erving Goffman called 'a phantom normalcy' (1990: 143), which reflects a model of society where the acceptance of difference is subject to conditions and deviation is sometimes associated with deviance. Like Marin and Dupuy, Czajkowska has transformed Beckett's works and turned the normative ghosts of *Quad* into 'creative bodies' (Dennis, 2018) with a sense of agency.

After *Quad version 6*, the company returned to Beckettian works in a different mood. By the time they embarked on the project *Beckett – Moves Me*, Czajkowska and her partner, Jacek Krawczyk, were more self-confident and had acquired greater artistic maturity. The dance video *All This This Here* was shot on location at various places in Sopot, a seaside town on the Baltic Sea near the city of Gdańsk. In this context, the choreographers recycle various motifs from the Beckettian universe that immediately beckon to the audience: the bowler hats from *Waiting for Godot*, the chairs from *Ohio Impromptu*, Flo Vi and Ru from *Come and Go* sitting in the catholic cemetery of Sopot or the walks in the square of *Quad* relocated to a park in the city. *Quad* is used a first time in the passage between 04' 02" and 05' 04", as the five female performers and the male performer move with jerky gestures that are reminiscent of puppets. The second time, in the passage between 11' 35" and 12' 19", they no longer avoid the centre but pass through it. A small jump marks the entry into the 'danger zone' (Beckett, 2009a: 95) of *Quad*, the third time in a sequence between 16' 40" and 18' 12", where the six performers dare to make contact, whether it is to bump into, to push back or to lean on each other, to fall or to get up, as in *Waiting for Godot*. They have faces, make eye contact and look upwards together at the end of this dance video, where the camera is not a fixed eye as in *Quad* but a very mobile one, free to move around.

This is an invigorating choreographic projection of *Quad* in which the Sopot Dance Theatre Company's performers display an energy that is very different from the 'exhaustion' that Gilles Deleuze (1992) saw in the figures. Their energy is harnessed in running, jumping, falling and recovering, which blows up the square and the combinative art originally at work in Beckett's *Quad*. In doing so, the dancers considerably transform the 'spectrovision', which results in a veritable ballet whose ghosts have metamorphosed into beings of flesh and blood now capable of shedding their 'normative normality', of seeing the other and rediscovering numerous gestures. It seems as though *All This This Here* had freed the four ghosts of *Quad* from their confinement through a form of re-embodiment. Like Dupuy and Marin before her, Czajkowska emancipates herself from the norms of dance, but also from the norms of Beckett's work and those of the critical discourse surrounding it. Indeed, through dance, she empowers Beckett's figures and reconceptualises *Quad*.

Conclusion

At the end of this journey exploring three Beckettian choreographic projections, which testify to a very diverse range of aesthetics from dance theatre to minimalism, we have seen that Beckett's work allows dance to interrogate itself and to renew dancers' performances. It leads them to question norms, both choreographic and social, and to break out of dominant formats and formatting. It allows dance to show what it has been barred from showing and dancing before, such as disabilities in *May B* or old age in *La petite dame*. Beckett's work makes it possible to continue to dance, by channelling kinaesthetic creativity and energy to the three choreographers discussed in this chapter: Maguy Marin, Dominique (and Françoise) Dupuy, and Joanna Czajkowska. By allowing itself to take liberties with Beckett's texts, to distort and condense them, dance gives new impetus to his works and reinvigorates them, perhaps reversing but at the same time enriching their potential meanings or interpretations. The three choreographic projections of Beckett's works highlighted in this chapter shift their centre of gravity, enabling less pessimistic, more joyful as well as hopeful, and finally more curative readings of them.

Notes

1. All translations are my own except otherwise stated.
2. 'écrivain de la résistance joyeuse' is an expression by Marin from an unpublished interview given at the Arsenal de Metz on 14 March 2012, before the performance of *Salves* (2011). In the interview, she attributed to Beckett the phrase 'Quand on est dans la merde jusqu'au cou, il ne reste qu'à chanter' (When you are up to your neck in shit, all you can do is sing), which a dancer writes on a blackboard in *Salves*.
3. *May B* premiered on 4 November 1981 at the Théâtre Municipal d'Angers. Music: Franz Schubert, Gilles de Binche and Gavin Bryars.
4. For a clarification of the term 'theatrality' and its relation to 'theatricality', see Alter (1981).
5. See *L'urgence d'agir* (2019), a film devoted to Marin by her son David Mambouch. An article about the 1983 American Dance Festival, written by Anna Kisselgoff in the *New York Times*, helped to make her work more known. See www.nytimes.com/1983/07/13/arts/dance-french-troupe-at-north-carolina-festival.html (accessed 13 August 2021).
6. A reference to a stock figure of the Carnival of Binche in Belgium, where Marin lived (in Brussels) while studying at Mudra. The five men and five women of *May B* dance to the fanfare tunes of this famous Carnival. Her figures, with their white clay-coated faces, are also reminiscent of the faces of the Gilles, and one woman wears their characteristic white bonnet.

7 *La jeune fille et la mort* (1979). Choreographer: Maguy Marin. Dancers: Corinne Barbara, Christiane Glick, Maguy Marin, Isabelle Rius, Sylvia Sadaoui, Daniel Ambash. Music: Quartet in D Minor 'Death And The Maiden' by Franz Schubert, performed by the Quartetto Italiano. Production: Ballet Théâtre de l'Arche. In *May B*, Marin used 'Death and the Maiden' again for the second part called 'L'anniversaire'. It also features in Beckett's radio play *All That Fall*.

8 *Winterreise* (*Winter Journey*) is a cycle of twenty-four lieder for piano and voice, composed by Franz Schubert in 1827 from poems by Wilhelm Müller. 'Der Doppelgänger' often recurs as a motif in Beckett's work, for example *Film* (see Beloborodova, 2019: 302–5; Van Hulle and Nixon, 2013: 95–6).

9 There is a fragment of text from *Three Dialogues* that Marin quotes in French in 'En vrac…' (2017: 35): 'Admettre qu'être un artiste c'est échouer comme nul autre n'ose échouer, que l'échec constitue son univers et son refus de désertion' (Beckett, 2012: 29). In Beckett's own words: 'to admit that to be an artist is to fail, as no other dare fail, that failure is his world and the shrink from it desertion' (1983: 145).

10 This beginning invokes Beckett's radio plays, famously described as 'coming out of the dark' and intended 'for voices, not bodies' (2014: 63), which he considered the domain of theatre.

11 Translated by Richard Wigmore. Original Text : 'Drüben hinter'm Dorfe, / Steht ein Leiermann, / Und mit starren Fingern / dreht er was er kann. / Barfuss auf dem Eise / Schwankt er hin und her; / Und sein kleiner Teller / bleibt ihm immer leer. / Keiner mag ihn hören, / Keiner sieht ihn an; / Und die Hunde knurren / um den alten Mann. / Und er lässt es gehen / Alles, wie es will, / Dreht, und seine Leier / Steht ihm nimmer still. / Wunderlicher Alter, / Soll ich mit dir geh'n? / Willst zu meinen Liedern / deine Leier dreh'n?' The original poem is by Wilhelm Müller (1824). See www.oxfordlieder.co.uk/song/2046 (accessed 23 August 2021).

12 This moment occurs between 17' 09" and 18' 22" in the film *May B* by Charles Picq and Luc Riolon (2000).

13 I am grateful to Dominique Dupuy for sending me a transcript of his unpublished text by e-mail on 17 April 2016.

14 'From their [Dominique Dupuy and his wife Françoise] first lecture entitled *Elaborating Modern Dance*, delivered on 24 May 1949 at The International Archives of Paris, to their most recent works, all their artistic actions and desires have tended to promote, one might say, the *act* of dancing, both in the cultural landscape as well as the mind of the audience' (Corsino and Corsino, 2017: 178; original emphasis).

15 *La petite dame* is the opening of *Seule?* (2003). Choreography by Dominique Dupuy, danced in silence with musical interludes. Set elements by Jean-Pierre Schneider. Performed at the studio Le Regard du Cygne in Paris as part of *Mémoire vive*.

16 See Beckett's letter of 9 July 1937 to Axel Kaun in which he introduced the concept of a 'Literatur des Unworts' (2009d: 515), translated into English by George Craig as 'literature of the non-word' (2009d: 520).

17 The full quote goes: 'Dans un texte truculent, succulent, Gordon Craig, grand homme de théâtre anglais, suggère de barrer la route à l'activité intempestive du danseur avec son corps, en l'emprisonnant dans une "armure légère" qui fasse obstacle aux débordements des gestes gratuits, inutiles et l'assigne à n'en produire que la part la plus essentielle' (Dupuy, 2011: 43). (In a truculent, succulent text, Gordon Craig, a great man of English theatre, suggests blocking the way to the dancer's untimely activity with his body, imprisoning it in a 'light armour' that prevents the overflowing of gratuitous, useless gestures and assigns it to produce only the most essential part of them.)
18 See Roquet (2019: 170–8). For her, this quality of presence emanates from older artists and is the result of a lifetime's work.
19 In reference to Paul Éluard's *Le dur désir de durer* (1946).
20 Tomasz Wiśniewski is the Associate Director of Research at the Institute of English and American Studies at the University of Gdańsk. He is the founder of the festival Between. Pomiędzy and of the Beckett Research Group at Gdańsk.
21 See www.youtube.com/watch?v=4ZDRfnICq9M (accessed 13 August 2021).
22 *Quad version 6* is the English translation by Johanna Czajkowska of *Kwadrat Wersja 6,* performed at the Sopot Theatre. Choreography and interpretation: David Cassel, Iwona Strupiechowksa, Jacek Krawczyk, Joanna Czajkowska. Music: Grzegorz Welizarowicz, Rafat Dektos. Lighting director: Adam Akerman.
23 Concept: Joanna Czajkowska. Music: Mariusz Noskowiak. Director: Piotr Czarnecki (Magenta Project). Choreography, improvisation, costumes: Joanna Czajkowska, Joanna Nadrowska, Barbara Pedzich, Kalina Porazinska, Grazyna Stabon. Consultant: Dr Tomasz Wiśniewski. Production assistant: Andrzrej Pawloski. See www.youtube.com/watch?v=aDdQITh7WNU (accessed 13 August 2021).
24 I borrow the term 'spectrovision' from Elfriede Jelinek: 'Die Leinwand ist der Ort, wo etwas erscheint und spurlos wieder verschwindet. ... Film ist überhaupt "Gespentersehen"' (1997) (The screen is the place where something appears and disappears without a trace. ... Films are actually 'spectrovisions').

References

Alter, J. (1981). 'From text to performance: semiotics of theatricality', *Poetics Today,* 2.3, 113–39.
Badiou, A. (1995). *Beckett. L'increvable désir*. Paris: Hachette.
Badiou, A. (2003). *On Beckett*. Trans. N. Power and A. Toscano. Manchester: Clinamen.
Beckett, S. (1983). 'Three Dialogues', in R. Cohn (ed.), *Disjecta: Miscellaneous Writings and a Dramatic Fragment*. London: John Calder, pp. 138–45.
Beckett, S. (2007). *Fin de partie*. Paris: Les Éditions de Minuit.
Beckett, S. (2009a). *All That Fall and Other Plays for Radio and Screen*. Pref. E. Frost. London: Faber and Faber.

Beckett, S. (2009b). *Company, Ill Seen Ill Said, Worstward Ho, Stirrings Still*. Ed. D. Van Hulle. London: Faber and Faber.
Beckett, S. (2009c). *Endgame*. Pref. Rónán McDonald. London: Faber and Faber.
Beckett, S. (2009d). *The Letters of Samuel Beckett Volume I: 1929–1940*. Ed. M. Dow Fehsenfeld and L. More Overbeck. Cambridge: Cambridge University Press.
Beckett, S. (2010). *Happy Days*. Pref. J. Knowlson. London: Faber and Faber.
Beckett, S. (2012). *Trois dialogues*. Trans. E. Fournier. Paris: Les Éditions de Minuit.
Beckett, S. (2014). *The Letters of Samuel Beckett Volume III: 1957–1965*. Ed. G. Craig, M. Dow Fehsenfeld, D. Gunn and L. More Overbeck. Cambridge: Cambridge University Press.
Beckett, S. (2016). *The Letters of Samuel Beckett Volume IV: 1966–1989*. Ed. G. Craig, M. Dow Fehsenfeld, D. Gunn and L. More Overbeck. Cambridge: Cambridge University Press.
Beloborodova, O. (2019). *The Making of Samuel Beckett's 'Play' / 'Comédie' and 'Film'*. Brussels and London: University Press Antwerp and Bloomsbury.
Bernold, A. (2006). *L'amitié de Beckett: 1979–1989*. Paris: Hermann.
Bolens G. (2016). *L'humour et le savoir des corps, Don Quichotte, Tristram Shandy et le rire du lecteur*. Rennes: Presses Universitaires de Rennes.
Clavier, E. (2018). 'Samuel Beckett and modern dance', in O. Beloborodova, D. Van Hulle and P. Verhulst (eds), *Beckett and Modernism*. London and New York: Palgrave MacMillan, pp. 193–205.
Clavier, E., and J. Czajkowska (2020). 'Entretien avec Joanna Czajkowska', *Recherches en danse*, 1–9, http://journals.openedition.org/danse/2967 (accessed 16 August 2021).
Cooper Albright, A. (1997). *Choreographing Difference: The Body and Identity in Contemporary Dance*. Middletown, CT: Wesleyan University Press.
Corsino, N., and N. Corsino (2017). 'Never in fashion, yet always modern', in F. Dupuy and D. Dupuy, *Françoise et Dominique Dupuy. Album*. Dijon: Éditions Analogues, p. 178.
Deleuze, G. (1992). 'L'Épuisé', in S. Beckett, *Quad et autres pièces pour la télévision suivi de L'Épuisé*. Paris: Les Éditions de Minuit, pp. 55–106.
Dennis, A. (2018). 'Compulsive bodies, creative bodies: Beckett and agency in the 21st century', *Journal of Beckett Studies*, 27.1, 5–21.
Dupuy, D. (2007). Untitled text written for the defence of Katerina Kanelli's doctoral thesis in general and comparative literature, 'L'effet Beckett: pour une nouvelle image du corps', defended at the Université Paris, 8 June. Unpublished.
Dupuy, D. (2010). 'Danse, théâtre, le souffle musagète', *Études théâtrales*, 49.3, 29–31.
Dupuy, D. (2011). *La Sagesse du Danseur*. Paris: Éditions Jean-Clause Béhar.
Dupuy, D. (2014a). Interview with E. Clavier, 8 March, Paris. Unpublished.
Dupuy, D. (2014b). '"Un adepte du cerf-volant", lettre ouverte adressée aux collégiens et collégiennes du collège Romain Rolland de Clichy-sous-bois', in *On n'en finit jamais avec Beckett*. Paris: Association Ode après l'Orage, pp. 19–20.
Dupuy, D. (2016). 'A propos d'*Acte sans paroles I*. Le miracle de l'encore ou l'art d'enfiler son caleçon un pied après l'autre au risque d'une implacable perte d'équilibre', *Samuel Beckett Today / Aujourd'hui*, 28.2, 331–7.

Dupuy, D., and F. Dupuy (2002). *Une danse à l'œuvre*. Pantin: Centre national de la danse.
Genette, G. (1982). *Palimpsestes. La littérature au second degré*. Paris: Seuil.
Genetti, S. (2011). 'Filiations chorégraphiques: Winnie selon Béjart et chez les Dupuy', *Samuel Beckett Today / Aujourd'hui*, 23, 49–62.
Genetti, S. (2015). 'Projections chorégraphiques beckettiennes: pour un corpus en danse', *Recherches en danse*, 1–19, https://journals.openedition.org/danse/1211 (accessed 16 August 2021).
Goffman E. (1990 [1963]). *Stigma: Notes on the Management of Spoiled Identity*. London: Penguin.
Jelinek, E. (1997). 'Zu *Carnival of Souls*', www.elfriedejelinek.com/fgrusel.htm (accessed 16 August 2021).
Jones, S. (2013). 'Samuel Beckett and choreography', in *Literature, Modernism, and Dance*. Oxford: Oxford University Press, pp. 279–309.
Juliet, C. (1999). *Rencontres avec Samuel Beckett*. Paris: Editions P.O.L.
Knowlson, J. (1996). *Damned to Fame: The Life of Samuel Beckett*. London: Bloomsbury.
MacDougall, J. (1998). *Plea for a Measure of Abnormality*. Routledge: New York.
Mambouch, D. (2018). *L'urgence d'agir*. DVD. Naia Productions, la Compagnie Maguy Marin, le CNC, la Région Auvergne Rhône-Alpes Cinéma.
Marin, M. (1994). '"May B. Maguy Marin": intervention retranscrite par J.C Lallias, à l'occasion d'un débat organisé par Tom Bishop, le vendredi 18 juin 1993, consacré aux relations de Samuel Beckett avec les autres arts', *Théâtre d'aujourd'hui*, 3, 77.
Marin, M. (2002), 'Capacités d'agir…', in G. Daret and S. Lebard (eds), *La danse, corps manifestes. Lyon Biennale de la danse*. Lyon: Artha, pp. 76–9.
Marin, M. (2012). Interview with E. Clavier, 14 March, Arsenal of Metz. Unpublished.
Marin, M. (2015). Interview with E. Clavier. 20 April, Ramdam, Sainte-Foy-les-Lyon. Unpublished.
Marin, M. (2017). 'En vrac…', *Théâtre / Public (Maguy Marin)*, 226, 28–37.
Morin, E. (2017). *Beckett's Political Imagination*. Cambridge: Cambridge University Press.
Picq, C., L. Riolon and Compagnie Maguy Marin (2000). *May B*. DVD. Angers: 24 Images.
Rancière, J. (2004). *Politics of Aesthetics: The Distribution of the Sensible*. Trans. G. Rockhill. London and New York: Continuum.
Roquet, C. (2019). *Vu du geste. Interpréter le geste dansé*. Pantin: Centre national de la danse.
Van Hulle, D., and M. Nixon (2013). *Samuel Beckett's Library*. Cambridge: Cambridge University Press.

12

'I'll give you just enough to keep you from dying': power dynamics disclosed in Tania Bruguera's *Endgame*

Luz María Sánchez Cardona

In April 2017 Cuban artist and activist Tania Bruguera had her directorial debut at the Biennial of Contemporary Arts (BoCA) in Porto (Portugal), introducing her personal take on Samuel Beckett's *Endgame*, a play that she has been acquainted with since 1998, from her early years as an art student and practitioner.[1] The international visibility that Bruguera's short- and long-term projects have obtained in recent years makes her approach to Beckett's *Endgame* interesting to follow. It is placed at the centre of the political discourse of a practitioner whose artistic strategies reveal situations in which citizens live within a permanent state of control, and *Endgame / Fin de partie* deals with shifting power roles, confinement, psychological torture, imposed scarcity and famine politics.

Bruguera's adaptation of *Endgame* is a culmination of some of her recurring ideas about power dynamics in contemporary society, and especially in Cuba, her home country. One of her most visible political gestures was her refusal to participate in the 13th Havana Biennial of 2019, openly criticising the Cuban Government's need to 'whitewash' its image, after imposing Decree 349 that criminalises artists' activities in Cuba. Her continuous denunciations of the lack of freedom of speech in her home country have placed her under arrest on several occasions, most notoriously in July 2021, framed by demonstrations that ended in a series of detentions of artists and activists. She also received the 2018 Hyundai Commission for the Turbine Hall at the Tate Modern in London, for which she presented an artwork that addressed global immigration, and in 2021 she was awarded the Documenta15/Arnold Bode Prize.[2]

Bruguera's approach to *Endgame* is a clear example of how artists may choose to include Beckett's works as *strategies within* their own practice, allowing them to stress specific ideas that place the artwork outside of the contemporary art landscape and move it into a transdisciplinary arena within the social and political reality as a background. In this chapter, I examine Bruguera's ongoing interest in *Endgame* and her take on it as director of the play. When she approaches, examines and 'appropriates' *Endgame*, she builds upon a strategy that has been fundamental to establishing and expanding the boundaries of her art practice: 'I don't want art that points to a thing. I want art that is the thing' ('Activist Art', n.d.). By adapting and re-enacting *Endgame*, Bruguera is looking to create an art 'that *is* the thing', bringing Beckett's work to the lingua franca of contemporary art practices.

Bruguera's political gestures

In order to help us understand her art practice while trying to avoid confusion and reduction, Bruguera developed 'theoretical terms' such as 'Arte de Conducta [Behavior Art], Political Timing Specific Art, Arte Útil [Useful Art], Est-Ética [Aest-ethics]' and the 'borrowed' term 'Artivism' (Bishop, 2020). It constitutes an attempt to discuss her artwork outside of genres and mediums. For Patricia Phelps de Cisneros, these terms *invoke*

> an art that produces energy over objects; one that builds awareness of problems and discrepancies and solves those problems creatively; one that directly confronts power; one that discovers the vernacular processes of art legible to those 'outside' of art history; an art that emphasizes ethics over aesthetics and has the capacity to achieve greater social justice. (qtd in Bishop, 2020: 7)

Bruguera divides her practice depending on the *momentum* it takes to build up in short-term artworks. These can be understood as timely interventions with political glimpses that consist of performances/participatory actions installed in a given place to address socio-political situations. These actions run parallel to her long-term, community-based projects that 'go beyond representation to create democratic institutions and platforms' ('Tania Bruguera', n.d.) and that Bruguera pairs with her instigation of concepts such as the Hannah Arendt International Institute for Artivism, a school and exhibition space in Havana (since 2016); the Escuela de arte útil (School of Useful Art, since 2013) that looks at art as a tool for social and political change; the *Immigrant Movement International* (since 2010), in which Bruguera addresses the contemporary migration crisis; and the Cátedra Arte de Conducta (Behaviour Art School) that she ran in Havana from 2003 to 2009. For Bruguera, changes in contemporary art practices cannot be explained with 'medium-specific terminology', since 'art is redefining itself in terms of its function (what is art for?), its relationship to the audience (participants, collaborators, co-authors, users), the resources it works with (legislations, civic society, direct politics), its impact (populism, modes of alternative governance, dissolution in culture) and its preservation (reenactment, delegation, sustainability)' (qtd in Bishop, 2020: 11).

Among Bruguera's short-term projects is *Tatlin's Whisper*, a series of works named after the Soviet constructivist artist Vladimir Tatlin addressing 'the relationship between artists and power at certain historical moments' while evoking 'the mandate of art for social change' (Bishop, 2020: 75). For Bruguera '[the] idea behind the series is that people get anesthetized to news from other places', so she 'decided to work with an image that represented such news and bring it to the people's real experience, so they could no longer be indifferent' (2020: 38). 'Tatlin's Whisper #5' (2008), made for London's Tate Modern, requires two mounted police officers to use crowd control techniques on the audience. In contrast to 'Tatlin's Whisper #6', this intervention 'is not political timing specific' (2020: 74). Nevertheless, its political dimension becomes clear when Bruguera observes that point 3.i of the contract with the Tate states: 'The work can be shown in places where abrupt social and political events have happened either in their recent history, in the significant history of the place, at the moment when such events are an overwhelming presence in the media or when the tension leading to the conditions for sudden civilian uprise are present' (2020: 74). That is the moment when, in the words of Bruguera, 'the audience will be in the right psychological mind-set to react to the piece the way they should' (2020: 74). In the case of 'Tatlin's Whisper #6' (2009), made for the Havana Biennial, Bruguera 'set up an official-looking stage, presided over by two men in military uniform. Anyone could step up to the podium and say what they wanted for one minute. A white dove was placed on each speaker's shoulder – a reference to the dove that landed on Fidel Castro's shoulder in Havana in 1959 when he spoke amid the triumph of the new-minted revolution'. With '#6' she presented a brief opportunity for free speech, testing the limits set by Raúl Castro's promise of a 'greater degree of open debate in Cuba' (Higgins, 2018). Both 'Tatlin's Whisper #5' and '#6' go beyond the concept of performance, entering the realm of political interventions, as they are actions to be *performed* after a set of instructions, designed to interact with specific audiences within extremely politically charged situations.

For her *10,148,451* Turbine Hall 2018 commission, Bruguera introduced a series of interventions outside and inside Tate Modern. The work has a shifting title, since it is linked to data supplied by the Missing Migrants Project that is constantly tracking 'incidents involving migrants, including refugees and asylum-seekers'.[3] Outside, Bruguera collaborated with twenty-one people living and working in the neighbouring area, inviting them to 'explore how the museum can learn from and adapt to its local community'. One of the first actions by the so-called 'Tate Neighbours' was to rename Tate's

Boiler House as Natalie Bell, after a local activist. Inside, at the Turbine Hall, a heat-sensitive floor was installed where the face of a Syrian refugee in London appeared and an adjacent gallery was filled with non-toxic chemicals that made visitors cry, thus creating what Bruguera has called 'forced empathy' ('Hyundai Commission', n.d.). Through these examples we see how short- and long-term projects intertwine within Bruguera's political art practice. While her long-term projects aim for community (re)organisation in order to 'imagine other, more inclusive political futures' ('Tania Bruguera', n.d.), her short-term projects are made to nail down her concrete point of view regarding art as a tool for social change.

However, within Bruguera's art practice there is a particular body of work that is explicitly related to Beckett's *Endgame* and that, at first sight, does not quite fit the two general strategies that Bruguera otherwise follows: her *Endgame Studies* or *Studies for Endgame*. Made in 2005 and exhibited in Chicago in 2006, Bruguera's 'Study for Endgame #1' to '#6' were created for the Rhona Hoffman Gallery,[4] and '#7' for the Museum of Contemporary Art (MCA) Chicago. Maquettes '#1' to '#5' for Hoffman detail how she was planning to stage *Endgame* as a 'participatory installation' (Camper, 2006).

In 'Study for Endgame #2 (Gia)' Bruguera presents an elongated corridor with seven doors on each side and a light bulb protruding from the centre of the maquette, while a video monitor is installed in an adjacent pedestal. 'Study for Endgame #3 (Blue Velvet)' is a two-storey miniature structure made of plywood with two adjacent monitors. A cylinder is the central point – the stage – with a central light bulb and at least three holes in which heads of small mannequins mimicking members of the audience are placed, and we can see Hamm lying down in a two-wheeled stretcher – the actual stage that twelve years later Bruguera would develop for the BoCA Biennial. Back in 2006, from the information she presented in her *Endgame Studies* exhibition, it appears that she was planning to have a twelve-hour performance that left the audience free to 'decide how long they'll stay'. Since Bruguera was 'worried that her maquettes at Hoffman wouldn't convey *Endgame*'s emotional content' (Camper, 2006), she paired each stage prototype with a film that had 'similar dilemmas to those of the play' (Bruguera qtd in Camper, 2006), including *The Bicycle Thief* (Vittorio De Sica, 1948) and *Blue Velvet* (David Lynch, 1986). 'Study for Endgame #6 (MCA Chicago)' is a maquette that shows how this piece was being presented in parallel at the MCA Chicago, with an adjacent video monitor and a light bulb dimly illuminating the whole model. We see words engraved in the floor with the *Endgame* quotation 'I'll give you just enough to keep you from dying' (Beckett, 2009: 8) and three mannequins standing, one on top of the engraved words, one at the edge of the maquette and one in a balcony looking into the whole gallery. The same *Endgame* quotation was printed on the floor of the gallery space at MCA Chicago. 'Endgame Study #7' belongs to Bruguera's short-term projects linked to the *Tatlin's Whisper* series, as it offers a space for free speech within a political context. Bruguera installed a loudspeaker and a microphone on each of two balconies next to the main gallery space at MCA Chicago. The microphones were wired to the loudspeakers installed on the opposite balcony, so that when visitors spoke into the microphone, 'their voices were projected only into the opposite balcony's speaker and heard by someone who could not fully be seen. Likewise, the speaker adjacent to the microphone registered the sounds of the auditor' (Israel, 2013: 263).

How can we explain Bruguera's deep interest in Beckett's *Endgame*? Why cling to a play from 1957 and introduce it into her own explorations of political art practice? For an art practitioner who is so fond of coining concepts to specifically address her art strategies, to go and situate a 'white European author' (Thompson, 2010: 38) in the middle of her political discourse is not an equivocal act. Bruguera confirmed that she got acquainted with *Endgame* as far back as 1998, developing an obsession with the play: 'I read it five times in a row and still didn't understand a lot of things. At first I saw it in terms of power relationships between the two main characters. Now it seems more emotional, about a dysfunctional relationship' (qtd in Camper, 2006). Bruguera is an astute reader of Michel Foucault,[5] and her response to Cuban reality through her artwork comes from a first-hand understanding of political power[6] and enduring 'panoptic conditions of artistic production' (Quiles, 2016). She has openly expressed that 'Cuba is a point of reference' in her work as she is 'interested in understanding how power uses people, and all the complicity involved in this process'. Acknowledging that this phenomenon is universal, she adds: 'but in Cuba, as it is a small island, things become ridiculously clear'. If we follow Bruguera's statement that adapting *Endgame* is not 'anything different from what I've been doing' (qtd in Queirós, 2017), then her appropriating *Endgame* is a solid strategy used to explore Beckett's work and locates it at the centre of her own political discourse.[7]

Endgame as a tale of 'controlled' famine

Beckett's *Endgame* has become a key work to approach the aftermath of political strategies pre-and post-Second World War, such as degradation, famine politics and imposed scarcity, in addition to the role of the tyrant/perpetrator as self-proclaimed victim. James McNaughton precisely introduces

Beckett as a 'writer who is politically alert in specific historical moments and who addresses the failed political, aesthetic and philosophical solutions to modernity' (2018: 3). McNaughton states that *Endgame* 'excludes history' (2018: 9), stressing that if history is reduced to 'permanent Catastrophe', we are facing a *historical crisis* where the individual has lost 'the power of consciousness to think history' so that their 'historical salvation is unavailable' (Adorno qtd in McNaughton, 2018: 10). For McNaughton it is evident that 'Beckett's work builds from recent political history' (2018: 140), and from this perspective he proposes to understand *Endgame* within the period 1930–40, reminding us that extermination through famine as a governmental policy did not appear only as part of the Nazi strategies in the concentration camps but also as part of the postcolonial strategies implemented by Hitler's Germany and Stalin's Soviet Union. During Beckett's lifetime, 'mass starvation was purposefully brought about with the revolutionary transformation of the Soviet economy and with Nazi promises to secure German standards of living' (2018: 140). What is more: 'Visions of paradisiacal plenitude – that is, dreams of solving the imperative of national self-sufficiency – lead in different ways to the justification of murdering millions of civilians by withholding food' (2018: 140).

The line chosen by Bruguera for her 'Study for Endgame #6' – 'I'll give you just enough to keep you from dying' – explicitly points to the control of human life through withholding or managing food. Even if Beckett did not introduce 'a realistic account of famine, and he avoids a pitiful or even emphatic account of the victims' (McNaughton, 2018: 161), nevertheless *Endgame*, in McNaughton's opinion, 'performs, with devastating failure, the rhetorical contortions needed to make weaponized famine appear natural' (2018: 161). If *Endgame* can be regarded as a tool for examining and discussing mind-structures around and about control and power, Bruguera's production becomes an extension of her own practice – through the proxy of Beckett – in which she addresses issues such as domination, servitude, authority, biopolitical control, but also transgression and the possibility of confronting Power.

Bruguera made a strong connection with *Endgame* early on in her career, and she keeps coming back to it:

> I was fascinated that I could visualise the play so clearly, but I couldn't understand the power dynamics among the characters. Every time I read it, it looked like a different power struggle scenario, one between a father and son, a master and slave, a boss and an employee, a privileged person and an underprivileged one. In terms of agenda and knowledge, I imagined so many different outcomes and saw the relevance of the piece every time. (qtd in Sharp, 2017)

But other than her short-term political performative constructs, and some of her long-term participatory theatrical installations, Bruguera did not have any prior experience as theatre director. She worked with those elements she found more 'flexible' within Beckett's play: 'With Beckett, the estate won't let you change a comma of the text: nothing' (qtd. in Allen, 2017). Therefore, actors followed Beckett's lines. It was within the experience of the audience and the shape of the stage that Bruguera decided to expand her strategies and thus modify Beckett's directorial specifications: 'I found a way to add a little twist. The author never says anything about where the audience is. That's where I saw my chance' (Allen, 2017). Bruguera links the reference for positioning the spectators with her decision to make a round stage and place the audience in a scaffold to have an aerial view of the play, poking their heads inside a white cylinder (see Figure 12.1): 'I follow the stage instructions precisely, but I made the stage circular. He [Beckett] never speaks of the spectator's perspective, so I proposed an aerial perspective. The audience views the play from above, looking down' (Allen, 2017). However, Beckett *does* refer to the placement of the audience in his stage directions, the scenography, and through the line for Clov '[*He gets down, picks up the telescope, turns it on auditorium*]' (Beckett, 2009: 20).[8] The fact that Beckett removed this reference some time before 1974, yet kept it in the rest of the editions, describes a movement that first shatters

Figure 12.1 *Endgame*. A production by BoCA Biennial (Lisbon).

the fourth wall but is later undone again, 'thus creating a stronger sense of confinement at the cost of a loss of metatheatricality' (Van Hulle, 2019: 47).[9] Bruguera's double directorial decision permanently breaks the fourth wall of the play as well as the carceral implications of the cylinder, with the audience constantly being reminded that they are standing in a scaffold watching actors perform inside of a white circular space. I propose that Bruguera disarms the theatrical construction through a formula: she eliminates the *audience* by making it part of the artwork – stripped of their spectator role, their heads protruding through the white fabric as muted witnesses – like in 'Tatlin's Whisper #5', in which visitors were not aware of being part of an 'action' while they were forced to move around the space by mounted police. Audience, actors, cylinder, scaffold, Beckett's text, all become part of Bruguera's artwork, building a metareflexive layer.

Anna McMullan reminds us that 'when involved in the staging of his plays as director or advisor, Beckett was concerned not only with the actor's performance but also with visual and practical details of the stage design which defines the stage world for both the actors and the audience' (2012: 1). And Beckett's stage directions reflect the fact that his 'radically minimalist dramaturgy necessitated a new, distilled scenographic approach, one attuned to his intense focus on the performing body in an almost bare stage, where every detail of the costume, props, visible environment and lighting signifies and resonates' (2012: 2). By proposing a circular stage,[10] Bruguera's placement of specific elements and actors changes the way the play develops. In addition, costume design and props – armchair and step-ladder – modify the signifiers of those proposed by Beckett: '*Left and right back, high up, two small windows, curtains drawn. Front right, a door. Hanging near door, its face to wall, a picture. Front left, touching each other, covered with an old sheet, two ashbins. Centre, in an armchair on castors, covered with an old sheet,* HAMM' (2009: 5).

Bruguera's circular stage was limited by the 'dark and severe block of scaffolding' with '[f]our discrete entrances [that] bring audience members deep into and up the structure to their viewing spots, where they peer through slits in the cylinder to watch the play unfold below'. Inside this structure the audience discovers a 'pristine white cylinder' ('Endgame Itinerant Theater', 2017) made from white fabric that has a double role of 'walls' for the stage and viewing placements for the public. The elements Beckett called for – the door and the picture – are made of the same white textile, the door being slightly open – since it is just a piece of loose fabric – and the picture a frame made of the same white material. The two windows are suppressed; instead, we have two structures that Clov uses to climb up the white fabric wall. The curtains are two long pieces of white fabric suspended from the top of the structure to the floor level. There is no step-ladder but a plywood step. The two ashbins are made of grey fabric. Within this circular setting and without a point of reference, left and right depend on the place of the public at a certain moment, always from an aerial view. The door, picture and two climbing structures/curtains – the windows – are arranged in one half of the circular shaped stage, with the placement of the ashbins opposite to the door – instead of *'Front left'* (Beckett, 2009: 5). Beckett asked for Hamm to be *'[i]n a dressing-gown, a stiff toque on his head, a large blood-stained handkerchief over his face, a whistle hanging from his neck, a rug over his knees, thick socks on his feet'* (2009: 6). Instead, we see him in an immaculate white shirt, a white toque and a small blood-stained handkerchief; yes, the whistle is hanging from his neck, but there are no socks and his legs are covered by the plywood structure of the stretcher while his feet are dangling. Placed in this two-wheeled plywood stretcher – just like in Bruguera's 2005 'Study for Endgame #3 (Blue Velvet)' maquette – Hamm is lying on his back, facing the audience. Clov is dressed in white pyjama trousers, wearing no shirt, and his movements within the stage go from walking to crawling to laying down, facilitating a full aerial view for the public. Nagg and Nell are played by children who carry the performance through recorded adult voices (Sardin, 2020: 77).

In McMullan's opinion, Beckett's theatre 'foregrounds scenographic space, which is affected by the phenomenological presence of the actors on stage, by the animation of the space by voice, other sounds and lighting, and by the audience in the auditorium. Indeed, we might argue that scenography translates Beckett's interest in the visual arts into the plastic medium of the stage' (2012: 3). Bruguera's take on staging Beckett goes beyond visual arts and performance practices, the white monochrome cylinder in which the play took place, nine metres high, being the most prominent visual aspect of her proposal, 'a kind of clinical chamber where the lighting was stark throughout the performance' (Sardin, 2020: 74). As stated before, Bruguera changed elements regarding the directions for the actors to comply with the aerial view. The audience was allowed to move through the scaffold, thus having 'multiple perspectives on the performance' (Tubridy, 2018: 81). By poking their heads through the slits in the fabric, the public physically entered the cylinder and integrated themselves into the stage. According to Bruguera, 'you can only know about performance through redoing it and feeling it' (qtd in Bishop, 2020: 55), and she establishes three forms of re-enactment, as explained to Claire Bishop: 'First, as a pedagogical act, in which the goal is to learn through experiencing it' or *learning through doing*; second, the 'reenactment for historical research'; and, finally, a re-enactment that 'uses the original performance as a point of departure but updates the image, the symbols, or the references so it becomes relevant to the present' (2020: 55–6). It is in these three forms that Bruguera appropriates and re-enacts Beckett's *Endgame*.

Endgame as a tale of surveillance and power

The construction of the stage brings to mind Beckett's *Le Dépeupleur / The Lost Ones*, which takes place '[i]nside a cylinder fifty metres round and sixteen high' (Beckett, 2010: 101), while Bruguera's cylinder 'is a 14m x 14m x 9m structure which contains both the stage and 82 audience members' ('Endgame Itinerant Theater', 2017). It is a structure in which Hamm, Clov, Nagg and Nell are being watched, as in Foucault's Panopticon, by the public who, far from being seated in the dark, are forced to participate while individually glancing at the play by having their heads inside the brightly lit cylinder. Thus, they 'are active observers of the actors who cannot escape their glance; but they are also part of the set and fixed in their positions in the room which makes them part of the game' ('Tania Bruguera Endgame', 2017). The audience, transformed into 'observers', become witness to an endless famine-induced game. Foucault states: 'Not only must people know, they must see with their own eyes. Because they must be made to be afraid; but also because they must be witnesses, the guarantors, of the punishment, and because they must to a certain extent take part in it' (1995: 58). *Endgame* is Bruguera's exploration of the political dimension of the play, in which the audience witness strategies of control and death by famine exerted over the inhabitants of the cylinder by a blind and dying dictator. Spectators are fully aware of their condition as witnesses of 'the aftershadow of the purported collapse of the natural world, matched on the inside by self-defeating cruelty and a residue of denial for ill-defined culpability' (McNaughton, 2018: 145–6).

The white pristine circular *habitaculum* – in contrast with the dark scaffold structure – is also reminiscent of the Panopticon prison system designed by Jeremy Bentham in the eighteenth century, as described by Foucault: 'at the periphery, an annular building; at the centre, a tower; this tower is pierced with wide windows that open onto the inner side of the ring' (1995: 200). This 'peripheric building is divided into cells, each of which extends the whole width of the building; they have two windows, one on the inside corresponding to the windows of the tower; the other, on the outside, allows the light to cross the cell from one end to the other' (1995: 200). Within Bruguera's structure, spectators are on full view from within the white cylinder and also from outside of the scaffolding, illuminated by the light coming from the tubular stage. In this sort of *reversed* Panopticon we have the *witnesses* poking their heads in to observe incessantly the action taking place below in the central cell, which also has inner cells that are kept out of sight: Clov's kitchen, Nagg and Nell's bins. Surveillance comes from the *witnesses*, that is the spectators, which adds a further layer to Bruguera's complex staging of *Endgame*.

More than an architectural space, the Panopticon is where Power takes place 'as a generalizable model of functioning; a way of defining power relations in terms of the everyday life of men' (Foucault, 1995: 205). Actually, for Foucault – and this is a direct link to Bruguera's strategies – one of the central constructs of panopticism is the complicit subject, 'whereby cooperation with the power structure becomes so ingrained and automatic that the subject requires little, if any, supervision' (Swanson, 2011: 5). The prisoners believe they can be seen by the guards even when the guards are not present, so, ultimately, the guards are unnecessary. For Bruguera, *Endgame* is a clear example of self-policing, self-regulation and self-imprisoning, especially in Clov's constant state of panopticism, as he 'epitomizes Foucault's panoptic subject because he polices himself; he self-regulates' (Swanson, 2011: 6). The Panopticon in Bruguera's staging introduces confinement, immobility, self-regulation, the controlling gaze – the annulated gaze of Hamm – and food as elements of control and annihilation.

Power relations, surveillance, confinement and control are also elements that naturally pertain to Bruguera's extended art practice and which she has been subjected to first-hand. Like some of the characters of Beckett's plays, Bruguera has experienced the restraint of her movements through house arrest and confinement when taken to police stations in Havana. She has spoken openly about her experiences with the surveillance and control system in Cuba and has even had an assigned officer/interrogator (Higgins, 2018), a situation that reminds us of Beckett's *Rough for Radio II*. Citizens in Cuba are being stripped of their right to freedom of speech – among other basic human rights. Through an open panoptical system – no need of any tower or any specific construction – each *revolutionary* inhabitant will tell the head of the block what happens in all households from their block, and this head of the block will in turn communicate the information to the next link in the control system. In the words of Coco Fusco, author of *Dangerous Moves: Performance and Politics in Cuba* (2015), it is a sort of 'Cuban panopticism' (qtd in Quiles, 2016). As Foucault states: 'The power in the hierarchized surveillance of the disciplines is not possessed as a thing, or transferred as a property; it functions like a piece of machinery' (1995: 177). This Foucauldian control machinery is in place in Cuba. If surveillance is the state apparatus looking at its citizens, and sousveillance is an act of rebellion – the citizens looking back at the apparatus – *surveillance-by-proxy* will then be this looking at citizens by the state apparatus through the eyes of other citizens loyal to the so-called *revolution*. The 'panoptic conditions of artistic production' (Quiles, 2016) in Cuba imply that artists 'had three choices: demonstrate proper conduct and reap benefits, leave the country or risk enduring various forms of internal exile: expulsion from professional organisations and jobs, social marginalization or incarceration' (Fusco qtd in Quiles, 2016). Bruguera did not comply with the first and has found ways to gain international visibility and to pursue her art practice on the island, initiating participatory actions and breaking the *surveillance-by-proxy* cycle. Even if the control practices executed by the state are well known to Bruguera, she admits that during interrogation she has felt frightened when realising that in those situations there is an absence of law. But again, Bruguera knows *her* Foucault very well, and for power control the body 'serves as an instrument or intermediary: if one intervenes upon it to imprison it, or to make it work, it is in order to deprive the individual of a liberty that is regarded both as a right and as property' (Foucault, 1995: 11). This right, then, is what Bruguera is being stripped of when she has the sensation of an absence of law: 'punishment has become an economy of suspended rights' (1995: 11). It may very well be in this sense that *Endgame* speaks intimately to her.

Coming back to McNaughton's point made above: 'In *Endgame*, the atrocity invoked is not the [concentration] camp, but famine. Famine was the rhetorical warning of ecological devastation that spurred along World War II, and famine is the actual outcome of prophecies of plenitude: this horrific politics of food is deeply embedded in Beckett's play' (2018: 138). McNaughton clearly reminds us of the connection between *Endgame* and mass murdering through starvation, literally 'by withholding food' (2018: 140). As mentioned before, the play 'reckons with the famine politics of the 1930s and 1940s', when famine was 'deployed in rhetorical strategies designed to accrue political power and to exact submission through prophetic treats and promises of deliverance' (2018: 137). Bruguera's *Endgame* responds to similar questions that arise from her upbringing within the Castro regime in Cuba, and that mirror her experiences of a state that controls every single movement of the lives of Cuban citizens, including what and how much they eat within tougher permanent rationalisation policies; a regime characterised by attributing their limitations and flaws to the outside geopolitical situation – either the withdrawal of Soviet military after the collapse of the Soviet Union in 1991, the tightening of the US embargo since 1993, the exodus of refugees to the US in 1994, and so on. The critical interpretation that Bruguera undertook of *Endgame* might coincide with McNaughton's concept of famine control. The phrase she has been introducing within her work ever since her school days at the MCA Chicago – 'I'll give you just enough to keep you from dying' – is perfectly compatible with McNaughton's reading of *Endgame*, a play that 'suggests that those sentimental narratives – we did everything we could – are obscene when applied to modern man-made famines which contradict them so brutally' (2018: 161). It is not only the lack of freedom that citizens endure in Cuba; it is the promise of a communist paradise in which reality comes down to extreme scarcity that has been draining Cuban society for decades. Thus, when Bruguera got the invitation from BoCA Biennial, the timing was appropriate for the play to be staged, especially during a moment when 'democracy is abused instead of enacted' (Bruguera qtd in Sharp, 2017).

Conclusion

Contemporary art practitioners 'have turned to Beckett in order to better understand the motivations and consequences [not only] of state oppression and paranoia' (Kinkaid, 2013: 169) but also to acknowledge other realities of the present. Such realities are linked with policies to halt global immigration, biocontrol policies that force populations to accept high levels of mortality and inequalities due to controlled famine. *Endgame* may be a play that looks back to a pre-Second World War world, but it opens up to other interpretations – for example, Nazism as 'applied colonialism' (McNaughton, 2018: 161) and Hitler's *Hungerpolitik* strategies using 'food security as the logic for colonial war that took aim at Soviet Ukraine' and 'to withhold grain from others, thereby planning to starve millions' (2018: 13). But there is another scope of interpretation that necessarily brings the Soviet Union and Cuba into the game, hence Bruguera's approach. In the 1930s, 'Stalin's design for "socialism in one country" became in reality colonialism in one country' (Brown, 2003: 115). Those policies could thirty years later be translocated to Cuba, an ally of the Soviet Union from 1961 until 1991. These 'colonial stories allow Hamm to keep the cause of famine entirely under the sign of an exhausted "earth," a class of scarcity that apparently avoids the suspicion of being humanly engineered, even if cruelly bungled after it has arrived' (McNaughton, 2018: 154).

If Beckett's work 'maps out and anticipates … a terrain all-too-easily recognised, even appropriated, by the paranoid state apparatus of the present' (Kinkaid, 2013: 181), contemporary art practitioners like Bruguera are trying to explore while re-enacting Beckett, learning the code and the aesthetics of his work, to challenge the present. Giorgio Agamben reminds us that *performance* – one of the Greek senses of *liturgy* – 'is not a "representation" … of an event: it is itself the event' (2019: 14), and Bruguera is attuned to this: 'I don't want art that points to a thing. I want art that is the thing'

('Activist Art', n.d.). So, when she says that *Endgame* is 'a revenge against totalitarian dictators' (qtd in Sharp, 2017), she is not merely using Beckett's play to 'point' to a thing. If we follow the Agambean meaning of performance, we perhaps find the reason for Bruguera's clinging to Beckett: *Endgame* is not an artwork that 'points at' famine and policies of controlled starvation; rather, it 'is' famine and policies of controlled starvation, re-enacted every time the *performance* takes place.

Notes

1 Samuel Beckett, *Endgame*. Concept and direction: Tania Bruguera. Architects: Dotan Gertler Studio. With: Brian Mendes, Jess Barbagallo, Pedro Aires and Lara Ferreira. Light design: Rui Monteiro. Sound design: Rui Lima and Sérgio Martins. Assistant direction: John Romão, Mitchell Polonsky. Technical director: Patrícia Gilvaia. Production: BoCA. Executive producer: Francisca Aires. Co-production: São João National Theatre (Oporto, PT), Colectivo 84 (PT), Kunsten Festival des Arts (Brussels, BE), Théâtre Nanterre-Amandiers (Nanterre, FR), Festival d'Automne à Paris (Paris, FR), Fondation d'Enterprise Hermès (Paris, FR), International Summer Festival Hamburg (Hamburg, DE), Estudio Bruguera. World premiere: Mosteiro São Bento da Vitória/Teatro Nacional São João (Porto), 20 April 2017.
2 See https://documenta-fifteen.de/en/news/arnold-bode-prize-2021-goes-to-instar-and-tania-bruguera/ (accessed 12 August 2021).
3 See https://missingmigrants.iom.int/ (accessed 12 August 2021).
4 For images, see www.latinamericanart.com/en/artist/tania-bruguera/ (accessed 12 August 2021).
5 'After I left the school and after a heavy Foucault induction, I called what I was doing Arte de Conducta, to make sure that any analysis would start with the social and political implications of the work' (qtd in Eccles, 2016).
6 'Daughter of one of the founders of the Communist Party of Cuba, Miguel Brugueras del Valle, later a diplomat and deputy foreign minister of Fidel Castro, Tania lives inside and outside the country and maintains a tense and complex relationship with the Cuban authorities' (Queirós, 2017).
7 All quotations from Quiles are my own English translations from Portuguese.
8 In Bruguera's production, Clov looks at the audience through the telescope following the shape of the round structure (BoCA, 2020: 1h 27' 01"–1h 27' 14").
9 For a more detailed study of metatheatricality in *Fin de partie* / *Endgame* and how Beckett revised this element for the various productions of the play he was involved in, see Van Hulle and Weller (2018: 335–8).
10 In reference to the 1957 and 1958 productions of *Endgame,* scenographer Jocelyn Herbert recalls: 'The French set was completely circular, whilst mine was angular' (qtd in Courtney, 1993: 28).

References

'Activist Art' (n.d.). *Tate Gallery*, www.tate.org.uk/art/art-terms/a/activist-art (accessed 12 August 2021).

Agamben, G. (2019). *Creation and Anarchy: The Work of Art and the Religion of Capitalism*. Trans. A. Kotsko. Stanford, CA: Stanford University Press.

Allen, E. (2017). 'The fabulist. Tania Bruguera', *Aesop*, 21 December, www.aesop.com/ch/fr/r/the-fabulist/tania-bruguera (accessed 10 April 2021).

Beckett, S. (2009). *Endgame*. Pref. R. McDonald. London: Faber and Faber.

Beckett, S. (2010). *Texts for Nothing and Other Shorter Prose, 1950–1976*. Ed. M. Nixon. London: Faber and Faber.

Bishop, C. (2020). *Tania Bruguera in Conversation With / En Conversación con*. New York and Caracas: Fundación Cisneros/Colección Patricia Phelps de Cisneros.

BoCA Bienal (2020). 'BoCA Online, Tania Bruguera, "Endgame" by Samuel Beckett', private video.

Brown, K. (2003). *A Biography of No Place: From Ethnic Borderland to Soviet Heartland*. London and Cambridge, MA: Harvard University Press.

Camper, F. (2006). 'Performance provocateur', *Chicago Reader*, 20 January, https://chicagoreader.com/arts-culture/performance-provocateur/ (accessed 12 August 2021).

Courtney, C. (1993). *Jocelyn Herbert: A Theatre Workbook*. London: Art Books International.

Eccles, T. (2016). 'Tania Bruguera', *ArtReview*, 9 February, https://artreview.com/december-2015-feature-tania-bruguera/ (accessed 12 August 2021).

'Endgame Itinerant Theater' (2017). *Dotan Gertler Studio*, https://dotangertlerstudio.cargo.site/Endgame-Itinerant-Theater (accessed 13 August 2021).

Foucault, M. (1995). *Discipline and Punish: The Birth of the Prison*. Trans. A. Sheridan. New York: Vintage.

Higgins, C. (2018). 'Detained, grilled, denounced: Tania Bruguera on life in Cuba – and her Turbine Hall show', *Guardian*, 26 September, www.theguardian.com/artanddesign/2018/sep/26/tania-bruguera-interview-cuba-tate-modern-turbine-hall (accessed 12 August 2021).

'Hyundai Commission, Tania Bruguera: 10,148,451' (n.d.). *Tate Gallery*, www.tate.org.uk/whats-on/tate-modern/exhibition/hyundai-commission-tania-bruguera (accessed 13 August 2021).

Israel, N. (2013). 'Contemporary visual art', in A. Uhlmann (ed.), *Samuel Beckett in Context*. Cambridge: Cambridge University Press, pp. 255–65.

Kincaid, A. (2013). 'Mapping the future: *Endgame*, premediation, and the war on terror', *Samuel Beckett Today / Aujourd'hui*, 25, 169–82.

McMullan, A. (2012). 'Samuel Beckett's scenographic collaboration with Jocelyn Herbert', *Degrés: Revue de Synthèse à Orientation Sémiotique*, 149–150, 1–17.

McNaughton, J. (2018). *Samuel Beckett and the Politics of Aftermath*. Oxford: Oxford University Press.

Queirós, L. M. (2017). 'Uma dança de poder e manipulação com vista para a Cuba dos Castro', *Público*, 20 April, www.publico.pt/2017/04/20/culturaipsilon/noticia/danca-de-poder-num-tubo-de-ensaio-1769284 (accessed 13 August 2021).

Quiles, D. R. (2016). 'The vicissitudes of conduct', *Third Text: Critical Perspectives on Contemporary Art and Culture*, September, http://thirdtext.org/vicissitudes-of-conduct (accessed 13 August 2021).

Sardin, P. (2020). 'Beckett performed in the context of the globalisation of contemporary performance: Robert Wilson's *Endspiel* and Tania Bruguera's *Endgame*', *Francosphères*, 9.1, 71–84.

Sharp, R. (2017). 'Master and servant: how Tania Bruguera is using Beckett to dismantle power', *Guardian*, 11 April, www.theguardian.com/stage/2017/apr/11/tania-bruguera-samuel-beckett-endgame-boca-porto (accessed 12 August 2021).

Swanson, V. (2011). 'Confining, incapacitating, and partitioning the body: carcerality and surveillance in Samuel Beckett's *Endgame*, *Happy Days*, and *Play*', *Miranda*, 4, 1–17, http://journals.openedition.org/miranda/1872 (accessed 12 August 2021).

'Tania Bruguera' (n.d.). *MUAC Contemporary Art University Museum*, https://muac.unam.mx/exposicion/tania-bruguera?lang=en (accessed 13 August 2021).

'Tania Bruguera Endgame' (2017). *Kampnagel Sommerfestival*, www.kampnagel.de/media/file/Sommerfestival_2017/Abendzettel_TANIA_BRUGUERA_fuer_Web.pdf (accessed 12 August 2021).

Thompson, N. (2010). 'Destroyer of worlds', in P. Chan (ed.), *Waiting for Godot in New Orleans: A Field Guide*. New York: Creative Time, pp. 38–49.

Tubridy, D. (2018). 'Theatre and installation: perspectives on Beckett', *Contemporary Theatre Review*, 28.1, 68–81.

Van Hulle, D. (2019). 'The pentimenti principle: the draft and the draff in Beckett's critique of narrative reason', *Samuel Beckett Today / Aujourd'hui*, 31.1, 37–52.

Van Hulle, D., and S. Weller (2018). *The Making of Samuel Beckett's 'Fin de partie' / 'Endgame'*. Brussels and London: University Press Antwerp and Bloomsbury.

13

Godot noir: Beckett in black and whiteface

S. E. Gontarski

On 'this adaptation business'

Although he was savvy enough to warn his French publisher of 'this adaptation business' as requests for English-language rights for *En attendant Godot* began to arrive in Paris in mid-1953, Beckett seems to have had only the scantest idea of how completely commercial theatre was imbricated in it (2011: 379). As early as 'before' 18 May 1953, Beckett was responding to a proposition from American writer and director Garson Kanin, who was already working with his Broadway colleague, Thornton Wilder, to adapt *Godot*. After Beckett's warning, his French publisher, Jérôme Lindon, communicating through French producer and intermediary Denise Tual, acknowledged that English-language performance rights were still available (Beckett, 2011: 380n1). Two days later he received another inquiry, this directly from a London agent, Rosica Colin, asking about the English-language rights to all of his work and, further, proposing a club performance of *Godot*. Beckett replied on 19 May: 'Re English and American rights to my work in French I think you would be well advised to get in touch with my editor [i.e. publisher] Monsieur Jérôme Lindon .... He knows better than I how things stand. I am not even sure that they are still available' (2011: 380, 381n1). The strictures he would subsequently impose on performances of his theatre works were one response to such reservations about adaptation as he was beginning to be drawn into the world of commercial theatre where adaptation was the norm, although he would be less than consistent, even whimsical at times, in enforcing those strictures. In 1953, however, Beckett's response to the possibility of 'adaptation' now seems mild or understated. He seems to have intuited, at least, that theatre works always have an elasticity – in short, an adaptability – to the point, at times, of multiple configurations. Producers, theatre directors, actors and translators have been theatre's chief reconfigurers, but the author himself would eventually recast his own work through his various and multiple creative roles, and he understood finally – if slowly, perhaps – that all performance is adaptation.

Beckett would plunge into 'this adaptation business' himself by 1962, as he reconfigured Robert Pinget's radio play *La Manivelle* as *The Old Tune* with the acknowledgement: 'English adaptation by Samuel Beckett'. We might say the same of his directorial debut, re-rendering Pinget's *L'Hypothèse*, which he directed with actor Pierre Chabert in 1962. As a theatre director, Beckett would freely 'adapt' his own works for the stage and vary productions for different actors and stage configurations. As both an aesthetician and a hands-on, practical man of the theatre, Beckett would wrestle with such theoretical and philosophical issues as he immersed himself in the world of practical performance. He would accept that theatre, subject to a myriad of cultural forces and the collaborative nature of performance itself, necessitates adaptation, which is by definition a change in response to altered or shifting ecologies as well as a synonym for interpretation, and more so, perhaps, in the hands of commercial theatre managers who are explicitly driven by economic and political forces. In the world of performance, then, questions of production and reproduction, of originals and copies, of essences and simulacra, of purity and corruption are questions of adaptation and so matters of degree rather than of kind.

One such commercial theatre manager was American producer Michael Myerberg, who has become something of a maligned figure for summarily discharging Alan Schneider after the Miami *Godot*,[1] but also as a force trying to adapt, that is to commercialise, *Waiting for Godot* to fit the Broadway market. Most of that distrust, if not resentment, was driven by the spurned director, who saw the producer as someone keen to reconfigure this new sort of play written by a neophyte, Hiberno-French author by bringing in a major American writer and another theatre professional, Thornton Wilder, to refashion it. Beckett's American publisher, Barney Rosset, recounted his experience with Myerberg in a letter to Beckett of 6 February 1956:

> I am very happy that you wrote [to British producer, Donald] Albery to instruct Myerberg and tell him that there can be no unauthorized deviations from script. Myerberg once told me on the phone that he considered the translation to be a poor one and that he would very much like to have Thornton Wilder re-do it. I think it entirely possible that he may be messing around with it. (Rosset, 2017: 112)

By the time of Rosset's writing, however, Beckett's script had already been considerably re-rendered, according to Schneider's Miami notes, and what Beckett characterised as 'the queer kind of English that my queer French deserves' had been significantly altered (Beckett, 2011: 592). Rosset, not known for his patience, was also uncomfortable with the business of Broadway and particularly Myerberg's secretive methods. Thinking subsequently in terms of an American producer for *Endgame*, Rosset would finally write to Beckett on 19 March 1957, 'I would prefer almost anyone to Mr. Myerberg', and he followed with a PS, asking: 'Are there any limitations to the length of time Myerberg will continue to hold the rights to GODOT' (2017: 112). Rosset was reinforcing, yet again, the all-out campaign that the spurned director, Alan Schneider, launched against Myerberg, his own lawsuit against the producer still in litigation. Rosset recounted Schneider's phone call with its litany of complaints to Beckett on 27 January 1956:

> Myerberg is not the man to produce Godot. Godot should be put on off-Broadway, preferably at the Theatre de Lys [where Schneider had connections]. Schneider would like to direct it, but beyond that, he would like to see Godot put on as well – that means no Myerberg and no Bert Lahr. ... Myerberg plans to turn it into a vehicle for Lahr. This will be disastrous. In Miami Lahr and Ewell played two different plays. Ewell at least tried to work for the play. The London production should not be brought over here. It is inferior to American standards. ... And so it went. Obviously what Schneider had to say was music to my tinny ears. ... I do hope you will pass along Schneider's opinions to Albery. ... I told Schneider that I feared I was being thought of as the village crank by you and Albery because I have conducted this monstrous diatribe about [i.e. in favour of] off-Broadway. (2017: 110–11)

As Rosset notes further: 'The Myerberg contract does not provide for an off-Broadway production' (2017: 111).

Schneider's anti-Myerberg screed reflects the ongoing civil lawsuit *Schneider* v. *Myerberg*. Actor Tom Ewell wrote in full support of the Miami director. Lahr's letter in the case, on the other hand, offered only the weakest of support for Schneider, the legal issue being how conscientiously Schneider rehearsed the play, particularly given Myerberg's request, in response to the disastrous reviews, that rehearsals be continued after the opening. In New York, Ewell would be replaced by E. G. Marshall and Schneider by Herbert Berghof, a charter member of the Actors Studio since its inception in 1947.[2] The off-Broadway option favoured by Schneider and Rosset, however, had serious economic implications, as Myerberg knew well; off-Broadway theatres were smaller than those on Broadway, so box office revenues would suffer and actors would be asked to work at a reduced, off-Broadway pay scale. Such economic reductions would make off-Broadway productions less attractive to investors and mitigate against the preference of many producers for star actors like Lahr (see Tallmer, 1957a).

A 'Negro *Godot*'

Myerberg's theatrical credentials as a Broadway insider were, if not impeccable, at least strong. He had unconventional theatrical interests, evident in his 1947 revival of *The Cradle Will Rock: A Play in Music*, a Federal Theatre Project production from 1937, originally directed by Orson Welles at the Mercury Theatre for the politically adventurous Federal Theatre group. He followed up this musical production with the premiere of Wilder's 1942 experimental drama *The Skin of Our Teeth*, which, according to Henry Morton Robinson and Joseph Campbell, is a recasting of James Joyce's *Finnegans Wake* (qtd in Gibbs, 1942: 42). The Wilder premiere was something of a hit. In 1950, Myerberg went on to produce another politically charged musical (or opera), Langston Hughes's *The Barrier: A Musical Drama* that Hughes adapted from his earlier Broadway success, *Mulatto*, the story of a southern white plantation owner living conjugally with his black housekeeper. Although the 'Musical Drama' ran for only four performances, Myerberg's interest in race relations also led to a second production of *Waiting for Godot*, *Godot* II, a year after its Broadway debut, the so-called 'Negro *Godot*'. The idea may have originated with Beckett himself, or at least he wrote to Rosset on 30 August 1956:

> I spent a rather dismal evening with Myerberg (nice man) and his lady friend. I mentioned to him that I thought Godot by an all-negro cast would be interesting. He said he had had the same idea but was nervous about telling me, fearing I wd not like it. ... I had a letter from him some days ago in which he says that Lahr is not available ... and that he is getting going with preparations for performance with all negro cast. This pleases me, rightly or wrongly, much. (Beckett, 2011: 647)

Beckett's comment reminds us that as early as 1934 he contributed nineteen translations to *Negro: An Anthology*, Nancy Cunard's groundbreaking, 822-page collection of prose, poetry, music and polemics by African American and international black artists and cultural commentators, celebrating their voices of joy and rage.

While the all-black *Godot* was in keeping with Myerberg's political leanings, *Godot* II seems to have hit the difficulty of enticing middle-class, white Americans to cross a colour line in a still segregated America and to pay Broadway ticket prices to watch an all-black cast perform not minstrelsy with Jim Crow characters but an experimental European drama, and not in Harlem, the predominantly black section of New York City, but on Broadway, dubbed The Great White Way.[3] Myerberg had high hopes for this new 'Negro' *Godot*. Interviewed by Jerry Tallmer for the *Village Voice*, he noted: 'The Negro has had no theater literature of his own. Marvelous in dance, in music, but always had to play second fiddle in the formal theater. Now for the first time he'll have a chance to appear in a work of classic structure and represented by the BEST POSSIBLE CAST' (Tallmer, 1957a: 9). When Tallmer asked whether this production would be 'better than the other version; I mean closer to the play written?', Myerberg answered astonishingly: 'No, different' (1957a: 9). To which of the two questions that Tallmer posed did Myerberg's response apply remains ambiguous. The nature of the response, furthermore, hinges on Tallmer's inserted comma. With it, Myerberg's reply is probably the strongest indication we have that Beckett's play had become part of the economic engine that is commercial theatre. Myerberg was taking phone calls and impatiently checking his watch during the questioning, so Tallmer had no chance to follow up and ask what would be 'different', the cast, the staging, the interpretation or the text.

The play would preview from 10–19 January 1957 at the Shubert Theatre in Boston, where Rosset saw it and issued an enthusiastic report to Beckett on 14 January 1957:

> The Boston production went off very well. To me the new Vladimir is incomparable – better than Marshall, and this greatly changes the whole play. The new Lucky is absolutely different from the other one [Alvin Epstein] and the descriptions of the Boston critics, wherein they say that he [Rex Ingram] is 'astounding', is about the best adjective available. Estragon [Mantan Moreland] has some lamentable Negroisms, which disturb me and I hope they somehow tone him down before it opens on Broadway. (Rosset 2017: 128)[4]

Rosset's phrase 'some lamentable Negroisms' refers to Jim Crow performances of stereotyped African American behaviour, with bulging eyes and chattering teeth, that Moreland honed in his performances as Birmingham Brown, the chauffeur in the Charlie Chan films, which themselves also played on Asian American stereotypes (Padgett, n.d.). *The Harvard Crimson* shared Rosset's enthusiasm:

> But on one point there can be no equivocation. The acting and direction which this production displays is in every way superb, and very likely is the best work to come along this season. Each of the members of the all-Negro cast is an actor of unsurpassed stature. I am not in a position to compare Mantan Moreland with Bert Lahr, who played Estragon in the original American production, but it is difficult to imagine any performance which embodies slapstick drollery and technical subtlety to a higher degree of perfection. Earle Hyman as the more intelligent Vladimir suggests just the right amount of dignity, and Rex Ingram makes a beautifully fearsome and pathetic Pozzo. As for Lucky, the part demands a pantomimist, and in Geoffrey Holder it has found a master of this form. Herbert Berghof, who also directed the original production, molded the four performances into a superbly balanced whole, and accomplished his job with imagination and no little daring. The merits of Samuel Beckett's contribution to the evening may be debated, but the work of these five men stands far above the possibility of reproach. (Schwabacher, 1957)

Rosset's editorial assistant, Judith Schmidt, lamented the play's closing to Beckett on 30 January 1957: 'We all thought this production was very good – in some ways better than the first production. Earle Hyman [Vladimir] was wonderful'.[5] And *Village Voice* theatre critic Tallmer agreed, defending at least the play and its bold, politically charged new staging. Nick Lucchesi of the *Village Voice* characterised the New York 'production at the Barrymore Theatre on 47th Street west of Broadway' as an 'encore to the prior year's blockbuster New York premiere that starred Bert Lahr. It was helmed by the same producer, Michael Myerberg, and touted in the [*Village*] *Voice* (and, presumably, elsewhere) as "Negro *Godot*": Under the direction of Herbert Berghof (who'd also directed the original), all the cast members were black' (Lucchesi, 2014).

While Brooks Atkinson praised Moreland's comic performance in the *New York Times* for 'a suspicious joyousness of manner, a crack-voiced laugh, a teetry walk, a general feeling that he is the one who is going to be slapped' (1957: 25), the production was generally panned by New York theatre critics, Atkinson among them. Tallmer opened his riposte with some heavy-handed irony on 30 January 1957:

> *'Godot II' had already been handed over to the embalmers the night before I sat down to start this, but since then a half a day has somehow gone into other affairs, with the copy paper sitting idle in the typewriter, and now I see over my coffee that Mr. Myerberg has pumped at least a second week into the show. This is good for all concerned, except perhaps for Mr. Brooks Atkinson of the* New York Times, *dean of American drama critics, to whom I feel I must tonight pay my respects if I do not wish to blow my brains out, for many incredible present reasons but especially these.* (1957b: 7; qtd in Lucchesi, 2014; italics in original)

Tallmer then goes after Atkinson's review: 'There are seven sentences in the foregoing, only six of them in total error. That is batting .143'.[6] Tallmer goes on to detail the misconceptions that Atkinson has unleashed on the public about Beckett and his first produced play, which Atkinson calls a 'rigadoon', suggesting a French musical form. Atkinson's dismissive judgement came at a time when theatre critics had considerable sway over, at least, the Broadway stage, and Tallmer, not among them, is incisive in his ridicule of how Atkinson's traditionalism and conventionalism pass for insights into Beckett's play. While he takes issue with Berghof's vision of *Godot*, Tallmer himself deflects the racial issue, avoiding questions of what black actors might bring to Beckett's European drama in the racially segregated United States of the 1950s, or, on the other hand, whether or not race might shift, distract from or distort its thematic focus. Instead, he goes on to suggest, by omission perhaps, that race has little or no effect on the thematic thrust:

The new version, though it makes the main lines clearer, is actually as great a distortion as before. When 'Godot' is finally staged here as one great slow throbbing mortal pulse, we shall for the first time see Beckett's text at least partially justified in action. (I do not *mean that the humor must be deleted. It must remain and intensify.*) Also I am afraid I now find even more to disapprove of in Herbert Berghof's direction, or rather in his second-time-round innovations: intermittent heavenly choral music, for instance, or the way Lucky's tirade is both blurred into total gibberish – for the words in it are very important – and 'dramatically' broken up with little punctuating moans and utterances from the sidelines. (1957b: 7; qtd in Lucchesi, 2014; italics in original)

The Free Southern Theater: 'no more water / but the fire next time'

But a black cast inevitably injects a political edge into performances, especially in the US, and, although Tallmer missed or avoided this most salient feature of the new production, that racial thread was picked up as the 1950s melded into the 1960s and issues of race moved from invisibility to high visibility, from the North of the country to the South, and so from background to foreground as the push for equal civil rights gained momentum predominantly (but not exclusively) in the American South. The early days of the American Civil Rights movement saw theatre become a major platform for and instigator of change, most directly with the formation of the Free Southern Theater (FST). Six years after the 'Negro *Godot*' or *Godot* II appeared on Broadway, the FST was formed in September 1963 by activists involved in the Civil Rights movement, namely Gilbert Moses, a journalist for the *Mississippi Free Press*, and John O'Neal, a leader in the Student Non-Violent Coordinating Committee (SNCC). The FST was part of the 'Radical Black Theater' movement that not only focused on race relations but was committed to rethinking theatre itself, as a cultural force for a new, more just social order.[7] Their founding document established an African American, or 'Negro', cultural, political and aesthetic focus:

> Our fundamental objective is to stimulate creative and reflective thought among Negroes in Mississippi and other Southern states by the establishment of a legitimate theater, thereby providing the opportunity in the theater and the associated art forms. We theorize that within the Southern situation a theatrical form and style can be developed that is as unique to the Negro people as the origin of blues and jazz. ... Through theater we think to open a new era of protest. One that permits the development of playwrights and actors, one that permits the growth and self-knowledge of a Negro audience, one that supplements the current struggle for freedom. (Dent et al., 1969: 3–4)

Such an aesthetic refocusing would feed into, complement and finally merge with the broader Black is Beautiful movement of the 1960s that reinvoked some of the Pan-African spirit earlier in the century called 'Negritude' and questioned the broadly accepted principle that white characteristics and culture were the standards against which all beauty and aesthetics were to be measured.

The emphasis of the FST was also on the nature and function of theatre itself: 'we are seeking a new kind of liberation from old forms of theatre, old techniques and ideas. A freedom to find new forms of theatrical expression and to find expression in people who have never expressed themselves in theatre before' (Schechner, 1964: 65–6).[8] Their specific geographical and racial emphases aside, the project and its goals might have been taken as something of a gloss on *Godot*, and, surprisingly, given their American regional focus, one of the first plays that the FST chose to perform was indeed *Waiting for Godot* (see Figure 13.1). Organisers and activists behind the FST could not know that in the earliest, mimeographed pre-publication copies of *Godot*, in circulation among potential producers and actors, the geographical reference in Lucky's speech was not to Connemara (Beckett, 2010: 41–2), as it is in all published versions of the text, but to Mississippi's neighbour, Alabama (see Van Hulle and Verhulst, 2017: 303). Beckett revised the location of Lucky's invocation of atavistic or underdeveloped humanity from Alabama (stronghold of American slavery and hotbed of resistance to civil rights when *Godot* was written) to the west of Ireland.

The FST's targeted audiences were not socialites, nor the New York intellectuals that Myerberg appealed to for support of the original Broadway run, although the FST would eventually look to those groups for financial support. The FST's audiences were, on the contrary, predominantly sharecroppers, impoverished farm workers labouring under subsistence conditions, and those audiences behaved differently from those on Broadway, more in keeping with their own interactive religious heritage in black fundamentalist churches. They responded verbally, shouted out responses, asked questions: 'Maybe in this race relations business we should take the rope off our necks after the master goes blind. Who is Godot? Where does he fit in? Was the boy Stanley [Taylor, the Boy but doubling as the stage manager] playing [someone] different [each time]? Was he the same?' These are among the comments recorded in the company's 'Discussion Notes', made by someone identified simply as 'Negro Woman' (Dent et al., 1969: 64). The political climate in the southern United States at the time was explosive: 'The church we played in had been shot into the week before we came with *Purlie Victorious* [a play by actor and activist Ossie Davis] and *Waiting for Godot*. There were bullet holes above the door. Yet when we played, they all came out' (Schechner, 1964: 64).

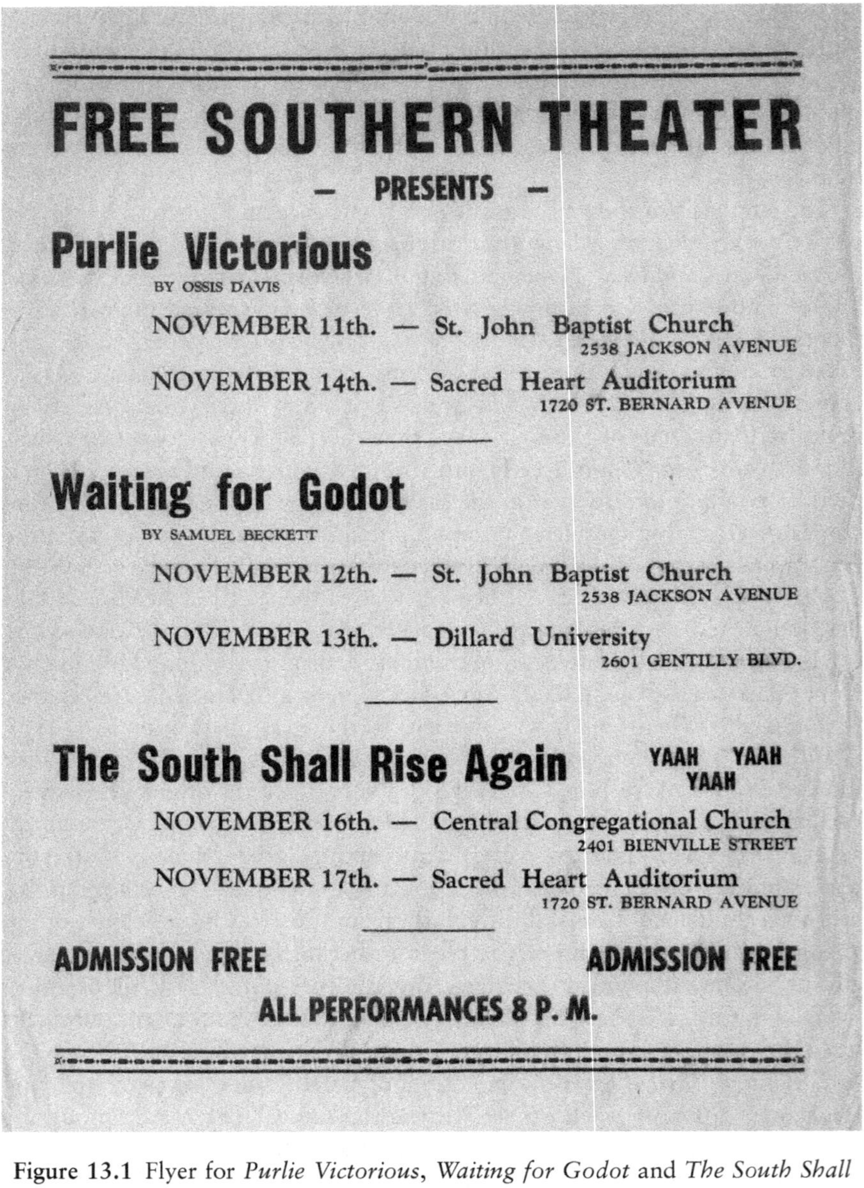

FREE SOUTHERN THEATER

— PRESENTS —

Purlie Victorious

BY OSSIS DAVIS

NOVEMBER 11th. — St. John Baptist Church
2538 JACKSON AVENUE

NOVEMBER 14th. — Sacred Heart Auditorium
1720 ST. BERNARD AVENUE

Waiting for Godot

BY SAMUEL BECKETT

NOVEMBER 12th. — St. John Baptist Church
2538 JACKSON AVENUE

NOVEMBER 13th. — Dillard University
2601 GENTILLY BLVD.

The South Shall Rise Again

YAAH YAAH YAAH

NOVEMBER 16th. — Central Congregational Church
2401 BIENVILLE STREET

NOVEMBER 17th. — Sacred Heart Auditorium
1720 ST. BERNARD AVENUE

ADMISSION FREE ADMISSION FREE

ALL PERFORMANCES 8 P. M.

Figure 13.1 Flyer for *Purlie Victorious*, *Waiting for Godot* and *The South Shall Rise Again*.

The group created its own racial controversy as well by highlighting, manipulating and playing against what was then called the 'colour line':

> 'Purlie Victorious' by Ossie Davis and Samuel Beckett's 'Waiting for Godot' were among the first plays produced by the company, and they toured in repertory through Mississippi, Tennessee, Georgia, and Louisiana in 1964 and 1965. The company, however, often adapted well-known plays to suit their purposes. The company sparked controversy when actors performed 'Waiting for Godot' in whiteface. (Handy, n.d.)

The company's schedule was arduous. From 11 November 1964 to February 1965 the group performed in twenty-six cities, mostly in Mississippi but in Tennessee and Georgia as well. The final two performances of the tour were in New York City: on 5 February at the New School for Social Research and on 12 February at the American Place Theatre, created in 1963 in St Clements Church as an off-Broadway theatre but in Hell's Kitchen (Dent et al., 1969: 51–2; see also Minor, 1965). The theatre was receptive to and encouraged the African American theatre movement, Tennessee Williams being among its original Board of Directors.

Although the FST was associated with the SNCC (see 'Free Southern Theater', n.d.), its approach was less passive than proactive, invoking at times the critique of race in America as detailed by James Baldwin in two longish essays collected as *The Fire Next Time* (1963), its title a direct evocation of the spiritual or gospel song – originally a slave song – 'Mary Don't You Weep': 'God gave Noah the rainbow sign / No more water but the fire next time'. As Moses wrote on 9 March 1964, on his way to New York to raise funds to support the FST for the tour outlined above: 'It will be a very difficult trip. I picture myself prancing around New York, talking about the theater in Mississippi …. I feel like a vaudeville barker. Exhorting people to pay their dues. Step right up and see the fire next time in Mississippi' (qtd in Dent et al., 1969: 8). As Moses goes on: 'A large part of the excitement generated by the idea for the theater was centered around the fact that it would be integration operating in the deep South, and integration operating in the largely unintegrated American Theater' (1969: 9). The group's adaptation of *Godot* would become central to this political mission, this 'new approach to civil rights', as it would be again in South Africa's battle against Apartheid in the 1970s and 1980s ('Waiting for Godot', 2020). Baldwin's 1962 *New Yorker* article 'Down at the Cross, a Letter from a Region of My Mind', which became part of *The Fire Next Time*, laid out his hope for a future: 'If we – and I mean the relatively conscious whites and the relatively conscious blacks, who must, like lovers, insist on, or create, the consciousness of others – do not falter in our duty now, we may be able, handful that we are, to end the racial nightmare, and achieve our country, and change the history of the world' (Baldwin, 1962). In 2016, however, a musical, *Can I Get A Witness? The Gospel of James Baldwin*, staged as a church service, was based on *The Fire Next Time* and premiered at the Harlem Stage in Harlem, New York, to suggest that we had faltered in our duty, that race was still divisive and that the struggle for human justice and equality remained unachieved.[9]

The Classical Theatre of Harlem: 'Can these bones live?'

In August 2005, Hurricane Katrina devastated the greater New Orleans area, and low-income, predominantly African American neighbourhoods in the Lower Ninth Ward in particular. Some 1,836 people died, and for a protracted period the city and surrounding parishes remained flooded. Emergency responses from government agencies seemed slow as many locals, now homeless, were displaced. When attention needed to be focused on the plight of those displaced, some thought, once again, in terms of art as a messenger, a generator of change and a political weapon. Writing in the New Orleans newspaper the *Times-Picayune* on 6 November 2007, Ann Maloney laid out one artistic response to that natural disaster: 'Christopher McElroen's concept of setting Samuel Beckett's "Waiting for Godot" in post-Katrina New Orleans seemed inspired when the director staged it last June in New York at the Classical Theatre of Harlem, on a roof in a 15,000-gallon swimming pool' (2007).[10] No arid country road with dying tree here; this *Godot* was under water, at first in a simulated flood on the rooftop of the theatre, but then on the devastated streets of what was left of the Lower Ninth Ward, once artist and activist Paul Chan got involved in what became *Paul Chan's Waiting for Godot in New Orleans: A Play in Two Acts, A Project in Three Parts* as Chan's *Creative Time* website has it ('Creative Time', 2007). In an 'Arts and Leisure' feature for the *New York Times* on 2 December 2007, Pulitzer Prize-winning arts editor Holland Cotter noted that

> Christopher McElroen had directed a well-received run of 'Godot' for the Classical Theater of Harlem using the agonizing wait for help after Katrina as central metaphor. He agreed to rework the production for an outdoor setting. Three actors from the New York cast would appear, including Mr. [Wendell] Pierce, a New Orleans native familiar from the television show 'The Wire.' Others would be hired locally. Mr. Chan would design new props. There would be two performances at each location, admission first come first served, and free. (2007)

Cotter foregrounded the context of this production: 'part of a larger project conceived by the New York artist Paul Chan, 34, who is well known to the international art world for his video animations of paradises embattled and lost, and to law enforcement officials for his activist politics' (2007). The specific issues of devastation and continued racial tensions again seemed a perfect match with the experimental play that emerged from a post-Second World War, European context. 'Writing is everywhere in the Lower Ninth Ward', Cotter continues: 'A board propped against a ruined church carries a hand-painted text: "Can these bones live? Behold, I will cause breath to enter you, and ye shall live." The words, evoking an apocalyptic future, are from Ezekiel' (2007). The New Orleans performances received massive national attention, due to the collaboration of Chan and the support of the New York arts advocacy group, Creative Time, an organisation 'committed to presenting important art for our times and engaging broad audiences that transcend geographic, racial, and socioeconomic barriers' ('Creative Time Statement', n.d.).[11]

Moreover, the impact of this site-specific production of Beckett's play was extended far beyond the limits of performance, with Chan's various preparatory outreach programmes and university lectures, and the publication of his *Waiting for Godot in New Orleans: A Field Guide* (2010). The *Field Guide*'s photographic record alone ensures that the New Orleans *Godot* is the most documented production of a Samuel Beckett play in history. The volume, available in hard copy and in PDF online, contains an essay by McElroen in which he says:

> Directing a post-Katrina *Godot*. In May 2006, eight months after Hurricane Katrina, I had the opportunity to stage Samuel Beckett's *Waiting for Godot* at the Classical Theatre of Harlem. Prior to my work on the play I had seen several productions of *Godot*. And, despite the varying quality of these productions, there was always one constant: the play seemed remote. (Chan, 2010: 50)

Not only did McElroen and Chan counter the play's perceived remoteness with a shift from the abstract to the concrete, from the timeless to the timely, they put the performances in direct succession to the FST productions. The play became part of a larger event as well, something of a Dionysiac symposium, with gumbo reception, live music and parades, a theatre festival and celebration of the human spirit that 'will cause breath to enter you, and ye shall live'. The *Elosticity* blog carried the following evocation of the evening:

> The city, and, more specifically, the front porch and gutted interior of one of a row of ruined houses near the London Street Canal breach, is as appropriate a stage set as Sarajevo was for a Susan Sontag production during the war in Bosnia. The audience followed a Second Line brass band towards the bleacher seats along Pratt Street that served as a theater. The brass band of course always leads celebrations and funerals. ('Waiting for Godot', 2007)

Writing for the *NOLAFugees blog*, Anne Giselson evokes the poetry of the evening:

> The immediate 'stage' where most of the action occurred had its own stirring composition. Left to right: an upright utility pole, a north-leaning storm-bent pole, an upright artificial stage 'tree' in the center of the road as a sort of visual fulcrum and to the right another north-leaning signless post, and a rusty fire hydrant, used for full comedic effect. The soundscape was just as integral: distant police sirens, tugboat and train horns, some sharply wailing birds, all pulsing quietly in the background, muted by the once treacherous canal and surrounding empty lots of former homes. ... Beckett's characters seem to emerge from this landscape, to have always been there. ('Waiting for Godot', 2007)

But Giselson also cites the concomitant elitism of such high-profile, well-funded events:

> while hundreds of us stood around in line for a ticket, some for over an hour, joking around, grumbling, spraying ourselves with the free mosquito repellent, VIPS with lanyards sailed past us, as did some neighborhood residents who tried to argue that they'd lived there their whole lives and they shouldn't have to wait. ... I had a moment's sense of unease while in line for the port-a-let across from a graffiti-riddled storm-trashed house. Down one side of the road were hundreds of people in a soup line and on the other side was a mob crowding some police barricades, waiting. ('Waiting for Godot', 2007)

Such initiatives, however, often extract a cultural price as well, Giselson notes:

> With all this post-Katrina cultural boosterism, I feel as though we're in danger of self-parody and provincialism, always pointing our fingers back at our own 'uniqueness' but always the same uniquenesses, which become more and more commodified, less and less attached to their origins and ultimately threatening the true cultural strength of the city. ('Waiting for Godot', 2007)

Such free events, touted as such, are, moreover, never 'free', and Gilbert Moses must have realised as much in 1964 as he headed to New York to raise funds for the Free Southern Theater tour, which included New Orleans among its stops. Economic forces are always in play in the arts, in theatre and other visual arts more so than in others, perhaps. That said, such black *Godot*s, or performances of what I am calling '*Godot* Noir', have altered the landscape for Beckett's art over a fifty-year span, at least from 1957 to 2007, from the New York intellectuals of Myerberg's appeals to the dispossessed of Mississippi and 'Nawlins', those performances without an inevitable dumbing down of the art that characterises most attempts to make Beckett accessible. Such adaptation and site-specificity hardly diminish Beckett's art but, on the contrary, suggest its elasticity, its adaptability, its potential for reconfiguration, even along political lines. In San Quentin and other prisons, in churches and makeshift theatres of Mississippi and Soweto, on the battlefield of Sarajevo, amid the political divide of the West Bank, in a 2012 revival of the play by a black-led theatre company in West Yorkshire (see Dickson, 2012; Eve, 2012) – or in the still-devastated streets of New Orleans (see McDonald, 2015: 56–9) – Beckett's bones live.

Notes

1 A newspaper advert for this try-out production, called 'the International Comedy Sensation', is available in Rosset (2017: 99).
2 These documents are part of the University of California, San Diego, Alan Schneider Papers, box 74.
3 Although the nickname 'The Great White Way' indicated that Broadway was one of the first New York City streets to be illuminated in the 1890s, see also, for example, Hoffman (2014).
4 Portions of Rosset's letter are included in Beckett (2014: 12), but the editing jumbles its coherence. The letter is here quoted from Rosset (2017: 128). A full copy is also available in the Stanley E. Gontarski Grove Press Research Collection at Florida State University, catalogued under 'Archives' in the FSU Library's Special Collections, 'Correspondences'. See https://archives.lib.fsu.edu/repositories/10/resources/1064 (accessed 16 September 2021).
5 As above, this letter is available in the Stanley E. Gontarski Grove Press Research Collection at Florida State University. The original copies are held in the Grove Press Records at the Syracuse University Libraries Special Collections Research Center. See https://library.syr.edu/digital/guides/g/grove_press.htm (accessed 16 September 2021).
6 The figure is a baseball term suggesting a success rate of merely 14 per cent.
7 See the special issue on 'Black Theatre' of the *The Drama Review* (12.4, 1968) for responses by theatre groups to the assassination of Martin Luther King, Jr.
8 Ruby Cohn (1967: 79–89) includes short excerpts about the FST *Godot*.
9 See Als's 2016 *New Yorker* review. Baldwin's *Amen Corner* of 1954 was revived by London's Royal National Theatre in June 2013. Set in Harlem in a storefront or corner church, hence the title, it featured considerable gospel and spiritual music (see Billington, 2013).
10 For more critical responses to the staging of *Godot* in post-Katrina New Orleans, see, for example, Duerfahrd (2013), Moody (2013) and Rose (2017).
11 For more information about Creative Time and the New Orleans production of *Godot*, see http://creativetime.org/programs/archive/2007/chan/actor_bios.html and http://creativetime.org/programs/archive/2007/chan/play.html (accessed 16 September 2021).

References

Als, H. (2016). 'James Baldwin, onstage', *New Yorker*, 25 November, www.newyorker.com/magazine/2016/12/05/james-baldwin-onstage (accessed 5 February 2021).

Atkinson, B. (1957). 'Theater: "Godot" is back: Beckett play staged with negro cast', *New York Times*, 22 January, 25, www.nytimes.com/1957/01/22/archives/theatre-godot-is-back-beckett-play-staged-with-negro-cast.html (accessed 5 February 2021).

Baldwin, J. (1962), 'Letter from a region in my mind', *New Yorker*, 10 November, www.newyorker.com/magazine/1962/11/17/letter-from-a-region-in-my-mind (accessed 6 February 2021).

Beckett, S. (1962). 'The Old Tune', *New Writers* 2. London: John Calder, pp. 96–127.

Beckett, S. (2010). *Waiting for Godot*. Pref. M. Bryden. London: Faber and Faber.

Beckett, S. (2011). *The Letters of Samuel Beckett, Volume II: 1941–1956*. Ed. G. Craig, M. Dow Fehsenfeld, D. Gunn and L. More Overbeck. Cambridge: Cambridge University Press.

Beckett, S. (2014). *The Letters of Samuel Beckett, Volume III: 1957–1965*. Ed. G. Craig, M. Dow Fehsenfeld, D. Gunn and L. More Overbeck. Cambridge: Cambridge University Press.

Billington, M. (2013). 'The Amen Corner – review', *Guardian*, 12 June, www.theguardian.com/stage/2013/jun/12/the-amen-corner (accessed 5 February 2021).

Chan, P. (ed.) (2010). *Waiting for Godot in New Orleans: A Field Guide*, http://creativetime.org/programs/archive/2010/godotbook/PDF/godot_sec2_picture.pdf (accessed 6 February 2021).

Cohn, R. (1967). *Casebook on Waiting for Godot*. New York: Grove Press.

Cotter, H. (2007). 'A broken city. A tree. Evening', *New York Times*, 2 December, www.nytimes.com/2007/12/02/arts/design/02cott.html (accessed 6 February 2021).

'Creative Time Presents Paul Chan's *Waiting for Godot* in New Orleans: A Play in Two Acts, A Project in Three Parts' (2007). *CreativeTime.org*, https://creativetime.org/programs/archive/2007/chan/welcome.html (accessed 14 February 2021).

'Creative Time Statement of Commitment to Universal Human Rights and Free Expression' (n.d.). *CreativeTime.org*, https://creativetime.org/about/ (accessed 6 February 2021).

Dent, T., R. Schechner and G. Moses (eds) (1969). *The Free Southern Theater: A Documentary of the South's Radical Black Theater*. New York: Bobbs-Merrill.

Dickson, A. (2012). 'The waiting game: Beckett with an all-black cast', *Guardian*, 31 January, www.theguardian.com/stage/2012/jan/31/all-black-waiting-for-godot (accessed 6 February 2021).

Duerfahrd, L. (2013). *The Work of Poverty: Samuel Beckett's Vagabonds and the Theater of Crisis*. Columbus: Ohio State University Press.

Eve, M. P. (2012), 'Talawa's Waiting for Godot', 11 March, https://eve.gd/2012/03/11/talawas-waiting-for-godot/ (accessed 6 February 2021).

'Free Southern Theater' (n.d.). *Digital SNCC Gateway*, https://snccdigital.org/inside-sncc/culture-education/free-southern-theater/ (accessed 6 February 2021).

Gibbs, W. (1942). 'Finnegans teeth', *New Yorker*, 18 December, 42, www.newyorker.com/magazine/1942/12/26/finnegans-teeth (accessed 6 February 2021).

Handy, H. (n.d.) 'Free Southern Theatre Records, 1960–1978, Amistad Research Center', http://amistadresearchcenter.tulane.edu/archon/?p=collections/findingaid&id=48&q=&rootcontentid=26623 (accessed 6 February 2021).
Hoffman, W. (2014). *The Great White Way: Race and the Broadway Musical*. New Brunswick, NJ: Rutgers University Press.
Lucchesi, N. (2014). 'Here's late *Voice* theater critic Jerry Tallmer doing a proto-takedown of the *Times*', 11 November, www.villagevoice.com/2014/11/11/heres-late-voice-theater-critic-jerry-tallmer-doing-a-proto-takedown-of-the-times/ (accessed 6 February 2021).
Maloney, A. (2007). 'For New Orleanians, "Waiting for Godot" hits the spot', *NOLA.com/The Times-Picayune/The New Orleans Advocate*, 2 November, www.nola.com/entertainment_life/article_c848cf77-1a67-56dc-837d-48bbb70b5724.html (accessed 16 September 2021).
McDonald, R. (2015). '*Waiting for Godot* and Beckett's cultural impact', in D. Van Hulle (ed.), *The New Cambridge Companion to Samuel Beckett*. Cambridge: Cambridge University Press, pp. 48–59.
Minor, W. F. (1965). 'They are waiting for Godot in Mississippi, too', *New York Times*, 31 January, X3, www.nytimes.com/1965/01/31/archives/they-are-waiting-for-godot-in-mississippi-too.html (accessed 6 February 2021).
Moody, A. (2013). '*Waiting for Godot in New Orleans*: Modernist Autonomy and Transnational Performance in Paul Chan's Beckett', *Theatre Journal*, 65.4, 537–57.
Padgett, K. (n.d.). 'Mantan Moreland 1902–1973', *Blackface!*, http://black-face.com/Mantan-Moreland.htm (accessed 6 February 2021).
Rose, A. (2017). 'Beckett in New Orleans', *Samuel Beckett Today / Aujourd'hui*, 29.2, 337–49.
Rosset, B. (2017). *Dear Mr. Beckett: Letters from the Publisher, The Samuel Beckett File*. Ed. L. Oppenheim. Cur. A. M. Rosset. New York: Opus.
Schechner, R. (1964). 'Dialogue: the Free Southern Theatre', *Tulane Drama Review*, 9.4, 63–76.
Schwabacher, T. K. (1957). '*Waiting for Godot* at the Shubert', *The Harvard Crimson*, 15 January, www.thecrimson.com/article/1957/1/15/waiting-for-godot-pwhen-the-curtain/ (accessed 6 February 2021).
Tallmer, J. (1957a). 'Negro "Godot" readies on 2nd St. as Myerberg keeps on the go', *Village Voice*, 16 January, 7, 9, https://news.google.com/newspapers?nid=KEtq3P1Vf8oC&dat=19570116&printsec=frontpage&hl=en (accessed 6 February 2021).
Tallmer, J. (1957b). 'Godot: still waiting', *Village Voice*, 30 January, 7–8, www.scribd.com/doc/246271718/Village-Voice-Jerry-Tallmer-on-Waiting-for-Godot (accessed 6 February 2021).
Van Hulle, D., and P. Verhulst (2017). *The Making of Samuel Beckett's 'En attendant Godot' / 'Waiting for Godot'*. Brussels and London: University Press Antwerp and Bloomsbury.
'Waiting for Godot' (2007), *Trydersmith.org*, http://trydersmith.org/theatre/waiting-for-godot-2/ (accessed 6 February 2021).
'Waiting for Godot' (2020). *Encyclopaedia of South African Theatre, Film, Media and Performance (ESAT)*, https://esat.sun.ac.za/index.php/Waiting_for_Godot (accessed 6 February 2021).

14

Deferred dreams: waiting for freedom and equality in Nwandu and Beckett

Graley Herren

Antoinette Nwandu's provocative play *Pass Over* premiered at Chicago's Steppenwolf Theatre in 2017 and has since been produced to great acclaim in several other cities. The script specifies the setting as 'a ghetto street. a lamppost. Night' (Nwandu, 2018: 5), consciously emulating the iconic set of *Waiting for Godot*: 'A country road. A tree. Evening' (Beckett, 2010: 5). Nwandu described the play to T. J. Armour of *N'Digo* as 'a mashup of the biblical Exodus story and *Waiting for Godot* in a modern urban setting. It concerns two young black men wrestling with whether or not there is a promised land for black men in the United States'. Asked about her inspiration, she reflected:

> I wrote *Pass Over* as a response to the senseless killings of young black men that have plagued our country of late, most expressly Trayvon Martin's death. For every step forward the black community makes – specifically young black men – there is this equal and opposite violence that resists that forward progress. And that journey, that lack of unobstructed progress seems absurdist and existential. (qtd in Armour, 2017)

Pass Over is layered with overlapping strata of history, allegory, and intertextuality. All of the characters and action are simultaneously set in contemporary urban America, in 1855 on an American plantation and in thirteenth-century BCE Egypt among the enslaved children of Israel (Nwandu, 2018: 5). The two main characters, Moses and Kitch, also function as transplanted and transculturated reincarnations of Vladimir and Estragon, Beckett's exhausted but ever-vigilant tramps steadfastly awaiting rescue by Godot. Nwandu's young African American protagonists are stuck on the corner of their blighted neighbourhood block. They make plans, provide company and diversion, re-enact familiar routines and figuratively kill time while trying to avoid being literally killed by a stray bullet or an overzealous police officer. *Pass Over* also features Mister and Ossifer, two white characters played by the same actor. They represent different sides of the power structure oppressing Moses and Kitch and keeping them in bondage. Mister and Ossifer simultaneously stand in for American slave masters and the Pharaoh's army, but they also serve structural purposes comparable to Pozzo and the Boy in *Waiting for Godot*. Like his namesake, Nwandu's Moses aspires to escape captivity and pursue dreams of a Promised Land. Exodus generates the hopeful forward-moving propulsion towards freedom and equality in *Pass Over*, while *Godot* supplies counterforces of cyclical inertia, deadening habit and moral atrophy.

Nwandu is uniquely qualified to orchestrate this ingenious dialectic. Raised in the Christian Church, she is intimately familiar with the Exodus story and understands its inspirational role in the African American freedom movement. As a graduate of Harvard with a major in English who wrote her senior thesis on Beckett, she also appreciates him as the poet laureate of alienation, impotence and stagnation. Most importantly for the purposes of the present volume, Nwandu both channels and challenges approaches to adaptation in Beckett. Although he was notoriously (if inconsistently) opposed to mixing genres or departing from the strict cast, set and stage directions of his plays, Beckett freely incorporated and adapted the works of other artists as inspirations for original dialectical hybrids – what Nwandu calls 'mashups'. For instance, almost all of Beckett's teleplays incorporate seminal works by influential artists (Beethoven in *Ghost Trio*, Yeats in ... *but the clouds* ..., Schubert in *Nacht und Träume*) only to adapt them for his own radically different purposes. In this same spirit, *Pass Over* is a theatrical experiment to discover what happens when the incompatible worldviews of *Godot* and Exodus are mashed together and forced to share a single stage. In Nwandu's hands, *Godot* becomes a scalpel with which to dissect the Moses myth as an archetype for African American freedom and equality. *Pass Over* also provides a sharp blade for excising the continuing policies of exclusion that have prevailed far too long in staging Beckett's drama.

Passed over

'What happens to a dream deferred?', asks Langston Hughes in his poem 'Harlem' (1995: 426). Nwandu follows the deferred dream of a Promised Land as it festers, crusts, dries up and finally explodes without ever being realised. Her play's title evokes the Jewish Passover, a celebration commemorating the liberation of the children of Israel from slavery. Passover also honours God's mercy in passing over Jewish households during the final plague, when the angel of death killed all the first-born children of Egyptian families. Moses and Kitch are eager to follow this precedent. They dream of fleeing to freedom and equality as God's chosen people. Moses declares that he has 'got plans to rise up to my full potential / be all i could be' (Nwandu, 2018: 11). He aims to 'git my ass up off dis block' and move forward to 'dat promised land' (2018: 12). Moses and Kitch may be young, but they are not naive. They can see the evidence all around that they are trapped in a world designed to control, discourage, humiliate, incarcerate and potentially kill them. They recognise that, so far at least, they have been *passed over* for their share of the American Dream and suffer instead from the 'red white blues' (2018: 74, 76). Nevertheless, for as long as they can, they cling to the dream that a better world lies beyond this block/plantation, calling for them to pass over:

> Moses. We gon git off dis plantation
> git up off dis block
> then we gon walk
> walk right up to dat river …
> den dat river man
> iss gon part
> gon open up jess for us …
> dis life right here
> ain't gon be no jail no more
> you hear me
> ain't gon be no ghetto
> no plantation
> gon be sweet …
> Kitch. like milk and honey (2018: 56–7)

This is Moses's 'I Have a Dream' speech, his 'Let My People Go' spiritual. At such moments, Nwandu indulges hopes that the dream will not be deferred forever, that the milk and honey will not sugar over before Moses and Kitch make it to the Promised Land.

Other signs point in less optimistic directions. This is literally true of the set for the original Chicago production. Director Danya Taymor and set designer Wilson Chin used street signs to locate Moses and Kitch's lamppost at the corner of Martin Luther King Drive and East 64th Street (see Figure 14.1). The allusion to King acknowledges the play's debts to his frequent rhetorical appropriation of Exodus as a prototype for African American freedom (Selby, 2008), a strategy Nwandu borrows, if only to refract it through the existentialist prism of *Godot*. The Chicago context is also crucial. The city has been one of the epicentres of the Black Lives Matter movement because of an epidemic of shootings of young black men, a history of systemic violence and mutual distrust between the police and the black community, and a deep-seated legacy of economic disparity stretching back generations. The creative team of *Pass Over* alludes to that sordid

Waiting for freedom in Nwandu and Beckett 221

Figure 14.1 Jon Michael Hill (left) as Moses and Julian Parker (right) as Kitch in Antoinette Nwandu's *Pass Over* (Steppenwolf Theatre, Chicago).

legacy by placing Moses and Kitch at the corner of MLK Drive and 64th Street. This situates the action specifically in the Washington Park section of Woodlawn, the setting of Lorraine Hansberry's *A Raisin in the Sun* (1959). The title of this groundbreaking play is again taken from Langston Hughes's 'Harlem': 'What happens to a dream deferred? / Does is dry up / Like a raisin in the sun?' (1995: 426). The autobiographical roots of Hansberry's play are planted specifically in the Woodlawn neighbourhood, where Hansberry's family bought a house only to face resistance from white property owners opposed to racial integration. That house sits only a few blocks from MLK and 64th. A map will tell you that Steppenwolf Theatre in the Lincoln Park neighbourhood of Chicago's North Side is only about thirteen miles away from Washington Park on the South Side. But Moses and Kitch know better. They occupy a different world from those Steppenwolf patrons. These two men are as stuck as their Woodlawn lamppost, as rooted to the spot as the tree in *Waiting for Godot*. The lamppost and tree are constant reminders of immobility, incarceration, deprivation and sacrifice.

Nwandu is well aware that the tree in *Godot* gestures back to the crosses on Calvary, where Christ was crucified alongside two thieves. Vladimir and Estragon are the descendants of those crucified thieves, as are Moses and Kitch. 'One of the thieves was saved', Vladimir reminds Estragon: 'It's a reasonable percentage' (Beckett, 2010: 7). Didi and Gogo wager that the surest path to salvation involves faithfully hoping and patiently waiting for

Godot. Countless scriptural encomia endorse precisely this patience from faithful Christians. For example, the Book of Lamentations decrees: 'The Lord is good unto them that wait for him, to the soul that seeketh him. / It is good that a man should both hope and quietly wait for the salvation of the Lord' (3:25–6). The ex-Protestant Beckett knew this theological tradition well and drew upon it for his critique of Christian patience (Gontarski, 2018: 125–43). Nwandu is likewise familiar with this Christian theology, and she knows the nefarious ways it has been co-opted to caution African Americans against moving too quickly or too radically towards seizing a full measure of freedom and equality. Julius B. Fleming terms this obstructionist ideology 'black patience': 'By this I mean a racialized system of waiting that has historically produced and vitalized antiblackness and white supremacy by compelling black people to wait and to capitulate to the racialized terms and assumptions of these forced performances of waiting' (2019: 589). From their respective cultural, historical, political and theological vantage points, *Waiting for Godot* and *Pass Over* interrogate the internalised rationalisations and coercive external forces that keep their central pairs passively waiting for deliverance.

Nwandu recognises that the solution is not as simple as summoning up the courage and motivation to get up off the block and march into the Promised Land. The heavy baggage of history weighs down Moses and Kitch, and they are trapped within an oppressive system that continues to conspire against their hopes and exploit their black bodies. Nwandu is part of a movement among African American artists and intellectuals to refocus attention on the material embodiment of racism. Ta-Nehisi Coates is best known for articulating this position in his powerful extended letter to his son, *Between the World and Me* (2015). Coates enumerates the many ways throughout American history in which black bodies have not mattered – have instead been subjugated, denied, destroyed and reduced to expendable fuel for the American Dream. He contends: 'It is hard to face this. But all our phrasing – race relations, racial chasm, racial justice, racial profiling, white privilege, even white supremacy – serves to obscure that racism is a visceral experience, that it dislodges brains, blocks airways, rips muscle, extracts organs, cracks bones, breaks teeth. You must never look away from this' (2015: 10). The question that drives *Between the World and Me*, much as it drives Nwandu's *Pass Over*, is 'how do I live free in this black body?' Coates asserts: 'The question is unanswerable, which is not to say futile. The greatest reward of this constant interrogation, of confrontation with the brutality of my country, is that it has freed me from ghosts and girded me against the sheer terror of disembodiment' (2015: 12). As Coates bluntly puts it later in the book: 'In America, it is traditional to destroy the black body – *it is heritage*' (2015: 103; original emphasis).

Two faces of oppression

The beneficiaries and enforcers of that heritage of white supremacy and black subjugation are represented in *Pass Over* by Mister and Ossifer. Nwandu elaborated on her aims in an essay for *American Theatre*:

> My play *Pass Over* ... engages a majority white audience in a conversation about the violent effects of white oppression on black bodies. The embodiment of that oppression has two faces: Mister, a genteel, upper-middle-class man on his way to his mother's house, and Ossifer, a menacing beat cop. My play argues that while Ossifer's overt aggression is pernicious, Mister's complacent privilege is far more lethal. That one actor plays both parts demonstrates the connection between them: Ossifer's menace fertilizes the soil necessary for Mister's wide-eyed entitlement to thrive. (2017)

The first of these figures to emerge on the scene is Mister. Midway through the first act, a lost white man wanders onto stage with a picnic basket, unmistakably echoing the arrival of Pozzo and Lucky in *Waiting for Godot*. With his immaculate suit and his frequent exclamations of 'oh goodness' and 'gosh golly gee', he is obviously not from this neighbourhood nor from this era. He may share a street corner and stage with Moses and Kitch but, like the majority white audiences at Steppenwolf, he really comes from a different world. Some of the play's detractors have criticised its caricatured depictions of Mister and Ossifer, but this misses Nwandu's point and fails to engage the play on its own terms.[1] Of course they are types: how else can a single character simultaneously represent the Pharaoh's son, an 1850s plantation owner, a 1950s cartoon of suburban affluence, Pozzo from *Waiting for Godot*, Dorothy from *The Wizard of Oz* and Little White Riding Hood? Mister gets lost on his way to his mother's house to bring her food. He offers to share his bounty with Moses and Kitch, an inexhaustible cornucopia of every delicacy imaginable. The meal and its pleasantries end abruptly, however, when Mister corrects Moses' pronunciation of his name: 'master / my name is master' (Nwandu, 2018: 39). Embarrassed by the chilling effect this has on Moses and Kitch, he insists: 'it's just a name / a family name' (2018: 39). It is not just a name but also a potent signifier, the calling card of his white privilege and patriarchal power.

The issue of naming takes an even more sinister turn when Mister calls out Moses and Kitch for their repeated use of the 'n-word'.[2] He finds this word offensive and was taught by his mother never to use it. He asks: 'if i don't get to say / the n-word / why do you?' (2018: 45). Moses explains that some people have earned the right to use the word and some have not; Mister has not: 'iss not'chors' (2018: 45). This is where Little White Riding Hood is revealed as the Big Bad Wolf. Mister/Master roars: 'EVERYTHING'S

MINE!' (2018: 45). He claims ownership over everyone and everything. He is the slave master of this plantation, the Pharaoh of this Egypt and the Pozzo looking for a Lucky to hang his noose around and sell at the market for a good price.

As the smiling face of white oppression, Mister generally keeps his racism hidden. As the snarling face of white oppression, however, Ossifer bares his fangs like a badge of honour. He patrols this block with impunity, torturing and dehumanising its residents at leisure. He is ripped from the headlines as a brutal urban cop; he is ripped from the history books as a slave catcher; and he is ripped from the scriptures as a soldier in the Pharaoh's army. Mister tried to coax and bribe Moses and Kitch into behaving the way he wanted them to, but the heavy-handed Ossifer does not bother with such niceties. He delights in emasculation, he demands immediate compliance and he will punish any behaviour short of total submission. As soon as Kitch says something Ossifer deems insufficiently deferential, he forces both men to the ground. Then he commences with his familiar nightly routine: 'we're going to do this / nice and gentle / just like we always do' (2018: 54). The interrogation always consists of two questions: 'Who are you?' and 'Where are you going?' Moses knows the drill and supplies the mandatory responses: 'stupid / lazy / violent / thug' and 'nowhere / sir' (2018: 54). Although the vicious Ossifer bears no overt resemblance to the timid Boy who arrives near the end of Acts One and Two in *Godot*, both characters deliver messages that no Exodus is forthcoming. Ossifer also communicates another message loud and clear: black lives do not matter here.

Moses gets the message. Suffocated beneath a pall of despair, he abandons all hope for earthly escape, deciding that he can only achieve freedom through death. He convinces a reluctant Kitch to kill him, but before they can follow through with the plan they are interrupted by Ossifer's return. Kitch immediately 'assumes the position', but Moses is done following orders. He resists arrest and prepares for 'suicide by cop', telling Ossifer:

> i'm standin here
> sayin i'd rather die
> than put up wit'cho shit
> for one mo day
> but'chu won't do it
> wuss da matter
> you scared? (2018: 83)

Ossifer takes the bait and unleashes his fury, assaulting first Moses then Kitch in a staged scene of police brutality that is hard to watch. This violent climax seems headed towards certain murder as Ossifer draws his gun and points it at Moses.

Then a completely unexpected and magical thing happens. According to the stage directions, '(*The space changes.*) / (*Then,* Moses *changes too.*) / (*Then, the plagues against* Ossifer *begin.*)' (2018: 84), Moses is suddenly empowered with righteous authority. He disables Ossifer's weapon and demands the dignity and respect long denied him by this racist policeman:

> cuz we are not
> the people that'chu
> think we are
> not stupid
> not lazy
> not violent
> not thug
> We Are Men
> Two Black Men (2018: 86)

Finally, Moses performs an exorcism. Chanting with increasing intensity 'STOP KILLING US', he '*purges the evil from* Ossifer's *body*' as 'Ossifer *spews black bile from his mouth*' (2018: 86). Ossifer miraculously recognises Moses and Kitch as free human beings for the first time: 'YOU'RE MEN! / (*The plagues stop.*) / ... you're men / and you are free to go' (2018: 87).

Ossifer exits, and Moses and Kitch celebrate. They are awestruck and elated by this superhuman display, not only defeating but also curing their oppressor. It temporarily seems that black lives do matter, 'a change is gonna come' and the deferred dream is about to be realised. There is certainly no precedent for this turn of events in *Godot*. Moses enacts a perfect power reversal where the wicked are punished and the virtuous rewarded, a fantasy which Didi and Gogo never come anywhere near enjoying. Moses receives divine grace and exercises holy power; God exists and delivers his chosen people from bondage; good wins over evil.

Then Mister enters, and with him any hope of a happy ending quickly exits. The snarling face of white oppression may finally have been tamed, but the smiling face proves the more lethal threat. Mister poses the interrogation questions asked by Ossifer: 'Who are you?' and 'Where are you going?' Before Moses has a chance to answer, Mister shoots him dead on the spot (2018: 90–1). The dream deferred explodes in a bloody assassination.

Nothing to be done?

The initial Chicago run of *Pass Over* came in the immediate aftermath of Donald Trump's election as President of the United States. Trump's inflammatory rhetoric, his reactionary Obamaphobia and his repugnant tolerance of white supremacist ideology all signalled a regressive backlash against civil rights advances, heralding the dawn of a terrifying new era of racist bigotry and renewed persecution against non-white Americans. The wounds were raw when Nwandu finished writing the play, and it shows in her original conclusion. Mister is given the final word, and it is a triumphalist manifesto. He proclaims that what has 'passed over', in this play and in America, is the aberrational blip in white dominance briefly represented by the Obama administration:

> it's passed because we have done
> what we were meant to do
> we stood our ground
> we caught the bad guys
> we took back what was ours
> and now
> together
> we will make sure
> that no one ever
> ever
> ever
> takes it back from us again[3]

While Mister never quotes the Trump rally cry 'Make America Great Again', the same message comes through unmistakably:

> all that we once had
> is ours again
> this country
> is ours again
> isn't it great

Mister's old-fashioned 1950s hokum was largely used for comic effect in Act One, but it is no laughing matter at the play's conclusion. He hails from the pre-civil-rights era and speaks for a frighteningly large faction of Americans nostalgic for that period of invincible white hegemony.

Nwandu's vision of America had shifted by 2018, and accordingly she revised the closing speech when *Pass Over* transferred to New York's Lincoln Center Theater. Mister still gets the last word, but his jingoistic bravado is replaced with ambivalence. After shooting Moses, Mister weirdly expresses concern over the recurring murders of young men of colour. He laments that 'another black fella was killed' and wonders why this keeps happening (2018: 91). He claims to be sad and confused by the epidemic of violence and injustice. But he also confesses to sympathy-fatigue and admits to feeling 'helpless / to change / or intervene' (2018: 92). In contrast to Chicago

Mister's victory speech, New York Mister ends on an irresolute note of resignation:

> (*Then a big performative sigh; self-conscious without being ironic.*)
> (*A moment.*)
> (*Then his demeanor brightens.*)
> anyway...
> (*Blackout.*) (2018: 93)

It is difficult to square Mister's tepid sympathy and paralysed inaction in this closing monologue with his cold-blooded murder of Moses. But this is not realism, after all, so rational logic is not the right lens through which to view the conclusion. The New York ending resonates more closely with Nwandu's absurdist source text. Mister's 'anyway...' essentially closes *Pass Over* on the same resigned note with which Beckett begins *Godot*: 'Nothing to be done' (2010: 5).

Nwandu sends different signals to different segments of her audience in the conclusion of *Pass Over*. In her 2017 think piece for *American Theatre*, the playwright reflected on her desired impact upon African American audience members: 'Reconciliation is impossible without an honest conversation about who is angry at whom, and I am deeply grateful for the opportunity to present a reality that most black audience members identify with and find cathartic in a historically white institutional space'. *Pass Over*'s transition from the sadistic 2017 Steppenwolf Mister to the impotent 2018 Lincoln Center Mister reflects Nwandu's revised diagnosis about the deepest sources of the problem. She shifts attention from the overtly threatening officer with a badge and gun to the comparatively benign white civilian with a season subscription, one whose privilege and apathy silently contribute to perpetuating systemic racial injustice. Nwandu may have little opportunity to reach the Ossifers of the world through her play, but she encounters ambivalent, conscious-stricken, yet fundamentally ineffectual Misters at every performance. She confronts these audiences in a 'historically white institutional space' and challenges them to face down an uncomfortable worldview in which 'black lives do not matter and white lives remain unburdened by the necessary work of reckoning with white privilege and the centuries-long legacy of violence by which it is secured'.

Nwandu provides the impetus for that reckoning in *Pass Over*, and she appropriates *Waiting for Godot* as a clarion for her wakeup call. Vladimir uses sleep and dream imagery late in the play as he confronts the dire consequences of doing nothing. After Pozzo and Lucky exit for the last time, and as an exhausted Estragon drifts back to sleep, Vladimir muses with self-lacerating poignancy: 'Was I sleeping, while the others suffered?

Am I sleeping now? Tomorrow, when I wake, or think I do, what shall I say of today? That with Estragon my friend, at this place until the fall of night, I waited for Godot? That Pozzo passed, with his carrier, and that he spoke to us? Probably. But in all that what truth will there be?' (Beckett, 2010: 87). Vladimir admits to sleepwalking through life, and he confronts his callous disregard for the suffering of others: 'The air is full of our cries. [*He listens.*]' (2010: 87). However, he also identifies a counterimpulse of inertia that makes it easier to stop up his ears and remain wilfully deaf to those cries: 'But habit is a great deadener' (2010: 87). Nwandu tries to make her audience recognise that unchecked privilege and entitlement are likewise great deadeners. Whether the root cause is apathetic adherence to habitual routine, or whether it is uncritical acquiescence to the racially biased status quo, the result is a lethal case of moral atrophy. Deferred dreams of salvation will not cure this illness and neither will permanently ignoring these problems in hopes that they will simply go away.

Wakeup call

Following Nwandu's cue, and accepting her challenge to confront difficult truths, it is time to face some hard facts about Beckett's own theatrical legacy. Simply put, Beckett has a problem with inclusiveness. For decades now, theatrical practitioners have bemoaned the interventionist tactics, first of Beckett himself and later of his executors, of condemning, forbidding, disavowing or shutting down certain productions of his work that depart from the playwright's exacting specifications about cast, set and stage directions. It has long been observed, however, that Beckett and his proxies have been lax in enforcing these expectations if the artist knew Beckett personally or if the artist's aesthetic instincts were deemed trustworthy. As biographer James Knowlson observes, 'it made a tremendous difference if he liked and respected the persons involved' (1996: 608). The truth is that those artists liked and respected enough to be permitted creative liberties in adapting Beckett's work have almost always been white men while those denied equal artistic autonomy – not always, but far too frequently – have been women and/or people of colour.

Notice the conspicuous patterns of discrimination in productions singled out for rejection, denunciation or legal injunction:

- A proposed (and denied) 1973 production of *Waiting for Godot* featuring Estelle Parsons and Shelley Winters [Beckett's justification to Linda Ben-Zvi for his refusal to grant permission: 'Women don't have prostates' (qtd in Ben-Zvi, 1990: x)].[4]

- JoAnne Akalaitis's *Endgame* for ART in 1984, directed by a woman with a multiracial cast [according to Beckett: 'The American Repertory Theater production which dismisses my directions is a complete parody of the play as conceived by me. Anybody who cares for the work couldn't fail to be disgusted by this' (qtd in Kalb, 1989: 79)].
- De Haarlemse Toneelschuur's all-female cast of *Godot*, which the Beckett Estate unsuccessfully sued to prevent in 1988 ('Dutch to defy Beckett', 1988).
- The Denver Center Theatre's *Godot* starring two women [with this disclaimer inserted in the programme: 'Samuel Beckett wrote *Waiting for Godot* for five male characters and has never approved otherwise' (qtd in Ben-Zvi, 1990: xvii)].
- The Beckett Estate's successful lawsuit against Bruton Boussagol for staging an unauthorised all-female production of *Godot* at the 1991 Avignon Festival (Baldwin, 2014: 2).
- Deborah Warner's transgressive production of *Footfalls*, mounted at the Garrick Theatre in 1994 but prevented by the estate from a follow-up European tour (Bedell, 1994).
- The estate's attempted injunction against Studio Theatre's 1998 production of *Godot* in Washington, D.C., featuring African American performers as Didi and Gogo (McGrath, 1988).
- The forced cancellation of a 1998 Edinburgh Festival Fringe production of *Godot* featuring two women [from a Grimey Up North Theatre Company spokesperson: 'The Beckett estate just thought we were a gay rights group or that we had a political motive, but that wasn't the case. The women were tramp-like, but they thought it was a transvestite production' ('Waiting for no woman', 1998)].
- The estate's unsuccessful attempt to shut down the Pontedera Theatre's 2006 Italian production of *Godot* with two women in the lead roles (Billington, 2006).
- The Estate's notification to director Christopher McElroen in 2011 to cease all future Classical Theatre of Harlem productions of *Godot*, widely praised for its multiracial, site-specific productions in hurricane-ravaged New Orleans [McElroen's response: 'There is no doubt that I have pushed the boundaries of the text by placing the show in New Orleans .... But that is the very thing that has been celebrated about the production, which has garnered international acclaim for its faithfulness, its sense of contemporary relevance and immediacy, its artistic merit, and for introducing Samuel Beckett into communities that would otherwise never experience his work' (qtd in Shanahan and Goldstein, 2011)].
- The cancellation of Oberlin College's all-female *Godot* in 2019 [after hastily replacing *Godot* with Jen Silverman's queer play *Collective Rage*, director Tlaloc Rivas asked Oberlin audiences to '[c]ome out and support this production and throw up a middle finger to all the toxic masculinity that still manifests itself when women and people of color try to assert artistic expression anywhere' (qtd in Simakis, 2019)].

This list is selective, not exhaustive, but it certainly is damning. And it does not account for all of the productions which were never even contemplated for fear of facing the certain wrath and targeted profiling tactics of Beckett's gatekeepers. Given this deplorable track record, how can theatrical communities comprised chiefly of women, people of colour and their allies – which is to say, the majority of contemporary theatrical communities – feel anything but unwelcome? It is time for those of us who value Beckett's work to confront and rectify this inclusivity problem. 'Women don't have prostates' can no longer be brushed aside as clever or cute or quaint and then be accepted as a valid rationale for permanently barring half the world's population from performing in *Godot*. In her seething article for the *Cleveland Plain Dealer*, 'It's 2019 and women still can't wait for Godot, even in Oberlin', Andrea Simakis tells it straight: 'Now, nearly 30 years after his death, the Nobel prize-winner has reached his hoary hand from the grave to strangle off opportunities for actors with ovaries at Oberlin College' (2019). Listen to that tone of contempt and register her righteous indignation. But also pay close attention, my fellow Beckettians, because she is right to be angry – and the future is on her side.

Antoinette Nwandu's *Pass Over* challenges audiences, critics, scholars and practitioners to confront the consequences of white institutional bigotry in theatre. The short-sighted protectionism of Beckett and his estate, which has all too often insulated his work from experimental adaptations, especially by women and people of colour, is an outdated remnant of that systemic bigotry. It is time to face this problem and fix it, not merely permitting but fully embracing creatively and demographically diverse adaptations of Beckett's work. This dream has been deferred too long and, if not remedied in the near future, then Beckett's theatrical legacy may dry up like a raisin in the sun.

Notes

1 For the most controversial example, see Weiss (2017). Nwandu's supporters in the Chicago theatre community were so outraged by Weiss's tone-deaf review that a protest petition was circulated against her and many venues cut off her access to reviewing their productions. For an overview of the contretemps, see Tran (2017) and Nwandu's own reflections (2017).
2 In addition to the controversial Weiss review, *Pass Over* was also subject of another offensive review by Katy Walsh for the blog *Fourth Walsh* with the cringe-worthy title 'The n-word is Nwandu'. Walsh quickly amended the original piece, changed the title and issued an apology (2017). The experience with Weiss and Walsh motivated Nwandu to insert 'A note about the language in this play' in the published script. The n-word is uttered over 200 times during the performance

of *Pass Over*. Nevertheless, in her note Nwandu explicitly declares: 'Let me be crystal clear: Aside from the actors saying lines of dialogue while in character, this play is in no way shape or form an invitation for anyone to use the n-word. Not during table work, not during talkbacks, not during after-work drinks' (2018: 7).

3 All quotations from this original ending are transcribed from Spike Lee's filmed version of the Steppenwolf production of *Pass Over* (2018). The revised New York ending is in the published script.

4 See also Beckett's justification to Barney Rosset: 'I am against women playing GODOT and wrote to Miss Parsons to that effect. Theatre sex is not interchangeable and GODOT by women would sound as spurious as HAPPY DAYS or NOT I played by men. It was once performed in Israel, without our authorisation, by an all-female cast, with disastrous effect' (2016: 335–6).

References

Armour, T. J. (2017). 'Q&A with Antoinette Nwandu, playwright of "Pass Over"', *N'Digo*, 29 May, https://ndigo.com/2017/05/29/16593/ (accessed 5 February 2021).

Baldwin, P. (2014). *The Copyright Wars: Three Centuries of Trans-Atlantic Battle*. Princeton, NJ: Princeton University Press.

Beckett, S. (2010). *Waiting for Godot*. Pref. M. Bryden. London: Faber and Faber.

Beckett, S. (2016). *The Letters of Samuel Beckett, Volume IV: 1966–1989*. Ed. G. Craig, M. Dow Fehsenfeld, D. Gunn and L. More Overbeck. Cambridge: Cambridge University Press.

Bedell, G. (1994). 'Profile: disturbing the picnic: Deborah Warner', *Independent*, 17 July, www.independent.co.uk/voices/profile-disturbing-the-picnic-deborah-warner-the-director-who-shocked-glyndebourne-is-bold-emotional-1414397.html (accessed 5 February 2021).

Ben-Zvi, L. (ed.) (1990). *Women in Beckett: Performance and Critical Perspectives*. Urbana and Chicago: University of Illinois Press.

Billington, M. (2006). 'Beckett estate fails to stop women waiting for Godot', *Guardian*, 4 February, www.theguardian.com/world/2006/feb/04/arts.italy (accessed 5 February 2021).

Coates, T. (2015). *Between the World and Me*. New York: Spiegel & Grau.

'Dutch to defy Beckett on women in "Godot"' (1988). *New York Times*, 12 April, www.nytimes.com/1988/04/12/theater/dutch-to-defy-beckett-on-women-in-godot.html (accessed 5 February 2021).

Fleming, Jr., J. B. (2019). 'Transforming geographies of black time: how the Free Southern Theater used the plantation for civil rights activism', *American Literature*, 91.3, 587–617.

Gontarski, S. E. (2018). *Revisioning Beckett: Samuel Beckett's Decadent Turn*. New York: Bloomsbury Academic.

Hansberry, L. (1959). *A Raisin in the Sun*. New York: Random House.

Hughes, L. (1995). *The Collected Poems of Langston Hughes*. Ed. A. Rampersad. New York: Knopf.

Kalb, J. (1989). *Beckett in Performance*. Cambridge: Cambridge University Press.

Knowlson, J. (1996). *Damned to Fame: The Life of Samuel Beckett*. New York: Simon & Schuster.

McGrath, S. (1998). 'Beckett estate probes D.C. Studio's *Godot*', *Playbill*, 18 November, www.playbill.com/article/beckett-estate-probes-dc-studios-godot-com-78532 (accessed 5 February 2021).

Nwandu, A. (2017). 'When critics don't like their reflection', *American Theatre*, 27 June, www.americantheatre.org/2017/06/27/when-critics-dont-like-their-reflection/ (accessed 5 February 2021).

Nwandu, A. (2018). *Pass Over*. New York: Samuel French.

Pass Over (2018). Writ. A. Nwandu. Dir. (stage) D. Taymor. Dir. (film) S. Lee. Star. J. M. Hill, J. Parker, R. Hallahan and B. DeLong. 40 Acres & a Mule Filmworks and Amazon Studios.

Selby, G. S. (2008). *Martin Luther King and the Rhetoric of Freedom: The Exodus Narrative in America's Struggle for Civil Rights*. Waco, TX: Baylor University Press.

Shanahan, M., and M. Goldstein (2011). 'No more "Waiting"', *Boston.com*, 25 January, http://archive.boston.com/ae/celebrity/articles/2011/01/25/no_more_waiting/ (accessed 5 February 2021).

Simakis, A. (2019). 'It's 2019 and women still can't wait for Godot, even in Oberlin', *Cleveland Plain Dealer*, 17 November, www.cleveland.com/news/2019/11/even-in-oberlin-in-2019-women-still-cant-wait-for-godot-andrea-simakis.html (accessed 5 February 2021).

Tran, D. (2017). 'The review that shook Chicago', *American Theatre*, 27 June, www.americantheatre.org/2017/06/27/the-review-that-shook-chicago/ (accessed 5 February 2021).

'Waiting for no woman: acting in Godot is strictly for males' (1998). *Herald*, 26 July, www.heraldscotland.com/news/12255770.waiting-for-no-woman-acting-in-godot-is-strictly-for-males/ (accessed 5 February 2021).

Walsh, K. (2017). 'Review "Pass Over" (Steppenwolf Theatre): didn't pass over, impaled me!', *The Fourth Walsh*, 12 June, http://thefourthwalsh.com/2017/06/review-pass-over-steppenwolf-theatre/ (accessed 5 February 2021).

Weiss, H. (2017). '"Pass Over" envisions a Godot-like endgame for young black men', *Chicago Sun-Times*, 13 June, https://chicago.suntimes.com/entertainment/pass-over-envisions-a-godot-like-endgame-for-young-black-men/ (accessed 5 February 2021).

15

'How can you photograph words?': expanding the *Godot* universe from adaptation to transmedia storytelling

Luciana Tamas and Eckart Voigts

Adaptations frequently raise questions of cultural power. This chapter looks at two specific cases that recontextualise Samuel Beckett's most powerful play, *Waiting for Godot*, in this regard. Beginning with an overview of inter- and transcultural revisionings of *Godot*, we show how its adaptations initiate a two-way process of transcoding: adapters 'exert power over what they adapt' (Hutcheon, 2013: 150), but they also use what they adapt to intervene in situations of cultural encounter. *Godot* is at the same time a largely 'universal' commentary on the existential, absurd human condition – whether in the UK, the US, China, France or Romania – but it also becomes a recontextualised intervention specific to the various moments when it re-emerges. For what purpose is whatever cultural power that has accrued to *Godot* used and what adaptations do these different contexts require? We begin by showing how the adapted *Godot*s are transformed into a tool for political or social engagement. Addressing issues of violence as well as of cultural and semiotic transcoding, our chapter focuses on two works that represent different phases in intertextual and intermedial engagement: Matei Vişniec's theatrical appropriation, *Le dernier Godot* (1987, published 1998), and Rudi Azank's filmed web series adaptation *While Waiting for Godot* (2013). We also show how the ambiguous, arguably violent vocabulary of *Godot* led to the play being censored or prohibited by totalitarian regimes, which we discuss with reference to Vişniec's appropriation.

Beckett's *Godot*s, 'tradaptation' and transmediation

There is no definitive version of *Waiting for Godot*, as even the 'authorised versions' exist in two languages, French and English, and Beckett collaborated intensely on a third, Elmar and Erika Tophoven's German translation. Beckett wrote *En attendant Godot* in French between October 1948 and January 1949 as a recreational exercise after the painful composition of the trilogy

– *Molloy*, *Malone meurt* and *L'Innommable* (Knowlson, 1996: 376–8) – but it took years until its first stage appearance. After a preliminary abridged studio production for the French Club d'Essai de la Radio on 17 February 1952 (Feldman, 2015: 157), *Godot*, directed by Roger Blin, who also played the part of Pozzo, subsequently premiered on 5 January 1953 at the Théâtre de Babylone in Paris. The first English-language production took place later, on 3 August 1955 at the Arts Theatre in London (see Knowlson, 1996: 413–17). While the initial response to the play was general incomprehension (although the reviews were mixed rather than hostile), it is now the best-known text by Beckett and his most widely produced play.

As Richard Rorty remarks, '"the world becomes view" as the intellectuals (and gradually, everyone else) realize that anything can be made to look good or bad, interesting or boring, by being recontextualized, redescribed' (1993: 113). Beckett's transformation of theatrical vocabulary, too, has incited playwrights and directors to redefine his work – either in more simplified, graspable 'formulas' or in reinterpretations that add to its initial connotations. *Godot* thus has a rich and varied global production history on the stage. We can note several cases of extravagant, irreverent, parodic or appropriative stagings of the play. It has been 'tradapted' as far away as mainland China – as *Dengdai Geduo* in Shanghai in 1987. In 1998, Lin Zhaohua merged Beckett and Chekhov in *Sam Jiemei – Dengdai Geduo* (*Three Sisters – Waiting for Godot*) at Beijing's People's Art Theatre and, more recently, Contemporary Legend Theatre staged a *xiqu* (Chinese opera) adaptation in 2005 (Jianxi and Ingham, 2009: 131–7). In Japan, there were Shingeki and Noh adaptations of *Godot* as well as *Yattekita Godot* (*Godot Who Has Come*, Minoru Betsuyaku, 2007), originating one of the most recurrent adaptational motifs: the introduction of Godot as a character. Seikou Ito turns *Godot* into the waiting entity in his *Godot Being Awaited* (*Godot wa Matarenagara*, 1992) (see Tajiri and Tanaka, 2009: 152–9). Roger Assaf tradapted *Godot* in Lebanese at Ain al-Mreisseh's Beirut Theatre. In India, Aligarh Muslim University's Raleigh Literary Society staged an adaptation in 2016, *Waiting for Good Days*, which referenced political issues in India and renamed Pozzo and Lucky Mr Ban and Mr Question. A few months before his death, Bertolt Brecht even planned to adapt *Godot*, which had had its first West German premiere as *Wir warten auf Godot* at the West Berlin Schlossparktheater in September 1953. His adaptation would have juxtaposed documentary film depicting revolutionary movements with the characters embodying social types – Estragon as an industrial worker, Vladimir as an intellectual, Lucky as a police officer and Pozzo as an aristocrat (see Hartel et al., 2009: 89).

As a media-specific artist, Beckett was not always welcoming towards adaptations of his plays, and the majority of the few existing transpositions of *Godot* to other media have been 'reverent' and 'faithful'. When Roman Polanski and Jack MacGowran approached Beckett about a film adaptation of *Godot*, he explained his rejection in no uncertain terms: 'I'm terribly sorry to disappoint you and Polanski but I don't want any film of *Godot*. As it stands it is simply not cinema material and adaptation would destroy it. Please forgive me. And don't think of me as a purist bastard' (qtd in Hutchings, 2005: 18). When Peter O'Toole suggested another movie adaptation by Tom Stoppard shot in western Ireland, Beckett made a clear medium-specific argument that tied his play to the stage as an oral institution, to use Ginka Steinwachs' pun on Schiller's 'moral institution' (qtd in Lippert, 2013): 'How can you photograph words?' (qtd in Hutchings, 2005: 18). Responding to Donald McWhinnie's television adaptation, Beckett explained medium-specificity in terms of size: 'My play wasn't written for this box. My play was written for small men locked in a big space. Here you're all too big for the place' (qtd in Knowlson, 1996: 487–8).

There are, however, a few medium-specific film adaptations, appropriations, prequels and sequels, often by amateurs, students or semi-professionals. Richard Becker's *Finding Godot* (2012), for example, presents Vladimir and Estragon on a bench after the final curtain has fallen on the play in performance. The Greek fifteen-minute *Godot Came* (Leyteris Tsatsis and Thanassis Scroubelos, 2019) presents a single old man called Mistos (but addressed as Estragon by Godot) who relates his encounter with both Godot and a transvestite boy to his father's suit.[1] Just as in Rudi Azank's adaptation discussed below, this *Godot* is set in an urban milieu of vagrant musicians and artists. Marc Nadal's 2011 'micromovie' *Marionetas* features two female puppets abandoned by Godot, among other instances of more or less educational videography on social media.[2] We also find several transpositions into audio-only productions such as Herbert Berghof's, based on his 1956 Broadway production at the John Golden Theatre. Having received the English translation from Beckett in 1953, the staff at the BBC's Third Programme noted after some internal debate that *En attendant Godot* was 'a "basically radiogenic" work suitable for immediately [sic] translation and adaptation on radio' (qtd in Feldman, 2015: 156).

Even considering Beckett's evident dislike of adaptation and insistence that art must be medium-specific, it is quite surprising that there have been relatively few adaptations of *Godot* in other media, and even less research in the field. Linda Hutcheon argues that experimental texts – such as Beckett's – are less easily and less frequently adapted than linear realist novels (2013: 15). The idea that there are 'difficult' or even 'unfilmable' texts, however, has come under scrutiny in recent adaptation studies, and we illustrate two ways in which such adaptations or appropriations of *Godot* have been accomplished.

Le dernier Godot

The Romanian-French playwright Matei Vişniec, an acclaimed (Oică, 2017: 561) and self-declared (Vişniec, 2019) successor of Beckett and Eugène Ionesco, wrote the one-act play *Le dernier Godot*, which constructs a setting that enables Godot and Beckett to meet. Here, Godot calls Beckett to account for not allowing him to appear onstage, as in the following exchange:

> Samuel Beckett: You don't call me Judas! You've no right to call me to account!
>
> Godot: I've no right to call you to account? Oh, let's get this straight. I am *the only one* who has this right. Just who do you think you are? Look at Shakespeare! All of his characters appear onstage. Even the ghost does! Everything that's on paper goes onstage. ... Do you think it's been easy for me all these years? After all, who am I? What am I? How can you possibly play with me like this? (*Gradually starts whining.*) One minute would've been enough... Even just one second... I could've said one word. Any word... I could have said, 'no'. (Vişniec, 2020: 58–9)[3]

Godot's saying 'one word, any word' onstage, however, would create a breach in Beckett's original dramatic intentions, since the play's theatrical composition and vocabulary rest upon Godot's absence.

Beckett's *Godot* gravitates around the eponymous character, a named but absent entity who never engages in direct action. In this sense, he is the reverse of Beckett's unnamed (and unnameable) protagonist in *L'Innommable*. Unlike the latter, Godot does have a name, be it one abusively invoked, yet he never materialises as a palpable being. Rather, Godot is generated by the other protagonists' projections, and whenever we search for evidence of his existence, we can rely solely on the testimony of a boy with slippery memory, who claims to have interacted with him. Godot's very absence, however, and the repetitive invocation of his name paradoxically turn him into an omnipresent entity.

We may arguably identify another unnamed, yet equally omnipresent, entity in Beckett's text, which has been almost fully omitted from Vişniec's appropriation: violence – verbal, physical or ontological – appears as an inerasable element in the characters' language and behaviour.[4] There is an inherent interrelation between language, violence and Godot, since the latter two stem primarily – though, in the case of violence, not exclusively – from language. Godot requires language and violence to gain apparent materiality; to the other characters, violence becomes a means of communication through which they can enact their waiting. While Godot gives them an existential purpose, a 'pretext' that feeds their illusions (Oică, 2017: 564), violence appears as its manifestation and means – for instance, as they decide to 'hang [them]selves immediately' while they wait (Beckett, 2010: 13). Violence also occasionally becomes a pastime, for instance when Vladimir and Estragon decide to 'play at ... Pozzo and Lucky' (2010: 68). Furthermore, it is a manifestation of the power relations among the characters, as seen, for example, in the verbally – 'You're being spoken to, pig! Reply!' (2010: 24) – and physically – 'LUCKY *kicks him violently in the shins*' (2010: 29) – abusive interaction between Pozzo and Lucky. The same applies to the relationship between Vladimir and Estragon, who are engaged in persistent verbal or physical aggression. Since both violence and Godot appear solely as manifestations of the other characters' language and behaviour – and not as palpable characters in their own right – they appear to have an important symbolic value. In their absence, the other characters' existence would be devoid of meaning, which thus secures Godot and violence in positions of power. Simultaneously, it is precisely the characters' indulging in meaningless violent acts as well as their fruitless waiting for Godot that inhibits them from advancing. In this sense, Godot – who becomes synonymous with waiting, so that Vladimir remarks they are 'waiting for Godot, waiting for... waiting' (2010: 173) – and violence are the other characters' common language, which constitutes and informs their microcosm. It is thus violence as well as Godot's absence that appear to be the guiding principles of the play. If Godot were to appear onstage for 'just one second', as Vișniec's Godot demands, he would gain palpable reality and lose his metaphorical omnipresence (as indeed he does in Vișniec's appropriation).

Godot's absence and the ensuing violence paradoxically enhance his power over the other characters and enable him to create a 'dictatorship' to which he subjects them. His status as a constant yet never embodied promise of something can explain why, after the play's 1957 production at San Quentin Prison, the convicts saw 'Godot [as] society' or 'the outside' (Esslin, 2001: 20). Similarly, he can represent the power structures of New York in Azank's adaptation, discussed below. This reading also explains the distaste of the censors from the communist bloc for this play, as it dangerously 'spoke eloquently to those early audiences of the absurdities and frustration of life under a totalitarian regime' (Bradby, 2003: 165). Thus, the communist bloc (as well as fascist Spain) 'had surveillance systems that hindered the production of Beckett plays' (Fernández Quesada, 2011: 193). In Romania (Esrig, 2018), for example, where Vișniec originates from, the play was met with aggressive, ideologically informed criticism, as a 'disintegrative' example of the 'decadent productions' of the West (Călin, 1958: 30).[5] *Godot* made reviewers of the time 'realise with shattering certainty the moribund character of this [Western] literature'; such plays made 'the human condition disappear, transform[ed] the individual either into a haunted animal, into a neurotic paralysed by the force of obsessions, or into a non-being' (1958: 30). The author of the review, as was habitual in such journals (see Miłosz, 1955), draws from an ideological discourse based on stark dichotomies: the depravity of the West versus the moral purity of the East. Under the guise of literary criticism, reviewers claimed that the Western mentality led not only to the negation of 'any constructive élan, but also to the disappearance of humanity, and ... to the self-destruction of man through abulia, existential nausea, despair, and fear' (Călin, 1958: 30). Later, the malleability of Beckett's play enabled readings of it to become tools for political engagement or subversion, as, for instance, with Susan Sontag's 1992 direction of the play in Sarajevo, 'at the height of the Serb bombardment of the city' (Bradby, 2003: 165).

It was in this socio-political context that Vișniec wrote *Le dernier Godot* in 1987, a much less (overtly) violent interpretation of Beckett's original. We can trace this 'toning down' back to the impact of communist censorship. Authors were constantly under censors' scrutiny, and expressing thoughts that contradicted the collective ideology jeopardised authors' freedom or lives (see, for instance, Miłosz, 1955; Simuț, 2008). This often led to self-censorship – writers' and artists' instinctive gesture of eliminating 'forbidden' ideas and notions, such as 'loneliness, hesitations, thoughts of death, doubts, love, ... the hope in God', which were seen as 'reminiscences of a demobilizing bourgeois thinking' that obstructed the creation of a new proletarian society (Simuț, 2008).[6] As Czesław Miłosz explains, writers would often 'get halfway through a phrase, and already ... submit it to Marxist criticism', imagining 'what X or Y will say about it, and ... change' the text so that it would fit the ideology, because 'the objective conditions [necessary to the realisation of a work of art] ha[d] disappeared' (1955: 14). Other authors describe self-censorship as a humiliation and a daily dissimulation within families and society or as a generalised alienation (Nedelcovici qtd in Pascu-Oglindă, 2016). Some writers nevertheless dared to attempt vague textual subversions through a ciphered language that tried to evade censors' reading and invited like-minded readers to search beyond the text's surface-level interpretations (Simuț, 2008).

Vișniec defines *Le dernier Godot* as the only postmodern play he has written, along with *Mașinăria Cehov* (2008), but interprets postmodernism only in terms of intertextuality (Cheianu, 2001). Yet, as Vișniec's generational peer, writer and theorist Alexandru Mușina explains, postmodern literature during or immediately after communism was impossible in Eastern Europe, where to speak of postmodernism was like 'speaking of the "paradise" of consumerist society, "remade" in and through the "materials" found in a garbage bin [because], with the Russian occupation ..., the entire East was pulled back approximately half a century' (1996: 123).[7] Attempts at a postmodern literature in the East could therefore only be made by 'authors who "remake" ... a paradise inside the trash bin into which they were born ..., or by hyper-refined authors who find refuge within the text, and away from reality' (1996: 124). Whether or not Vișniec's play is 'postmodern', it is an intertextual gesture of subversion. While he never praised the regime through his texts – shown also by the fact that his career on Romanian stages began only after the fall of the Iron Curtain (Nelega, 2001) – neither was he a declared opponent. Yet in writing – two years before the 1989 revolution – the appropriation of a play that was unacceptable to the regime (Esrig, 2018), Vișniec indirectly exercised a form of subversion. As shown above, there have been interpretations of Beckett's *Godot* as representing 'the outside' – as the act of waiting for something that fails to arrive, with its ensuing alienation. This summarises the lives of numerous people subjected to communist dictatorship and, in this regard, Vișniec is an 'expert' on *Godot*'s microcosm, as well as on 'the existential experience of waiting' (Bradby, 2003: 165). Furthermore, considering that *Le dernier Godot* is 'one of the last plays he wrote in Romanian, just a few weeks before he left for France' for political reasons (Lecossois, 2008: 93), his *Godot* can be seen as an exercise in getting to know the 'outside'.

Le dernier Godot presents the eponymous character in a constellation different from Beckett's: while Godot continues to exist outside any interaction with the other – now erased – characters of the original play, he is no longer absent. Instead, he now appears 'behind the scenes', in a dialogue with Beckett. *Le dernier Godot* reverses the original patterns in accordance with Vișniec's stance towards the 'model', which he sees as a starting point that informs the subsequent work written by another author. The 'model', to him, functions as the impulse for a creation which needs to distance itself aesthetically from the source (Vișniec, 1994: 149). His reinterpretation of *Godot* indeed transforms the elements he borrowed, and in this sense we can see *Le dernier Godot* as an appropriation, which 'affects [sic] a more decisive journey away from the informing source into a wholly new cultural product and domain' (Sanders, 2006: 26).

Vișniec reduces the play to one act, and this dramatic decision is arguably an ironic stance towards Beckett's largely repeating the first act in his second (a hint of which we can read in the title of another play by Vișniec, *Mais maman, ils nous racontent au deuxième acte ce qu'il s'est passé au premier*). While Beckett has suppressed the world in his version of *Godot*, reducing it to a few (male) characters and a tree, Vișniec sacrifices the play's characters entirely and recontextualises only the previously absent Godot. *Le dernier Godot* borrows elements from both the textual and extratextual levels of Beckett's *Godot* which allows Godot and Beckett to meet and to thus symbolically transgress the textual boundaries that had separated them. As Oică notes, Godot and Beckett appear in a literary '(extra)-reality' and in a 'fictional meta-reality' (2017: 563). The originally fictional character is now given a 'real' presence that allows him to exist on the same level as his creator. This gives the former a voice – and therefore the authority – to question and defy the latter's dramatic choices. Yet, at the same time, Godot's presence and voice dispossess him of his previously enigmatic aura; instead, he now appears as a tired, aged man. His voice and presence are at first more tangible than Beckett's, but Beckett becomes a fictional character and thus receives a sliver of Godot's mysterious power:

> Godot: Extraordinary! I see that you exist.
>
> Samuel Beckett: I do. I exist, of course. Who made you think I didn't?
>
> Godot: ... for some years, I have been asking myself whether you exist or not. ... There were days on which I thought maybe you don't. (Vișniec, 2020: 58)

Godot does here what the characters in the original play do not – he doubts Beckett's existence, which, in turn, grants the latter a mythic aura.

Furthermore, Vișniec constructs a meta-theatrical setting that is reminiscent of Beckett's *Godot*: Beckett-the-character and Godot are the only remaining spectators left of a now deserted theatre, from which they have both been evicted. The two men, both described in the same manner – '*GODOT, a skinny man, but decently dressed ... and a second skinny man – but decently dressed*' (Vișniec, 2020: 57) – have a conversation outside the theatre, gradually discovering each other's identity. Here, Vișniec simplifies the power relations present in the source text: violence, one of the catalysts in Beckett's play, is replaced by a polite mimicking thereof – a few threats and swearwords the two do not act upon: 'you numb nut', 'I'll punch you one', 'Go on, punch me! ... You know, Mister, you've punched me enough ... so far' (2020: 58). Godot reveals the act of aggression that Beckett had been allegedly exerting over him by not allowing him to appear onstage: 'You've been boiling me like a rat .... Night after night, every second, for years and years. You've ... destroyed me. You've made a ghost out of me, a dummy, you've humiliated me. ... You bastard! Now you'll pay for everything! (*Crushingly*.) I am Godot!' (2020: 58), or 'How is it possible ... to be and not to be, at the same time?' (2020: 59). Lamentation then quickly replaces the verbal violence, as Godot begs Beckett to change his script: 'Perhaps it was ... A bad day... But things could heal ... Something could be done ... I only need a minute, a word, to be myself ... Just squeeze me in somewhere, anywhere ... Open a parenthesis ... Do something!' (2020: 59). The power relations further change towards the end of the play, as the two, under the pressure of a crowd that starts assembling around them, gradually morph into Vladimir and Estragon. Those familiar with Beckett's play recognise textual cues that announce this metamorphosis, even though 'Vladimir' and 'Estragon' remain unnamed. The beginning of Beckett's *Godot* is re-enacted at the end of Vișniec's, under the guidance of Beckett-the-character, who is starting to regain his power over a now gradually submissive and claustrophobic Godot:

> Godot: ... If we stay another minute, it'll be too late. They'll suffocate us. ...
>
> Godot (*watching, terrified, the crowd that's gathered on the sidewalk*): God, what should I say?
>
> Samuel Beckett: Ask me if they beat me ... Meanwhile, I'll take off my boot and look at it. Afterwards you ask me what I'm doing here. (*Takes off his boot.*)
>
> Godot (*in a self-confident tone*): What are you doing?
>
> Samuel Beckett: Taking off my boot. Did that never happen to you? (2020: 61)

This transfer of identity enables Vișniec's play to appear in a loop that sets it in close intertextual connection to Beckett's and indirectly explains why Godot, in the original version, had to remain absent. In this regard, *Le dernier Godot* becomes a postscript to *En attendant Godot*, and the two plays, face to face, complete, intensify and explain each other as negative images.

While Waiting for Godot

Rudi Azank's monochrome web series *While Waiting for Godot*, which is now (in a concession to the integrity of the work) available as a full ninety-minute video on Vimeo,[8] emerges from a cultural setting quite different to Vișniec's *Le dernier Godot*, namely early twenty-first-century New York. *Godot*'s ageing and ailing characters emerge rejuvenated in a recognisable, specific and contemporary rather than sparse, abstract and universalised setting – in a way, they are precisely the small men in a big space required by Beckett, but here appearing on the variously-sized screens of social media. The web series reformats the stage play for a present-day audience, as the claim on the official website states in an advertising parody: 'Brand New Translation. Brand New Setting. Good old-fashioned Waitin'' (Azank, 2013a).

While Waiting is a student production by Azank – obsessed with *Godot* since his early youth – and a few friends at NYU Tisch School of the Arts (Roveri, 2014) which has won web programming awards but was rejected for film festivals (Corozine, 2018). The project is representative of current modes of independent low-budget filmmaking. Azank claims to have translated Beckett's original unpublished manuscript of *En attendant Godot* as a thesis at NYU and to have received the blessing of the Beckett Estate for his project (Roveri, 2014). Based on Azank's new translation of the uncensored

French ur-*Godot*, it appears that the script validates both his initial claim ('brand new translation') and his title, as it records the original text that emerged while Beckett was waiting for *Godot* to be produced.

The language is modernised, and Estragon's use of it conforms to New York's violent street speech: his 'people are bloody ignorant apes' (Beckett, 2010: 9) is turned into 'People are cunts', and he says, 'Fuck it, let's go'. There are also nods to the location when the conversation on the English pronunciation of 'cawm' (2010: 12) is Americanised to the Boston pronunciation, and the Eiffel Tower (2010: 6) to the Empire State Building. Instead of conceiving the play in two separate acts, with the second one a shorter, more exhausted repetition of the first, the filmmakers condensed the text into one sequence, as Vișniec did in his play, while adding a distinctly cinematic quality to *Godot*. Azank describes his project on his Kickstarter page as a loose adaptation that tries both to go for the most original urtext and is upfront about its sitcom-inspired innovation:

> Conceived as more accessible to a 21st century culture, familiar with the popular styles of 'meta films' and a Larry David-Jerry Seinfeld brand of 'entertaining nothingness' – after an 8 year study of the untouched original text by Samuel Beckett, and with the Beckett estate's approval of his translation, Rudi Azank has completed the first fully cinematic adaptation of Godot. (Azank, 2013b)

Paying heed to Beckett's warning that one cannot photograph words, to work on screen *Godot* crosses the border from filmed theatre into a truly cinematic aesthetic. Azank's trajectory is to apply a neo-realist cinematography to the play that not only relies on the words but also pays attention to the specificity of recording the real New York while filming *Godot*. This makes the endeavour weaker in universalising abstraction and stronger in the specificity of spaces and actors. In less obvious ways, but not entirely dissimilar to Vișniec's play, Azank has included an element of metacommentary. At various times, the performers speak directly to the camera, and the *mise en scène* features blurry close-ups, handheld cameras, whip pans, high and low angle shots, expressive side- and backlit lighting schemes and (during Lucky's speech) rapid cuts. Estragon even has a dream sequence set in a verdant field, filmed in colour, so that Azank's version foregrounds filmic vocabulary.

This media transposition amounts to a remix of a straightforward evening street performance on a public bench in NYC, framed by epigraphs, prologues of a plethora of found footage and homeless people. Also, the adaptation first restructured the play according to the norms of web TV into seasons, with a pilot and episodes, before Azank decided to leave the play as a whole on the Vimeo platform. It has a diverse soundtrack as well as a variety of sound effects and applies various modes of cinematic narration. Twice, a speech is followed by a canned laughter track well known from sitcom, and the music is frequently synchronised to the characters' actions, highlighting the timing in the comic routines and segueing from extradiegetic mood music to ostensible interaction with the performers. Azank's film version follows the norms of televisuality by adding music to the soundtrack, which expands the narrating time of the film considerably and supplies extradiegetic intrusions into the supposedly neo-realist recording of street life.

Godot's setting is based on the principle of reduction and indeterminacy and suggests a recurrent 'void' (Beckett, 2010: 61). It was important to Beckett to leave the setting unspecific and therefore ambiguous. The stage directions merely read: '*A country road. A tree. Evening*' (2010: 5). The tree is leafless and dead in the first act, but, miraculously, has grown '*four or five leaves*' in the second act, although this takes place '*Next day. Same time. Same place*' (2010: 52). The most important prop is the tree, which has invited commentators to speculate on its meanings in the Bible (as a symbol of life and knowledge) or on its function in suicide (for instance, of Judas) or at the Gates of Hell in Dante. The characters even imitate this crucial object; they 'do the tree' (2010: 72). In performance, it is often modelled on Alberto Giacometti's slender design in the famous 1961 production of the play.

Azank, however, relying on very specific New York locations (which include a tree), has little interest in the abstract space of Beckett's theatre. Didi and Gogo are a pair of very concrete vagrants passing their time on the streets, representing the all-too-frequent homelessness in neoliberal capitalism of the early twenty-first century. The New York street locations become a key player in this adaptation, highlighted by an instantly recognisable neo-realist aesthetic that seems at odds with the abstraction of the Theatre of the Absurd. As Azank explained: 'It was shot in black and white on vintage Pentax lenses for an older look, aiming to replicate the Italian Neo-Realist look, particularly the cinematographic work of Gianni Di Venanzo'.[9] He points out that it was filmed 'entirely on location, in Manhattan during the middle of the night, for an abandoned, urban surreal look'. The New York street locations may remind viewers of street art experiments such as Hal Fischer's *18th Near Castro Street* (1978), which records street life on a bench in San Francisco's gay neighbourhood for twenty-four hours. The monochrome shot of Brooklyn Bridge and other Hudson River locations most clearly references Woody Allen's *Manhattan* (1979) – in conjunction with swing jazz era music (Fats Waller, Dave Brubeck, Henry Mancini and others). The monochrome may also reference the vaudeville film contexts that have been frequently invoked with reference to *Godot*. Vladimir and Estragon, who call each other Didi and Gogo, bring to mind classic pairs of vaudeville acts and slapstick comedy such as Laurel and Hardy, and are paralleled by the appearance of Pozzo and Lucky. In Beckett's play, their ethnicity and background are unclear, and their decontextualised appearance, fluid names and fragmentary stories about their past never add up to comprehensive character outlines. Generally, they are dressed and played as unkempt vagrants, with Vladimir lanky and Estragon stocky in stature, both wearing bowler hats (suggesting Dublin dress codes or Laurel and Hardy props). Azank's web series, however, rejuvenates both characters (while keeping, symbolically, the bowler hats), and also presents Pozzo and Lucky as two rich sisters: Pozzo appears as a black woman in a scanty evening dress who pops off to a Chase Manhattan bank branch to get some money, while Lucky is a pale Goth girl in black marine uniform and a navy hat.

Azank's *Godot* references the brutality of life on the street, which causes suffering to the poor but also pleasurable consumption, as indicated in Pozzo's outfit and the background consisting of banks, entertainment industries and urban architecture. The New York setting in Azank's version works as an emblem of the diversity of metropolitan characters, as well as a scenario for 'bums' reduced to a precarious and tedious existence. As the final scene – the rejection of suicide here acted out on Brooklyn Bridge – suggests, the vagrants' friendship appears as the antidote to the city's encroaching violence. The fact that the shooting occurs at night guarantees a relative scarcity of passers-by and highlights the nocturnal atmosphere that puts the vagrants explicitly at odds with more usual city dwellers. While Beckett suppresses the world indefinitely, Azank's world only awaits sunrise to restart its usual dynamics.

The failure of Godot to appear has acquired proverbial status and now is the greatest cliché that has emerged in the play's reception. The *absence présente* of Godot as a God or as a projection of the characters is at the very heart of the play. In Azank's media update, Godot keeps sending messages to the cell phones Gogo and Didi retrieve from a suitcase that also houses a saxophone, directing them to come to 375 Park Avenue (that is, Mies van der Rohe's Seagram Building; see Figure 15.1).[10] Here, Didi and Gogo are obviously vagrant street musicians, as indicated, for instance, in the scene in which the turnip is pulled from the tube of the saxophone in Vladimir's suitcase, which is full of stolen cell phones; also, perhaps in a Beckettian metareference, they steal bikes.

This urban *Godot* is very mobile, active, and clearly rooted in the Jewish bohemia of New York:

> I wanted a kind-of 'don't worry, be happy, version,' … a kind-of antithesis of the play's opening line of 'Nothing to be done' …, because as the two wander around the night-time City … they do many things: talk, kibbitz, some vaudeville schtick … and just meander around the liquid black and white metropolis.

From adaptation to transmedia storytelling 245

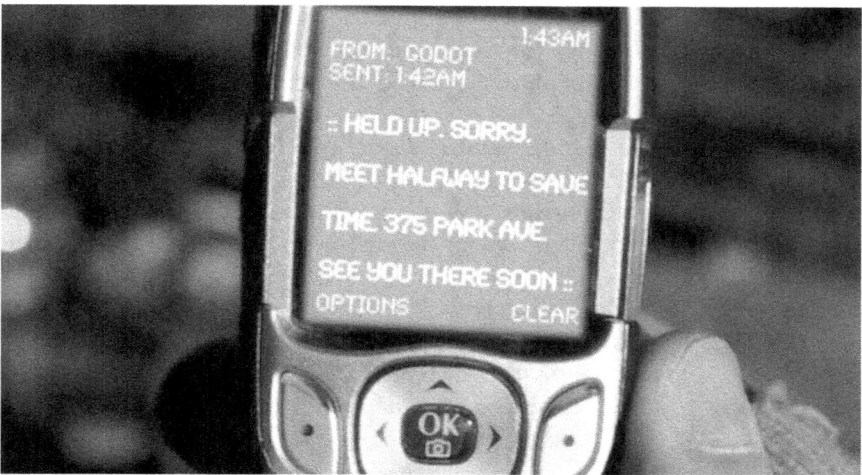

Figure 15.1 Close-up of a text message Godot sends to Vladimir and Estragon. Screenshot from *While Waiting for Godot* (director Rudi Azank, 2013).

... I wanted a portable 'Godot', with multiple trees, multiple venues, showing their friendship, their relationship. (qtd in Corozine, 2018)

The series also employs elements of humorous cultural remix, for instance when Pozzo makes Lucky dance to Daft Punk's 'Get Lucky' (1h 02' 50"). Her directions are 'Dance, misery!', as in Beckett (2010: 37), and Gogo, to support his claim that he can dance just as well, starts dancing to Wham's 'Wake Me Up Before You Go-Go' – an obvious riff on his nickname. In these scenes, *Godot* is remixed with the vestiges of late capitalist consumer culture. This is a very specifically American *Godot* – from the locations and accents to the sound design: 'One idea that Azank drew on was the striking similarity between the homelessness of post-Recession New York and its counterpart in the 1930's Depression Era, using period music. Didi and Gogo as street people, as men looking for something... anything... even an unknown Godot' (Corozine, 2018). The violence in Azank's play is clearly the neoliberal product of urban poverty after the capitalist crisis of 2008–9 and is emphasised by the neo-realist film aesthetic that informs his film adaptation.

Conclusion

Our discussion of Azank's *While Waiting for Godot* has focused on the dominance of audio-visual, cinematic narration over Beckett's dialogue in this transcoding of *Godot* to the vocabularies of transmedia storytelling, adapting the theatrical play for a web audience. While not an 'intersemiotic' (Jakobson, 1959: 233) adaptation, Vișniec's *Le dernier Godot* recreates and recontextualises Beckett's play by overtly toning down the violent vocabulary originally employed. This restraint is arguably informed by an automatic incorporation of self-censorship applied by writers in the former communist bloc and leads to a possible interpretation of the play as a dissident reaction to that political context, from which the author fled in the same year. Much more subtly than Azank, who seeks to de-censor and update Beckett, highlighting the violence in the New York language and cityscape, Vișniec nevertheless performs an act of (inter)textual violence by creating a breach in Beckett's dramatic intentions, which allows a transfer of identity between Beckett, now become a character, and the now-present Godot.

Notes

1 See www.youtube.com/watch?v=PRIGoQPnHTo&list=FLNrGjGy8ccB2Hc8ha84s5Sg&index=5&t=0s (accessed 28 February 2021).
2 See www.youtube.com/watch?v=BaD8tuyiWPI (accessed 16 September 2021).
3 All quotations from the play are Luciana Tamas's translations from the Romanian edition.
4 As will be explored in more detail in Tamas's PhD thesis (in progress).
5 Translations of Romanian from Călin (1958) are by Tamas.
6 Translations of Romanian from Simuț (2008) are by Tamas.
7 Translations of Romanian from Mușina (1996) are by Tamas.
8 See https://vimeo.com/252586094 (accessed 29 April 2022).
9 Private email communication with Eckart Voigts, 19 July 2019. Di Venanzo worked as cinematographer with Antonioni and Fellini on *La Notte* (1961), *L'Eclisse* (1962) and *8 ½* (1963).
10 This might be significant, as Beckett admired Mies van der Rohe's Neue Nationalgalerie in Berlin (Knowlson, 1996: 569) and Gontarski (1995: xv) links his early rejection of ornament to van der Rohe's architectural theory.

References

Azank, R. (2013a). *While Waiting for Godot*, www.whilewaitingforgodot.com/ (accessed 28 February 2021).
Azank, R. (2013b). 'While Waiting-for-Godot, the webseries, season 2', *Kickstarter*, www.kickstarter.com/projects/1750314357/while-waiting-for-godot-the-webseries-season-2/description?lang=de (accessed 28 February 2021).
Beckett, S. (2010). *Waiting for Godot*. Pref. M. Bryden. London: Faber and Faber.

Bradby, D. (2003). *Beckett: Waiting for Godot*. Cambridge: Cambridge University Press.
Călin,V. (1958). 'Anxietate și neant', *Teatrul*, 3.6, 26–30.
Cheianu, C. (2001). 'Postmodernismul – o nouă/veche mișcare literară la sfârșitul secolului XX – începutul secolului XXI', *Atelier Contrafort*, 9–11, 83–5, www.contrafort.md/old/2001/83-85/230_10.html (accessed 7 March 2021).
Corozine, R. (2018). 'Personally speaking: filmmaker Rudi Azank', *Hudson Valley One*, 2 July, https://hudsonvalleyone.com/2018/07/02/personally-speaking-filmmaker-rudi-azank/ (accessed 28 February 2021).
Esrig, D. (2018). 'Cenzura a dezvoltat în mediul cultural o mentalitate de sclavi', *Revista Scena*, 28 February, https://revistascena.ro/interviu/david-esrig-cenzura-a-dezvoltat-in-mediul-cultural-o-mentalitate-de-sclavi/ (accessed 28 February 2021).
Esslin, M. (2001 [1960]). *The Theatre of the Absurd*. New York: Vintage Books.
Feldman, M. (2015). *Falsifying Beckett: Essays on Archives, Philosophy, and Methodology in Beckett Studies*. Stuttgart: Ibidem.
Fernández Quesada, N. (2011). 'Under the aegis of the Lord Chamberlain and the Franco Regime: the bowdlerisation of *Waiting for Godot* and *Endgame*', in C. O'Leary and A. Lázaro (eds), *Censorship across Borders: The Reception of English Literature in Twentieth-Century Europe*. Newcastle upon Tyne: Cambridge Scholars Publishing, pp. 193–210.
Gontarski, S. E. (1995). 'Introduction', in S. Beckett, *The Complete Short Prose, 1929–1989*. New York: Grove Press, pp. xi–xxxii.
Hartel, G., K. Völker and T. Irmer (2009). 'The reception of Beckett's theatre and television pieces in West and East Germany,' in M. Nixon and M. Feldman (eds), *The International Reception of Samuel Beckett*. London: Continuum, pp. 75–96.
Hutcheon, L. (2013 [2006]). *A Theory of Adaptation*. London and New York: Routledge.
Hutchings, W. (2005). *Samuel Beckett's Waiting for Godot: A Reference Guide*. London: Praeger.
Jakobson, R. (1959). 'On linguistic aspects of translation', in R. A. Brower (ed.), *On Translation*. Cambridge, MA: Harvard University Press, pp. 232–9.
Jianxi, L., and M. Ingham (2009). 'The reception of Samuel Beckett in China', in M. Nixon and M. Feldman (eds), *The International Reception of Samuel Beckett*. London: Continuum, pp. 129–46.
Knowlson, J. (1996). *Damned to Fame: The Life of Samuel Beckett*. London: Bloomsbury.
Lecossois, H. (2008). 'Samuel Beckett and Matéi Visniec: from one Godot to the last', in P. E. Carvalho and R. C. Homem (eds), *Plural Beckett Pluriel: Centenary Essays / Essais d'un centenaire*. Porto: Faculdade de Letras da Universidade do Porto. pp. 93–104.
Lippert, L. (2013). 'Das theater als oralische anstalt', *nachtkritik.be*, www.nachtkritik.de/index.php?option=com_content&view=article&id=8232:die-schwarze-botin-wiener-festwochen&catid=127&Itemid=100058 (accessed 1 May 2020).
Miłosz, C. (1955). *The Captive Mind*. New York: Vintage Books.
Mușina, A. (1996). *Unde se află poezia?* Târgu-Mureș: Editura Arhipelag.

Nelega, A. (2001). 'Piese noi si proiecte "de resuscitare"', *Observator Cultural*, 57, 27 March, www.observatorcultural.ro/articol/piese-noi-si-proiecte-de-resuscitare/ (accessed 28 February 2021).

Oică, I. (2017). 'Matei Vișniec: beyond the iron mask', *Journal of Romanian Literary Studies*, 12, 561–8.

Pascu-Oglindă, M. (2016). 'Cenzura și autocenzura în scris în perioada comunistă pornind de la 3 cărți', *Bookaholic*, 10 March, www.bookaholic.ro/cenzura-si-autocenzura-in-scris-in-perioada-comunista-pornind-de-la-3-carti.html (accessed 28 February 2021).

Rorty, R. (1993). *Contingency, Irony, and Solidarity*. Cambridge: Cambridge University Press.

Roveri, M. (2014). 'Rudi Azank and While Waiting for Godot on Italish!', *Italish!*, 9 August, https://italish.eu/rudi-azank-waiting-godot-italish/ (accessed 28 February 2021).

Sanders, J. (2006). *Adaptation and Appropriation*. London: Routledge.

Simuț, I. (2008). 'Literatura subversivă', *România literară*, 18, https://arhiva.romanialiterara.com/index.pl/literatura_subversiv (accessed 7 March 2021).

Tajiri, Y., and M. H. Tanaka (2009). 'The reception of Samuel Beckett in Japan', in M. Nixon and M. Feldman (eds), *The International Reception of Samuel Beckett*. New London: Continuum. pp. 147–62.

Vișniec, M. (1994). 'Poezia într-o lume normală', in G. Crăciun (ed.), *Generația 80 în texte teoretice*. Pitești: Editura Vlasie, pp. 149–51.

Vișniec, M. (2019). 'Întâlniri esențiale: Teatrul și simbolurile sale', *Teatrul Municipal 'Matei Vișniec' Suceava*, 30 May, www.teatrulmateivisniec.ro/ro/stiri/matei-vi-niec-in-dialog-cu-george-banu/ (accessed 28 February 2021).

Visniec, M. (2020). 'Ultimul Godot', *Feedback*, 1–2, 57–61.

16

The figure of Beckett in four contemporary novels

Paul Stewart

In recent years, four novelists have either included a version of Beckett in their works, entirely premised a novel on what is known of his life or created characters based on Beckett and his acquaintances. In each case, but in a variety of ways, these novelists were faced with the challenge of fully realising a version of Beckett based on sketchy, or absent, archival evidence which they often supplemented with recourse to his own fiction and drama, as if assuming that these were in turn based on his lived experience in some way. As such, a dynamic relation was created between real-life events, historical traces of those events, the works of Beckett as well as subsequent writers and, above all, between biography, autobiography, fiction and authenticity.

Lucia (2018) by Alex Pheby is predicated on an act of literary destruction and absence. Pheby's work reimagines the life of Lucia Joyce, a promising dancer and artist who succumbed to mental illness and was known primarily as the daughter of that most prominent of authors, James Joyce. Pheby deploys a host of narrative perspectives whilst Lucia's own voice (as in her life, perhaps) is omitted, partly due to the destruction of her letters as detailed in an early chapter of the novel. At the behest of a character whose name is redacted – a black block replaces the name of Stephen Joyce, the author's grandson and often controversial defender of Joyce's estate, privacy and reputation – an unnamed youth burns a trunkful of letters and photographs which appear to be those of Lucia. The youth is instructed not to read anything: 'He was prohibited from reading them. So now, suddenly, he wanted to read them. The interdiction provoked its own transgression. It defined it. Enforced it' (Pheby, 2018: 21).

Later, and only briefly, Samuel Beckett is mentioned when an unnamed narrator speculates on Lucia's reaction to finding herself in Beckett's fiction: 'It is painful to live within the pages of a book, and/or to be recognised, for example to be a pair of eyes removed and placed on a dish. Would you like it, Samuel Beckett?' (2018: 145). The text is alluding to the Syra-Cusa in Beckett's posthumously published *Dream of Fair to Middling Women*

(1992) and, as *Lucia* points out, it would not have been hard for readers of that novel in manuscript to identify that the Syra-Cusa was based on Lucia (see Knowlson, 1996: 150–1). The Saint of Syracuse is, of course, St Lucy or Lucia, whose martyrdom in many accounts includes her eyes being gouged out. Given that Lucia was deeply aware of her own slight astigmatism, one could accuse Beckett of at least a lack of tact in this regard.

These two moments from Pheby's novel offer useful parameters to consider how Beckett has been portrayed in fiction in recent years. Moreover, these moments outline not only the theoretical and ethical concerns of fictionalised representations of the author but also Beckett's practice of basing some of his own early fictions on such personages as Lucia Joyce and Peggy Sinclair. His 'afterlife' in the pages of other writers might therefore also help us gauge how he used the lives of others.

Fictionalising from the archive

Pheby's *Lucia* does not fully characterise Beckett as such, but three other contemporary novels in English feature fictionalised versions of him: *The Joyce Girl* (2016) by Annabel Abbs, *A Country Road, A Tree* (2016) by Jo Baker and *Jott* (2018) by Sam Thompson. All of these have appeared following an increased accessibility of biographical material. Whilst James Knowlson's authorised biography of Beckett first appeared in 1996, as did Anthony Cronin's biography *The Last Modernist*, the greater impact may well have been the publication of Beckett's letters in four volumes from 2009 to 2016. Although these letters are highly selective in many respects, they have given greater access to the Beckett behind the works and opened up archives that were once the preserve of the specialist academic researcher. In the case of Pheby and Abbs – whose primary interest is in Lucia Joyce – the groundbreaking biography of her by Carol Loeb Schloss (2003) has surely had no less of an impact.

However, as the destruction of Lucia's letters in Pheby's novel indicates, these adaptations from the life owe as much to the absence of archival material as to its presence. Pheby's and Abbs's novels, although radically different in conception and execution, are both concerned with bringing Lucia's life to the fore, a life which had so often been overshadowed by her father and her mental illness. However, as Loeb Schloss details, letters and documents pertaining to Lucia were routinely omitted or abridged before Stephen Joyce destroyed the bulk of the extant material in 1988 and urged Beckett to also destroy his letters from Lucia. Given Lucia's long-term hospitalisation, interviews with her in person were also fraught with difficulties. For example, when Richard Ellmann spoke to Lucia whilst she was in St Andrew's Hospital, Northampton, he 'expected no information, sought none, got none' (qtd in Loeb Schloss, 2003: 15). However, he did encourage her to write a brief essay on her life. James Joyce's published letters (1957, 1966a, 1966b) and Ellmann's monumental biography (1983) therefore only provide the barest of outlines concerning the Lucia and Beckett relationship.

This situation continued even with the publication of Beckett's letters. Across the four volumes of published correspondence, there is only one addressed to Lucia and those that mention her are rare. Nevertheless, these letters demonstrate a basic problem with the documentation of any ongoing, lived relationship. In July 1930, Beckett writes to Thomas McGreevy[1] that he has heard from Lucia and that she 'is unhappy she says. Now that you are gone there is no one to talk to about that' (2009e: 27). Again to McGreevy, on 10 March 1935, Beckett mentions: 'The Lucia ember flared up & fizzled out. But more of that viva-voce' (2009e: 260). Some things, it seems, are best said in person. One can only speculate as to what such enigmatic phrases as 'flared up & fizzled out' might mean within a lived reality. As Loeb Schloss puts it: 'Hidden amongst such facts as these are the familiar threads of human interaction – the smiles, the touches the personal admissions' (2003: 187). In other words, the documented (and documentable) historical figure cannot necessarily grant access to the actual person in their lived experience.

If this is true for Abbs and Pheby, it is no less true for Thompson in *Jott* and Baker in *A Country Road, A Tree*, albeit for slightly different reasons. Thompson's book is based on the relationship between Beckett and Geoffrey Thompson, his longtime friend who recommended Beckett take a course of psychotherapy in London and who was at that time working at the Bethlehem Hospital before going into practice himself. Again, the documented evidence is scarce, precisely because Beckett and Thompson were frequently seeing each other face-to-face during that period. So, there are no directly addressed letters between the two within the published correspondence, although Beckett frequently mentions Thompson in letters to McGreevy in particular. In later years, Geoffrey Thompson's presence is felt more as a marked absence because Beckett frequently complains of not seeing or hearing from Geoffrey for long periods. For Sam Thompson, this represented a problem, but also an opportunity: 'I felt there was enough, there was a cue to imagine that here was a friendship in which there was quite a lot at stake' (2019). Baker's problem, as she focuses on Beckett's activities during the war, is more the interruption of documentary evidence than the upheaval of the conflict created. As there is a substantial hiatus in the published letters between 1941 and 1945, Baker had to draw more on the biographies as 'a quite practical resource, to establish timelines, events, cast of characters, who was where when' (qtd in Stewart, 2019: 295).

For a variety of reasons, therefore, all four contemporary authors were faced with the task of fully realising events that were only sketched out by documentary evidence. The Beckett that was available to history in this way was but a trace of the Beckett as he lived, and the Beckett that lived was no doubt less a single subject than a conglomeration of impulses, motives and subjectivities. However, one must be careful not to confuse biographical accuracy (if such a thing were possible) with the deployment of aspects of biography in the creation of a character in fiction. As Linda Hutcheon reminds us, any 'history' is already inevitably textual: 'The issue is no longer "to what empirically real object in the past does the language of history refer?"; it is more "to which discursive context could this language belong? To which prior textualizations must we refer?"' (1988: 119). In what some might see as an unwelcome correlation between two disciplines, she claims that the 'intertextual parody of historiographic metafiction enacts, in a way, the views of certain contemporary historiographers: it offers a sense of the presence of the past, but a past that can be known only from its texts, its traces – be they literary or historical' (1988: 125). In the present case, the traces and texts are at once literary *and* historical, as the paucity of historical documentation has led the authors to supplement their own fictions by using elements of Beckett's.

In addition, as Naomi Jacobs argues in *The Character of Truth*, the author of such historically based fictions is operating under a certain restriction: 'Since the verisimilar effects of the recognizable figure depend upon shared stereotypes in the minds of numerous readers, the portrayal of a historical figure must not conflict with what is commonly known or might reasonably be expected of the original' (1990: 20). Jacobs's use of the word 'original' should not obscure her sense that the biographical object in the mind of the readers is already a shared stereotype, a text rather than an 'actual' person. Nevertheless, the 'shared stereotype' operates as a marker of authenticity – the character in the novel should behave in ways that are congruent with the image of the figure that has already been inculcated in the mind by other texts. However, this is further problematised by the period of Beckett's life that is under consideration, a period which spans from 1928 (with the Lucia-based novels), to the mid-1930s (*Jott*) and the war years (*A Country Road, A Tree*). In effect, the Beckett of this early period has not yet become the 'shared stereotype' of Beckett in his post-*Godot* public incarnation. However, such a stereotype might still retroactively condition the fictionalised character of Beckett in the works and the reader's reception of those characterisations. It might well be that the reader's

The figure of Beckett in contemporary novels 253

knowledge or image of Beckett in his later years allows for, but also somewhat restricts, the versions of Beckett put forward by Baker, Thompson, Abbs and Pheby.

This is perhaps most apparent in *The Joyce Girl*. In the mid-1980s, Lucia Joyce confided to a friend, Dominique Maroger: 'My love was Samuel Beckett. I wasn't able to marry him' (qtd in Loeb Schloss, 2003: 188). This concept of Beckett as Lucia's great romance certainly seems to have been the inspiration for Abbs's detailed and sustained speculations about their relationship. From the bare bones that are known and contested, Abbs's novel assumes that Beckett was of crucial emotional importance to Lucia. Indeed, her first seeing Beckett is marked as a moment of 'the first stirrings of desire and ambition that pushed their way, like the greedy tendrils of a weed, into my young heart. Because that was the beginning. No matter what anyone else says, *that* was the beginning' (2016: 6; original emphasis). From Lucia's perspective (and in her assumed voice), their relationship is a matter of destiny from the very moment they first meet and she is 'struck by overwhelming emotion' (2016: 27). In many ways, in respect of the Beckett and Lucia relationship, *The Joyce Girl* reads like, and employs many of the idioms of, traditional romantic fiction. So, Lucia is often rapt by signs that 'we were meant to be together' (2016: 102), and when Beckett drunkenly asks for a kiss, Lucia is transported: 'He loves me, I whispered to our lucky Greek flag. He loves me!' (2016: 137). She imagines being Beckett's muse and their initial awkward physical moments of contact are thrillingly illicit: 'it finally happened. Without warning, Beckett lurched across the sofa and pressed his face against mine, his lips against my lips. I felt the contour of his body against me, … my desire was as great as his' (2016: 147). Their physical relationship culminates in a deliberately ambiguous, yet passionate, embrace on the parlour floor: 'I peeled off a stocking. … Pressed myself to him. Felt the press of him against my hips, my ribs, my stomach. Felt his hands seeking out my breasts. Felt my nipples spring up at the brush of his fingertips. All the while encouraging him to the floor, to that slice of light that called so urgently to me' (2016: 158).

There is a degree of discomfort here, as if Beckett – or at least the shared stereotype of him – has been placed in the wrong genre. Here, the Beckett character functions as a romantic hero upon whom Lucia's hopes of sexual, professional and marital fulfilment are pinned, and which are ultimately dashed. Yet, why could not the twenty-three-year-old Beckett have been a passionate, if initially awkward, lover who wants to learn to dance the Charleston as much as he wants sexual gratification with a woman he finds 'beautiful'? After all, Peggy Guggenheim wrote of a Beckett who was 'drunk all the time', who wanted nothing more than to 'remain in bed' with her, but who within ten days of the beginning of their affair had already allowed 'a friend of his from Dublin to creep into his bed' (2005: 164). Guggenheim also attests to Beckett's ability to inspire 'love' and 'passion' in her. Interestingly, it is from Guggenheim that Abbs appropriates the words with which Beckett breaks up with Lucia: 'It's as though I'm dead inside. I don't have any human feelings ... that's why I can't fall in love with you. I tried' (2016: 245). This is Abbs's version of Guggenheim's recollection: 'He always denied [having any capacity for intensity], saying he was dead and had no feelings that were human and that was why he had not been able to fall in love with Joyce's daughter' (2005: 175).

The discomfort one feels with the Beckett portrayed in *The Joyce Girl* is that it does not quite match with the conception of Beckett to which one has become accustomed. Partly, this is because the Beckett of the 1920s and 1930s has yet to become the Beckett of the postwar era who is more fixed within the imagination. However, Abbs feels it necessary to point in the direction of that Beckett, leading to some degree of anachronism. Just before the possible 'lesion of Platonic tissue' (Beckett, 1992: 19) in the parlour scene of *The Joyce Girl*, Lucia and Beckett discuss his nascent writing career, and he informs her: 'Language has failed us. ... Words have failed us' (Abbs, 2016: 154). He then goes on to implicitly distance himself from Joyce's aesthetic: 'You see what I mean, Lucia. About words. How inadequate they are. I know your father believes in the absolute power of words' (2016: 156). This, we are told, occurred in July 1929, at a time when Beckett was writing *Dream of Fair to Middling Women*, his most Joycean of works, and fully eight years before the famous Axel Kaun letter in which he expresses his mistrust of words (see 2009e: 512–21).

Jo Baker's *A Country Road, A Tree*, which focuses on the war years, is similarly caught between portraying Beckett as he then might have been and recognising the established writer and iconic figure he was to become. Baker's novel is very well researched, but the inevitable archival gaps give her a means of 'thinking and finding connections; how the real world inhabited his fictions' (qtd in Stewart, 2019: 292). This means a certain degree of 'casting forward' (2019: 291), to use Baker's terms, as the fiction and plays are seen to be embedded in, or emerging from, the lived experience, albeit often in distorted or attenuated forms. Wisely, Baker does not attempt a first-person narration as Abbs does for Lucia, but lets the subtleties of her own prose play across the years that separate Beckett's experience from the distillation of that experience in his art. As the novel ends with Beckett beginning the 'siege in the room' of prolific creation, the premise is that the wartime experiences marked a sea change in Beckett's life and art. As such, many of the experiences detailed by Baker have resonances with the postwar works, and Baker is adept at grounding Beckett's aesthetics within the mundane world, as when he is at home at the time of the declaration of war and this thoroughly middle-class and secure world is thrown into an immediate experience of dislocation: 'They cannot say anything worth saying, but that does not stop them talking, and the soft words accumulate, like sand trickling through an hourglass. They are up to their knees in it and cannot stop' (Baker, 2016: 25). In the context of Baker's novel, the issues and images deployed here make perfect sense, as the shock of the beginning of the war starts to sink in. Yet for those attuned to Beckett's works, a number of chords are struck: the seemingly pointless banter of Didi and Gogo in *Waiting for Godot*; the speech/silence dichotomy that propels the novels from *Molloy* onwards; the 'impossible heap' derived from Zeno's paradoxes in *Endgame* (Beckett, 2009b: 6); or the mountain of sand into which Winnie sinks in *Happy Days*. On a larger scale – and with a more ambitious projection forward – Baker also integrates the closed-space prose pieces of the 1960s with Beckett's wartime experiences. According to Knowlson, Beckett set up a tentlike structure in his apartment to try to keep Suzanne and himself warm. Baker picks up the cue: 'He folds himself up, knees and elbows. It's warmer, yes, inside the shelter, in the shared warmth. They are toe-to-toe. The fabric drapes above his shoulders. His neck is bent. He can feel her breathe. The world closed down to this. To body and breath' (2016: 97).

On occasion, this effect is achieved on a much smaller scale, even with the use of just a single word. For example, Baker habitually uses 'footfalls' rather than the more common 'footsteps', as if to suggest that the sounds heard in 'real life' that the novel describes finally find their way into the imagery of the play *Footfalls* years later. Indeed, with careful word choice, Baker manages to bridge the trials of life in Paris in the winter of 1940 with Beckett's emerging aesthetic: 'He can't sleep: he is haunted by absences, by things unsaid. He can't keep account of everyone; he can't *accommodate* it all' (2016: 103; emphasis added). As Beckett supposedly (and famously) said in his interview with Tom Driver: 'To find the form to accommodate the mess, that is the task of the artist now' (Driver, 2006: 219).[2] To the Beckett of 1940, the mess is self-evident, but the aesthetic response to it has not yet arrived.

Fiction, biography and the authentic

Baker's work is, then, replete with Beckettian motifs and, in keeping with her life/work assumptions, she expertly weaves these signatures into the fabric of mundane experience. However, the blurring of the fictional and the biographical texts can lead to an ontological circularity whereby Beckett's texts become evidence for the historical figure of the author and so elements of those texts are used in the fictionalised portrayal of him. Indeed, Baker's novel begins with one such moment, as in the spring of 1919 the young Beckett jumps from a tree at Cooldrinagh, his childhood home: 'He let go of the branch; he let go of the trunk. He lifted his arms and opened them wide. The pause on the cusp, the brink. He dived into the empty air' (2016: 11). In *Company*, this is rendered as: 'You climb to near the top of a great fir. You sit listening to all the sounds. Then throw yourself off. The great boughs break your fall. The needles' (Beckett, 2009a: 13). There are no needles in Baker – Beckett jumps from a larch, not a fir. Whose then is the invention? Knowlson is rather ambiguous here, since he uses the version in *Company* as the touchstone for what might have actually happened (1996: 19), and Cronin quotes *Company* directly as evidence for the supposed event (1997: 15). Neither biographer addresses the circularity of this process nor emphasises that the premise of *Company* is '[t]o one in his back in the dark a voice tells of the past' of which 'by far the greater part of what is said cannot be verified' (Beckett, 2009a: 3).

Sam Thompson's *Jott* seems to be keenly aware of this dynamic form of circularity whereby fiction feeds into a biography which is itself informed by that fiction. Rather than portraying Beckett and others under their own names and tying them to whatever historical incidents are available, Thompson uses the historical Beckett and Thompson as the basis for the fictional Louis Molyneux and Arthur Bourne. He also makes use of Beckett's fictions. Towards the end of the novel, Arthur is handed a copy of Louis's novel, *Jott*, which readers of Beckett would recognise as primarily patterned on *Murphy*. As he reads, Bourne comes across a familiar passage:

> The young Jott walked along a stony strand, holding hands with his mother and looking at the sea. *With wonder he saw the sea colours and longed to know the words for what was beautiful and endless and always changing. He asked her: What colour is the sea?* His mother looked at him with contempt and replied that the sea was grey. (Thompson, 2018: 259; original emphasis)

Although all the details are altered, this passage is unmistakeably an adaptation of a recurring motif in Beckett's work to be found with variations in *Malone Dies* (2010: 98), *Company* (2009a, 6), but initially in 'The End': 'A small boy, stretching out his hands and looking up at the blue sky, asked his mother how such a thing was possible. Fuck off, she said' (2009d: 39). When asked about this adapted vignette, Thompson replied that it 'seemed key to me. I find that story in Beckett deeply touching and upsetting. Clearly one of those moments that I assume is straight from the life, although I don't know. It is so odd and potent, so it has always stuck with me' (2019). The working assumption is that because this vignette occurred repeatedly in Beckett's fiction, it must therefore have a basis within Beckett's actual life. In order, then, to make his fictional Beckett as authentic as possible, some similar vignette needed to be included in Molyneux's fiction. Importantly, though, Thompson is fully aware that he is only making an assumption: he cannot know whether or not such an incident ever happened. When interviewed, Thompson was also keen to emphasise his working practice when dealing with the vagaries of supposed biographical fact:

> My sense of it, and I may be deceiving myself actually, was that I was quite systematic in wilfully distorting the historical record, at least in small ways. … So that was the kind of torsion of things; out of the biographical space and into the fictional space was just a slight, small twisting all the time. (2019)

There is a paradox here, of course, whereby fictional authenticity is dependent on a distortion of biographical actuality. However, one is no less aware that such an apparent actuality is not Beckett as he was from moment-to-moment, but a Beckett who was accessible through historical documentation.

This 'small twisting' of the historical space was something Beckett himself engaged in, especially in supposedly more autobiographical texts such as *Krapp's Last Tape* or *Company*. When Baker's Beckett returns to Ireland after the end of the war, he has a revelation about the direction his art must take, but she carefully distances herself from the version in *Krapp's Last Tape* that is often supposed to represent just such a moment:

> There is nothing grand about it; no waves, no wind, no briny spray. The world is not and never was in sympathy with him, nor with anybody else. But this is the moment when the wide chaotic chatter and stink of it, all that Shem-beloved hubbub, falls away, and his eyes are trained on darkness and his ears on silence. (2016: 292)

The myth that Krapp's experience was directly patterned on Beckett himself having an epiphany on some pier has long been debunked, with Knowlson claiming that Beckett had wanted him to make it 'clear once and for all' that the moment of realisation occurred in his mother's room (1996: 352). Again, we have a pattern of circularity: Beckett applies a 'small twist' to the autobiographical material as it works its way into his art, and this in turn is twisted back into a biographical moment for the fictional Beckett of Baker's book. This relation between the historical, biographical moment and the written work of art is one which exercised Thompson as well, as 'you also have the realm of the work to play with' (2019). Yet the precise nature of the biographical and aesthetic relation is one that remains tantalising: 'That little kind of gap between the writer and their writing is a sort of unbridgeable gap in a way, but also a gap in which you can feel a kind of voltage going' (2019). The intangible life/work connection is, in Thompson's metaphor, no less powerful for being ill-defined, or perhaps indefinable.

Thompson's novel is deeply involved in the life/work dichotomy, as the fictional Beckett (Molyneux) is seen to be dependent on the fictional Thompson (Bourne) for the material which will be translated into the novel *Jott* and, prior to that, a short story entitled 'A Routine Procedure', which somewhat resembles Beckett's 'A Case in A Thousand' of 1934. In this instance, Arthur had mentioned a case of a young girl who was convinced she would die during an operation, as indeed she does. In Louis's hands this becomes a 'horror tale, with the physicians and surgeons as pompous professional clowns who in treating the girl seemed ... to be acting out strange, unacknowledged desires of their own' (Thompson, 2018: 21). Arthur thinks that Louis has got it 'all wrong', but he fails to upbraid Louis as 'he was no longer sure that he knew what had really happened. If Louis's version hadn't displaced the reality, it had at least confused matters' (2018: 22). Fictional versions of reality are seen to infect and distort actuality, and this dynamic is carried forward into the story based on Arthur's most enigmatic patient, Walker, whom readers will identify as a version of Mr Endon in *Murphy*. Louis is granted access to, and spends a lot of time with, Walker before Louis abruptly ends the visits claiming: 'I've got what I need now. ... No reason to keep seeing him' (2018: 108). Louis's cavalier and somewhat crass attitude towards Walker is made no better by the story he writes based on Walker's life. Arthur's reaction is ambivalent: 'The fictitious young man certainly resembled Walker on the surface .... Perhaps the inner life was Walker's also. It could be that Louis had somehow extracted a history from the patient and had set it faithfully down .... On the other hand, perhaps Louis had made it up' (2018: 122). Here we have Arthur's belief that fiction can just be fiction: that a set of circumstances, scenes and dialogues can be stitched together to offer some kind of plausible life story that has no claim to truth beyond its own limits. Yet, Arthur also entertains the possibility that the author of a fiction has succeeded where the psychoanalyst has failed, that the fictional character is a more accurate depiction of Walker's inner life than any therapy can aspire to.

When Arthur reads the final manuscript of Louis's *Jott*, whilst Louis is hospitalised for an unknown but near fatal condition, he finds himself included in the fiction as a Dr Bell. Arthur's professional capacity is thereby called into question and his personal life – a source of some contention between Arthur and Louis – is apparently ridiculed. It amounted to 'a thorough assassination of his private life. He ought to ask Louis why he was incapable of writing anything without slandering his friends. Why this compulsion to claw at those who cared for him?' (2018: 256). Thompson's version of Beckett is far from likeable, even as we might feel sympathy for his mental and physical problems. The locus of one's dislike, perhaps, is Louis's utter disregard for those around him as he plunders their lives for his fiction, only to then discard them as is the case with Walker, or distance himself from them, as with Arthur.

The question arises, therefore, whether or not people's lives are fair game for the novelist. This ethical issue is one of which Baker, Pheby and Thompson all seem to be keenly aware. To return to Lucia's complaint about being included in *Dream* as the Syra-Cusa, upon which Pheby dwells, one might also add Beckett's use of Peggy Sinclair as the Smeraldina in the same novel and in *More Pricks Than Kicks*. (Thompson, in turn, mentions Louis's relationship with 'Connie' who dies of tuberculosis, as Sinclair did.) As Knowlson details, a great many incidents in *Dream* are patterned on Beckett's and Sinclair's personal history: 'their first meeting in Ireland; Beckett's visit to Laxenburg, where she was studying music and dance; his later visit to Kassel, when their relationship inevitably went awry; and the flood of love letters that she sent him' (1996: 148). Much of the tone towards the Smeraldina is mocking and tinged with misogyny, yet Knowlson assures his readers that the 'real-life Peggy was, in any case, merely the starting point for [an] extravagant exercise in language' (1996: 150). That might be the case, but the figure of Peggy was recognisable enough for her depiction to cause dismay to the Beckett and Sinclair families on the publication of *More Pricks Than Kicks*. Peggy had died not long before.[3] It is this callousness that Thompson adroitly identifies and captures.

The ethical issue of basing fiction on a historical personage – a 'real' person – exercises Thompson, Baker and Pheby more than it appears to have bothered the young Beckett. It has certainly prompted a number of critical reactions, in particular to Baker's book. For example, Eoin McNamee of the *Irish Times* has questioned the right of Baker's book to exist at all, asserting: 'There is transgression here. There's no point in asking whether Beckett would have liked it. He wouldn't' (2016). There is a certain critical naivety in this notion whereby a fiction is felt to invade the 'true' private space of the subject, Beckett. As we have seen, no such direct correlation can be made, since versions of Beckett – the 'real', the historically available, the author deduced from the works and the author of popular stereotype – all play across each other in an elaborate tapestry. But, as Thompson has claimed, 'in a way all the Beckettian stuff is like the reverse, like the hanging threads on the back of the fabric and what should really be of interest is the front' (2019).

If the front of the tapestry is what should concern us when assessing any literary artist, then Thompson's decision to include passages of Louis's output is a significant one, as a fictional version of Beckett writes fictional versions of Beckett's fiction. This somewhat dizzying prospect should not deflect one from recognising the bravery of Thompson's decision, especially as *Jott* includes pastiches of Beckett's style not only from *Murphy* but also *Dream* of *Fair to Middling Women* and other early works. In Thompson's terms, creating Louis's work is 'an exercise in characterising' (2019), therefore the small twisting that applies to the historical Beckett in the novel is also apparent in Louis's prose. Thompson manages to capture something of the *More Pricks Than Kicks* period of Beckett's style, as a single paragraph merges allusion, erudite diction, slang and Dublin reality. There is a sneering tone, almost, which captures Louis's character and which, by extension, makes one aware of this within Beckett's prose. Yet it is with the Beckett of *Murphy* that Thompson engages most fully. The last few pages of the novel move between Arthur's reality and his reading of *Jott*, and many Beckettian motifs are apparent, not least Jott's habit of encasing himself in a trunk, which has much the same effect as Murphy tying himself to a rocking chair. However, it is the small things of Beckett's style that Thompson has captured most impressively. The opening words of *Jott* manage to hint towards, but not be restrained by, *Murphy* (2009c: 3): 'The first of April and a fine spring morning. A day to make one glad to be alive, if so inclined' (2018: 235). There is a sly quality here (for example, one might easily miss that the novel begins on April Fool's Day), but it is the rhythm of the second sentence, hinged so delicately on the comma, that most effectively evokes the Beckett of 1936.

Circling biography

In keeping with the playfulness of Thompson's approach, and in keeping with much that this chapter has discussed, the most obvious borrowing from *Murphy* in *Jott* is not found within the novel Louis writes but within the life he lives. In a Lyons tearoom, Louis has just broken the news that he shall not be seeing Walker anymore:

> Arthur was dumbfounded, as much by Louis's offhand manner as by the news itself.
> Which to eat first, which next, which next, and which last, Louis said. Usually the ginger is reserved until the end, of course, but there are arguments to be made for the petit beurre and even for the digestive.
> What are you talking about? Arthur said. Why? (2018: 108)

Arthur is no doubt responding to the news about Walker, but we might equally hear him as responding to Louis's disquisition on biscuits. Without any prior knowledge of *Murphy*, in which the eponymous hero considers his biscuit options in much the same way (2009c: 61–2), this section of the novel functions to characterise Louis's eccentricities and lack of empathy for Walker. Yet, for the reader steeped in Beckett, the moment is an uncanny one: the incident is at home in *Murphy* but has been dislocated, adapted and found a somewhat familiar home in the life of Molyneux, Thompson's fictional version of a historical Beckett, but who is in this case based on an incident from Beckett's fiction.

This disquisition on the biscuits is a vivid reminder of the deeply blurred lines that fictions based on Beckett traverse. As we have seen, a gap in archival knowledge has led the authors considered to supplement their work with Beckett's own fictions and dramas, and this is a practice, one should add, in which Beckett's biographers also sometimes indulge. This circularity from fiction to (assumed) life and back to fiction is open to the play of differences, to the 'small twisting' of events and people that leaves a trace of a possible Beckett. How successful that depiction of Beckett might be is largely a matter of how it accords with the Beckett we carry with us in our own imagination.

Notes

1 I have kept the original spelling of McGreevy's surname as this is the policy adopted by the editors of the first volume of Beckett's letters. His surname is more commonly given as MacGreevy.
2 Driver acknowledged that the actual words used might not have been Beckett's: 'I reconstruct his sentences from notes made immediately after our conversation. What appears here is shorter than what he actually said but very close to his own words' (2006: 218). Whether or not Driver is quoting verbatim, the phrase has itself become part of Beckett lore.
3 Knowlson cites a letter from Beckett to Morris Sinclair, Peggy's brother, expressing regret for the publication (1996: 183). The letter is not among those included in Beckett (2009e).

References

Abbs, A. (2016). *The Joyce Girl*. Exeter: Impress Books.
Baker, J. (2016). *A Country Road, A Tree*. London: Doubleday.
Beckett, S. (1992). *Dream of Fair to Middling Women*. Ed. E. O'Brien and E. Fournier. Dublin: Black Cat Press.
Beckett, S. (2009a). *Company, Ill Seen Ill Said, Worstward Ho, Stirring Still*. Ed. D. Van Hulle. London: Faber and Faber.
Beckett, S. (2009b). *Endgame*. Pref. R. McDonald. London: Faber and Faber.
Beckett, S. (2009c). *Murphy*. J. C. C. Mays. London: Faber and Faber.
Beckett, S. (2009d). *The Expelled, The Calmative, The End, First Love*. Ed. C. Ricks. London: Faber and Faber.
Beckett, S. (2009e). *The Letters of Samuel of Samuel Beckett Volume I: 1929–1940*. Ed. M. Dow Fehsenfeld and L. More Overbeck. Cambridge: Cambridge University Press.

Beckett, S. (2010). *Malone Dies*. Ed. P. Boxall. London: Faber and Faber.
Cronin, A. (1997). *Samuel Beckett: The Last Modernist*. London: Flamingo.
Driver, T. (2006 [1979]). 'Tom Driver in "Columbia University Forum" Summer 1961, 21-5', in L. Garver and R. Federman (eds), *Samuel Beckett: The Critical Heritage*. London: Routledge, pp. 217–23.
Ellmann, R. (1982). *James Joyce*. London: Oxford University Press.
Guggenheim, P. (2005). *Out of this Century: Confessions of an Art Addict*. London: Andre Deutsch.
Hutcheon, L. (1988). *A Poetics of Postmodernism: History, Theory, Fiction*. New York and London: Routledge.
Jacobs, N. (1990). *The Character of Truth: Historical Figures in Contemporary Fiction*. Carbondale and Edwardsville: Southern Illinois University Press.
Joyce, J. (1957). *The Selected Letters of James Joyce*. Ed. S. Gilbert. London: Faber and Faber.
Joyce, J. (1966a). *Letters of James Joyce: Volume II*. Ed. R. Ellmann. New York: Viking.
Joyce, J. (1966b). *Letters of James Joyce: Volume III*. Ed. R. Ellmann. New York: Viking.
Knowlson, J. (1996). *Damned to Fame: The Life of Samuel Beckett*. London: Bloomsbury.
Loeb Schloss, C. (2003). *Lucia Joyce: To Dance in the Wake*. New York: Picador.
McNamee, E. (2016). 'A Country Road, a Tree by Jo Baker: Beckett proves elusive in forced resurrection', *Irish Times*, 7 May, www.irishtimes.com/culture/books/a-country-road-a-tree-by-jo-baker-beckett-proves-elusive-in-forced-resurrection-1.2637853 (accessed 8 February 2021).
Pheby, A. (2018). *Lucia*. Norwich: Gallery Beggar Press.
Stewart, P. (2019). '*A Country Road, A Tree*: an interview with Jo Baker', in P. Stewart and D. Pattie (eds), *Pop Beckett: Intersections with Popular Culture*. Stuttgart: Ibidem, pp. 289–304.
Thompson, S. (2018). *Jott*. London: JM Originals.
Thompson, S. (2019). Interview with P. Stewart, 27 September. Unpublished.

Index

Page numbers in italics refer to illustrations; those followed by *n*. and a number refer to information in a note. Beckett's works are indexed by title as individual index entries. Titles of works are plays unless otherwise indicated and given in English first. Works by others appear as subheadings under their name.

Abbs, Annabel: *The Joyce Girl* 15, 250, 251, 253–4
Abrams, M. H. 148–9
Act Without Words II 26, 37, 39
actors
    Beckett's veto on women in *Godot* 7, 27, 92–3n.5, 228, 229, 230
    neurodiversity and Thom's performance 13, 126, 131–6, 137
    women in Azank's *While Waiting for Godot* 244
    see also black productions of *Godot*
'adaphatroce' (*adaphatrôce*) 10, 19
adaptation
    and author's canon 8
    Beckett and adaptations by others of own work 6–7, 10, 19–28, 53, 70–1, 85, 98–9, 173–4, 202, 203–4, 205, 228–30
    Beckett's adaptations of work of others 21, 203
    Beckett's responses to adaptations across media 20–1, 98–9, 235
    and creativity 16, 96–7, 103, 108–9
    criteria for and 'borderline' forms 140–1, 151
    dance and choreographic projections 14, 171
    evolutionary effects 8–9
    and 'fluid texts' 155–6, 158, 160, 166
    forms of adaptation 5–6
    as ongoing process 12, 96, 97, 98, 108, 147, 151, 152
    and performance 22, 98, 104, 198–9, 202, 203
    posthumous nature of adaptations 29–30
    theory of 1–6, 97–8, 140–1
    see also Hutcheon, Linda
African Americans
    young men and Nwandu's *Pass Over* 218–28, 230
    see also black productions of *Godot*
Agamben, Giorgio 198, 199
age *see* old age
Akalaitis, JoAnne 27, 82, 83, 229
Albery, Donald 203, 204
Albright, Ann Cooper 173
All That Fall (radio) 11, 21, 25, 26, 50–63, 57, 73, 173
    Mouth on Fire 11, 50–1, 53, 54, 56–63
allusion 5, 14
Almena, Maria 133
American Civil Rights movement 208–9, 211–12
American Repertory Theater 229
Anderson, Wes: *The Grand Budapest Hotel* 150, 151

appropriation 3–4, 5–6, 7
  and Bruguera's *Endgame* 14, 187, 190
  Vişniec's *Le dernier Godot* 5, 15, 239–41, 246
  see also Nwandu: *Pass Over*
Aran Islands and Scaife's *Laethanta Sona* (*Happy Days*) 74–5
Áras an Uachtaráin 11, 50, 55, 59–62
art *see* contemporary art
Arte Concert 85
Assaf, Roger 234
Atkinson, Brooks 207
Audi, Pierre 160, 165, 166
audience
  and Broadway venue for all-black *Godot* 205
  in Bruguera's *Endgame* 192–4, *192*, 195–7
  and gaze 12, 81–2, 83–6, 87, 88–91
  and Gare St Lazare Ireland's *How It Is* 96, 102, 105
  inclusivity and Thom's performance 132
  and intermediality in Gare St Lazare Ireland's *How It Is* 96, 98
  masks and blindfolds 11, 50, 54, 55, 56, 59, 62
  Nwandu's *Pass Over* and urban settings 226–7
'authorised' texts 37, 38, 39
  self-translations as new texts 233–4
authorship and 'fluid text' 155–6, 158, 160, 166
Avignon festival 67, 68, 77, 229
Azank, Rudi: *While Waiting for Godot* (web series) 15, 233, 235, 237, 241–6, *246*

Babbage, Frances 111
Badiou, Alain 175
Baker, Jo: *A Country Road, A Tree* 15, 250, 251–2, 253, 254–6, 257, 259
Baldwin, James: *The Fire Within* 211–12
Barnbaum, Deborah 135, 136
Barthes, Roland 2, 29, 30
Bazin, André 47, 146
BBC 20, 21, 24

BBC Radio 3 21, 51, 57, 58, 235
Becker, Richard: *Finding Godot* 235
Beckett, Edward 59
Beckett, John 21
Beckett, May 52
Beckett, Samuel
  absence of biographical material 249, 250, 251–2
  appearance and *Beckett* video game 149, 150
  biographies of 28, 250, 256, 257, 261
  biography in fiction 6, 15–16, 249–61
  canonical status of work 8
  as character in Vişniec's *Le dernier Godot* 239–41
  death and posthumous nature of adaptations 29–30
  'grey canon' 29, 147, 148
  as Irish writer 11, 69, 73
  and Lucia Joyce 249–51, 253–4
  national honours and celebrations 60–1
  publication of letters 28, 250, 251–2
  religion and Protestantism 52, 60, 222
  see also Beckett estate and legacy *and individual plays and works*
Beckett, William 52
Beckett (video game) 141, 148–50, 151–2
Beckett Centenary Festival (2006) 11, 28, 60, 61, 66–7, 71, 142
Beckett Digital Manuscript Project (BDMP) 28–9
Beckett Estate 7–8, 55, 85, 91, 101, 192
  and Azank's translation 241, 242
  and *Beckett on Film* 11, 28, 37, 38, 39
  exclusions and restrictions 7, 92–3n.5, 228, 229, 230
  and festivals 71–2, 74, 75, 77–8
  and libretto for Kurtág's opera 160–1
  and new media 147
  and Thom's performance of *Not I* 133

Beckett family and Foxrock 50, 51, 52–3
Beckett Festival (1991) 10, 11, 34, 37–8, 45, 69–71
'Beckett in Foxrock' 11, 52–3
Beckett in the City project 112
Beckett on Film project 10–11, 12, 34–47
    and 'authorised' versions 28, 37, 38, 39
    DVD and online release 28, 34, 38, 41, 44–7
    Rozema's *Happy Days* 12, 40, 82, 86–7, 89, 92
Beckles Willson *see* Willson, Rachel Beckles
Behrens, Alfred 27
Beirut: Lebanese *Godot* production 234
Beloux, François 20
Benjamin, Walter 108–9
Benstock, Shari 84, 90
Berghof, Herbert 15, 204, 206, 207, 208, 235
Berkeley, Bishop George 81
Berlin (West): *Wir warten auf Godot* in 19, 234
biographical fiction 15–16, 249–61
Bird, Dúnlaith 117, 120
black actors and *Godot* 14–15, 202, 205–15, 229
    Free Southern Theater 15, 208–12, 210
    Myerberg's *Godot II* 15, 205–8, 209
    Nwandu and black youth 218–28, 230
Black is Beautiful movement 209
Black Lives Matter movement 15, 220
Blin, Roger 20, 177, 234
blindfolds *see* masks and blindfolds
Blue Angel Films 34, 41
body *see* embodiment/bodies
Boulter, Jonathan 127
Boussagol, Bruton 229
Braidotti, Rosi 126–7, 137
Breath: *Beckett on Film* production 37
Brecht, Bertolt 82–3, 234
Breuer, Lee 82, 83, 84, 90, 92
Brighton, Shane 144

Brokenshire, Mark 97
Brook, Peter 12, 81–2, 84–6, 92
Brooklyn Bridge Festival (1970) 12, 83
Brown, Terence 58
Bruguera, Tania 186–99
    Endgame and power dynamics 14, 186–7, 190–9
    Endgame Studies/Studies for Endgame 14, 189–90, 191, 194
    Immigrant Movement International 187
    Tatlin's Whisper series 14, 188, 190
    10,148,451 14, 188–9
Bryant, John 13–14, 155–6, 158, 160, 166
Bryden, Mary 155
...but the clouds... (TV) 37, 70, 219
Bunraku performance 119, 121

Cage, John 136
Caldwell, John T. 45
canonical status of work 8
    'aesthetic canonizing' 45
    festivals and adaptation 69–78
    festivals and experimental approaches 67–8, 70, 71–2, 75–6
    and 'grey canon' 29, 147, 148
Cardwell, Sarah 35
Carroll, Rachel 2
'Cartesian Theatre' 165
Cascando (radio) 26, 27, 157
'Case in A Thousand, A' (prose) 258
Catastrophe 29, 35–6, 73, 78n.1
censorship
    artists in Cuba 14, 186, 196–7
    Beckett's work in Ireland 61
    totalitarian states 233, 237, 238, 246
Centenary Festival *see* Beckett Centenary Festival
Cette fois 70
Chabert, Pierre 203
Chaikin, Joseph 23–4, 27
Chamfort, Nicolas 21
Chan, Paul 93n.8, 212–14
Channel 4 (C4) 28, 34, 41–2, 43–4, 46
Chapple, Freda 98, 103, 106
Check the Gate (*Beckett on Film* DVD) 45

Chin, Wilson 220
China: *Godot* productions 234
choreography *see* dance and choreography
cinema *see* film productions
citation 5, 141
Classical Theatre of Harlem 212, 229
Cluchey, Rick 23, 24
Coates, Ta-Nehisi: *Between the World and Me* 222
Coester, Edouard 157
Cohn, Ruby 6, 29, 83
Colgan, Michael 37, 38, 39, 41, 45, 70–1
Colin, Rosica 202
collaboration and transmediality 6, 99, 156, 157, 160
Come and Go 112, 173, 175, 180
  Brooks and Estienne 12, 81–2, 84–6, 92
  Mabou Mines 12, 82–4, 90
  Offshore Drama Club 147
Comment c'est see *How It Is*
'Comment dire' (poem) 29
Company (novel) 12–13, 25, 70, 111–22, 256, 257
Company SJ 12, 13, 111–12, 112–13, 114, 115, 117–22
computer games 13, 140, 141, 148–50, 151, 152
computer simulations 13, 141, 142, 143–6, 148, 151
Connor, Steven 90, 115–16
contemporary art 5, 13, 99
  and festivals 71, 73–4, 75
  new technologies and sound 136, 137
  posthuman and prosthetic art 126, 128–30, 137
  sculpture on stage 12, 89, 90, 91, 112, 117, 118–19, *118*
  see also installation practices
Contemporary Legend Theatre: *Godot* opera 234
copyright issues 7, 16, 37
  see also Beckett estate
Cotter, Holland 212–13
Creative Time 213
creativity and adaptation 16, 96–7, 103, 108–9

Cronin, Anthony 250, 256
cross-dressing in *Come and Go* 85, 86, 92
Cuba: Bruguera and *Endgame* 14, 186–7, 190–9
cultural power and *Godot* 233
cultural revision and 'fluid texts' 14, 156, 164
Culture Ireland 41
Culture Night 11, 59
Cunard, Nancy 205
Curry, Julian 70
Czajkowska, Joanna
  All Seen. OHIO 179
  All This Is Here 14, 171, 178–80, 180, 181
  Beckett Poruszenie (Beckett – Moves Me) 179, 180
  Quad 178–80
  Quad version 6 178, 179, 180

dance and choreography 14, 171–81
Darwin, Charles 8, 9
Datson, Will 134
Davidson, Donald 135–6
Davidson, Joyce 135
Davis, Ossie: *Purlie Victorious* 209, *210*, 211
De Haarlemse Toneelschuur 93, 229
Debussy, Claude 157, 159, 163
Deleuze, Gilles 145, 180
Dennett, Daniel 165
Denver Center Theatre 229
Dépeupleur, Le see *Lost Ones, The*
digital platforms 34, 35, 43–4, 44–7
  see also new media
Dillane, Stephen 102, 104–5, 106–7, 108
Doran, Paul 57, 59
Doran, Seán 72, 73, 74, 75, 77
Dream of Fair to Middling Women (novel) 16, 249–50, 254, 259–60
Driver, Tom 255
Dublin 69, 70, 71
  see also Beckett Centenary Festival; Beckett Festival; Gate Theatre
Dublin Theatre Festival 61–2, 70–1
Duckworth, Colin 22
Duerfahrd, Lance 10
Dunbar, Adrian 55, 73

Index

Dupuy, Dominique: *La petite dame* 14, 171, 176–8, 181
Dupuy, Françoise 14, 176–8
Duras, Marguerite: *Le Square* 10
DVD and *Beckett on Film* 28, 34, 38, 41, 44–7

Edinburgh International Festival (EIF) 67–8, 71, 77
  Fringe *Godot* 92–3, 229
Effinger, Elizabeth 127
Egoyan, Atom 41, 71
  Steenbeckett 73, 152
Eh Joe (TV) 24, 25, 37, 70, 71
Eleutheria 47n.1, 70
Eliot, T. S. 73
Ellmann, Richard 251
embodiment/bodies
  Beckett's minimalisation of bodies 142–3, 144
  black bodies and oppression in America 222
  Dupuy and 'dancing old' 176, 178
  inclusivity and Marin's *May B* 172–3, 175–6
  intermediality and *Company* 12–13, 111, 113, 114, 117, 120–1
  non-normative agency and Thom's performances 13, 132–6, 137
  posthumanism and non-normative agency 13, 126–37
  prosthetics and Beckett's work 13, 127, 128–30, 131
emotion and performance 119–20
  Beckett's minimalisation of 142–3, 144
En attendant Godot see *Waiting for Godot*
'End, The' ('La Fin') (prose) 256
Endgame (*Fin de partie* / *Endspiel*) 14, 98–9, 129, 165, 203–4, 255
  Akalaitis production 82, 229
  Beckett on Film production 39
  and Bruguera's work 14, 186–7, 189–99
  Kurtág's opera 13, 14, 155, 156, 158–66
  Marin and *Fin de Partie* 172–3, 175

Enniskillen, Northern Ireland 11, 73
  see also Happy Days Enniskillen Beckett Festival
'Epilogue' (abandoned prose-theatre piece) 29
Estienne, Marie-Hélène 12, 81–2, 84–6
Everyman Theatre, Cork 96, 101, 105
Ewell, Tom 204
exclusion
  Beckett and politics of 219, 228–30
  inclusivity and Thom's performance 132
Exodus and Nwandu's *Pass Over* 15, 218–25
experimental approaches 67–8, 70, 71–2, 75–6

Fahy, Catherine 160, 161–2
famine politics 190, 191, 197–9
Fenton, Andrew 135
Festival d'Avignon 67, 68, 77, 229
festivals 11–12, 66–78
  experimental approaches 67–8, 70, 71–2, 75–6
  in Ireland and adaptation 69–78
  site and Beckett adaptations 72–3, 74–5, 76
  time and festival events 75–6
fiction and adaptation 6, 15–16, 249–61
Film (film) 24, 25, 47n.3, 81, 130
film festivals and *Beckett on Film* 34, 38, 40, 46
film productions 20–1, 23
  Azank's web film 241–5
  Beckett's resistance to 20, 26, 235
  see also Beckett on Film project; *Film* (film)
Fin de partie see *Endgame*
First Love (*Premier amour*) (prose) 27, 101
Fischer, Iris Smith 83, 84
Fisher, Mark 141–3, 143–4, 146
Fitch, Brian T. 141
Fleming, Julius B. 222
'fluid text' 13–14, 155–6, 158, 160, 164, 166
Footfalls 112, 116, 149, 173, 229, 255
For to End Yet Again (*Pour finir encore*) 144

Foucault, Michel 14, 190, 195–6, 197
4Learning (C4 brand) 43, 44
Foxrock, Ireland 51–3
  'Beckett in Foxrock' 11, 52–3, 62
  see also Tullow Church, Foxrock
Fragments 85
Frangos, Mike 46, 146–7, 147–8, 152
Free Southern Theater (FST) 15, 208–12, 210, 214
From an Abandoned Work (prose) 21, 23
Frost, Everett 19
Frow, John 37
Fusco, Coco 196, 197

Galway Arts Festival 74–5
Gambon, Michael 39, 40
Gare St Lazare Ireland (GSLI) 71
  How It Is 12, 96–8, 101–9, 111
Garneau, Michel 5
Gate Theatre, Dublin
  Beckett Centenary Festival (2006) 11, 28, 60, 61, 66–7, 71, 142
  Beckett Festival (1991) 10, 11, 34, 37–8, 45, 66, 69–71
Gaudreault, André 113–14
gaze in theatre 12, 81–2, 83–6, 87, 89–91
gender and agency 12, 81–92
  cross-dressing in Come and Go 85, 86, 92
  see also women
Genette, Gérard 6, 147, 171
Genetti, Stefano 171
Georgi, Claudia 114–15
Gerrard, John 142, 148, 151
  Exercise (Djibouti) 13, 141, 143–5
  Exercise (Dunhuang) 13, 141, 145–6
Ghost Trio (TV) 123n.15, 219
Giselson, Anne 214
Goad, The (film by Paul Joyce) 26
Godot Came (Greek short film) 235
Goffman, Erving 180
Gontarski, S. E. 122, 147
Gormley, Anthony: Tree for Waiting for Godot 73
Grand Budapest Hotel, The (Anderson film) 150, 151
Grau, Oliver 148
'grey canon' 29, 147, 148

Grice, Paul 135
Griggs, Yvonne 3
Grimey Up North Theatre 229
Guggenheim, Peggy 253–4

Hall, Peter 20
Hansberry, Lorraine: A Raisin in the Sun 221
Happy Days (Oh les beaux jours) 81, 119, 149, 255
  Dupuy's La petite dame (dance) 176–8
  Rozema's film 12, 40, 82, 86–7, 89, 92
  Scaife's Laethanta Sona 74–5
  Shechet's Passing By 12, 82, 87–91, 92
Happy Days Enniskillen Beckett Festival 11, 55, 67, 71, 72–7
Haraway, Donna 128, 136
Harmon, Maurice 19
Harris, Claudia 70
Harvie, Jen 67–8
Haubenstock-Ramati, Roman: Credentials 167n.4
Hayles, N. Katherine 136–7
Herbert, Jocelyn 142, 199n.10
Heron, Jonathan 20, 67
Herren, Graley 145
'heterocosm' and new media 13, 141, 148–50, 151–2
Higgins, Michael D. 11, 50, 56
Hirst, Damien 37
historical fiction and Beckett 6, 15–16, 249–61
history and Beckett's work 190–1, 197–8
  Beckett's own history and work 254–5
'Hörendspiel' (radio) 29
Horn, Rebecca 126, 128–31, 133, 137
  Buster's Bedroom (film) 130–1
  Finger Gloves (Handschuhfinger) 128–9
  The Little Painting School Performs a Waterfall 130
  The Lost Ones, Samuel Beckett 130
  Pencil Mask (Bleistiftmaske) 128–9, 129–30
  Performances II 129
  Touching the Walls with Both Hands Simultaneously 129

Houben, Jos 85, 86
How It Is (*Comment c'est*) (novel) 12, 23, 27, 96–8, 99–109, 111
Howe, Mary Manning: *The Voice of Shem* 21
Hughes, Enda 37, 39
Hughes, Langston: 'Harlem' 219, 221
Human Wishes 16
Hunzinger, Stefani 98–9
Hurricane Katrina 212, 213
Hutcheon, Linda 1–2, 3, 4, 6–7, 13, 22, 97, 140
  adaptation and evolution 8, 9
  and *Beckett on Film* project 28
  and Bryant's 'fluid texts' 156, 160
  experimental texts and adaptation 235
  'heterocosms' 148, 150, 151
  on history and fiction 6, 252
  opera and adaptation 14, 160
  on sequels and prequels 5–6
Hutcheon, Michael 160
Hyman, Earle 206, 207

India: *Godot* production 234
Innommable, L' see *Unnamable, The*
installation practices 5, 13
  and Beckett's work 142, 146, 152
  Gerrard's simulations 143–6, 148
  visual art and festivals 71, 73–4, 75
intellectual property *see* copyright issues
intermediality 13, 25, 37, 67, 112–13, 113–14
  Beckett's views on 99
  and *Company* 12–13, 111–12, 113, 115–22
  and Gare St Lazare Ireland's *How It Is* 12, 96–109, 111
  media convergence 35, 42, 43, 46–7, 146–7
  metamediality 114–15
  and non-normative and posthuman agency 13, 126–37
  see also transmediality
intertextuality 5–6, 14, 22, 37, 102, 140–1
  Vişniec's subversion 239, 246
intratextual relationships 6, 141

Ireland
  Beckett's embargo on performances 61–2, 70–1
  Beckett's relationship with 60–2, 62–3, 69
  censorship of Beckett's plays 61
  festivals and adaptation 69–78
  see also Dublin; Enniskillen; Foxrock; Gare St Lazare Ireland
Irish Film Board (later Screen Ireland) 28, 41
Irish Gamelan Orchestra 105, 106
Ito, Seikou: *Godot Being Awaited* 234

Jackson, Michael 42, 43
Jacobs, Naomi 252
Japan: *Godot* productions 234
Jenkins, Henry 146
Jermyn Street Theatre, London 11, 50, 54–5, 56, 62
Johnson, Nicholas E. 20, 67, 71, 82
Jones, Netia 73, 75–6
Journal of Beckett Studies 10
Joyce, James 6, 61–2, 69, 249, 251, 254
  Finnegans Wake 21, 205
  Ulysses 25, 69, 71, 163–4
Joyce, Lucia 249–51, 253–4, 259
Joyce, Paul: *The Goad* (film) 26
Joyce, Stephen 249, 250

Kalb, Jonathan 88, 89
Kalman, Jean 73–4
Kanin, Garson 202
Karmitz, Marin 21
Kattenbelt, C. 98, 103, 106
Kaun, Axel 85, 254
Kaye, Nick 74
Keane, Raymond 112, 113, 117, 118–19, *118*, 120, 121
Keaton, Buster 130
Kenner, Hugh 165
Kid, Le: Beckett as actor in 21
Kleist, Heinrich von 26, 119–20
Knowlson, James 20, 28, 52, 93n.5, 119, 157, 228, 250, 255, 256, 257, 259
Kosuth, Joseph: *Texts (Waiting for-) for Nothing* 73
Krahn, Tim 135

Krapp's Last Tape 21, 41, 72, 102, 152, 257
  Mihalovici's opera 25, 158, 159
Krawczyk, Jacek 180
Kristeva, Julia 2
Kuball, Michael 27
Kurtág, György: *Samuel Beckett: Fin de partie, scènes et monologues* (opera) 13, 14, 155, 156, 158–66

Lahr, Bert 204, 205, 206, 207
'Last Soliloquy' (dramatic fragment) 29
Lavery, Carl 121
Laws, Catherine 155, 159
Lee, Spike 15, 231n.3
Leitch, Thomas 1
Lessness (prose) 21, 25
Letters of Samuel Beckett 28, 250, 251–2
Lewis, David 135
Lhermitte, Corinne 96, 103
Ligeti, György 26, 159
lightscapes 98, 102, 104, 107–8, 111, 118
Lindon, Jérôme 20, 24, 27, 202
location
  Azank's web series in New York 242, 243, 244, 245
  Beckett on Film productions 35–6, 86–7
  Chicago context for Nwandu's *Pass Over* 220–1
  Godot in post-Katrina New Orleans 212–15, 229
  inner-city locations for Scaife's work 112, 113
  and Mabou Mines' *Come and Go* 83
  Nwandu's *Pass Over* in Chicago and New York 226–7
  Shechet's *Passing By* in public space 87–91
  site and festival productions 72–3, 74–5, 76, 77–8
Loeb Schloss, Carol 250, 251
Loftis, Sonya Freeman 149
Long After Chamfort (poem cycle) 21
Lost Ones, The (*Le Dépeupleur*) (prose) 13, 24, 26–7, 82, 83, 116, 117, 131, 146, 195

Lovett, Conor 101, 102, 103, 104, 106–7, 108
Lovett, Judy Hegarty 96, 98, 102, 105

Mabou Mines 12, 26–7, 82–4, 90
MacDougall, Joyce 179
McElroen, Christopher 15, 212, 213, 229
McGovern, Barry 69, 70, 71
MacGowran, Jack 235
  Beginning to End 67, 111
  End of Day 67
machinic in Beckett 13, 127, 128, 130, 131, 136
Mackay, Robin 146
Magee, Patrick 21, 26, 58
Magni, Marcello 85, 86
Maleczech, Ruth 83, 84
Malone Dies (*Malone meurt*) (novel) 21, 37, 70, 234, 256
Maloney, Ann 212
Mamet, David 35–6
Manning Howe, Mary *see* Howe, Mary Manning
Maquisard (video game) 150
Marble Arch Caves, near Enniskillen 72
Marin, Maguy: *May B* 14, 73, 171, 172–6, 181
Marion, Philippe 113–14
Marshall, E. G. 204, 206
Martin, Tim 121, 122n.6
'mash-ups' 5, 15, 218
masks and blindfolds
  audiences 11, 50, 54, 55, 56, 59, 62
  Horn's work 129–30
Maude, Ulrika 127–8
McMullan, Anna 19, 101, 103, 104, 193, 194
McNamee, Eoin 259
McNaughton, James 190–1, 197–8
McPherson, Conor 39
McTighe, Trish 69
McWhinnie, Donald 57, 235
media convergence 35, 42, 43, 46–7
  see also intermediality; transmediality
mediations 4
  digital mediations 117, 152
  see also intermediality; remediations

Meek, Simon: *Beckett* (video game) 13, 141, 148–50, 151–2
Mendel, Deryk 19
Mercier, Mel 102, 104, 105
'metamediality' 114–15
Mihalovici, Marcel 21
  Krapp's Last Tape (opera) 25, 158, 159, 167n.12
Miłosz, Czesław 238
Minghella, Anthony 36
mirrors in Beckett's work 83–4, 90
Mitrani, Michel 21
Mittelalterliches Dreieck (dramatic fragment) 21
Molloy (novel) 20, 21, 101, 138n.8, 149, 151, 234, 255
Moloney, Alan 38, 41, 45
Moody, Alys 127, 128
More Pricks Than Kicks (prose) 16, 259, 260
Moreland, Mantan 206, 207
Moses, Gilbert 208, 211, 214
Mouth on Fire 11, 50–1, 53, 54, 56–63
movement and Kleist's theories 119–20
Mukaiyama, Tomoko 73–4
multiple billing of (short) plays 76
Murphy, Caroline 56, 59
Murphy (novel) 26, 27, 256, 258, 259–61
music and Beckett's work 155
  Beckett's dislike of opera 157
  Beckett's views on music in *Godot* 157
  Schubert lieder 105–6, 174
  see also opera; sound
Muşina, Alexandru 238–9
Myerberg, Michael 15, 203–8, 209, 214

Nacht und Träume (TV) 113, 219
Nadal, Marc: *Marionetas* (micromovie) 235
'Negritude' 209
Negro: An Anthology (Cunard) 205
neurodiversity and performance 13, 126, 131–6, 137
new media and technologies
  art and sound 136, 137
  and 'borderline' adaptations 13, 140–52
  see also digital platforms; video games; web series
New Orleans: *Godot* in 15, 93n.8, 212–15, 229
New York as setting 226–7, 242, 243, 244, 245
Niemetz, Anne: *Dark Side of the Cell* (with Pelling) 13, 126, 136, 137
Nixon, Mark 29
non-normative agency and Thom 13, 132–6, 137
Not I 13, 21, 36, 72, 112, 116, 142
  Thom and Touretteshero production 13, 126, 131–6, 137
novels and Beckett's life 15–16, 249–61
Nunn, Trevor 54
Nwandu, Antoinette: *Pass Over* 15, 218–30, *221*

Oberlin College, Ohio 93, 229, 230
Offshore Drama Club 147
Oh les beaux jours see *Happy Days*
O'Hara, Dan 128
Ohio Impromptu 25, 73, 142, 180
Oică, Iuliana 239
old age: Dupuy and 'dancing old' 176, 178
Old Tune, The (radio) 21, 203
O'Loughlin, Cian 78n.8
O'Neal, John 208
opera 13–14, 21, 25, 155, 156, 158–66, 234
  Beckett's dislike of opera 157
  libretto and Beckett's text 160–4
O'Reilly, Édouard Magessa 101
O'Toole, Peter 235
Out of Joint 11, 50, 55, 56, 62, 73

Pacey, Ben 134
Padmore, Mark 105–6, 108
Pan Pan Theatre 63n.3, 73
'Panopticon' and Bruguera's *Endgame* 14, *192*, 195–7
Paraskeva, Anthony 119
paratexts 34, 43, 46, 147, 151, 152
Park, Chan 15
Paska, Roman 117

PBS: *Waiting for Godot* production 23
Pelling, Andrew: *Dark Side of the Cell* (with Niemetz) 13, 126, 136, 137
performance and adaptation
  limitations of performing prose works 98, 104
  performance as adaptation 22, 202, 203
  performance as event 198–9
  politics and Bruguera's work 188–90
  possibilities of AI 142–3
performative voice in *Company* 116
Pethö, Ágnes 114
Pheby, Alex: *Lucia* 15, 249–50, 251, 253, 259
Phelps de Cisneros, Patricia 187
Philippe (for Philipe), Gérard 27
Piece of Monologue, A 25
Pike Theatre, Dublin 20, 53
Ping (prose) 116, 127, 128
Pinget, Robert
  L'Hypothèse 203
  La Manivelle 21, 203
Play 21, 36, 81, 82, 83, 116
Polanski, Roman 235
politics
  Bruguera and power dynamics 14, 186–99
  communist states and *Godot* 233, 237–8, 246
  Godot and cultural power 233
  Nwandu's *Pass Over* and Trump 225–7
  subversion in Vişiec's *Le dernier Godot* 239
  see also power dynamics; race issues
Pontedera Theatre 93, 229
posthumanism 13, 126–37
postmodernism and post-communist states 238–9
Pountney, Matthew 13, 131, 134
Power, Nina (Infinite Thought/I.T.) 142
power dynamics
  and Bruguera's *Endgame* 14, 186–7, 191–9
  and Vişniec's *Le dernier Godot* 233, 237, 240–1
  see also politics; race issues

prequels 5–6
prisons: *Godot* performances 22, 23, 215, 237
prose pieces
  advantages in lack of stage directions 12, 75, 111
  challenges of theatrical stagings 98, 101–2, 104, 107–8, 111
  and festival performances 75, 76
  see also individual works
prosthetics 13, 127, 128–30, 131
Proust (essay) 157
Puchner, Martin 75

Quad (TV) 14, 25, 144–5, 145–6, 151, 176
  Czajkowska's dance versions 178–80
Quinn, Cathal 53, 56, 57, 58, 59, 61

race issues
  black lives and Nwandu's *Pass Over* 15, 218–28, 230
  and Civil Rights in US 208–9, 211–12
  see also black actors and *Godot*
radio productions 21, 25, 37
  All That Fall theatrical productions 50–63
  Beckett and qualities of radio plays 53–4
  Waiting for Godot 235
  see also individual works
Rancière, Jacques 173
recorded voices 12, 25, 96, 116, 121
Reinboth, Ernst: *Der Sucher* (film) 26
remediations 4, 13, 73–4, 127, 140, 146–7
  see also intermediality; transmediality
'remixes' 5, 102, 242, 245
Renel, Will 13, 134
Resnais, Alain 21
'rewrites' 5
Rhys, Jean: *Wide Sargasso Sea* 5
Rivas, Tlaloc 93, 229
Rockaby 112, 116, 119, 142
Romania: responses to *Godot* in 237–8
Rorty, Richard 234
Ross, Alex 159, 164

Rosset, Barney 50, 53, 61–2, 203–4, 205, 206
Rothwell Group 21
Rough for Radio II (radio) 196
'Roundelay' (poem) in Kurtág's opera 161–2, 165
Rozema, Patricia: *Happy Days* film 12, 40, 82, 86–7, 89, 92
RTÉ
  and *Beckett on Film* 28, 34, 36, 37, 39, 41, 42–3
  and Gate Beckett Festival (1991) 70

Salkind, Wendy 82
Samuel Beckett Today / Aujourd'hui (journal) 10
San Quentin prison: *Godot* in 22, 23, 215, 237
Sanders, Julie 1–2, 2–3, 4–5, 6, 7, 8, 9, 22
Sarajevo: *Godot* production in 213, 238
Scaife, Sarah Jane 12, 74, 98, 111, 117, 119, 121
  Fizzles 112–13
  The Women Speak 112
Schloss, Carol Loeb *see* Loeb Schloss
Schmidt, Judith 25, 207
Schmidt, Katharina 129
Schneider, Alan 19, 20, 21, 23, 27, 203, 204
Schopenhauer, Arthur 157
Schubert, Franz: lieder 105–6, 174, 219
sculpture 12, 89, 90, 91, 112, 117, 118–19, *118*
seeing and being seen 12, 81–2, 83–4, 87–91
self-translation by Beckett 22, 25, 100, 108, 233–4
sensory experience 121
  see also blindfolds and masks; lightscapes; sound
sequels 5–6
Shades (BBC TV programme) 21
Shakespeare, William 7, 8, 68, 71, 163
Shechet, Arlene
  Full Steam Ahead installation 88, 90
  Passing By 12, 82, 87–91, 92

sign language interpreters 132, 134
silence 145, 157
  and the neurodiverse body 126, 134, 135
  sound and new technologies 136
Silent Faces: *Godot is a Woman* 7–8
Simakis, Andrea 230
Simpson, Alan 20, 53, 61
simulations 13, 141, 142, 143–6, 148, 151
Sinclair, Peggy 250, 259
Singleton, Brian 66, 69
sites *see* location
Solo 70
Sone, Yuji 119, 121
Sontag, Susan 213, 238
Sopot Dance Theatre Company 171
  Quad 178–80
  Quad version 6 178, 179, 180
sound
  art and new technologies 136, 137
  Azank's web film 242–3
  recorded voices 12, 25, 96, 116, 121
  sound effects in radio plays 53, 57–8
  soundscape and Gare St Lazare Ireland's *How It Is* 96, 98, 101–2, 102–4, 105–6, 111
  see also music and Beckett's work
'spin-offs' 5–6
Stafford-Clark, Max 55, 56, 73
Staging Beckett project 10
Steppenwolf Theatre, Chicago 15, 218, 221
Stirrings Still (prose) 70, 73, 75, 76
Stone, Kris 104
Stoppard, Tom 235
Studio Theatre 229
Sucher, Der (*The Seeker*) (film) 26
surveillance and Bruguera's *Endgame* 14, *192*, 195–7

Tajiri, Yoshiki 128
Tallmer, Jerry 205–6, 207–8
Tate Modern, London: Bruguera's work at 188–9
Taymor, Danya 15, 220

television productions 21, 25–6, 37, 98–9
  Beckett on space and scale 22–3, 235
  digital channels 43–4
  see also Beckett on Film project *and individual works*
text: on-screen projection 120–1
Texts for Nothing (prose) 23–4, 27
That Time 25, 116
Theatre Group 20, 23
Theatrical Notebooks series 28
Thom, Jess
  in *Not I* 13, 126, 131–6, 137
  10 Minutes of Nothing 13, 134, 136
Thomas, Dylan: *Under Milk Wood* 21
Thompson, Geoffrey 251, 256
Thompson, Sam: *Jot* 15–16, 250, 251, 253, 256–61
Three Plays by Samuel Beckett (Channel 4 TV programme) 41
time
  and festival events 75–6, 77–8
  festivals and shorter works 75–7
  infinite scale and new media 141
Tophoven, Elmar and Erika 233
Touretteshero 13, 126, 131–6, 137
transhumanism 126, 127, 130, 137
translation 4–5, 20
  Azank's *Godot* translation 241–2
  self-translation 22, 25, 100, 108, 233–4
transmediality 10, 13, 25, 146–50, 151, 152
  and collaboration 6, 99, 156, 157, 160
  Godot and 'tradaptations' 15, 233–46
  see also intermediality
Trinity College Dublin 21, 60, 70, 71
Trump, Donald 225–6
Tual, Denise 202
Tucker, David 119
Tullow Church, Foxrock 11, 50, 51–3, 55, 56–9, 57, 60, 62
Turk, Edward Baron 68
Tyrone Productions 28, 39

Uhlmann, Anthony 119, 120
United States
  all-black productions 14–15, 203–15, 229
  Civil Rights movement 208–9, 211–12
  English-language rights and *Godot* 202–4
  Nwandu's *Pass Over* 15, 218–28, 230
  see also New Orleans; New York
Unnamable, The (*L'Innommable*) (novel) 21, 100, 127, 136, 141, 165, 234, 236

Van Hulle, Dirk 25, 138n.8
video games 13, 140, 141, 148–50, 151, 152
Vilar, Jean 68
violence in *Godot* 233, 236–7, 240, 244, 245, 246
Vișniec, Matei: *Le dernier Godot* 5, 15, 233, 236–41, 242, 246
visual art *see* contemporary art
voices: recorded voices 12, 25, 96, 116, 121
Vouyoucas, Adonis 27

Waiting for Godot (*En attendant Godot*) 10, 99, 107
  all-black productions 14–15, 93n.8, 202, 205–15, 229
  Beckett on Film production 46–7
  Beckett's resistance to film version 235
  Beckett's veto on women actors 7, 27, 92–3n.5, 228, 229, 230
  and Beckett's wartime experiences 255
  and dance works 73, 180
  early productions and Beckett's responses 20
  first performance in Paris 176–7, 234
  global productions 234
  and Marin's *May B* 173, 175
  and music 157–8
  Nwandu's *Pass Over* 15, 218–28, 230
  performance rights 7–8, 202–4

radio productions 235
and television adaptations 22–3, 25–6
transmediality and 'tradaptation' 15, 233–46
violence as entity in 233, 236–7, 240
Vişniec's appropriation 25, 233, 236–41, 246
Walsh, Jack 113
Walsh, Katy 230–1n.2
Warner, Deborah 229
Warrilow, David 24, 70, 82
Was Wo (German TV adaptation) 6, 25
Watt (novel) 130
WDR 21
web series as medium for *Godot* 241–5
Weidt, Jean 177
Weiss, Hedy 230nn.1&2
West, Sarah 116, 117
'what is the word' (poem) 179
What Where (Quoi où) 6, 25, 149
see also *Was Wo*
white supremacy in Nwandu's *Pass Over* 222, 223–5
Whitelaw, Billie 24, 133, 142, 168n.15
Wiest, Dianne 88, 90, 91

Wilcox, Dean 114, 120
Wilder, Thornton 202, 203, 205
Wilkinson, Marc: *Voices* 158
Wills, David 128
Willson, Rachel Beckles 159–60, 161
Wilson, Robert 72, 74
women
and agency 81–92
in Azank's *While Waiting for Godot* 244
Beckett's veto as actors in *Godot* 7, 27, 92–3n.5, 228, 229, 230
and gaze 12, 81, 82, 83–6, 87, 89–91
real-life characters in work 249–50, 259
words: on-screen projection 120–1
Words and Music (radio) 25, 73, 157
Worstward Ho (prose) 24, 165–6
Woycicki, Piotr 145

Yeats, W. B. 69
YouTube 45–6, 147

Zhaohua, Lin: *Sam Jiemei – Dengdai Geduo (Three Sisters – Waiting for Godot)* 234
Zweig, Stefan 150, 151
Zweite, Armin 130

EU authorised representative for GPSR:
Easy Access System Europe, Mustamäe tee 50,
10621 Tallinn, Estonia
gpsr.requests@easproject.com

www.ingramcontent.com/pod-product-compliance
Lightning Source LLC
Chambersburg PA
CBHW051605230426
43668CB00013B/1986